Understanding the Chinese Language

Understanding the Chinese Language provides a vibrant and comprehensive introduction to contemporary Chinese linguistics. Combining an accessible style with an in-depth treatment of the topics at hand, it uses clear, full descriptions and vivid, modern examples to systematically take students through the phonology, vocabulary, grammar, discourse structures and pragmatics of modern Chinese. No prior knowledge of Chinese or linguistics is required.

Features include:

- Six detailed chapters covering the core linguistic aspects of the modern Chinese language, such as words, content units, sentences, speech acts, sentence-final particles and neologisms.
- User-friendly comparisons and contrasts between English and Chinese throughout the text, helping to clearly explain important complexities and nuances of the Chinese language.
- Clear, accessible explanations and insightful analysis of topics and linguistic devices, supported by many helpful examples, diagrams and tables.
- Lively and relevant examples drawn from real-life contemporary sources such as internet news reports, social networks like Sino Weibo, online forums and TV reality shows, offering fascinating perspectives on modern Chinese media, culture and society.
- Pioneering coverage of new Chinese words and the social phenomena they reveal.
- Additional exercises and four supplementary chapters covering Chinese syllables, idioms, discourse and culture are available for free download at www.routledge.com/9780415634885.

Written by a highly experienced instructor, researcher and linguist, *Understanding the Chinese Language* will be essential reading for undergraduate and post-graduate students taking courses in Chinese linguistics. It will also be of interest to anyone interested in learning more about Chinese language and culture.

Chris Shei is Associate Professor at Swansea University, UK.

'*Understanding the Chinese Language* is an excellent introductory textbook for Chinese linguistics. This book provides a systematic, in-depth, and seminal explanation of Chinese linguistics and its efforts in comparing English and Chinese using vivid and authentic examples make it very accessible.'

Han Luo, *Northwestern University, USA*

'Teaching Chinese linguistics can be very challenging but this book has made the task a lot easier. Dr Shei's use of authentic data (language used on TV reality shows and messages on social networks) to illustrate how the Chinese language really works is highly effective. He skilfully adopts various linguistic frameworks to examine Chinese sentence types. He also proposes new approaches, which include using concepts to define Chinese lexical items (i.e. words). Anybody who is interested in understanding how the Chinese language works will benefit from reading this book.'

Kan Qian, *The Open University, UK*

Understanding the Chinese Language

A comprehensive linguistic introduction

Chris Shei

 Routledge
Taylor & Francis Group

LONDON AND NEW YORK

First published 2014
by Routledge
2 Park Square, Milton Park, Abingdon, Oxon OX14 4RN

and by Routledge
711 Third Avenue, New York, NY 10017

Routledge is an imprint of the Taylor & Francis Group, an informa business

British Library Cataloguing in Publication Data
A catalogue record for this book is available from the British Library

Library of Congress Cataloging in Publication Data
Shei, Chris, 1956–
    Understanding the Chinese language / Chris Shei.
        pages cm
    1. Chinese language–Textbooks for foreign speakers–English.
2. Chinese language–Grammar.   3. Chinese language–Syntax.
4. Chinese language–Study and teaching–English speakers.   I. Title.
    PL1129.E5S54 2014
    495.182′421–dc23

2014000294

ISBN: 978-0-415-63486-1 (hbk)
ISBN: 978-0-415-63488-5 (pbk)
ISBN: 978-1-315-76722-2 (ebk)

Typeset in Berthold Akzidenz Grotesk
by Graphicraft Limited, Hong Kong

Printed and bound in the United States of America by
Edwards Brothers Malloy on sustainably sourced paper

Contents

List of figures

List of tables

Foreword

This book aims to introduce the Chinese language in an understandable way. It uses simple English and abundant examples to explain Chinese phonology, vocabulary, grammar and discourse. Linguistic theories are kept in the background, guiding the development of knowledge about the language and familiarity with the use of the language.

The book is written with the following readers in mind:

- university/college level students using the book as a Mandarin course/ reference book
- undergraduate or postgraduate students taking a course in Chinese linguistics
- anyone interested in learning Mandarin and knowing how it works in society
- researchers in arts and humanities requiring a working knowledge of Chinese
- Chinese or English-speaking researchers looking for fresh ideas in Chinese linguistics or Chinese media and political studies.

This book takes a discourse functional approach and draws on the web for hundreds of examples to illustrate the contemporary usage of the Chinese language. Spoken language samples are transcribed from unscripted talks from current TV reality shows; written data are selected from online news reports and messages posted on social networks.

For convenience, the term 'Chinese' or 'Chinese language' used in this book refers exclusively to Mandarin – that is, Putonghua (普通话) in China, Guoyu (國語) in Taiwan, or the more general Hanyu (汉语) worldwide – bearing in mind that there are at least seven major dialect groups in Chinese, each of which is worthy of a book-length introduction.

The book offers an accessible overview of the Chinese language and its functions in society (notably, in the TV media and the web). Chapters 1–3 introduce the fundamental linguistic components, including Chinese sounds, lexical units, functional items, and sentences. Chapter 4 discusses how Chinese is used to perform speech acts; that is, to give commands, offer promises, assert opinions, express feelings, and so on. Chapter 5 offers a comprehensive survey of sentence-final particles (SFPs) which play an important role in Chinese discourse. Finally, an up-to-date introduction to Chinese neologisms since the end of the twentieth century is offered in Chapter 6.

The key concepts in Chinese linguistics are introduced in relatively understandable ways, often using corresponding parts in English for comparison and contrast. The large number of authentic examples help establish the credibility of the theory, increase learning interest, and are valuable data for content studies in their own right.

List of abbreviations

Linguistic terms

*	(ungrammatical) or (unacceptable)		Num	number word
AD	*de5* as adjective marker		OB	object marker *ba3*
AM	aspect marker		OD	ordinal morpheme *di4*
Aux	auxiliary		PB	passive marker *bei4*
CFP	constituent final particle		PD	*de5* as possessive marker
Cla	classifier		PF	pause filler
Com	complement (of verb)		PoS	part of speech
Conj	conjunction		Pos	possessive case
Dem	demonstrative		Pro	pronoun
ED	*de5* as emphatic marker		PM	plural marker
Hon	honorific item		QM	question marker
IP	independent particle		QN	quantity word
Mea	measure word		SFP	sentence final particle
Neg	negation word			

Media programs

aqllk	Ai Qing Lian Lian Kan	爱情连连看
aywdm	Ai Yao Wo De Ma	哎哟我的妈
fcwr	Fei Cheng Wu Rao	非诚勿扰
ggbbm	Guo Guang Bang Bang Mang	国光帮帮忙
jwsdj	Jin Wan Shei Dang Jia	今晚谁当家
kxll	Kang Xi Lai Le	康熙来了
mrthk	Ming Ren Tai Hui Kao	名人太会考
SSxyzy	SS Xiao Yan Zhi Ye	SS小燕之夜
wmyhb	Wo Men Yue Hui Ba	我们约会吧
WOWhmj	WOW Hou Ma Ji	WOW侯麻吉
ylbfb	Yu Le Bai Fen Bai	娱乐百分百
zsydt	Zhuan Shen Yu Dao TA	转身遇到TA

Introduction

This chapter briefly introduces Chinese phonetics, morphology and syntax. There is also a discussion of the relationship between China and Taiwan as background knowledge for understanding the linguistic differences between the two Chinese communities referred to in this book.

0.1 CHINESE PHONETICS

The phonemic inventory (i.e. all the vowels and consonants used in a language) of Chinese is not dramatically different from that of English. While English makes use of 24 consonants and approximately 12 vowels, Chinese uses 25 consonants and 10 vowels. Chinese and English roughly share 14 consonants and 7 vowels, so there are only 11 Chinese consonants and 3 Chinese vowels, at most, that are unfamiliar to English speakers. Figure 0.1 shows the consonant sets and vowel sets, encoded in IPA (International Phonetic Association) symbols, used by Mandarin and English respectively and their intersections.

As Figure 0.1 shows, there are 14 consonants which Chinese and English share. The three voiceless aspirated stops [pʰ] [tʰ] [kʰ] are enclosed by a dotted rectangle to show their special status in this intersection. That is, although they are used to distinguish meanings in Chinese (i.e. saying [pʰ] means something different from saying [p]), they do not have such functions in English. In other words, although [pʰ] [tʰ] [kʰ] are independent sounds (or phonemes) in Chinese, they are not treated as such in English, but are phonetic variants of [p] [t] [k] respectively – sounds that are pronounced in different ways under different conditions which do not result in a difference in meaning. That is why we say there are 13 + 11 = 24 consonants in English, rather than 13 + 14 = 27 if interpreting the consonant intersection in Figure 0.1 incorrectly. However, these three sounds are indeed separate phonemes in Chinese, which means there are 11 + 14 = 25 consonants in Chinese, including the three semivowels [j], [w] and [ɥ]. Among the 25, there are 11 Chinese consonants which are not normally used in English and which may cause difficulties for English speakers learning Mandarin.

Figure 0.1 also shows the intersection of vowels between Chinese and English, which is a set consisting of seven members. There are only three Chinese vowels, [y], [ɨ] and [ɤ], which are not found in English, among which only the first two may be difficult for English speakers to pronounce.

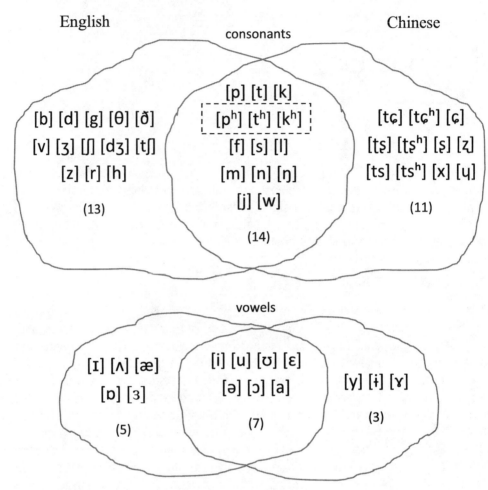

Figure 0.1 Intersections between Chinese and English consonants and vowels

All of the Chinese 25 consonants and 10 vowels will be explained in Chapter 1, which also discusses how sounds combine to form Chinese syllables and how tones are added to syllables to represent meaning.

'Syllable' is an important concept in the Chinese language. In English, a syllable is an intermediate structure between sound and word. For example, the word *ordinary* consists of four syllables – [ɔ.dɪ.nə.ri] – none of which makes sense when standing alone. Syllables in English normally become meaningful when they combine together to form words (with the exception of monosyllabic words such as *bed*, *cat* and so on). In Chinese, however, each syllable can stand alone and mean something. For example 电脑 'computer' consists of two characters, 电 [tjɛn] 'electric' and 脑 [nɑʊ] 'brain'; each character is exactly one syllable long and has its own meaning. Therefore, each syllable in Chinese is a 'brick of meaning'. They either carry out their semantic function individually or combine with other syllables to form larger meaningful units.

Phonetic transcription is another important factor to consider when learning the Chinese language. In the case of English, there is usually a certain degree of resemblance between the alphabet-based orthographical form of a word (e.g. *singer*) and the standard phonetic transcription of the spoken form, i.e. [sɪŋə]. In Chinese, however, there is no connection between the logographic system and the phonetic symbols normally used to transcribe Western languages. Although IPA has developed a set of symbols which aim to describe all human languages including Chinese, many symbols for the Chinese sounds are difficult to learn and inconvenient to type (i.e. most of the 11 Chinese consonants in Figure 0.1 which do not exist in English). This is where the Pinyin system comes in.

Pinyin is a Romanized system which represents Chinese sounds in a convenient way. Pinyin is also used to type Chinese characters as it is compatible with the English-based computer keyboard. Heselwood (2013) calls Pinyin a 'pseudo-transcription'. It is not a 'real' phonetic transcription system, nor is it a 'real' orthographic system, but it does carry out both functions in a partial sense. Pinyin is currently the most popular tool for encoding Mandarin sounds for language learners, who can use Pinyin to learn the Chinese sounds, to read Chinese text and later to key in the Chinese characters which they learn. Table 0.1 shows the relationships between the IPA and Pinyin symbols for the Chinese consonants and vowels.

Table 0.1 shows a good one-to-one correspondence between the Chinese Pinyin and the IPA symbols in the consonants section. This means a sound will not be ambiguously encoded by more than one symbol or vice versa. For example, the letter(s) *f*, *ph*, and *gh* can all stand for the sound [f] in English; whereas the alphabet combination *th* can stand for either the [θ] or the [ð] sound. For the Chinese Pinyin, this kind of ambiguity does not exist at the consonant level. In

Table 0.1 Chinese consonants and vowels in both IPA and Pinyin systems

Consonants										
IPA	p	pʰ	t	tʰ	k	kʰ	m	n	ŋ	f
Pinyin	b	p	d	t	g	k	m	n	ng	f
IPA	ts	tsʰ	s	ʐ	tʂ	tʂʰ	ʂ	tɕ	tɕʰ	ɕ
Pinyin	z	c	s	r	zh	ch	sh	j	q	x
IPA	l	x	w	ɥ	j					
Pinyin	l	h	w	yu	y					
Vowels										
IPA	a	ɛ	ə	ɤ	i	ɨ	ɔ	u	ʊ	y
Pinyin	a	e	e	e	i	i	o	u	o	yu

the vowels section, however, ambiguities do exist, which center around the use of the letter *e*. As can be seen from Table 0.1, the alphabet *e* is used to represent any of the three sounds: [ɛ], [ə], or [ɤ], presumably due to a shortage of common vowel alphabets.

In this book, as is the normal practice, Pinyin symbols are used to represent the Chinese sounds for convenience in typing. As will become clear, Pinyin not only indicates how the Chinese lexical items should be read, it also directly 'represents' the lexical item in an orthographic sense. That is, a lexical item represented in Pinyin can be directly connected to its meaning.

0.2 CHINESE MORPHOLOGY

The discussion of English morphology often starts with the concepts of morphemes, compound words, inflection and derivation, and so on.

- Morphemes: the smallest meaningful unit in a language. For example, the word *encouragements* is decomposable into four morphemes: *en-*, *courage*, *ment* and *-s*, each of which has a meaning (e.g. *courage*) or function (e.g. plural marker). Morphemes can be further classified into:

  ○ Free morphemes: a morpheme that can function on its own, such as *song* and *table*.
  ○ Bound morphemes: a morpheme that must be attached to another morpheme/word when used, e.g. *-ment*, *-ed*, *anti-* and so on. There are two kinds of bound morphemes:

    ◆ Inflectional morphemes: a bound morpheme assigned to a word to signify a certain grammatical property, e.g. *-ed*, *-ing*.
    ◆ Derivational morphemes: a bound morpheme added to a word to create a new form of the word, e.g. *-er*, *-ful*.

- Compound words: a word which is a combination of two or more words, such as *strawberry*, *football*, *blackboard* and so on.

In Chinese, the above notions either are inapplicable or have to be modified in some way in order to remain functional. Firstly, the idea of a morpheme is conceptualized differently in Chinese. In English, a morpheme is defined solely by the meaning disregarding the number of syllables it contains. A morpheme could be as long as *crocodile* (3 syllables) or as short as *dog* (1 syllable). In Chinese, however, any of the 400 or so usable syllables can mean something, after being assigned a tone and used in an appropriate context. A morpheme in Chinese can thus be defined not only by the meaning (i.e. the smallest meaningful unit in the language) but also in phonetic terms (i.e. each morpheme in Chinese is exactly one syllable in length).

Secondly, all morphemes are more or less of equal status in Chinese since almost all usable syllables are used as free morphemes. That is, they can stand alone to mean something, given appropriate circumstances. For example, *zhu1* (or [ʈʂu] in 1st tone) means 'pig' and *rou4* (or [ʐoʊ] in 4th tone) means 'meat'. There is only a very small number of syllables in Chinese which behave like bound morphemes. This is different from English, where there is a fixed set of inflectional morphemes like *-ed* and *-ing* and a large number of derivational morphemes like *re-, un-, co-, -er, -ish, -ness* and so on, which are used to create many new forms of existing words.

In Chinese, a morpheme (or a syllable) also corresponds to a character, e.g. *zhu1* 'pig' is written as 猪 and *rou4* 'meat' as 肉. Although both are free morphemes, they are not normally called 'words'. The concept of 'word' is notoriously difficult to define in Chinese. More than half of the lexical units thought to be 'words' in Chinese consist of two morphemes. For example, 'the meat of pig' in English is represented by a single word, *pork*. In Chinese, 'pork' is simply the combination of two morphemes, *zhu1* 'pig' and *rou4* 'meat', written as 猪肉. The same is true for beef (*niu2rou4* 'cow meat' 牛肉), lamb (*yang2rou4* 'sheep meat' 羊肉) and so on. The dilemma is that although we can call monosyllabic units like *zhu1, niu2, rou4*, etc. 'morphemes', they are also 'words' in their own right – just like free morphemes such as *garden, church, school* and so on in English. Thus, although the concept of 'morpheme' is relatively clear in Chinese, the concept of 'word' is not.

For English, there are distinct levels on the morpheme → word → compound word continuum. However, in Chinese, the boundaries between these categories are not so clear. If *zhu1* and *rou4* are treated as morphemes and not words, then *zhu1rou4* is a word. But if *zhu1* and *rou4* are both words, then *zhu1rou4* must be a compound. In practice, most practitioners treat lexical units like *zhu1rou4* 'pork' and *dian4nao3* 'computer' as words. The term 'compound word' has very little relevance in Chinese, then, since many words already look quite 'compound-like', having been assembled together from two or more stand-alone morphemes.

There is a good-sized literature in Chinese linguistics on the internal structure of disyllabic 'words', concentrating on the relationships between the two morphemes. For example, within the word 猪肉, the first morpheme describes the second morpheme (i.e. the meat is from the pig). The relationship between the two is said to be an 'endocentric' one (the first morpheme modifies the second). There are other kinds of word-internal structures manifesting different relationships between the participating morphemes, as indicated below:

- Endocentric: The first element modifies the second.

    白天 *bai2tian1* 'white-day (day time)'
    飞机 *fei1ji1* 'fly-machine (airplane)'
    勇气 *yong3qi4* 'brave-air (courageous)'
    新闻 *xin1wen2* 'new-hear (news)'

- Coordinative: The two elements are equal or closely related in meaning.

> 身体 *shen1ti3* 'body-body (body)'
> 贫穷 *pin2qiong2* 'deficient-destitute (poor)'
> 照顾 *zhao4gu4* 'shine-look (take care of)'
> 死亡 *si3wang2* 'die-die (die)'

- Subject-predicate: The second element is the predicate (verb or adjective) of the first.

> 地震 *di4zhen4* 'ground-shake (earthquake)'
> 脸红 *lian3hong2* 'face-red (blush)'
> 油炸 *you2zha4* 'oil-explode (deep fry)'
> 心酸 *xin1suan1* 'heart-sour (grief-stricken)'

- Verb-object: The first element is a verb and the second is its object.

> 下雨 *xia4yu3* 'send down-rain (raining)'
> 吃饭 *chi1fan4* 'eat-rice (have meal)'
> 打球 *da3qiu2* 'hit-ball (play ball)'
> 失业 *shi1ye4* 'lose-career (unemployed)'

- Verb-complement: The first is a verb and the second is its complement (the resultant state of an action).

> 说明 *shuo1ming2* 'say-bright (explain)'
> 推翻 *tui1fan1* 'push-turn over (overthrow)'
> 解开 *jie3kai1* 'solve-open (untie)'
> 昏倒 *hun1dao3* 'faint-inverse (pass out)'

- Noun-classifier: The first element is the noun and the second is the classifier (a monosyllabic item used to categorize a noun).

> 车辆 *che1liang4* 'car-classifier for land vehicles (vehicle)'
> 房间 *fang2jian1* 'room-classifier for rooms and buildings (room)'
> 花朵 *hua1duo3* 'flower-classifier for flowers and clouds (flower)'
> 水桶 *shui3tong3* 'water-classifier for large quantity of liquid (bucket)'

An inflection-like bound morpheme in Chinese is *men5* 们 'plural marker', which attaches itself to a certain type of noun to make it plural. For example, *hai2zi5* 孩子 'child' becomes *hai2zi5men5* 孩子们 'children'. Morphemes like this are extremely rare in Chinese. Their application to existing words or morphemes is also fairly restricted. For example, *猪们 'pig-plural' is not a good expression in Chinese, as 们 is normally only added to certain categories of human nouns. The noun alone (e.g. 猪) can be interpreted as either singular or plural depending on context. Plural marking for common nouns is not mandatory in Chinese.

There are more derivation-like morphemes in Chinese than inflection-like ones, but their application is also very limited and certainly not as productive as the English derivational morphemes such as *con-*, *dis-*, *-ive*, *-tion*, *-ment* and so on. Like English, these morphemes can occur at the beginning or at the end of a lexical unit. A suffix-like morpheme (which is a free morpheme itself, not a bound one) in Chinese is 痛 *tong4* 'ache' which, like its counterpart in English, *-ache*, can be added to a body part to mean a discomfort in that region. Thus, we have 头痛 'headache', 牙痛 'toothache', 胃痛 'stomach ache', 心痛 'heartache', 肚子痛 'tummy ache', 喉咙痛 'sore throat', 偏头痛 'slanting-headache (migraine)' and so on.

A prefix-like Chinese morpheme is 电 *dian4* 'electricity'. Examples are 电视 'electric-see (television)', 电话 'electric-words (telephone)', 电影 'electric-image (cinema)', 电灯 'electric-lamp (electric light)', 电冰箱 'electric-ice box (refrigerator)' and so on.

There are more derivation-like morphemes like 痛 and 电 in Chinese, with different degrees of productivity. Again, the combinations of these morphemes (bearing in mind they may also be called 'words' in Chinese) with other morphemes or words can be conceptualized as word-formation rules in Chinese. Yet they can also be said to follow phrase-structure rules in Chinese. The distinctions between morphemes, words, and phrases are far from clear in Chinese.

0.3 CHINESE ORTHOGRAPHY

Each Chinese character corresponds exactly to a Chinese syllable with a tone and a meaning. Only a small portion of Chinese characters are really pictographs; that is, the character resembles the concept it expresses in appearance. For example, the shape of 山 'hill' does resemble a mountain with three peaks. The character 羊 'sheep' originated from an oracle bone script which resembled the front of a sheep. Other character formation rules traditionally recognized include the following:

- Ideograph:
  - Simple ideograph: Simple strokes are used iconically to represent abstract ideas. For example, 上 'up' (an icon on a horizontal line), 下 'down' (an icon beneath a horizontal line), and 中 'middle' (a vertical line running through the center of a square).
  - Compound ideograph: The combination of pictograph(s) and ideograph(s) to represent more complicated concepts. For example, 休 'rest' (a person 亻 leaning against a tree 木).

- Phonetic loan: This is a 'borrowing' process where a character is said to be used to represent a homophone (same sound, different meaning) which as yet has no orthographic representation. For example, the verb meaning 'spend' had a spoken form, *hua1*, but initially was without a written form, so the character of its homophone, 花 *hua1* meaning 'flower', was used to represent it.

Table 0.2 Different vs. identical Chinese characters across the two systems

Sound/meaning	Traditional Chinese	Simplified Chinese
guo2 'nation'	國	国
xue2 'learn'	學	学
zhong1 'middle'	中	中
sheng1 'pupil'	生	生

- Phono-semantic compound: This is the combination of a phonetic loan and a meaning component. For example, the word 娶 *qu3* 'marry a woman' was created by adding a meaning component, 女 'woman', to a homophone, 取 *qu3* 'retrieve'.

There are currently two systems of Chinese characters used in various Chinese communities around the globe. The Traditional Chinese (正體字) is used mainly in Taiwan and in Cantonese-speaking communities such as Hong Kong and Macau. These are standardized character forms dating back to the Han dynasty. The Simplified Chinese (简体字) was developed by the People's Republic of China in 1954 and is now the official form used in China and by most overseas Chinese language teaching programs. Many native speakers in China also read Traditional characters and Taiwanese speakers also write some Simplified characters, although there may be few who read both kinds of characters equally fluently (each conditioned by their educational upbringing). Traditional and Simplified Chinese characters are not always different. Table 0.2 shows two characters which differ and two characters which remain the same across the two platforms.

For practical reasons and following reviewer feedback, this book has been printed in Simplified Chinese characters instead of Traditional Chinese characters.

0.4 CHINESE SYNTAX

Chinese and English are said to follow the same basic word order of SVO (Subject → Verb → Object) which differs from a language like Japanese where the SOV (Subject → Object → Verb) word order applies. Many of the phrase structure rules of English are equally applicable to Chinese; for example:

- S → NP VP

A sentence can consist of a noun phrase and a verb phrase.

- NP → Art Adj N

A noun phrase can consist of an article, an adjective, and a noun.

- VP → V NP

A verb phrase can consist of a verb and a noun phrase.

However, there are departures from English in certain aspects of Chinese grammar. For example, a prepositional phrase (PP), consisting of a preposition (Prep) and a noun phrase (NP), normally comes *after* a verb or a noun in English. In Chinese, however, the Prep can be to the left or the right of the NP within the PP. The PP itself usually comes *before* the noun and before or after the verb it modifies. Thus:

English	Chinese
- PP → Prep NP	- PP → Prep NP or PP → NP Prep
in the area on the table	在这地区 'at-this-area' 桌上 'table-up'
- NP → Art N PP	- NP → PP *de5* N
the fiddler on the roof	屋顶上的提琴手 'roof-on-*de5*-fiddler'
- VP → V PP	- VP → PP V
playing in the pub	在酒吧内演奏 'inside-pub-play music'

There are other differences between Chinese and English syntax in respect of word order. For example, an adverb describing a verb usually comes after the verb in English (e.g. He leaves *tomorrow*). In Chinese, the default position for 'tomorrow' would be between the subject and the verb (i.e. 他明天走 'he-tomorrow-walk (He leaves tomorrow)').

Just like Chinese words, a Chinese sentence is also difficult to define. Many Chinese sentences are either without subjects or without verbs, or have multiple verb phrases which are not well coordinated. In addition, the special Topic-Comment structure adds an extra dimension to the complexity of Chinese syntax. A Chinese sentence can start with two noun phrases, one representing the topic and the other the subject of the sentence.

0.5 CHINESE DISCOURSE

The problem of delineating Chinese sentences carries on to the reading of Chinese paragraphs. In reading an English paragraph, the unit of processing is normally a sentence (or a well-defined phrase if the sentence is relatively long). Both sentential grammar and punctuation marks are very helpful in defining English sentences. In Chinese, the punctuation marks do not help separate sentences as they do in English and the sentence seems to 'run on' forever. It is difficult for novice readers to know when to stop, 'wrap up' a structure and 'sum up the meaning' read so far. Take the following news text, for example (the translation is intentionally made 'structurally literal' so as to keep as many traits of the Chinese syntax as possible):

> 四川省泸州市一商场发生一起爆燃事故，商场负一楼和一楼起火，附近的多家店铺和一家宾馆也被殃及，事故现场玻璃碎片散落一地。截止到27日凌晨6时，事故造成4人死亡，35人被送往医院留院观察治疗。
>
> Sichuan Province Luzhou City a shopping mall occurred a deflagration accident, the mall first floor basement and ground floor caught fire, nearby many shops and a hotel were also involved, the accident scene shards of glass scattered on the ground. As at 6:00 on the 27th, the accident killed four people, 35 people were taken to hospital for observation and treatment.

There are six identifiable sentences in the above example, based on the conventional method of sentence analysis. However, there are only two Chinese period marks in the text. As will be explained in Chapter 3, Chinese-style periods (。) are used more for 'conceptual' rather than structural marking. Nor are the Chinese commas (，) used to mark sentences – although most of them do in this particular instance. The fourth comma, however, delineates a time phrase rather than a sentence. In Chapter 3, we analyze Chinese sentences in ways that will help readers understand not only the structure of the sentence itself but also how Chinese sentences are extended to become paragraphs.

On the spoken side of the language, we focus on a category of morphemes called sentence-final particles (SFPs) in Chinese, which are treated as discourse markers (DMs) in this book. Discourse markers are those 'small words' which play an important role in oral communication. In English, words like *oh*, *so*, *well*, *anyway*, *I mean*, *you know*, etc. help make sure conversation moves on in a smooth and efficient way. In Chinese, the same functions are carried out by a battery of linguistic devices called sentence-final particles. For example, the English expression *Well, that's it!* is often used to conclude something, with the discourse marker *well* showing the speaker's mood of relief, reluctance, disappointment, and so on. In the example below, the function of *well* is transferred to the SFP 了 *le5* in the Chinese translation.

> *Well,* that's it. Our show is over.
>
> | 就 | 这样 | 了。 | 我们 | 的 | 表演 | 到 | 此 | 为 | 止。 |
> |------|----------|------|----------|------|-----------|------|-------|--------|-------|
> | jiu4 | zhe4yang4 | le5 | wo3men5 | de5 | biao3yan3 | dao4 | ci3 | wei2 | zhi3 |
> | 'just' | 'like so' | SFP | 'our' | PD | 'performance' | 'reach' | 'this' | 'act as' | 'stop' |
>
> 'This is it then. Our show stops here.'

Note that, in the proper Chinese translation above, the discourse marker *well* is replaced by a sentence-final particle 了, which expresses the same sense of conclusion and the accompanying emotions. In Chinese, there are at least a dozen SFPs serving discourse marker functions, and these are discussed extensively in Chapter 5.

0.6 MANDARIN IN TAIWAN

Although Simplified Chinese and Pinyin seem to have become the mainstream encoding systems for Chinese orthography and phonology respectively, they are not the only option (just as communism is not the only possible political system for Chinese countries). The Traditional Chinese and the Zhuyin phonetic transcription system used in Taiwan deserve more of the world's attention.

The current government of Taiwan represents the political party (i.e. the Nationalist Party, or KMT) which led the revolution in 1911 that overthrew the Qing Dynasty. The Republic of China (中華民國) began in 1912, which was the first year in the country's independent calendar. This is still the official calendar system in Taiwan. Thus, Taiwanese year 103, or 中華民國103年 'year 103 of the ROC', is converted to year 2014 (= 103 + 1911) of the Western calendar.

The KMT (or 國民黨), after being defeated by Chinese Communist Party (CCP) in 1949 and relocating to Taiwan, initially ruled by single-party authoritarianism, just like the current CCP in China. However, with a series of successful democratic movements from the grassroots, a strong opposition party, the Democratic Progressive Party (民主进步党), was established in 1986, and the first direct Presidential election took place in 1996. From then on, Taiwan has become a fully democratic country with multi-party electoral competition, a parliament (called the Legislative Yuan), ideology-free education, unimpeded information flow, and the right to free speech and protests. Everything is regulated by law instead of being controlled by a long-standing party. The law is made by members of parliament who are directly elected by the people.

Communications between the two sides of the Taiwan Strait have become increasingly frequent in recent years due to the recent open policy of China and the need of Taiwanese people to develop businesses on the mainland. There was a period of some 40 years, however, in which interactions between Taiwan and China were few because of the continuing state of war after 1949 (with both sides wanting to regain lost territories). The Chinese languages evolved independently in both regions during this period, which resulted in some noticeable differences, especially in terms of the pronunciation of Mandarin and their vocabulary. However, the differences are mostly negligible and generally do not affect communication.

In Taiwan, Mandarin was made the official language after the KMT set up the government in 1949. The phonetic system used in Taiwan to teach Mandarin, called Zhuyin fuhao (注音符号) or simply Zhuyin, dated back to 1913 when the KMT was still in power in China. Zhuyin looks different from the Pinyin system released by the government of China in 1958. Table 0.3 contrasts the symbols used in both systems.

Initially, the Zhuyin system may seem difficult and an extra burden to learn. However, once the symbols are learned, and the correct phonetic associations made, the subsequent learning of Mandarin syllables, words and phrases using Zhuyin can be easier than with Pinyin (Flynn 2010).

Table 0.3 The Zhuyin and Pinyin symbols for consonants and vowels used in Mandarin

Consonants

Zhuyin	ㄅ	ㄆ	ㄇ	ㄈ	ㄉ	ㄊ	ㄋ	ㄌ	ㄍ	ㄎ	ㄏ	ㄐ	ㄑ	ㄒ
Pinyin	b	p	m	f	d	t	n	l	g	k	h	j	q	x

Zhuyin	ㄓ	ㄔ	ㄕ	ㄖ	ㄗ	ㄘ	ㄙ	ㄧ	ㄨ	ㄩ				
Pinyin	zh	ch	sh	r	z	c	s	y	w	yu				

Vowels

Zhuyin	ㄚ	ㄛ	ㄜ	ㄝ	ㄞ	ㄟ	ㄠ	ㄡ	ㄢ	ㄣ	ㄤ	ㄥ	ㄦ
Pinyin	a	o	e	e	ai	ei	au	ou	an	en	ang	eng	er

Note: The semivowels ㄧ, ㄨ and ㄩ are used both as consonants and as vowels

CHAPTER 1

Chinese sounds

In this chapter, we explore the range of sounds used in spoken Mandarin, how these sounds combine to form syllables, and how the tones are added onto the syllables to form meaningful spoken units. We first distinguish between consonants and vowels, explain some of their characteristics, and then analyze how a Chinese syllable is made using different combinations of consonants and vowels. In the second part, we introduce Chinese tones which are a necessary component in turning syllables into the basic unit of meaning in Chinese.

1.1 INTRODUCTION

Like English (and all other human languages), Chinese uses both consonants (C) and vowels (V) to construct meaningful units. In addition, when combining consonants and a vowel to form a syllable, Chinese uses a simpler method than English; that is, while English permits consonant clusters of up to three consonants each within a syllable, Chinese only allows one consonant per possible slot (i.e. before or after the vowel).

Three levels of linguistic structures are contrasted between English and Chinese in Figure 1.1: the word level, the syllabic level, and the sound level. In particular, the differences in structural complexity of syllables between English and Chinese are highlighted. The word *Christopher* comprises three syllables which differ from one another dramatically in terms of vowel-consonant configurations, as shown on the left side of Figure 1.1. The first syllable of *Christopher* consists of two consonant clusters surrounding a vowel – altogether five different sounds. The second syllable is a single vowel and the third syllable is made up of a consonant and a vowel. In contrast, when *Christopher* is transliterated into Chinese, the sounds adjust to the Chinese phonotactic system and the overall picture becomes more 'orderly', as the right half of Figure 1.1 shows. For example, Chinese phonotactics do not allow a syllable initial consonant cluster (excluding a consonant-semivowel combination), so a vowel has to be inserted between the beginning two consonants. Thus, the initial CCV configuration of *Christopher* is broken into two syllables in the Chinese translation, becoming *ke* and *li* (CV-CV structure). Secondly, the /s/ sound in Chinese cannot exist alone and must be supported by a following vowel. This is where *si* comes in

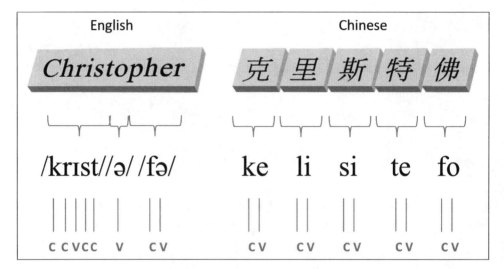

Figure 1.1 A rough comparison of English and Chinese syllabic structures

as the third syllable in the Chinese version. The rest of the word (i.e. -topher) generates a good CV-CV correspondence between the two languages so the syllabic structure remains unchanged.

Thus, any syllable comprising a CCV structure must be turned into a disyllabic CV-CV structure to conform to the Chinese phonotactic restriction, and a VC structure must be changed to V-CV, unless the ending consonant is a nasal. That is, the only final consonants allowed in Mandarin are two of the three nasal stops – the n (alveolar) or the ng (velar) sound.

1.2 CHINESE SOUNDS

We now turn to the Chinese phonemic inventory; that is, the list of consonants and vowels used in Chinese pronunciation. Again, there are abundant similarities between English and Chinese. We will use the Chinese Pinyin system to represent Chinese sounds. English sounds, where applicable, are represented by their IPA symbols.

There are 22 Chinese consonants altogether (in this discussion we will exclude the three semivowels), the same as English (if its two semivowels are also excluded). Chinese consonants are allocated in Table 1.1 to slots according to the manner and place of articulation. IPA phonetic symbols are provided in brackets where there are equivalent English consonants.

The places of articulation for the sounds in Table 1.1 are marked approximately in Figure 1.2, with straight lines connecting parts of the tongue to the roof of the oral cavity where the constrictions occur. For example, the bilabial sounds (b, p and m) are made by the upper and lower lips coming together. The labial-dental sound f is made by gently placing the upper teeth on the lower lip and letting the air flow through the narrow passage continuously. The dental

Table 1.1 Chinese consonants shown with English equivalents (where available)

Manner of articulation	Place of articulation	Bilabial −vd	Bilabial +vd	Labio-dental −vd	Dental −vd	Alveolar −vd	Alveolar +vd	Post-alveolar (Retroflex) −vd	Post-alveolar (Retroflex) +vd	Alveo-palatal −vd	Velar −vd
Plosive	−asp	b [p]				d [t]					g [k]
	+asp	p [pʰ]				t [tʰ]					k [kʰ]
Affricate	−asp				z			zh		j	
	+asp				c			ch		q	
Fricative				f [f]	s [s]			sh	r	x	h
Lateral							l [l]				
Nasal			m [m]				n [n]				ng [ŋ]

sounds (z, c and s) are made by bringing together the tip of the tongue and the back of the upper teeth.

There are five ways of making the consonants in Table 1.1, referred to as the *manner of articulation*. The plosives, also called 'stops', are made by building up air pressure (air drawn from the lungs) in the tightly shut mouth and releasing it by suddenly opening up the closure and releasing all the air. The closure may be made by the two lips (b, p, m), by the front of the tongue sealing the mouth at the alveolar ridge (d, t), or by the back of the tongue attaching to the velum (g, k).

The fricatives are made by allowing the air to flow freely from the lungs, up through a narrow passage in the oral cavity, to the outside. Again, the narrow passage may be formed in many places. In Chinese, the s fricative is made by bringing the tip of the tongue toward the back of the upper teeth, which is different from the English [s] whose constriction point is a little way back into the mouth, at the alveolar ridge. The h sound, on the other hand, is made through the narrow passage formed by the back of the tongue and the velum. The Chinese h is also different from the English [h] (e.g. *home*), which is generally characterized as a glottal fricative.

The affricates have both properties of plosives and fricatives as they involve both an initial closure and some trailing air flow through a narrow passage. There are six affricate sounds in Mandarin Chinese. The z and c share the same place of articulation with s – at the back of the front teeth. Both the zh and ch sounds are made by using the tongue (curled up like the bowl of a spoon) to enclose the oral cavity at the post-alveolar region. The mounted air is then released all of a sudden with a trickling hiss. The j and q sounds are similar to the [dʒ] (*giant*) and [tʃ] (*cheese*) sounds respectively in English. If you modify the two English sounds by 'flattening out' your lips (from the original rounded shape), the resultant sounds are very much like j and q.

Both the lateral sound (l) and the nasal sounds (m, n, ng) used in Chinese are basically the same as those in English.

According to Table 1.1, 12 of the 22 Chinese consonants are also used in English. The other 10 consonants (four fricatives and six affricates) will be unfamiliar to someone who speaks only English. Also, of the 22 Chinese consonants in Table 1.1, ng is only used in syllable-ending position. As in English, the sound ng is not used to begin a syllable. Conversely, all the other 21 consonants in Table 1.1 are only used in syllable-beginning position in Chinese – except for n, which can be used either to begin or to end a syllable.

Most Chinese consonants are voiceless; the voiced ones are the three nasals m, n and ng, the lateral l, and a retroflex r. The retroflex pair, r and sh, are the only pair of sounds in Chinese that offers a voiced-voiceless contrast. In English, by contrast, many pairs of sounds exist where one sound differs from the other only in voicing, such as [p]-[b], [k]-[g], [f]-[v], and so on. In Chinese, the plosive sounds are instead contrasted by the 'aspiration' feature, which is not used to distinguish phonemes in English. Voicing refers to the vibrating movement of the vocal cords when making the sound. Aspiration refers to the extra puff of air coming out of the mouth when articulating a sound, usually when uttering plosives or affricates, whose initial closure of the oral cavity enables aspiration.

In English, aspiration is a feature that distinguishes between allophones (variants of the same phoneme that are pronounced differently due to a different phonetic environment). For example, the same /p/ sound is pronounced with aspiration [pʰ] at word-initial position, such as *poet*, but it is pronounced unaspirated [p] in a word like *sport*. Although the two sounds are pronounced differently, they are both recognized by native speakers of English as the same phoneme /p/ at the conceptual level. One can articulate the /p/ in *sport* as [pʰ] and the word is still recognized as *sport* even though the pronunciation may be thought of as irregular. In Chinese, however, aspiration has a different status – it is used to distinguish meanings. For example, *ba* [pa] said in the fourth tone can mean 'father' (爸), but *pa* [pʰa] in the same tone can mean 'afraid' (怕) instead. Such a pair like [pa] and [pʰa] are called a 'minimal pair' in phonology – they differ only in one sound at the same position and their meanings are different. In this case, it is the aspiration feature that creates the semantic difference.

According to Table 1.1, there are 12 Chinese consonants which have (close) English equivalents and therefore can be pronounced relatively easily by an English speaker:

Chinese	b	p	m	f	d	t	n	l	g	k	h	ng
English	s*p*eak	*p*eak	*m*e	*f*or	s*t*eak	*t*oo	*n*o	*l*ow	s*k*y	*k*ey	*h*ot	si*ng*

On the other hand, there are also 10 Chinese consonants that differ from similar English sounds to different degrees. Some sounds only require minor adjustments, such as making the rounded lips unrounded. Some are more difficult to assimilate, such as the four retroflex sounds.

Chinese	j	q	x	z	c	s	zh	ch	sh	r
English	*j*eep	*ch*eap	*sh*eet	card*s*	*ts*unami	*s*un	*j*am	*ch*ain	*sh*ower	*r*aw

The approximate places of articulation of the 21 syllable-initial Chinese consonants are marked on Figure 1.2.

Of the 10 consonants that have no close equivalents in English, the *x* sound is similar to the English *s* in that they are both fricatives and both make high-pitched, intensive hissing sounds (called 'sibilants'), except that the constriction point for *x* (alveo-palatal) is further back than [s] (alveolar). Both *j* and *q* are affricates, which start like a plosive but release continuously like a fricative. The *j* sound can be made by 'unrounding' the [dʒ] sound of *J* in *Jack*; that is, it is much like the *j* sound in *jeep*. Likewise, to make the *q* sound in Pinyin, 'unround' your lips when saying the [tʃ] sound of the *ch* in *church*. Again, it is easier to

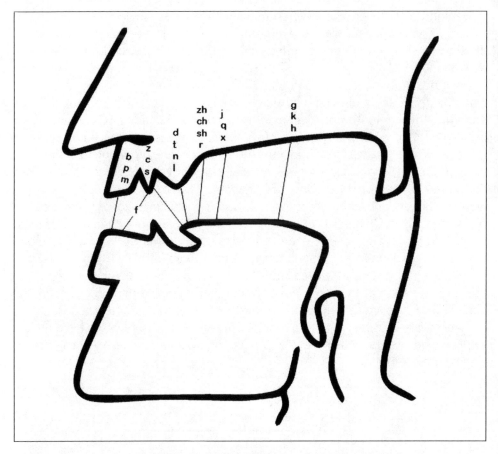

Figure 1.2 The 21 syllable-initial Chinese consonants (in Pinyin)

get the *q* sound when the *ch* sound is followed by a high front vowel as in *cheap*, which is less conducive to rounded lips.

Both *z* and *c* are also affricates. Both are made by bringing the tip of the tongue to the back of the teeth to form a closure and then releasing the air in an 'explosive' manner followed by a trailing hiss. The *z* sound is like the *ds* sound at the end of a word like *cards*. The *c* sound is similar except that it is aspirated. The *ts* at the beginning of *tsunami* sounds like the Chinese *c*. The Chinese *s* sound is again similar to the [s] sound in English except that *s*, like *z* and *c*, is made by the tongue approaching the teeth rather than the alveolar ridge.

The four Chinese retroflex sounds, *zh*, *ch*, *sh* and *r*, are probably the most difficult to assimilate for most learners (indeed, some of them are difficult even for many Chinese native speakers to master). These sounds are made by curling up the tongue toward the post-alveolar area. The tip of the tongue does not 'curl back' to any large degree as the word *retroflex* suggests. Instead, there is a general rise of all edges of the tongue when the tip of the tongue touches (in the cases of *zh* and *ch*) or approaches (in the cases of *sh* and *r*)

Table 1.2 Chinese vowels in Pinyin shown with English vowels (where applicable)

	Front		Center	Back	
	−rd	+rd	−rd	−rd	+rd
Close	i [i]	ü	ɨ	u (part of diphthong) [ʊ]	u (standing alone) [u]
Mid	e (part of diphthong) [ɛ]		e (before nasals) [ə]	e (standing alone)	o [ɔ]
Open	a [a]				

the post-alveolar area. The configuration of the oral cavity remains the same for all four sounds. They differ in *zh* and *ch* being affricates (release of air after initial blockage) and *sh* and *r* being fricatives (continual release of air through a narrow passage). The two sounds *zh* and *ch* differ in the former being unaspirated and the latter aspirated. The *sh*, on the other hand, is voiceless and the *r* is voiced.

In terms of vowels, there are 10 single vowels in Chinese, most of which have close English equivalents and cause few problems. Table 1.2 lists the 10 single vowels in Mandarin Chinese. Where available, their English counterparts appear in brackets in IPA symbols.

Vowels are classified by the tongue position being relatively 'front' or 'back', high (close) or low (open). They are also called rounded (+rd) or unrounded (−rd), based on the shape of the lips when uttering the vowels. Finely classified, there are 10 single vowels in Mandarin Chinese, seven of which have close English equivalents, as Table 1.2 shows. Two of the unshared vowels, *ü* and *ɨ*, due to the relative inconvenience in typing, are normally represented as *u* (or *v*) and *i* respectively in Pinyin, causing ambiguity as both *u* and *i* also represent other sounds. The third unshared vowel, [ɤ], is written in Pinyin as *e* (the standing alone *e* in Table 1.2) and is discussed in the next paragraph. The seven vowels used by Mandarin that have close English equivalents are shown below with English words containing the relevant vowel:

Chinese	a [a]	i [i]	e [ɛ]	e [ə]	u [ʊ]	u [u]	o [ɔ]
English	far	see	very	about	know	too	all

As Table 1.2 shows, the use of *e* is ambiguous in three ways in Pinyin. The first usage of *e* is equal to IPA symbol [ɛ]. When following a semivowel (e.g. *ye*), this kind of *e* sounds like the *e* in *cherry*. The same is true when *e* combines with other vowels to form a diphthong, such as *ei* and *üe*. This sound is sometimes expressed as *ê* in Pinyin, to distinguish it from the other forms of *e*. Second, when *e* is followed by a nasal sound such as *en* or *eng*, it is pronounced as [ə], like the *a* in *acute*. Third, when *e* stands as the sole vowel in a syllable, it is equivalent to IPA symbol [ɤ] and is pronounced like the *ir* in the English *sir*. Example Chinese syllables are *de*, *te*, *ne*, *zhe*, *che*, *she*, and so on. Some sounds in this category will 'look like' an English word – *me*, *he* and *she* – but when used in Pinyin, they only represent the sounds (which are pronounced differently from their English lookalikes) and may be associated with a number of different meanings depending on the tone.

Despite the high degree of similarity, two Chinese vowels are quite different from regular English vowels – the [y] sound and the [ɨ] sound in IPA symbols. The [y] sound is translated to *ü* as a relatively familiar alphabetic letter but the [ɨ] is still represented as *i* due to a lack of familiar corresponding letters.

Chinese	ü	ɨ
	(written as *v* or *u* in Pinyin)	(written as *i* in Pinyin and only appearing after *z*, *c*, *s* and *zh*, *ch*, *sh*, *r*)
English	m*ü*esli	zzz*i*...
	(German pronunciation)	(the vowel part of this buzzing sound)

Since the [ɨ] sound is written as *i* in Pinyin, the *i* symbol then comes to represent two sounds. It is pronounced as the *ee* in *see* in most cases (without the 'long' vowel ingredient), but it becomes a central (instead of front) high vowel when following the three dental sibilants (*z*, *c*, *s*) or the four retroflex (*zh*, *ch*, *sh*, *r*) sounds. The IPA symbol for this sound is *ɨ* (the letter *i* with a horizontal bar). This central vowel is not found in English and can be assimilated by making a *zzzi* buzzing sound (keeping only the 'vowel' part).

Another sound that does not exist in English is *ü*, a rounded front vowel, which is found not only in Chinese, but also in German and other languages. A way to make this sound is to start to say the *y* sound in *yellow*, while at the same time making your lips round (like the lips' shape in saying *u*), so *ü* is somewhat like 'the combination of [i] and [u]'. Because *ü* is not found on common English keyboards, in practice the Chinese input method normally accepts the *v* letter as *ü*. That is, if we want to type the Chinese character equal to *nü3* ('female'), we strike *nv3* on the keyboard and we will get the desirable character 女. It is also not uncommon to use *nv* (as in this book) or even *nu* in place of *nü* as surface Pinyin representations. However, since *nu* itself is a legitimate representation of other meanings, context is crucial for determining whether *nu* really means *nu* or, rather, *nü* on a given occasion.

There is, in fact, an additional vowel in Mandarin which is like the vowel version of the retroflex consonants. This is represented in Pinyin as *er*. Since it is an isolated vowel and only forms a syllable by itself (that is, it does not combine with consonants or other vowels to form a syllable), it is excluded from further discussions.

Apart from the 22 consonants and the 10 vowels described above, there are three semivowels (or glides) in Chinese, whose IPA symbols are [w] (voiced labialized velar approximant), [j] (palatal approximant) and [ɥ] (voiced labialized palatal approximant) respectively. The English counterparts for both *w* and *y* exist, e.g. the [w] sound in *wasp* and the [j] sound in *York*. But there is no English counterpart for *yu* [ɥ], just as there is no *ü* in English. IPA symbols like [j], [w], [ɥ] are adopted by Duanmu (2007) for dedicated discussions on Chinese phonology. In this book, however, like other consonants and vowels, we continue to use the Pinyin symbols – in this case, *w*, *y* and *yu* respectively – to represent these three sounds, taking advantage of Pinyin's connectivity between sounds and meaning.

1.3 CHINESE SYLLABLES

When analyzing Chinese syllables, it is customary to present models more complicated than the CV (consonant-vowel) structure seen in Figure 1.1. Normally, a Chinese syllable is said to comprise an Initial and a Final. The Initial can be one of the 21 consonants shown in Figure 1.2. It can also be absent in the case of a syllable consisting only of the Final. The Final itself consists of three parts: the Medial, the Nucleus and the Ending. The Medial, when present, is one of the three semivowels *w*, *y* or *yu*. The Nucleus is the only indispensable element in the syllable, which can be any one of the nine vowels given in Table 1.2 (i.e. excluding the 'part of diphthong' [ʊ] which only appears in the ending position). Finally, the Ending can be *i*, *o*, *u* or one of the two nasals *n* or *ng*. Figure 1.3 shows the Chinese syllable structure with all the possible sounds in each component and an overall example syllable.

Note that in Figure 1.3, the example syllable *qiao* makes use of a medial *y* [j], which is written as *i* instead of *y* (it will be written as *y* in a syllable-initial position such as *yan*). In the same vein, for a syllable like *kuan*, the *u* stands for the semivowel medial [w], which will be written as *w* in a syllable like *wang*. To take another example, the syllable *yuan* is analyzable into a Medial (*yu*) + Nucleus (*a*) + Ending (*n*) with *yu* standing for the semivowel *yu* [ɥ].

Another graphical illustration of the Chinese syllabic structure is given in Figure 1.4 to show more example syllables and how they are generated from each component.

Another way of analyzing the Chinese syllabic structure is using the Zhuyin convention adopted in Taiwan. The Zhuyin system introduces a different set of symbols, each standing for an Initial, a Medial or a Nucleus + Ending combination. Figure 1.5 shows how some example syllables are derived in the Zhuyin-based model.

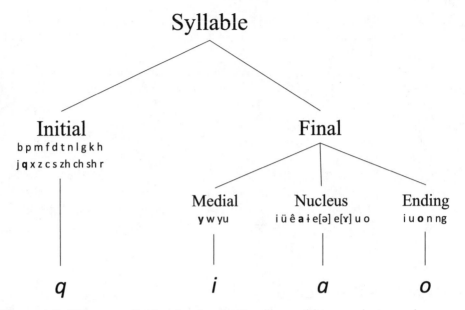

Figure 1.3 Chinese syllable structure with all possible sounds in each level/group

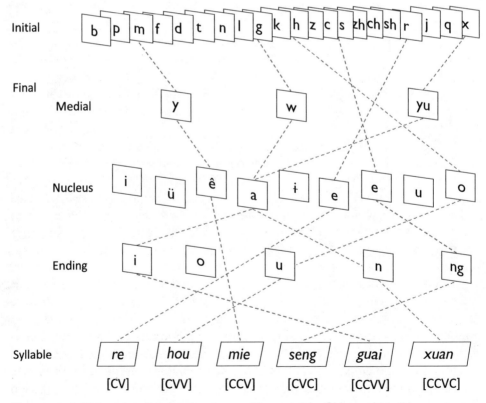

Figure 1.4 Chinese syllable structure with possible CV combinations

Initial

Final

Medial

Nucleus and

Ending

Syllable

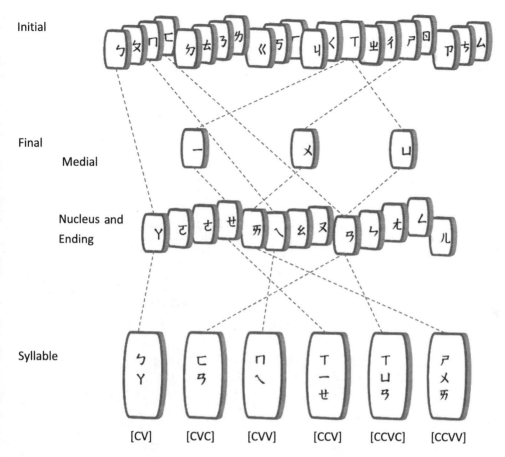

[CV]   [CVC]   [CVV]   [CCV]   [CCVC]   [CCVV]

Figure 1.5 Chinese syllable structure based on the Zhuyin system

As can be seen from Figure 1.5, the Zhuyin system clearly and unambiguously represents the three semivowels with distinct symbols — ㄧ (y in Pinyin), ㄨ (w in Pinyin) and ㄩ (yu in Pinyin). The Nucleus and the Ending portions are combined in the Zhuyin model so that some symbols in this category consist of only a vowel sound, while others each represent a diphthong or a combination of a vowel and an ending nasal. The symbols are very distinct and provide a good way for generating and remembering the Chinese syllables.

1.4 CHINESE TONES

For each syllable in Mandarin Chinese it is possible to distinguish four varieties based on tonal differences. More accurately, the difference lies in the pitch contour of each variety. For example, I recorded myself speaking *ma1*, *ma2*, *ma3* and *ma4* (with the numbers representing the first to the fourth tone respectively). The result is shown in Figure 1.6. While the time factor in Figure 1.6 (i.e. the horizontal bar) merits some attention, the pitch track (the vertical parameter) is the more important distinguishing factor.

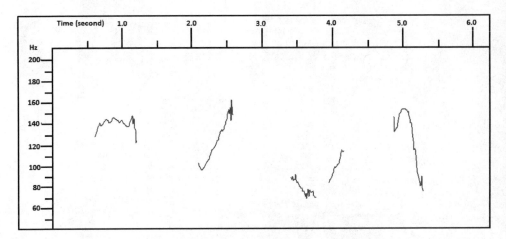

Figure 1.6 The pitch tracks of *ma1, ma2, ma3* and *ma4* spoken by the author of this book

Here is a summarized description of the four tones based on Figure 1.6 (that is, in terms of the author's voice range):

- First tone (high-level): maintaining a level and relatively high pitch through-out the articulation, concentrating on the 140Hz line.
- Second tone (rising): starting at a medium point and rising steeply, from around the 100 Hz point to approximately 160Hz.
- Third tone (falling-rising): starting from a medium pitch (90Hz), falling to a lower point (70Hz) and rising again to a higher point (120Hz).
- Fourth tone (falling): starting from a higher pitch (160Hz) and falling sharply to a low point (80Hz).

There is a standard method for encoding Chinese tones in Pinyin using tone marks of corresponding shapes; for example, *ma1* as mā, *ma2* as má, *ma3* as mǎ, and *ma4* as mà. However, this book adopts the number system for clearer presentation in later chapters when Pinyin annotations have to be given in smaller fonts for language examples. The Chinese language (teaching) literature normally represents the tonal differences in idealized ways like so:

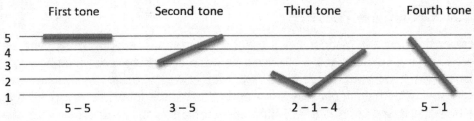

Figure 1.7 Tonal differences

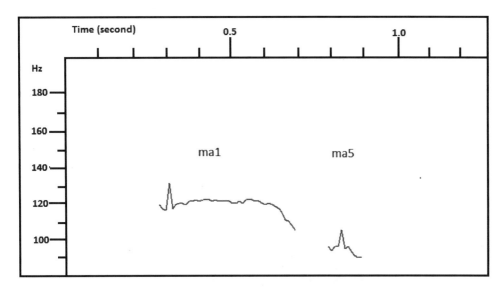

Figure 1.8 The pitch tracks of *ma1ma5* spoken by the author of this book

Note that, in practice, the third tone is rarely pronounced in full but normally ends 'at the bottom'; that is, with the pitch contour of 2-1 instead of 2-1-4. This is known as the 'half third' tone – see Norman (1988, p. 147), for example.

Also note that, apart from the four distinct tones, there is a fifth tone called the 'neutral tone' (or simply 'toneless'), which is a relatively low-pitched and short sound without a sustained or stable contour. In Figure 1.8, I said *ma1ma5* ('mother'). Note that the second *ma* is of the fifth tone and is lower in pitch as well as much shorter in duration. The fifth tone, however, is normally not used to distinguish meaning, but is merely a reduction at the phonetic level for certain syllables at an unstressed position. The two *ma*'s in Figure 1.8, for example, represent the same meaning, although the second *ma* is reduced to 'toneless' in that position.

The addition of tone means many different meanings can be expressed by each of the 400 or so syllables created via the process illustrated in Figures 1.4 and 1.5. Using the syllable *ba* as an example, we can have four different kinds of *ba*-based syllables, each of which represents one or more meaning. The most common meanings for each syllable-tone combination are shown in Table 1.3. More homophones of each of these varieties can be found in a complete Chinese dictionary.

Note that the pitch range for each tone is relative. Each person has a different voice frequency range. Their tones can be understood so long as the pitch contours are correct, disregarding the absolute pitch range. In other words, for a given syllable, there are prototypes (i.e. the most typical representations) for each tonal contour, but there are no absolute pitch levels to aim at. For example, Figure 1.9 shows two different people saying the same syllable with the same tone. The pitch contours are recognizable, even though the pitch tracks

Table 1.3 Different tones of the syllable *ba* and some examples for each tone variety

Different tones of the same syllable	Different meanings for the same syllable-tone combination	Character corresponding to the meaning
ba1	'eight'	八
	'to get close to', 'to long for'	巴
	'scar'	疤
ba2	'to pull out'	拔
	'cymbal'	钹
	'to travel'	跋
ba3	'handle', 'to hold', Object Marker	把
	'target'	靶
ba4	'father'	爸
	'a local chief', 'to dominate'	霸
	'dam'	坝
	'to cease'	罢

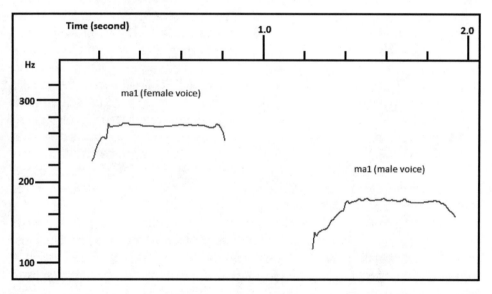

Figure 1.9 A male and a female saying the same syllable with the same tone

appear at very different frequency ranges (i.e. female between 220–270 Hz, male at a lower 120–180 Hz range).

Chinese tones are not as difficult to master as some would believe. Tonal contours are also witnessed in non-tonal languages such as English. The difference is that a non-tonal language does not use tonal variations to distinguish meaning. For example, in English, there are different ways of saying *no*, as in *No?*, *No!!*, or *No, I'm not*. Actually, Mandarin has the smallest number of tones in comparison to other Chinese dialects. Cantonese, for example, is said to utilize as many as nine tones (see Sun 2006 for a summarizing table of tones versus dialects and Lin 2001 for a detailed analysis of tonal differences between the dialects).

Another point to note about Chinese tones is the tonal change of syllables in certain contexts; this is also called 'tone sandhi'. We have already seen an example of tone sandhi in Figure 1.8, where the second instance of *ma1* in *ma1ma1* is reduced to the fifth (or neutral) tone in most contexts (i.e. we say *ma1ma5* instead of *ma1ma1*). In fact, this is a very common tone reduction process that weakens the tone of the second syllable for many disyllabic items. For example, the normal pronunciation of 西瓜 'watermelon' is *xi1gua1* but, on many occasions, it is changed to *xi1gua5*, especially when it is at the end of a sentence. This applies mostly to Mainland Chinese speakers and not to the Taiwanese ones.

Another frequently encountered tone sandhi is changing the first third tone to second tone when two third tone syllables form a lexical unit or a phrase of some sort. For example, when we combine *lao3* ('old') and *ma3* ('horse') to form 老马 'old horse', we say *lao2ma3* [23] instead of *lao3ma3* [33]. The latter seems more difficult to produce (and comprehend) if you insist on not changing the tone!

When there are three consecutive syllables all marked with the third tone, the process of sandhi is more complicated. Which syllable needs to change tone depends on the grouping of morphemes. For example, in the case of 女总统 *nv3zong3tong3* [333] 'female president', since *zong3tong3* [33] 'president' is a lexical item, it is also a sandhi unit and changes to *zong2tong3* [23], so the entire unit becomes *nv3zong2tong3* [323] when uttered. When no such internal grouping occurs within a trisyllabic unit, such as the syntactic combination 省点纸 'save some paper', the pronunciation changes from *sheng3dian3zhi3* [333] to *sheng2dian2zhi3* [223]. That is, the two third tones prior to the final third tone are changed to the second tone.

If a disyllabic unit has already undergone a sandhi process, i.e. it has changed from [33] tone to [23], but it is followed by another syllable in the third tone, then a further sandhi process is applied. For example, the phrase 总统好 [*zong3-tong3*] *hao3* '[president] good' ('How are you, president?'), is pronounced as *zong2tong2hao3* [223] rather than *zong2tong3hao3* [233]. That is, the end product is like a trisyllabic item without internal grouping, such as 省点纸 [223] mentioned above.

If a quadrisyllabic unit consists entirely of third tone syllables, the pronunciation also depends on how you group the morphemes based on semantic and syntactic properties. Some groupings are easier to say. For example, 总统好惨 is analyzed as [*zong3tong3*][*hao3can3*] '[president] [very miserable]' and is spoken in a rhythmic [23][23] pattern. But in the case of 水果酒好 [[*shui3guo3*]*jiu3*][*hao3*] '[[fruit] wine][good]', the sandhi process first needs to change the pronunciation of 水果 'fruit' from [33] to [23] as this is the core unit; then it changes 水果酒 'fruit wine' from [233] to [223]. The final step, however, is less decisive. Most native speakers from China being presented with 水果酒好 are not sure how to say it! It could be that the same process continues to change 水果酒好 from [2233] to [2223] but a process of sandhi as far-reaching as this is rare. Most native speakers I asked, who managed to settle on a more consistent pronunciation, replied they would say [2233] instead of [2223].

How do we pronounce an even longer five-syllable expression such as 总统你好惨 zong3tong3 ni3 hao3can3 'president, you are miserable'? Again, we analyze the phrase into groups of syllables based on semantic and/or syntactic properties, and then activate the sandhi process for each identified group. Thus, 总统你好惨 is grouped into ［总统］ 你 ［好惨］ '[president] you [very miserable]' and pronounced as zong2tong3 ni3 hao2can3 or [23]3[23]. The process is the same for even longer expressions. For example, 总统你好我很惨 can be grouped into ［总统］ ［你好］ 我 ［很惨］ '[president] [how are you] I [very miserable]' and pronounced as zong2tong3 ni2hao3 wo3 hen2can3 or [23][23]3[23]. Note that, in both cases, we have a condition where two third tone syllables are adjacent to each other. In other words, a [33] combination is still pronounceable and even inevitable when word grouping dictates it or in order to avoid 'unfavorable' sandhi results such as the [2223] configuration.

In very rare cases, the same sequence of syllables can be analyzed in more than one way, generating different readings. For example, 派出所有女主管 can be grouped in two ways:

a	［派出所］	有	［女主管］
	pai4chu1suo3	you3	nv3zhu3guan3 [original]
	pai4chu1suo3	you(2or3)	nv3zhu2guan3 [result of sandhi]
	'police station'	'have'	'female supervisor'

'There are female supervisor(s) in the local police station.'

b	［派出］	［所有］	［女主管］
	pai4chu1	suo3you3	nv3zhu3guan3 [original]
	pai4chu1	**suo2**you(2or3)	nv3zhu2guan3 [result of sandhi]
	'dispatch'	'all'	'female supervisor'

'Dispatch all the female supervisors!'

The crucial difference between the two analyses lies in the tone of the morpheme 所. If the speaker keeps the third tone for this syllable as in (a), then it is understood to be part of 派出所 'the police station' and the sentence is interpreted accordingly. If 所 is changed to the second tone as in (b), then it is understood to form a constituent with 有 to become 所有 'all', and a different interpretation applies. Tone sandhi, therefore, can help resolve ambiguous sentences occasionally.

Finally, special sandhi processes are applicable to two particular morphemes in Chinese — 一 *yi1* 'one' and 不 *bu4* 'not'. There are three situations:

- When standing alone or as an ending morpheme to a constituent, 一 and 不 are spoken with their original first and fourth tone respectively (e.g. 第一 *di4yi1* 'first'; 要不 *yao4bu4* 'otherwise').
- When followed by a syllable with the fourth tone, both 一 and 不 are changed to the second tone in their respective units (e.g. 一半 *yi2ban4* 'half', 不算 *bu2suan4* 'not-count').
- When followed by a syllable with all other tones (i.e. first, second and third tone), both 一 and 不 are changed to the fourth tone (e.g. 一生 *yi4sheng1* 'one lifetime', 一元 *yi4yuan2* 'one dollar', 一本 *yi4ben3* 'one volume'; 不高 *bu4gao1* 'not tall', 不穷 *bu4qiong2* 'not poor', 不矮 *bu4ai3'* 'not short').

Note: In this book, the tonal changes involving 一 and 不 are reflected in the Pinyin notations in the example sentences. The tone sandhi, which changes any syllabic combinations from [33] to [23], however, is not reflected. This is because there are plenty of lexical items which inherently come with a [23] tonal combination. If all [33] combinations are also presented as [23], then readers not familiar with a given disyllabic unit will not know whether the [23] marking is inherent or is a result of sandhi.

1.5 SUMMARY

In this chapter, we first identified the range of consonants and vowels used in Chinese. We noted that there are 22 consonants, three semivowels and 10 vowels used in Mandarin (excluding the isolated *er*). We then explored the important concept of syllable in Chinese, considering the structure of the syllable and investigating the process for generating Chinese syllables. As an integrated part of the Chinese syllable, the range of tones used in Mandarin were also investigated. We learned that, for any given syllable in Mandarin, there are four possible tones that can be assigned to it. There is a fifth tone (the neutral tone) to mark a weakened syllable without changing the meaning of the syllable. There are also sandhi processes which change the tones of some syllables under certain conditions; again, without affecting their meanings. With this fundamental knowledge of Chinese phonology, we move on to consider how syllables are combined into different kinds of meaning-making units in the next chapter.

CHAPTER 2

Chinese words

In this chapter, we discuss units of meaning of various lengths in Chinese on the basis of the number of syllables contained in each unit. We start by pointing out the importance of the syllable as a meaning-making unit in Chinese. We ponder the intriguing question of 'What is a word in Chinese?' and examine the relationship between the Chinese character, syllable, and morpheme. We first consider the lexical units which contain meanings by themselves, including the prevalent disyllabic units, the trisyllabic units, and the quadrisyllabic idioms which demonstrate some interesting syntactic properties of the Chinese language. We then move on to consider a number of functional items which mainly work at the grammatical level.

2.1 THE SYLLABLE AS THE BASIC UNIT OF MEANING

It is useful to highlight the association between 'syllable' and 'meaning' for understanding and learning the Chinese language. This is because almost all Chinese syllables come with individual meanings or functions. Figure 2.1 shows how the syllable stands at a pivot point, linking pronunciation and meaning.

There are two monosyllabic items which represent the Chinese view of what constitutes the basic unit of meaning:

- 字 *zi4* 'a Chinese character'
- 词 *ci2* 'a basic linguistic unit which can independently express a concept'. (definitions adapted from the *Dr.eye* dictionary)

Although we said earlier that each Chinese syllable/character has a distinct meaning, it is more frequently the case (in modern Chinese) that concepts are best expressed by combinations of syllables/characters. For example, although the character 礼 *li3* standing alone can mean 'gift', it is more customary to say and write 礼物 *li3wu4* 'gift-object' on most occasions. In contemporary Chinese, a two-character combination seems to represent a more complete concept and a more qualified lexical unit than a monosyllabic item. For one thing, the monosyllabic item is often combined with other items to form a different concept. Thus, 礼盒 *li3he2* means 'gift box', 礼饼 *li3bing3* means 'gift cake', 礼坊 *li3fang1* means 'gift shop' and so on. Such multisyllabic combinations with very specific

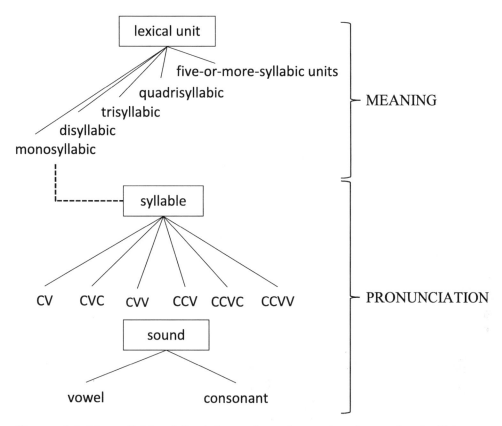

Figure 2.1 The syllable at the intersection of sound and meaning in Chinese

meanings seem to make the monosyllabic core ambiguous, abstract and incomplete when used alone.

It is therefore very difficult to decide what a 'basic unit of language' is in
Chinese. In fact, a fundamental challenge in explaining the Chinese language
using established English terminology is to define what a 'word' is in Chinese. In
Chinese a word is not a syllable (or character), as characters do not always stand
alone to make unambiguous meanings. But if words are multisyllabic items in
Chinese, what are the criteria for deciding the limit of syllabic expansion or the
boundary of a unit? An easy way to recognize what a word is in English is to see
if it is listed in an English dictionary as an entry. In a traditional Chinese dictionary,
however, the headwords are normally the individual characters. Below each character
are then listed a number of multi-character items which are habitually used together
to mean something. There are many kinds of multisyllabic items in Chinese. How
do we decide which are words and which are not? This is an open question.

For most people speaking English, *apple* is clearly a word. In Chinese, the
same concept is expressed as 苹果 *ping2guo3* 'apple', which is a disyllabic unit
consisting of two characters, the first of which means a kind of weed and the
second, fruit in general. Is *ping2guo3* one word or two words in Chinese? We
hate to say it's a two-word compound because it refers to a monolithic natural

kind of object. If we say it is a single word, on the other hand, then we seem to deny the wordhood of its two components, both of which are also undeniably 'a single unit of language which means something' (part of the definition for *word* in the Oxford Advanced Learner's Dictionary).

It may be useful to refer to another language, like English, for deciding on the lexical status of a particular unit in Chinese. For example, 抽烟 *chou1yan1* 'to smoke (a cigarette)' can be expressed by one word in English (*smoke*) and refers to an easily recognizable concept. Therefore, it is perhaps best treated as a Chinese word. 抽痰 *chou1tan2* 'to suck out phlegm (from patient)' is best characterized as a phrase, as *chou1* 'to suck' and *tan2* 'phlegm' both seem to maintain their individual meanings and the overall concept needs to be 'added up', so to speak.

Using concepts to define lexical items is workable in many cases. For example, 开飞机 *kai1fei1ji1* 'fly-airplane' does not represent a single concept but two ('operate' an 'aircraft'), so it is a phrase rather than a lexical unit (the disyllabic unit 飞机 'airplane', on the other hand, is a self-contained concept and can be categorized as a word). The same analysis applies to the phrase 打飞机 *da3fei1ji1* when it means 'to shoot down an airplane' in real battle or video game contexts. However, 打飞机 is also a colloquial term which means 'to masturbate'. In this case, it is clearly a lexical unit as it expresses a single concept. Moreover, its constituent elements (打 'hit' and 飞机 'airplane') also have not maintained their original meanings in the colloquial usage. This example illustrates the usefulness of using concepts to define wordhood.

Other definitions of the Chinese 'word' exist in abundance, each of which has its own merits. For example, Packard (2004) distinguishes between many kinds of words (semantic, lexical, phonological, psychological etc.) before deciding on the 'syntactic word' as the best term to characterize the Chinese word, which is defined as 'a form that can stand as an independent occupant of a syntactic form class slot' (p. 12). This definition presumably serves a good purpose in Packard's syntactically based analysis of 'word'. Our aim in this book, however, is to understand simply how different units of meaning in Chinese are formed from syllables and used pragmatically in the real world. Thus, 'word' is defined here as the minimum number of syllables *habitually used* by native speakers of Chinese to denote a *self-contained concept*. Some other English words like *term* and *unit* are also used interchangeably with *word* in this book to reflect the fuzzy nature of the concept of 'word' in Chinese.

2.2 CONTENT UNITS

In this section, we explore lexical units which can stand alone by themselves and represent meaning. These include meaningful units made of one, two, three, four or even more syllables. The monosyllabic items may often be referred to as 'morphemes'. The disyllabic items are most frequently referred to as 'words'. Units of meaning longer than three syllables in Chinese are more likely to be thought of as 'phrases'. The trisyllabic units can be words or phrases.

2.2.1 Monosyllabic items

A Chinese monosyllabic item corresponds to the linguistic concept of a 'morpheme', which is normally defined as the smallest meaningful unit of a language. Thus, syllable, character and meaning are the three sides of a pyramid, and represents the smallest meaning-making unit in Chinese where the sound, orthography and concept converge. A syllable is a spoken unit of meaning which may be ambiguous if it has homophones. A character is a less ambiguous representation of a meaning in written form. A morpheme is the sum of the syllable, the corresponding character, and the meaning(s) they represent. This idea is graphically expressed in Figure 2.2.

Thus, the tone-carrying syllable *qiang2* when heard as acoustic signals, may mean 'strong' (强) or 'wall' (墙) or something else. But when presented in the written form, as 强, it unambiguously means 'strong'. We can then refer to the unit [强 *qiang2* 'strong'] as a morpheme or simply use the syllable or character to represent the morpheme with the intended meaning.

Although most morphemes in Chinese can stand alone to represent a self-contained concept, they may not be habitually used to do so (that is, native speakers may be more inclined to integrate them into multisyllabic units). When a monosyllabic item frequently stands alone in a sentence or in a pragmatic context to mean something, it may qualify as a 'word' as well as being a morpheme.

Some common monosyllabic items include verbs like 说 *shuo1* 'say', 想 *xiang3* 'think', 跑 *pao3* 'run', 给 *gei3* 'give', 吃 *chi1* 'eat', 哭 *ku1* 'cry'; nouns like 钱 *qian2* 'money', 蛇 *she2* 'snake, 花 *hua1* 'flower', 光 *guang1* 'light', 路 *lu4* 'road'; and adjectives such as 美 *mei3* 'beautiful', 大 *da4* 'big', 冷 *leng3* 'cold', 新 *xin1* 'new' and so on. Most monosyllabic items can be used in a sentence

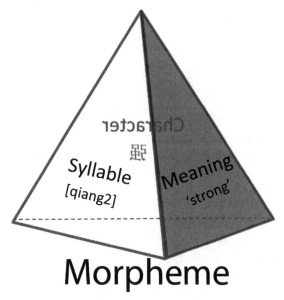

Figure 2.2 A Chinese morpheme consisting of sound, character and meaning

to form fresh combinations with other items. For example, the morpheme 爱 *ai4* 'love' normally functions as an independent verb and takes a morpheme like 钱 as an object to form a verb phrase 爱钱 'love money', or combine with a disyllabic unit to form a trisyllabic phrase like 爱音乐 'love music'. The same is true with a monosyllabic adjective such as 新, which works independently to describe another monosyllabic item, e.g. 新车 'new car', or a disyllabic item, e.g. 新朋友 'new friend'. Morphemes like these deserve the status of 'word' since they often function alone to represent a full concept.

Some monosyllabic units are rich in cultural connotations. For example, single characters like 春 *chun1* 'spring' or 福 *fu2* 'luck' are printed on diamond-shaped paper and hung in doorways in the Spring Festival period. Some Chinese characters can often be seen on foreigners' T-shirts or on their body parts as tattoos, including animal morphemes like 龙 *long2* 'dragon', 虎 *hu3* 'tiger' and 熊 *xiong2*, 'bear'; philosophical terms such as 爱 *ai4* 'love', 仁 *ren2* 'kindness' and 美 *mei3* 'beauty'; those relating to personal qualities or aspirations such as 力 *li4* 'strength', 胜 *sheng4* 'victory' and 忍 *ren3* 'endurance'; and religious terms like 神 *shen2* 'deity', 佛 *fo2* 'Buddha', 道 *dao4* 'way' and so on. A monosyllabic item (in the form of a Chinese character) can be a powerful symbol representing some essence of the Chinese history, culture or philosophy. In this respect, they also deserve to be called 'words', being frequently used independently, in pragmatic contexts, to embody self-contained meanings.

Most Chinese surnames are monosyllabic items – they usually also mean something when not serving as surnames. For example, Chairman Mao's full name is 毛泽东 *mao2ze2dong1* where *mao2* is the surname and means 'hair' and *ze2dong1* is the given name (where *ze2* means 'to benefit' and *dong1* means 'east'). Some common Chinese surnames are 王 *wang2* 'king', 李 *li3* 'plum', 黄 *huang2* 'yellow', 马 *ma3* 'horse', 孙 *sun1* 'grandson', 林 *lin2* 'woods', 高 *gao1* 'tall', 田 *tian2* 'field' and so on. Note that in Chinese, unlike in English, the surname comes before the given name. Also, while Chinese surnames are predominantly monosyllabic (with only a handful of disyllabic surnames) a person's given name could be either monosyllabic or disyllabic.

For foreigners wanting to adopt a Chinese name, the method is to find the equivalent sounds of the original name in syllabic terms, often involving supplying a vowel to any vowel-less consonants in a cluster to create a syllable. For example, *Andrew Strauss* can become *an1de2lu3 shi3te4lao2si1* 安德鲁·史特劳斯, where the consonants *d*, *s*, and *t* in the original names have become full syllables by adding vowels *e*, *i*, and *e* respectively in the Chinese version.

Some monosyllabic verbs in Chinese can behave like simple English command words such as Listen! (听 *ting1*), Look! (看 *kan4*), Come! (来 *lai2*), Sit! (坐 *zuo4*), Speak! (说 *shuo1*) and so on. In practice, however, monosyllabic verbs often take a noun object or a modifying adverb to form a verb phrase of some sort (or become an established lexical unit); for example, 吃饭 *chi1fan4* 'eat-rice (have meal)', 打球 *da3qiu2* 'hit-ball (play ball)', 抱住 *bao4zhu4* 'hold-stay (hold firmly)', 睡醒 *shui4xing3* 'sleep-wake (awaken)', 吃饱 *chi1bao3* 'eat-full', 躺下 *tang3xia4* 'lie-down' and so on. The resultant structure is similar to an English verb phrase where a verb is followed by an object (*talk business*) or an adverb (*talk endlessly*).

Monosyllabic nouns often serve as the basis for forming a larger nominal unit in a family of nouns with related meanings. For example, 车 *che1* 'vehicle' is the base morpheme for many kinds of vehicles, such as 汽车 *qi4che1* 'steam-vehicle (car)', 火车 *huo3che1* 'fire-vehicle (train)', 战车 *zhan4che1* 'war-vehicle (tank)' and so on. This is dramatically different from English where a different type of vehicle is more frequently referred to by a completely different noun, e.g. *car, truck, van, trailer*. This is also a distinctive trait of word formation strategy in Chinese, where syllables or characters are built upon each other to form new units of meaning in a largely compositional way.

Monosyllabic adjectives often precede a noun which they modify, thereby forming a frequently used phrase such as 好书 *hao3shu1* 'good book', 坏人 *huai4ren2* 'bad person', 女童 *nv3tong2* 'female-child' and so on. Another common form is for the adjective to follow a degree adverb such as 很 'very' or 非常 'extremely'; for example, 很美 *hen3mei3* 'very pretty', 非常难 *fei1chang2nan2* 'extremely difficult'. In both of these the word order of adjective → noun and adverb → adjective are the same as in English. Note that the popular monosyllabic unit 好 'good' can serve both as an adjective (好消息 *hao3xiao1xi2* 'good-news') and as a degree adverb (好笨 *hao3ben4* 'very-stupid').

As already mentioned, many monosyllabic items are used independently in structural or pragmatic terms. At the other extreme, there are a very small number of morphemes which cannot function alone and do not have independent meanings. For example, both morphemes in the respective pairs of 萝卜 *luo2bo5* 'carrot', 葡萄 *pu2tao5* 'grapes', 蜘蛛 *zhi1zhu1* 'spider' and 鹦鹉 *ying1wu3* 'parrot' are bound to each other. None of the morphemes can stand alone and they exist only in their respective disyllabic units (i.e. they do not form larger units with other morphemes). However, these monosyllabic items are comparatively few in number.

2.2.2 Disyllabic units

The disyllabic unit refers to a pair of syllables often used together to express a self-contained meaning. A short Chinese text found in 2013 on the Facebook page of Ma Ying-jeou, PhD, President of the Republic of China in Taiwan, illustrates the overwhelming dominance of the disyllabic unit in Chinese text.

The text in Figure 2.3 consists of 45 (Traditional Chinese) characters in total, among which 30 (67 percent) contribute to the formation of two-character units. That is, more than half of the text consists of disyllabic units. This is not a coincidence – it is the norm rather than the exception. The concluding paragraph of Mr. Hu Jintao's 2013 New Year speech as President of the People's Republic of China offers another piece of evidence for the ubiquitous presence of disyllabic words in Chinese.

The text in Figure 2.4 consists of 70 characters, 50 of which (71 percent) constitute 25 disyllabic units, slightly higher than the 67 percent of the text in Figure 2.3.

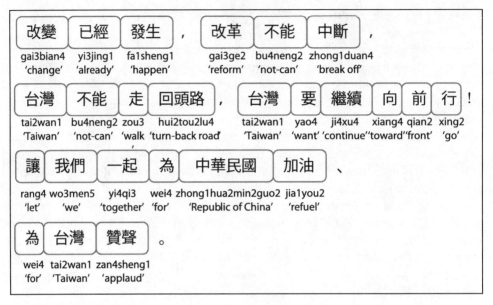

Figure 2.3 A short text illustrating the prevalence of disyllabic units

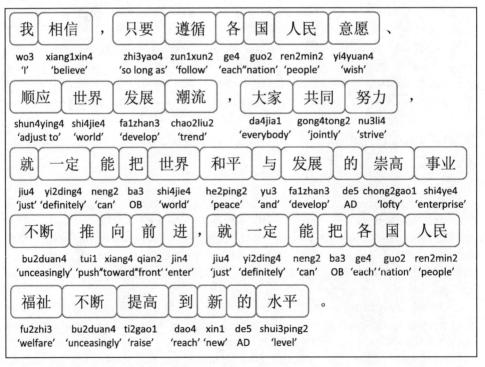

Figure 2.4 Another text illustrating the prevalence of disyllabic units

Table 2.1 Disyllabic units classified on the basis of overall and constituent parts of speech

Overall PoS	Constituent PoS	Constituent relation	Example
V	VV	Co	饲养 *si4yang3* 'feed-raise (to rear)'
	VN	VO	失踪 *shi1zong1* 'lose-track (to disappear)'
	VA	VC	长大 *zhang3da4* 'grow-big (to grow up)'
	NV	SP	草创 *cao3chuang4* 'grass-create (to start a business)'
	NN	En	鱼肉 *yu2rou4* 'fish-meat (to oppress)'
	NA	SP	心酸 *xin1suan1* 'heart-sour (to feel sad)'
	AV	En	苦干 *ku3gan4* 'bitter-do' (to work hard)'
	AN	En	美容 *mei3rong2* 'beautiful-looks (to improve looks)'
	AA	Co	菲薄 *fei3bo2* 'light-flimsy (to slight)'
N	NN	En	网路 *wang3lu4* 'net-road (network)'
	NA	SP	风险 *feng1xian3* 'wind-dangerous (risk)'
	NV	SP	利息 *li4xi2* 'profit-cease (interest)'
	AV	En	小说 *xiao3shuo1* 'small-speak (novel)'
	AN	En	博士 *bo2shi4* 'broad-learned person (a PhD)'
	AA	Co	忙乱 *mang2luan4* 'busy-confused (chaos)'
	VV	Co	变化 *bian4hua4* 'change-transform (transformation)'
	VN	En	报纸 *bao4zhi3* 'to report-paper (newspapers)'
	VA	VO	尊严 *zun1yan2* 'to respect-father (dignity)'
A	AA	Co	高兴 *gao1xing4* 'tall-cheerful (pleased)'
	AV	En	莽撞 *mang3zhuang4* 'rude-collide (impetuous)'
	AN	En	狠心 *hen3xin1* 'cruel-heart (heartless)'
	VV	Co	惊讶 *jing1ya4* 'to startle, to wonder (surprised)'
	VN	VO	离谱 *li2pu3* 'leave-music score (absurd)'
	VA	VC	痛苦 *tong4ku3* 'ache-bitter (painful)'
	NV	SP	性感 *xing4gan3* 'nature-feel (sexy)'
	NN	Co	狼狈 *lang2bei4* 'wolf-legendary wolf (wretched)'
	NA	SP	年轻 *nian2qing1* 'year-light (young)'

Note: En = Endocentric; Co = Coordinative; SP = Subject-Predicate; VO = Verb-Object; VC = Verb-Complement

Disyllabic units can be verbs, nouns, adjectives or adverbs. Their constituent morphemes can be any of the major parts of speech. Table 2.1 summarizes the range of disyllabic units in relation to overall and constituent parts of speech.

A significant difference between Chinese and English in terms of parts of speech is that, for Chinese, words revolving around the same concept but used in different grammatical settings (i.e. as noun or verb or adjective/adverb) can share the same form. For example, in English, the concept of 'being protected from danger' can be referred to by the word *safe* (the adjective form), while the word *safety* (the noun form) refers to the state of being safe. In Chinese, however, both noun and adjective concepts are represented by the same token 安全 'safety, safe', thus:

Example 1

a   维护　　　国际　　　　　和平　　与　　安全
wei2hu4 guo2ji4　　　he2ping2 yu3 **an1quan2**
'maintain' 'international' 'peace'　'and' **'safety'**
'maintain international peace and safety'

b   **安全**　　　性　　行为
an1quan2 xing4 xing2wei2
'safe'　　'sex' 'behavior'
'safe sexual behavior'

We can see from the characters and Pinyin representations in Example 1 that the Chinese word for the concept of 'safety' in both sentences is identical in form. In English, however, the appropriate word forms must be used depending on the grammatical context. This kinds of morphological-syntactic differences add to the difficulties of Chinese speakers learning English as an additional language, for the ideas of both inflection (talk → talked) and derivation (entertain → entertainment) are unfamiliar concepts. On the other hand, the difficulty for English speakers learning Chinese lies in the higher level comprehension and encoding, as there are fewer bottom-up clues in the morphological department to rely on when processing the Chinese language.

To understand how this 'hidden parts of speech' machinery works for Chinese, imagine a non-existent English word, *successal*, which can represent *succeed*, *success*, *successful*, and *successfully* depending on context. Example 2 presents an array of sentences containing different forms of the word *success*, which, however, have all been replaced by the non-word *successal* in order to give a 'Chinese flavor'.

Example 2

a   North Korea may have finally *successal* in putting a satellite into space. ('succeeded')
b   Officials said the launch appeared to have been a *successal*. ('success')
c   South Korea hails *successal* rocket launch. ('successful')
d   South Korea *successal* launches first rocket into space. ('successfully')

If the reader can derive the meaning of *successal* in the various contexts of Example 2 without much ado (or irritation!), they can start to appreciate how the Chinese get around the issue of grammatical categories by using a single form for all contexts. One such set of Chinese sentences centering around the same concept of 'success' is offered in Example 3 below, where the same form, 成功, is used as a verb, a noun, an adjective, and an adverb respectively.

Example 3

a 　如何　　在　40　　岁　　以前　　**成功**
　ru2he2 zai4 si4shi2 sui4　yi3qian2 **cheng2gong1**
　'how'　'at'　'40'　　'years 'before'　**'succeed'**
　'How to succeed before 40 years old?'

b 　失败　　为　　**成功**　　　之　母
　shi1bai4 wei2　**cheng2gong1** zhi1 mu3
　'failure' 'act as' **'success'**　　'its' 'mother'
　'Failure is the mother of success.'

c 　一　　个　事业　**成功**　　　的　男人
　yi2　ge5 shi4ye4 **cheng2gong1** de5 nan2ren2
　'one' Cla 'career' **'successful'**　AD 'man'
　'A man with a successful career'

d 　**成功**　　　移民　　　有问必答
　cheng2gong1 yi2min2　you3wen4bi4da2
　'successfully' 'immigrate' 'have-ask-must-answer'
　'Any questions answered regarding successfully immigrating'

We can therefore expect a lot of 'mistakes' in word forms when communicating with a Chinese person in English, when English is not their first language. Verbal interactions are especially difficult as these often involve conscious 'calculations' of which word forms to use in what sentential contexts. In Chinese, one is only concerned with which lexical items to choose from the mental lexicon, without worrying about further morphological processing.

Although disyllabic items account for more than half of the Chinese lexical units, the process for generating habitual meaning-making units does not stop there. As a trend in modern Chinese, more syllables can be added to existing items to form new, larger lexical or phraseological units.

2.2.3 Trisyllabic units

The majority of trisyllabic units are formed by adding one more syllable to an existing disyllabic unit. Few trisyllabic units comprise three separate monosyllabic items unknown to each other. For example, the trisyllabic unit 外交部 *wai4jiao1bu4* ('Foreign Office') is created by adding an extra syllable to an existing disyllabic unit 外交 'international diplomacy', which itself was previously formed by combining two syllables 外 'external' and 交 'to interact'. The same process can go on to create even larger units, each of which may express a self-contained concept and is habitually used by native speakers (e.g. 外交部长 'Minister of Foreign Affairs').

A word formation process for disyllabic units was mentioned in 2.2.2, where a head noun is used to generate a family of mutually related words. The same process also applies to trisyllabic units. Thus 外交部 means Ministry of Foreign Affairs, 教育部 is Ministry of Education, 国防部 is Ministry of National Defence and so on, which all share the same root morpheme 部 'department'. Table 2.2 shows two further examples where 人 'human' and 员 'member' are

Table 2.2 Trisyllabic units created by adding different disyllabic units to the same head noun

Head noun	Participating disyllabic unit	Resultant trisyllabic unit
人 *ren2* 'person'	阴阳 *yin1yang2* 'negative-positive'	阴阳人 *yin1yang2ren2* 'an intersex'
	隐形 *yin3xing2* 'hide-shape (become invisible)'	隐形人 *yin3xing2ren2* 'an invisible person'
	局外 *ju2wai4* 'bureau-outside (outside the bureau)'	局外人 *ju2wai4ren2* 'an outsider'
	过来 *guo4lai2* 'cross-come (come over)'	过来人 *guo4lai2ren2* 'an experienced person'
	中国 *zhong1guo2* 'middle-nation (China)'	中国人 *zhong1guo2ren2* 'a Chinese person'
员 *yuan2* 'member'	公务 *gong1wu4* 'public-affair'	公务员 *gong1wu4yuan2* 'a public servant'
	救生 *jiu4sheng1* 'save-life'	救生员 *jiu4sheng1yuan2* 'lifeguard'
	管理 *guan3li3* 'govern-manage'	管理员 *guan3li3yuan2* 'a superintendent'
	推销 *tui1xiao1* 'push-sell'	推销员 *tui1xiao1yuan2* 'a sales representative'
	足球 *zu2qiu2* 'football'	足球员 *zu2qiu2yuan2* 'a footballer'

the base morphemes, with various disyllabic units added to create new units of meaning.

Most of the examples in Table 2.2 are compositional. That is, the meaning of the trisyllabic unit is largely transparent and is the sum of the meanings of the disyllabic unit and the noun root. A few of them are not straightforward, and some imagination or learning is required to know what the trisyllabic items mean. For example, someone who has got both the 'shade' (dark side) and the 'sun' (bright side) is an intersexual person. Someone who has 'come over' to this side is an 'experienced person'.

Sometimes monosyllables like 人 and 员 are said to be 'derivational morphemes' in that they can be added to many existing words to create new meanings, somewhat like the suffixes -or (act → actor), -ment (move → movement) etc. in English. A derivational morpheme is usually restricted in some way in the range of words it can combine with. For example, assignment and equipment are fine, but not *allocatement or *affordment. The Chinese derivation-like process is even more selective. Most of the examples in Table 2.2 represent individual cases and the process is not very productive, with the possible exception of [nation + 人] = 'a citizen of that nation' and [ball game + 员] = 'a player of that game'. Examples are 美国人 'America-person (an American)' and 篮球员 'basketball-member (a basketball player)'.

Nouns are not the only grammatical category that can be the head of a series of derived words. Table 2.3 lists a group of trisyllabic units centering around a head verb. In this set of examples, the meaning of the monosyllabic head 打 ('hit') is depleted or neutralized when it combines with the disyllabic

Table 2.3 Trisyllabic units created by attaching disyllabic units to the head verb

Head verb	Participating disyllabic unit	Resultant trisyllabic unit
打 da3 'strike'	电话 dian4hua4 'electric-speech (telephone)'	打电话 da3dian4hua4 'make a phone call'
	招呼 zhao1hu1 'attract-exhale (greeting)'	打招呼 da3zhao1hu1 'say hello'
	喷嚏 pen1ti4 'spurt-sneeze (a sneeze)'	打喷嚏 da3pen1ti4 'to sneeze'
	领带 ling3dai4 'collar-belt (necktie)'	打领带 da3ling3dai4 'put on a tie'
	麻将 ma2jiang4 'hemp-general (mah-jong)'	打麻将 da3ma2jiang4 'play mah-jong'
	算盘 suan4pan2 'calculate-tray (abacus)'	打算盘 da3suan4pan2 'use abacus; be scheming and calculating'

noun. That is, it becomes a generic verb much like the *make* in *make a phone call* in English.

Not all trisyllabic units consist of an established disyllabic unit plus a head morpheme. Sometimes a trisyllabic unit is put together afresh by three independent morphemes. For example, 夜来香 *ye4lai2xiang1* 'night-come-fragrance (tuberose)' comprises a noun/adverb ('night'), a verb ('come') and a noun ('fragrance'), and together they form a noun denoting a flower name. Likewise, a number of established trisyllabic units seem to originate from a syntactic process. For example, 来不及 'come-not-reach (too late)', 差不多 'differ-not-much', 忍不住 'endure-not-live (cannot hold back)' are frequently used trisyllabic units which follow the [V not A] or [V not V] pattern.

Many trisyllabic units are pragmatically laden or culturally embedded. Some of them acquire the status of idioms; that is, their meanings become very different from the meanings of the individual words put together. For example, 三脚猫 'three-legged-cat' means 'a person who can do many things but specializes in nothing', and 三字经 'three-character-scripture' becomes an umbrella term for all the swear words consisting of three morphemes.

We have seen ways how trisyllabic units can be formed by putting together three monosyllabic items or by combining a disyllabic unit with a monosyllabic item. The meaning of the new unit can be either compositional or idiomatic. The idiomatic trisyllabic ones such as 打喷嚏 'to sneeze' and 仙人跳 'sex trap' each refer to a self-contained concept and are habitually used as a unit. They should therefore deserve the status of 'words'. To take another example, 三脚猫 'a superficial person' (idiomatic) seems more like a word than 兩頭蛇 'two-headed snake' (compositional) as the latter is easily decomposable into three concepts ('two', 'head' and 'snake') which retain their literal meanings in the new formation. Thus, idiomaticity also seems a useful criterion for helping to decide the word-hood of a multisyllabic unit.

2.2.4 Quadrisyllabic units

Broadly speaking, there are two kinds of quadrisyllabic units in Chinese: historically based units (commonly referred to as Chinese idioms) and usage based items (newly established, frequently used expressions). Chinese four-character idioms are a part of cultural heritage, each of which is normally associated with a particular historical tale or is adapted from a well-known classical work. They form a closed system and their number is unlikely to increase. The usage-based quadrisyllabic units, on the other hand, are being created daily, fixed in the mental lexicon as a result of repeated usage by native speakers. Among the 10,000+ claimed listed 成语 *cheng2yu3* 'established language' in He (2004), fewer than 300 entries (3 percent) are exactly three syllables or more than four syllables long. That is, around 97 percent of the 'established phrases' in Chinese may be quadrisyllabic units.

Most quadrisyllabic units listed in a phrase dictionary like He (2004) are either historical idioms (e.g. 三顾茅庐 *san1gu4mao2lu2* 'Warlord Liu Bei visiting Zhuge Liang three times to get his help in managing the country') or other commonly used four-character phrases that have been fixed for some time (e.g. 空中飞人 *kong1zhong1fei1ren2* 'a trapeze gymnast or a person who frequently flies'). New quadrisyllabic units are being created every day and disseminated through the media and social networks. 'Collocation' is a key factor in creating new quadrisyllabic units in Chinese, which involves putting together two disyllabic items to form a new expression, such as 维持原价 *wei2chi2yuan2jia4* 'maintain original-price', 破窗行窃 *po4chuang1xing2qie4* 'break-window-conduct-theft' and so on. (See Shei and Pain 2000 for a general discussion on collocation and Shei 2005 for a comparison between English and Chinese collocations.)

As can be imagined, with four syllables participating in the newly formed structure, the configuration of the components can be quite versatile. Many of the quadrisyllabic units are miniature sentences themselves, having a subject noun phrase (NP) and a verb phrase (VP) functioning as the predicate. Figure 2.5 shows such a case where a quadrisyllabic unit has the standard structure of a sentence complete with an NP (subject) and a VP (predicate). Here 铁树开花 *tie3shu4kai1hua1* 'iron-tree-open-flower' literally means 'the sago cycad blooms' and is normally used to refer to an unusual event, as the sago cycad is a plant which does not flower easily.

Although expressions like 铁树开花 seem 'self-contained' as a sentence-like structure, they do not always stand alone as isolated expressions in discourse. Instead, they are often embedded in a larger structure, supporting a higher order expression. For example, 铁树开花 in Example 4 clearly acts as a predicate for the entire sentence.

Example 4

埃弗拉　　**铁　　树　　开　　花**
ai1fu2la1　tie3　shu4　kai1　hua1
'Evra'　　　'iron'　'tree'　'open'　'flower'
'Evra bloomed like a sago cycad.'

The phrase (or miniature sentence) 铁树开花 in Example 4 is used to describe the footballer Evra's performance in the 2013 Premier League, when he scored the fifth goal in the Top 5 Goals competition. The Chinese commentator probably used this phrase to show how rare and brilliant this goal was in comparison with Evra's existing record (only 2 goals from when he joined Manchester United in 2005 up to 2012). The text in Example 4 shows how a sentence-like quadrisyllabic unit can be embedded in a larger sentence and serve as a predicate.

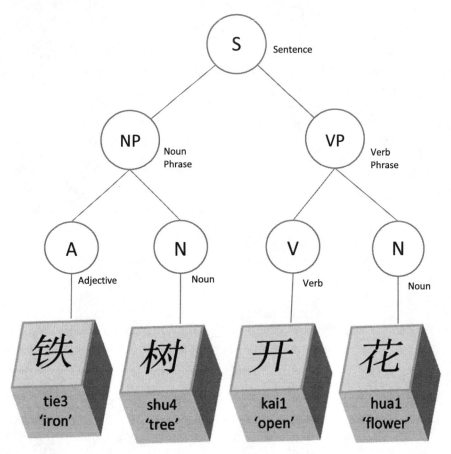

Figure 2.5 The syntactic structure of a four-character idiom

If we take the expression in Figure 2.5 as a sentence-like structure, since it comes with an NP and a VP, then a quadrisyllabic unit in Chinese may be a good frame to observe possible Chinese syntactic structures that are stripped to the very essence. In a four-character idiom, for example, the VP portion is often replaceable by an AP (adjective or adverbial phrase), like that in Figure 2.6.

The quadrisyllabic unit in Figure 2.6 does not contain a verb of any kind. Instead, it includes a disyllabic unit consisting of adjectives at the predicate slot, describing the state of the subject NP. This phrase is used to describe the anxious feelings of a group of people facing some kind of crisis. It can stand alone as an independent expression, or, like 铁树开花 in Example 4, it can be incorporated in a larger expression.

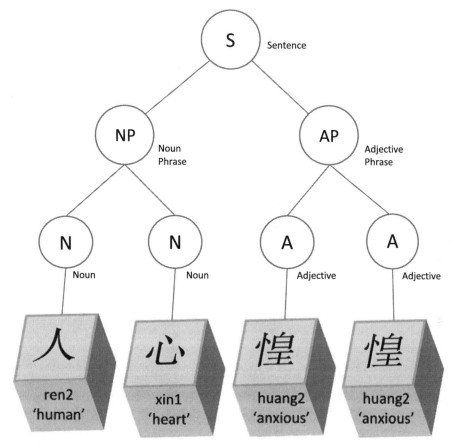

Figure 2.6 The syntactic structure of a quadrisyllabic unit with VP replaced by AP

Example 5

党	内	贪	官	人	心	惶	惶
dang3	nei4	tan1	guan1	ren2	xin1	huang2	huang2
'party'	'inside'	'corrupt'	'official'	'human'	'heart'	'apprehensive'	'apprehensive'

'Corrupt officials in the party are all on tenterhooks.'

In Example 5, 人心惶惶 serves as a predicate, even though it can also function as an independent expression, having both a subject and a predicate phrase, as Figure 2.6 shows.

So far we have seen how Chinese sentence-like structures work out in the quadrisyllabic framework. We have also seen how a four-character idiom can function as a predicate for a sentence. In fact, if we look into the constituent structure of some quadrisyllabic units, we can find an even smaller sentence-like structure (often consisting of two morphemes) embedded in the quadrisyllabic unit. Figure 2.7 shows such a structure.

The quadrisyllabic unit in Figure 2.7, 冤家路窄, means 'the road is especially narrow for people who don't like each other' (i.e. It is difficult to avoid your adversary). If the quadrisyllabic unit is a sentence (S), then 冤家 is the subject NP which means 'foes'. The other structure, 路窄 'road narrow', on the other hand, is a predicate to the subject, which is a miniature sentence itself, having the meaning of 'the road is narrow'. However, as will be pointed out later, in Chapter 3, another way to analyze this is to treat the sentence-initial NP as the 'topic' of the sentence. In contrast to the English Subject-Predicate structure, which is syntactically oriented, the Chinese Topic-Comment structure is more conceptually oriented. An example similar to 冤家路窄 is 洛阳纸贵 *luo4yang2zhi3gui4* 'Luoyang-paper-expensive', which literally means 'In Luoyang, paper is expensive'. Here, 洛阳 (the city), is not the subject of the quadrisyllabic unit in a syntactic

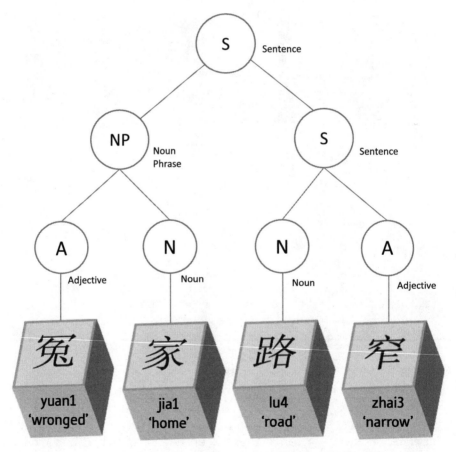

Figure 2.7 A sentence-like structure embedded in a quadrisyllabic unit

sense but 纸 'paper' is, since the predicate 贵 'expensive' is used to describe it. 洛阳, however, occupies the thematic position and is said to be the topic of the sentence. The miniature sentence structure, 纸贵 'paper is expensive', is offered as a comment on the topic. This is a special feature of the Chinese sentence. Thus, another structural property of the Chinese language is demonstrated by the four-character idiom.

Yet another kind of structure the quadrisyllabic unit illustrates is the juxtaposition of two sentence-like units without any conjunctive elements. Figure 2.8 shows such a structure.

The quadrisyllabic unit illustrated in Figure 2.8 does not consist of two existing disyllabic units, as neither 风吹 'wind blows' nor 草动 'grass moves' is an established lexical item (i.e. a habitually used unit with distinct meaning). They both consist of a subject noun and a verb predicate, however, and can both be said to be mini sentences. Here we witness another flexible syntactic arrangement of Chinese expressions – two sentences can often be juxtaposed

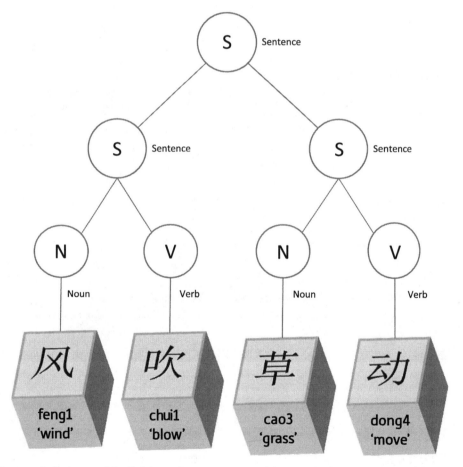

Figure 2.8 A quadrisyllabic unit consisting of two coordinate sentences

without any intervening conjunctive devices. This happens not only within a quadrisyllabic unit, but it is also a regular feature in Chinese texts.

Not all quadrisyllabic units exhibit sentence-like qualities (that is, having a subject-predicate structure). The unit 虎头蛇尾, for example, consists of two noun phrases, 虎头 *hu3tou2* 'tiger-head' and 蛇尾 *she2wei3* 'snake-tail'. Together the unit means 'having a fine start but a poor finish'. Despite the lack of a verb, the entire quadrisyllabic unit of 虎头蛇尾, however, can still function as a predicate, as Example 6 shows.

Example 6

反	腐	不	要	虎	头	蛇	尾
fan3	fu3	bu2	yao4	hu3	tou2	she2	wei3
'against'	'corruption'	'not'	'want'	'tiger'	'head'	'snake'	'tail'

'In combating corruption, do not be anticlimactic.'

In Example 6 we have a Topic-Comment structure where 反腐 'against corruption' is the topic, and the comment is an imperative sentence warning against a disappointing end when fighting against corruption.

Just as there are quadrisyllabic units made from two noun phrases, there are Chinese idioms consisting of two verb phrases, such as 种瓜得瓜 'reap what you sow', where each of the two verb phrases consists of a verb and its noun object. As could be expected, a quadrisyllabic unit consisting of two verb phrases is best used as a predicate in a sentence.

Example 7

芳	姨	种	瓜	得	瓜	有	收成
fang1	yi2	zhong4	gua1	de2	gua1	you3	shou1cheng2
'Fang'	'aunt'	'plant'	'melon'	'get'	'melon'	'have'	'receive-achieve'

'Aunt Fang reaped what she sowed and obtained a harvest.'

In Example 7, the verb phrase 有收成 'have harvest' is the main predicate to the subject 芳姨 'Aunt Fang'. The quadrisyllabic unit 种瓜得瓜 is also a verbal predicate to the subject NP but it sounds like an inserted sequence in this case. It is redundant in meaning but offers extra vivacity and metaphorical interest, a function often performed by Chinese four-character idioms.

Still another kind of phrase structure illustrated by the quadrisyllabic unit is a VP consisting of a prepositional phrase, a verb and a noun, such as 雾里看花 *wu4li3kan4hua1* 'fog-in-see-flower (blurred vision)'. The structure of this phrase illustrates another aspect of the Chinese language which is different from English – the prepositional phrase 雾里 'in the fog' consists of a noun (雾 'fog') followed by a preposition (里 'in'). The word order within this prepositional phrase is thus the reverse of English, where the preposition comes first and is followed by a noun. In Chinese, some prepositions prefer to come before the noun, while others habitually follow the noun.

Zhao's (2001) *Dictionary of Chinese Idioms* contains 4,639 entries, among which 4,214 (91 percent) are four-character units. The other 9 percent consist of multi-syllabic units of various lengths (i.e. trisyllabic units and units of between 5 and 14 characters). In the final part of this section, we visit some units of expression which are at least five characters in length.

2.2.5 Five-or-more-syllabic units

As we cross over the threshold of the quadrisyllabic unit and venture into fixed expressions over five characters long, we find fewer and fewer examples. The more syllables a unit consists of, the more likely it is an aphorism or a proverb. Due to their rare appearances, it is relatively difficult to determine whether a multisyllabic unit is an established idiom/proverb or a one-off 'poetic creation' of a language user. Shei (2008) introduces a good way of identifying fixed expressions through the use of web search engines to which interested readers can refer. Table 2.4 provides some examples of multisyllabic units ranging from 5 to 10 characters long.

Some of the examples of multisyllabic units in Table 2.4 are in the form of couplets, which is a common feature in Chinese language and literature. These are created under various meter and rhyme schemes and offer poetic reading as well as compact and cleverly encoded meaning. Some couplets are written in big characters on red paper and hung on the doors of homes and workplaces for good luck. Below is a sample of a couplet which is often written on paper scrolls to be pasted on door frames during the Chinese spring festival.

Example 8

花　　开　　富　　贵　　　　全　　家　　福
hua1　kai1　fu4　gui4　　　quan2　jia1　fu2
'flower' 'open' 'rich' 'expensive' 'all'　'home' 'lucky'
'Flower blossomed, fortune and social position bestowed, the whole family enjoy happiness.'

竹　　　报　　平　　安　　满　　堂　　春
zhu2　　bao4　ping2　an1　man3　tang2　chun1
'bamboo' 'report' 'flat' 'safe' 'full' 'hall' 'spring'
'Bamboo strips report safety and the entire living room is bathed in spring.'

Table 2.4 Examples of multisyllabic units

Multi-character idiom	Component analysis	Overall meaning
人穷志不穷 ren2qiong2zhi4bu4qiong2	人 *ren2* 'people' 穷 *qiong2* 'poor' 志 *zhi4* 'aspiration' 不 *bu4* 'not'	'Even though one is poor, one should still have ambition.'
杀鸡焉用牛刀 sha1ji1yan1yong4niu2dao1	杀 *sha1* 'kill' 鸡 *ji1* 'chicken' 焉 *yan1* 'herein' 用 *yong4* 'use' 牛 *niu2* 'cattle' 刀 *dao1* 'knife'	'Killing a chicken with an ox-cleaver' (The task is too trivial to handle with such inordinate fuss.)
情人眼里出西施 qing2ren2yan3li3chu1xi1shi1	情人 *qing2ren2* 'lover' 眼 *yan3* 'eye' 里 *li3* 'interior' 出 *chu1* 'produce' 西施 *xi1shi1* 'Xi Shi (a beautiful woman in Chinese history)'	'Any girl can look like a Xi Shi in her lover's eyes.' (Beauty is in the eyes of the beholder.)
豹死留皮，人死留名 bao4si3liu2pi2, ren2si3liu2ming2	豹 *bao4* 'leopard' 死 *si3* 'die' 留 *liu2* 'remain' 皮 *pi2* 'skin' 人 *ren2* 'person' 名 *ming2* 'name'	'When a leopard dies, it leaves its skin; when a person dies, they leave their reputation.'
做一天和尚，撞一天钟 zuo4yi4tian1he2shang4, zhuang4yi4tian1zhong1	做 *zuo4* 'do' 一天 *yi4tian1* 'one day' 和尚 *he2shang4* 'monk' 撞 *zhuang4* 'strike' 钟 *zhong1* 'bell'	'Being a monk one day, strike the bell one day.' (Do your duty as long as you remain in the post.)

2.3 FUNCTIONAL ITEMS

In this section, we examine a range of functional items in the Chinese language. Functional items normally refer to linguistic devices which perform syntactic or discourse functions rather than represent content meanings on their own. Most items discussed in this section are monosyllabic morphemes which generally do not represent meanings on their own. There are also disyllabic items, some of which may be more qualified as 'words' (e.g. 如果 'if').

Grammatical categories such as articles, pronouns, prepositions, and conjunctions are normally considered functional words in English. Most of the Chinese functional items carry out the same grammatical functions as their

English counterparts. Some of them, however, are either particular to Chinese (such as 'classifiers' and the sentence-final particles) or function in rather different ways from their equivalents in other languages. Functional words are also called 'closed classes' sometimes, as their numbers are unlikely to increase. The linguistic devices discussed in this section include:

- Pronouns
- Classifiers
- Number words
- Modal auxiliaries
- Prepositions
- Conjunctions
- Adverbial elements
- Verb accessories

Although adverbs are normally considered 'open classes' (that is, new items can be created and added to the lexicon), in Chinese, however, there is a fixed set of adverbial elements (e.g. 就, 才, 还, 又, 再) which seem very 'functional' in nature (i.e. bearing some influence on sentence formation and interpretation) and so are included in the discussion. The 'verb accessories', on the other hand, refer to monosyllabic items such as 在, 着, 了, 过 (used to mark verb aspects), 被 (as the passive marker) and 把 (as the object marker). Sentence-final particles (SFP) is a large category of functional items in Chinese and will be discussed separately in Chapter 5.

2.3.1 Pronouns

Just like English, the Chinese language has a full set of pronouns to refer to the first person, second person and third person. Table 2.5 lists the entire range of pronouns in Chinese, offering a comparison between Chinese and English pronouns in terms of number, case, gender and so on. Note that, in speech, all variants of the Chinese third person pronouns of the same number (i.e. all varieties of *ta1* for singular and all varieties of *ta1men5* for plural respectively) sound exactly the same. But in writing, different characters are used based on whether the third person referred to is human (male or female), an object, animal or spiritual being.

Two items are worth noting from Table 2.5: the possessive marker 的 *de5* and the plural marker 们 *men5*. The Chinese plural marker is fairly restricted in its applicability. It is nothing like the English plural marker -s which can be added to virtually all countable nouns (dog → dogs). The Chinese plural marker 们 can only be attached to certain types of countable nouns, notably nouns with the [+animate] feature and especially nouns with a [+human] attribute. This is not to say that objects like tables or trees cannot be referred to in a multiple sense. It simply means plurality is not an aspect to be signposted every time a countable

Table 2.5 English and Chinese pronouns

Person	Number	Case	English	Chinese
1st	Singular	Subjective	I	我 *wo3*
		Objective	me	
		Possessive	my, mine	我的 *wo3de5*
	Plural	Subjective	we	我们 *wo3men5*
		Objective	us	
		Possessive	our, ours	我们的 *wo3men5de5*
2nd	Singular	Subjective	you	你 *ni3*
		Objective		
		Possessive	your, yours	你的 *ni3de5*
	Plural	Subjective	you	你们 *ni3men5*
		Objective		
		Possessive	your, yours	你们的 *ni3men5de5*
3rd	Singular	Subjective	he	他 *ta1*
			she	她 *ta1*
			it	它 *ta1* (inanimate)
				牠 *ta1* (animal)
				祂 *ta1* (deity/spiritual)
		Objective	him	他 *ta1*
			her	她 *ta1*
			it	它 *ta1* (inanimate)
				牠 *ta1* (animal)
				祂 *ta1* (deity/spiritual)
		Possessive	his	他的 *ta1de5*
			her, hers	她的 *ta1de5*
			its	它的 *ta1de5* (inanimate)
				牠的 *ta1de5* (animal)
				祂的 *ta1de5* (deity/spiritual)
	Plural	Subjective	they	他们 *ta1men5*
				她们 *ta1men5*
				它们 *ta1men5* (inanimate)
				牠们 *ta1men5* (animal)
				祂们 *ta1men5* (deity/spiritual)
		Objective	them	他们 *ta1men5*
				她们 *ta1men5*
				它们 *ta1men5* (inanimate)
				牠们 *ta1men5* (animal)
				祂们 *ta1men5* (deity/spiritual)
		Possessive	their, theirs	他们的 *ta1men5de5*
				她们的 *ta1men5de5*
				它们的 *ta1men5de5* (inanimate)
				牠们的 *ta1men5de5* (animal)
				祂们的 *ta1men5de5* (deity/spiritual)

Note: The animal (牠) and spiritual (祂) representations are widely adopted in Taiwan but not in China noun is used. Thus 我买了花 *wo3 mai3 le5 hua1* 'I bought flower(s)' could mean one or more flowers. If it is important to mention the number of flowers, then a quantity word will be used, e.g. 我买了十朵花 'I bought 10 flowers'. Since 'flower' is not animate or human, *花们 'flowers' is not an acceptable term except in poetic contexts where the intention is to personify the flowers.

Another functional item in Table 2.5, *de5*, has two main usages: to mark the possessive case (annotated as PD in this book) or to mark a structure as an adjectival unit (annotated as AD in this book). When 的 follows a noun, it may mark the entire unit as a possessive case. Example 9 demonstrates this operation.

Example 9

63	岁	台商	的	57	岁	妻子
liu4shi2san1	sui4	tai2shang1	de5	wu3shi2qi1	sui4	qi1zi5
'63'	'year'	'Taiwan-merchant'	PD	'57'	'year'	'wife'

'The 63-year-old Taiwan merchant's 57-year-old wife'

The function of 的 in Example 9 is exactly like the possessive marker (') in English (e.g. *John's wife*). However, 的 has another function in Chinese which is to turn a lexical unit or a structure into a descriptor. This kind of structure is shown in Example 10:

Example 10

a

用	[轻松]	的	方式	呈现
yong4	qing1song1	de5	fang1shi4	cheng2xian4
'use'	'relaxed'	AD	'manner'	'present'

'To present (something) in a relaxed way'

b

[飘	着	细雨]	的	暗	夜
piao1	zhe5	xi4yu3	de5	an4	ye4
'float'	AM	'drizzle'	AD	'dark'	'night'

'A dark night when a drizzle was falling'

In Example 10a, 的 follows an adjective 轻松 'easy' to clearly mark the entire unit (轻松的) as an adjective. In Example 10b, on the other hand, 的 follows a sentence-like structure (飘着细雨 'drizzle is falling') again to mark the structure as performing a descriptive function. In English, a relative clause always follows the noun it describes (e.g. a person *who is afraid of taking risks*). In Chinese,

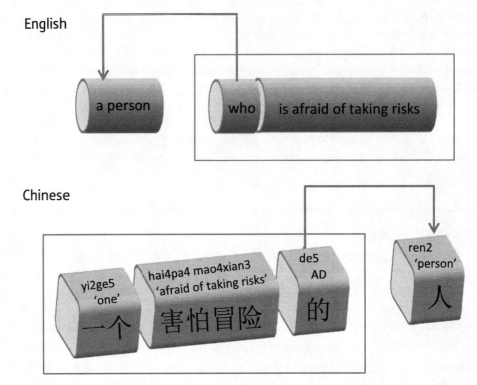

Figure 2.9 The different positions of relative clauses in English and Chinese

however, all noun descriptors, including the relative clause, have to be put ahead of the noun, with a mediating 的 clearly marking the structure as a pre-modifier of the noun (e.g. 害怕冒险的人 'afraid-of-taking-risk *de5* person'). The functional morpheme 的 itself has no meaning other than pointing out the relationship between the descriptor and the described. The different positions of relative clauses between English and Chinese in relation to the noun they modify are shown graphically in Figure 2.9.

As Figure 2.9 shows, English uses the relative pronoun *who* to wrap up the relative clause and post-modify the noun. Chinese, on the other hand, uses 的 to bundle up all the pre-modifiers and clearly indicate the relationship between the noun and its modifiers.

2.3.2 Classifiers

In English, counting or referring to objects is fairly straightforward; for example, *one man*, *two fish*, *three lions* and so on. In Chinese, a device called a 'classifier', normally in the form of a single morpheme, has to be used when referring to a noun. This monosyllabic item comes between the number word etc. and the noun to indicate the speaker's conceptualization of the category to which the noun belongs. This is like saying *one UNIT (of) man, two UNITS (of) fish, three UNITS (of) lions* in English, except that, in Chinese, the word *UNIT* is replaced by a different classifier in each case, based on the assumed category membership of the noun, and there is no other element (like *of* in English) intervening between the classifier and the noun. Also, there is no plural marker like the English *-s* to be added to the classifier or the noun in Chinese.

Table 2.6 Comparison of an English and a Chinese noun phrase

English		Chinese		
Determiner	Noun	Determiner	Classifier	Noun
a	man	— 'one'	个 *ge5* 'classifier (general)'	男人 'man'
two	fish	两 'two'	条 *tiao2* 'classifier (long object)'	鱼 'fish'
five	cats	五 'five'	只 (隻) *zhi1* 'classifier (animal)'	猫 'cat'

Note: The character 只 also means 'only'; the traditional 隻 is the unambiguous and recommended usage

The first classifier to appear in Table 2.6 is 个, which introduces the noun *man* in this instance. Apart from signaling the coming of human-related nouns, 个 is also the most general classifier in Chinese and can be used to introduce many kinds of nouns. For example, 一个家庭 'a family', 一个地方 'a place', 一个故事 'a story' are all common usages. The classifier 个 is also a relatively safe option to choose when not knowing which classifier to use. Although an incompatible classifier may cause disruption in communication, at least it fills in a slot and helps avoid total incomprehension; such as when a noun immediately and inappropriately follows a numerical item (e.g. *一礼物 rather than 一个礼物 'a present').

The second classifier appearing in Table 2.6 is 条, which is normally associated with long and narrow objects, e.g. 一条河 'a river'. Other members of this category include 路 'road', 蛇 'snake', 虫 'worm' and so on. The third classifier in Table 2.6, 隻(只), on the other hand, is most frequently associated with animals, e.g. 一只猴子 'a monkey', 两只老虎 'two tigers' and so on.

There may be as many as 100 commonly used Chinese classifiers. Some have meanings on their own and can be (part of) a lexical unit. Their usage as classifiers reflects their inherent meaning. Others, however, seem to be initially assigned arbitrarily to a category. Also, a given classifier may be able to introduce more than one category of entity and, vice versa, the same category of nouns may be associated with more than one classifier. Two further examples of classifiers are shown in Example 11.

Example 11

a 有   一   **头**   牛   挡住   了   我的   去路
   you3 yi4   tou2 niu2 dang3zhu4 le5   wo3de5   qu4lu4
   'have' 'one' Cla   'cow' 'block'   AM   'my'   'way forward'
   'There is a cow/bull blocking my way.'

b 如果   有   来生，   要   做   一   **棵**   树
   ru2guo3 you3 lai2sheng1 yao4   zuo4 yi4   ke1   shu4
   'if'   'have' 'future life' 'want' 'do'   'one' Cla   'tree'
   'If there is a future life, I would like to be a tree.'

In Example 11a, the classifier 头 originally meant 'head'. When used as a classifier, it collocates with large animals such as lions, elephants and so on. The meaning of the classifier and the meaning of the category it introduces are somehow related. In Example 11b, on the other hand, 棵 does not have meaning when standing alone, and its allocation to the 'plant' category is probably arbitrary.

Before ending this section, we should note a mass classifier, 些, which normally indicates the ensuing noun to be plural or of a larger mass. Examples of usage can be seen in Example 12.

Example 12

a **这些**   大学生   都   变   妈宝   了
   zhe4xie1 da4xue2sheng1   dou1 bian4   ma1bao3   le5
   'these'   'university students' 'all' 'change' 'mother's baby' SFP
   'All these university students have become mother's submissive children.'

b **那些**   年，   我们   一起   追   的   女孩
   na4xie1 nian2 wo3men5 yi4qi3   zhui1 de5   nv3hai2
   'those'   'year' 'we'   'together' 'chase' AD   'girl'
   'The girls we chased together in those years'

c 多数   的   凶宅   一般   都   是   有   **一些**
   duo1shu4 de5 xiong1zhai2   yi4ban1   dou1 shi4 you3 yi4xie1
   'most'   AD 'haunted house' 'in general' 'all' 'be' 'have' 'some'

   怪事   发生   的
   guai4shi4   fa1sheng1 de5
   'strange things' 'happen'   ED

   'Strange things normally occur in houses where homicide happened.'

As shown in Example 12, the item 些 collocates with the demonstratives 这, 那, and the number 'one' to become 这些 'these', 那些 'those' and 一些 'some'. These quantifying units can also be used to lead mass nouns (e.g. 一些水 'some water').

2.3.3 Numbers, ordinals and sequences

Like other languages, numbers in Chinese can be written either in the standard Hindu-Arabic form or in Chinese characters. In either case, they are of course pronounced in the same Chinese syllable-based style. Each number from 0 to 10 is represented by one syllable/character as below:

0	1	2	3	4	5	6	7	8	9
零	一	二	三	四	五	六	七	八	九
ling2	yi1	er4	san1	si4	wu3	liu4	qi1	ba1	jiu3

From 11 onward, it is a simple matter of adding 10 to 90 onto 1 to 9, much like the English way of saying 21 to 29:

10	11	12	13	14
十	十一	十二	十三	十四
shi2	shi2yi1	shi2er4	shi2san1	shi2si4
15	16	17	18	19
十五	十六	十七	十八	十九
shi2wu3	shi2liu4	shi2qi1	shi2ba1	shi2jiu3
20	21	22	23	24
二十	二十一	二十二	二十三	二十四
er4shi2	er4shi2yi1	er4shi2er4	er4shi2san1	er4shi2si4
25	26	27	28	29
二十五	二十六	二十七	二十八	二十九
er4shi2wu3	er4shi2liu4	er4shi2qi1	er4shi2ba1	er4shi2jiu3

The number 100 is represented as 一百 'one hundred' in Chinese. From 101 to 109 a morpheme representing 'zero' is explicitly pronounced:

101	102	103	104	105
一百零一	一百零二	一百零三	一百零四	一百零五
yi4bai3 ling2yi1	yi4bai3 ling2er4	yi4bai3 ling2san1	yi4bai3 ling2si4	yi4bai3 ling2wu3
106	107	108	109	
一百零六	一百零七	一百零八	一百零九	
yi4bai3 ling2liu4	yi4bai3 ling2qi1	yi4bai3 ling2ba1	yi4bai3 ling2jiu3	

From 110 to 999, the numbers are again represented in regular cyclic patterns. Some examples are given below:

110	125	304
一百一十	一百二十五	三百零四
yi4bai3yi1shi2	yi4bai3er4shi2wu3	san1bai3ling2si4
413	807	999
四百一十三	八百零七	九百九十九
si4bai3yi1shi2san1	ba1bai3ling2qi1	jiu3bai3jiu3shi2jiu3

The number 1,000 is represented in Chinese as 一千 'one thousand'. Anything below the thousand is pronounced in the same way as described above. For example, 1,105 is represented in Chinese characters as 一千一百零五 and pronounced as *yi4 qian1 yi4 bai3 ling2 wu3*.

It may be tempting for a westerner to represent 10,500 as *十千零五百 'ten-thousand-zero-five-hundred'. However, there exists an important difference between the Chinese number system and the one we are familiar with in English. This happens when the number to be said amounts to ten thousand (10,000) and over. In Chinese, ten thousand is seen as a separation point, a new unit given a new name (万 *wan4* 'ten thousand') rather than being treated as 'ten units of one thousand'. Thus, while English bundles up large numbers in three digits (thousand, million), Chinese does it in four digits, so 1,0000 has a name (万) and 1,0000,0000 has a new name (亿 *yi4*). In between these separation points, numbers are called 10 万, 100 万, 1000 万 and so on. It is therefore slightly difficult for a Chinese person to conceptualize large numbers in spoken English, and vice versa. For example, when someone says the number 100,000 (100 thousand) in English, the Chinese person probably has to mentally translate it to 10,0000 (10 万) in order to understand its magnitude.

Thus, the Chinese numbers from 10,000 onwards are represented in the following ways:

1,000	10,000	100,000	1,000,000	10,000,000	100,000,000
(1000)	(1,0000)	(10,0000)	(100,0000)	(1000,0000)	(1,0000,0000)
一千	一万	一十万	一百万	一千万	一亿
yi4qian1	yi2wan4	yi1shi2wan4	yi4bai3wan4	yi4qian1wan4	yi2yi4

As for Chinese ordinals, it is quite straightforward once you are familiar with the cardinal numbers. Add the syllable 第 *di4* in front of any number and the combination becomes an ordinal. For example, 第一 'first', 第二 'second' and so on. Normally, as in counting, when using the ordinal set a suitable classifier is also used before the noun. For example, 第三只眼 'the third eye', 第二次世界大战 'second world war' and so on. However, in some cases, especially with proper nouns, the classifier is disposed of and the ordinal precedes the noun directly; such as 第四中学 'The Fourth Secondary School', 第六人民医院 'The Sixth People's Hospital' and so on.

Another morpheme often used to indicate order is 号 *hao4* 'No.' which functions like 第 but comes after the number, as in 三号 'No. 3'. When 号 is used, 第 is normally omitted but it can also be present; for example, 第六号 'No. 6'. For easy distinction, we can call 第 an ordinal *prefix* and 号 an ordinal *suffix* in Chinese.

In Chinese, the seven days of the week and the 12 months of the year are each expressed as a numbered sequence, unlike in English where distinct names are given to each day or month. The names for the seven days of the week in both English and Chinese are contrasted below.

English	Monday	Tuesday	Wednesday	Thursday
Chinese	星期一	星期二	星期三	星期四
	xing1qi2yi1	xing1qi2er4	xing1qi2san1	xing1qi2si4

English	Friday	Saturday	Sunday	
Chinese	星期五	星期六	星期日	
	xing1qi2wu3	xing1qi2liu4	xing1qi2ri4 or	
			星期天	
			xing1qi2tian1	

The disyllabic unit leading the name of the day (i.e. 星期 'week') can be conceptualized as a 'prefix' attached to numbers 1 to 6 and 日 'sun'. Apart from 星期, two other items can serve the same purpose (i.e. as the prefix to name the day of the week). These are 礼拜 *li3bai4* 'ceremony-worship' and 周 *zhou1* 'circuit'. Thus, to refer to Wednesday in Chinese, one can use 星期三 (standard), 礼拜三 (colloquial), or 周三 (formal). Similarly, when we wish to say 'three weeks', we can say 三个星期, 三个礼拜 or 三周 (no classifier for this option), which all mean the same thing.

In contrast to days of a week, the month names in Chinese are based on a suffix 月 *yue4* 'moon' rather than a prefix. The rest is easy: just add a number before the suffix to form the name of a month. Thus, 六月 'six month' means the sixth month of a year, i.e. June. Note this is completely different from 六个月 'six UNIT month', which means 'six months'.

For a native speaker of Chinese, the first semantic property that springs to mind when the name of a month is mentioned (e.g. 五月 'May') is probably its numerical status among the 12 months of the year (the same may be true with other languages using the same system, such as Japanese). This is different from a language like English, where individual names such as *August* are more likely to trigger encyclopedic knowledge about the month such as weather, activities and so on.

2.3.4 Modal auxiliary verbs

Modal auxiliaries mark the properties of a verb in terms of possibility, obligation, ability and so on. This category of words includes *can*, *may*, *will*, *must* and so on in English. There are corresponding items in Chinese, some of which are shown in Example 13.

Example 13

a 我　说　　中文　　　　(7,630,000)
　 wo3 shuo1 zhong1wen2
　 'I'　'say'　'Chinese'
　 'I speak Chinese.'

b 我　**可以**　说　　中文　　(12,400,000)
　 wo3 ke3yi3 shuo1 zhong1wen2
　 'I'　'can'　'say'　'Chinese'
　 'I can/may speak Chinese.'

c 我　**能**　说　　中文　　　(10,900,000)
　 wo3 neng2 shuo1 zhong1wen2
　 'I'　'can'　'say'　'Chinese'
　 'I can speak Chinese.'

d 我　**应该**　　说　　中文　　(3,800,000)
　 wo3 ying1gai1 shuo1 zhong1wen2
　 'I'　'should'　'say'　'Chinese'
　 'I ought to speak Chinese.'

e 我　**会**　说　　中文　　　(2,830,000)
　 wo3 hui4 shuo1 zhong1wen2
　 'I'　'able'　'say'　'Chinese'
　 'I can speak Chinese.'

f 我　**必须**　　说　　中文　　(232,000)
　 wo3 bi4xu1　shuo1 zhong1wen2
　 'I'　'obliged to'　'say'　'Chinese'
　 'I must speak Chinese.'

The phrases in Example 13 include a basic expression 'I speak Chinese' in Example 13a followed by five other expressions each incorporating a different modal auxiliary. Each example also includes a number which is the number of Google hits for the expression (as a phrase) at the time of writing. The figures show, for example, that Example 13b may be the most frequently used expression among them and that Example 13f is the least popular.

Among the examples there, the item 可以 in Example 13b can express the 'permission' meaning of *may* or the 'ability' meaning of *can* in English. Therefore the expression in Example 13b is ambiguous — the word can mean either permission or ability. Context can disambiguate an expression such as this, as Example 14 shows.

Example 14

a 面试　　　的　时候　　是　不　是　**可以**　**说**　中文?
   mian4shi4 de5 shi2hou4 shi4 bu2 shi4 ke3yi3 shuo1 zhong1wen2
   'interview' AD 'moment' 'yes' 'not' 'yes' 'may' 'say' 'Chinese'
   'Can one speak Chinese at the interview?'

b 庞贝　　　有　**可以**　**说**　中文　　　的　导游
   pang2bei4 you3 ke3yi3 shuo1 zhong1wen2 de5 dao3you2
   'Pompeii' 'have' 'can' 'say' 'Chinese'   AD 'guide-tour'
   'There are Chinese-speaking tourist guides in Pompeii.'

From the context of the sentence, the expression 可以说中文 in Example 14a can be understood to mean 'allowed to speak Chinese' (permission) in an institution-controlled setting; while in Example 15b it refers to the existence of persons 'able to speak Chinese' (ability) for desirable functions.

The same ambiguous situation applies to other modal auxiliaries in Example 13. For example, 应该 can impose either an 'obligation' meaning to the main verb, or introduce a 'possibility' meaning.

Example 15

a 我们　　　**应该**　　每天　　　练习　　**说**　　中文
   wo3men5 ying1gai1 mei3tian1 lian4xi2 shuo1 zhong1wen2
   'we'   'should'   'everyday' 'practice' 'speak' 'Chinese'
   'We should practice speaking Chinese every day.'

b 德航　　　　　　上　　**应该**　　有　　**说**　　中文
   de2hang2   shang4 ying1gai1 you3 shuo1 zhong1wen2
   'German-airline' 'up'   'should'   'have' 'speak' 'Chinese'

   的　空姐　　　吧?
   de5 kong1jie3 ba5
   AD 'airhostess' SFP

   'There should be Chinese-speaking flight attendants on Lufthansa Airlines?'

Again, co-text can help disambiguate the ambiguous auxiliaries. In Example 15a, 应该 clearly expresses an 'obligation' attitude due to the first-person plural subject (to enforce group identity) and the nature of the predication (to enforce a routine). In Example 15b, both the 'possibility' and the 'obligation' meanings of 应该 are compatible with the co-text. The 'possibility' meaning applies if Example 15b is asked as a genuine question (i.e. requesting confirmation). The 'obligation' meaning applies if it is a rhetorical question (i.e. a challenge).

Chinese is a non-inflectional, discourse-oriented language. Many grammatical elements obligatory to a language like English can often be omitted in Chinese. A sentence-like structure in Chinese, for example, can often omit a subject. A complex sentence, on the other hand, can be without a subordinate conjunction. This can be illustrated by a short sentence incorporating the modal auxiliary 可以.

Example 16

感冒		可以	哺乳		吗?
gan3mao4		ke3yi3	bu3ru3		ma5
'common cold'		'may'	'breastfeed'		QM

'Can one breastfeed when one has a cold?'

The Chinese expression in Example 16 can be literally translated as 'Can common cold breastfeed?' which does not make much sense in English. In Chinese, however, an anonymous subject (a breastfeeding mother) is implied, as well as a subordinate conjunction like *when* (as in *when a mother gets cold*). The modal auxiliary 可以 plays a pivotal role here for 'cold' to be understood as a condition of 'breastfeeding' with the functionality of its 'permission' meaning.

Unlike English modal auxiliaries, Chinese modals can accept adverbial modifiers. In English, it is unacceptable to say *very can or *extremely must. In Chinese, it is perfectly alright to add intensifiers in front of a modal auxiliary. Some examples follow:

Example 17

a 很   会   抱   大腿   的 猫
   hen3 hui4 bao4 da4tui3   de5 mao1
   'very' 'able' 'hug' 'upper leg' AD 'cat'
   'A cat good at hugging (people's) thighs'

b 很   能   引发   人   思考   的 视频
   hen3 neng2 yin3fa1 ren2   si1kao3   de5 shi4pin2
   'very' 'can' 'trigger' 'person' 'speculate' AD 'video'
   'A thought-provoking video clip'

c 甲肝   定期   检查   很   必须
   jia3gan1   ding4qi2 jian3cha2 hen3 bi4xu1
   'Hepatitis A' 'regular' 'examine' 'very' 'necessary'
   'It is necessary for a Hepatitis A patient to take regular tests.'

d 感觉   很   可以，下次   还   会   入住
   gan3jue2 hen3 ke3yi3 xia4ci4   hai2 hui4 ru4zhu4
   'feel'   'very' 'can'   'next time' 'still' 'will' 'check in'
   'It feels quite alright. Will stay here again next time.'

All the examples in Example 17 incorporate an adverb 很, a typical intensifier in Chinese, attached to modal auxiliaries to intensify the degree of ability, possibility, obligation and so on.

2.3.5 Prepositions

A potential preposition (e.g. 'on'), when assumed to function as a preposition in a given situation, normally takes a noun phrase as its complement to form a prepositional phrase (e.g. on the beach), which then acts as a modifier to another word (*sunset* on the beach) or structure (When you *take your dogs* on the beach . . .). For both English and Chinese, we can only tell if a word is functioning as a preposition by the role it plays in a particular expression. For example, the word *on* is not a preposition in the sentence *Carry on with your work*, as it does not take any noun to form a prepositional phrase (but *with* is a preposition as it forms a prepositional phrase *with your work* to modify *carry on*). *On* is an adverb in *Carry on with your work* instead of a preposition. Therefore, whether a word is a preposition or an adverb in English depends on where you find it in a sentence or phrase.

In Chinese, an item which can serve as a preposition in an expression often can also take on other roles in different contexts, not only as an adverb as in English, but also as a verb or other categories. For example, the morpheme 对 *dui4* is a preposition meaning 'toward' in 对我有利 'to-me-advantageous' but is a verb meaning 'to match' in 对奖 'match-prize (to check lottery results)'. This makes it even harder to identify a Chinese preposition or prepositional phrase in running text. Some examples are offered in Example 18 with the prepositional phrases enclosed in brackets.

Example 18

a ［**向** 国旗］ 敬礼
  xiang4 guo2qi2 jing4li3
  'toward' 'nation-flag' 'salute'
  'Bow to the national flag.'

b 怎样 ［**用** 肉眼］ 判断 钻石 的 真假
  zen3yang4 yong4 rou4yan3 pan4duan4 zuan4shi2 de5 zhen1jia3
  'how' 'with' 'flesh-eye' 'judge' 'diamond' PD 'real-fake'
  'How can we judge the authenticity of the diamond with the naked eye?'

c 一段 美好 的 旅行 ［**从** 飞行］ 开始
  yi2duan4 mei3hao3 de5 lv3xing2 cong2 fei1xing2 kai1shi3
  'a section' 'fantastic' AD 'travel' 'from' 'flight' 'begin'
  'A beautiful travel experience starts from [with] flying.'

d 今天 ［**跟** 大家］ 分享 一下 我 丰胸
  jin1tian1 gen1 da4jia1 fen1xiang3 yi2xia4 wo3 feng1xiong1
  'today' 'with' 'everybody' 'share' 'a bit' 'I' 'enhance-breast'

  的 经验
  de5 jing1yan4
  AD 'experience'

  'Today (I will) share my breast enlargement experience with everyone.'

e ［**除了** 你］，我 谁 都 不要
  chu2le5 ni3 wo3 shei2 dou1 bu2yao4
  'except' 'you' 'I' 'who' 'all' 'not want'
  'I don't want anyone except you.'

f ［**关于** 维基百科］ 你 或许 不 知道 的
  guan1yu2 wei2ji1bai3ke1 ni3 huo4xu3 bu4 zhi1dao4 de5
  'about' 'Wikipedia' 'you' 'possibly' 'not' 'know' AD

  十 件 事
  shi2 jian4 shi4
  'ten' Cla 'matter'

  'Ten things about Wikipedia which you might not know'

All of the examples in Example 18 show the bracketed prepositional phrase as a kind of adverbial unit modifying the verb, which seems to be the main usage of Chinese prepositions (as opposed to adjectival usage modifying the noun). For example, the preposition 向 'toward' in Example 18a takes 'national flag' as its object and together they modify the verb 'salute' as a prepositional phrase, specifying the direction of the salutation. The morpheme 用 'use' in Example 18b serves as a preposition, forming a prepositional phrase with the noun 'naked eye' to modify the verb 'judge' by specifying the method used for evaluating diamonds. In Example 18c, 从 'from' takes 'flying' as object to form a prepositional phrase to modify the verb 'begin' by specifying a starting point for the journey.

As previously mentioned, a Chinese preposition can often serve more than one grammatical function, depending on the context. The preposition in Example 18d, 跟, for example, can also be used as a noun to mean 'heel' (高跟鞋 'high-heel-shoe') or as a verb to mean 'follow' (请跟我来 'please-follow-me-come'). The preposition 用 in Example 18b is also used as a verb, such as 学用筷子 'learn-use-chopsticks'. The examples in Example 18 also show that prepositions can be monosyllabic (Examples 18a–d) or disyllabic (Examples 18e–f).

Sometimes a preposition comes in two parts, surrounding a noun on both sides. Three examples are offered in Example 19:

Example 19

a   红酒   ［除了   美容   之外］，
    hong2jiu3 chu2le5 mei3rong2 zhi1wai4
    'red wine' 'except' 'cosmetics' 'outside'
    'Apart from cosmetic benefits,

    还   能   预防   多种   癌症
    hai2 neng2 yu4fang2 duo1zhong3 ai2zheng4
    'still' 'can' 'prevent' 'many-kind' 'cancer'
    red wine can also help prevent many kinds of cancer.'

b   法国   大选   ［对 美国   来说］   意味   着   什么？
    fa3guo2 da4xuan3   dui4 mei3guo2 lai2shuo1   yi4wei4 zhe5 shen2mo5
    'France' 'big-election' 'to' 'USA'   'come-speak' 'mean' AM 'what'
    'What does the general election of [in] France mean to the US?'

c   一   群   老人   ［在 舞台   上］ 传播   快乐
    yi4 qun2 lao3ren2   zai4 wu3tai2 shang4 chuan2bo4 kuai4le4
    'one' 'group' 'old-person' 'at' 'stage' 'up'   'disseminate' 'happiness'
    'A group of older people disseminate happiness on the stage.'

Like correlative conjunctions in English (*either...or, not only...but also*), the Chinese prepositions shown in Example 19 consist of two parts enclosing the noun and jointly carry out the mediating function of the preposition. For some pairs of prepositions like this, the second element of the pair is redundant and can be omitted at the speaker's discretion. For example, the preposition in Example 19a consists of two parts: 除了 'rid of' and 之外 'outside'. The use of 之外 strengthens the sense of exclusion but it can also be omitted. Similarly, in Example 19b, the second part (来说) of 对…来说 can be omitted without loss in meaning or functionality.

The prepositional pair 在…上 'at...up' in Example 19c represents a different kind of construction from Example 19a or Example 19b. For one thing, the second half of 在…上 is often necessary to its meaning and its replacement with another legitimate item changes the meaning of the preposition. For example, 在…下 means 'under' as opposed to 在…上, which means 'on'. In fact, there is a whole range of location items which pair with 在 to refer to all possible directions. Some examples are given in Example 20:

Example 20

a 杀害　　　蓝可儿　　的　凶手　　　仍　[在 酒店　　里]
　sha1hai4 lan2ke3er2 de5 xiong1shou3 reng2 zai4 jiu3dian4 li3
　'murder' 'Lan Ke-er' AD 'murderer' 'still' 'at' 'hotel' 'inside'
　'The murderer who killed Elisa Lam is still inside the hotel.'

b 伊能静　　　　[在 节目　　　中]　介绍　　　过　的
　yi1neng2jing4 zai4 jie2mu4 zhong1 jie4shao4 guo4 de5
　'Yi Nengjing' 'at' 'program' 'middle' 'introduce' AM AD

　涑口水
　shu4kou3shui3
　'rinse-mouth-water'

　'The mouthwash which Annie Yi introduced in a (TV) program'

c 男童　　　当场　　　受伤　　　躺　[在 马路　旁]
　nan2tong2 dang1chang3 shou4shang1 tang3 zai4 ma3lu4 pang2
　'male-child' 'at-venue' 'injured' 'lie' 'at' 'road' 'side'
　'The boy was injured on the spot and lay on the roadside.'

d 食物　[在 显微镜　　　　下]　的　惊人　　　细节
　shi2wu4 zai4 xian3wei2jing4 xia4 de5 jing1ren2 xi4jie2
　'food' 'at' 'show-tiny-mirror' 'below' AD 'astonishing' 'detail'
　'The amazing detail of food shown under the microscope'

Thus, we have 在 as part of a pair coupling with 里 or 中 to mean 'in (a building)' in Example 20a or 'on (a TV program)' in Example 20b. The morpheme 在 also pairs with 旁 to mean 'beside (the road)' as in Example 20c and with 下 to mean 'under (the microscope)' in Example 20d.

Many locational items shown in Example 20 can carry out the same pre-positional function without the introduction of 在. Some examples of this category appear in Example 21 below:

Example 21

a 男子　　［花园　　　　**里**］　　　睡觉　　　　被　　当成
　nan2zi3 hua1yuan2 li3　　　shui4jiao4 bei4 dang1cheng2
　'man'　'garden'　　'inside' 'sleep'　　PB　'take for'

　"死人"　　　吓坏　　　居民
　si3ren2　　　xia4huai4　ju1min2
　'dead-person' 'frighten'　'resident'

　'Local residents were frightened by a man sleeping in the garden who was taken for a corpse.'

b ［家　　**中**］　　堆　杂物　　　　　　　9旬　　　　　妇
　jia1　　zhong1　dui1 za2wu4　　　　　jiu3xun2　　　fu4
　'home' 'middle' 'pile' 'assorted objects' 'ninety-year-old' 'woman'

　住　　［路　**旁**］
　zhu4 lu4　pang2
　'live' 'road' 'side'

　'Her home littered with miscellaneous objects, the 90-year-old woman sleeps on the roadside.'

c 男子　　行窃　　　遇　　房主　　　　　回家
　nan2zi3 xing2qie4 yu4　fang2zhu3　　hui2jia1
　'man'　'steal'　　'meet' 'house-owner'　'return-home'
　'A man was stealing when the owner of the house returned home.'

d 躲　　［床　　**下**］　陪看　　　喜剧　　被　逗笑　　　露馅
　duo3 chuang2 xia4　pei2kan4　xi3ju4　bei4 dou4xiao4 lou4xian4
　'hide' 'bed'　'below' 'accompany-　'comedy' PB　'elicit-　'expose-
　　　　　　　　　watch'　　　　　　　　smile'　　stuffing'
　'(He) hid under the bed and co-watched the (TV) comedy and exposed himself while laughing.'

The four bracketed prepositional phrases in Example 21 all come with a locational morpheme to indicate the spatial relationship between two objects (the first PP in Example 21b) or the location of an action (Example 21a, the second PP in Example 21b, and Example 21c). For all four prepositional phrases in Example 21, the morpheme 在 can be added redundantly to the beginning of the phrase, like those in Example 20. The fact that 在 is omitted from all the expressions in Example 21 may be because they are all news headlines which emphasize succinctness. In spoken versions, 在 would have been added to all prepositional phrases in Example 21.

We have seen how 在 can be omitted from a prepositional phrase containing a more specific locational item. Conversely, 在 can also be used as a preposition on its own without other locational support. In this case, its meaning is roughly the same as *at* in English. The two examples in Example 22 illustrate this usage.

Example 22

a 北京　　　人　　　[在 纽约]　　　奋斗　　与　　挣扎　　　　的
　 bei3jing1 ren2　　 zai4 niu3yue1　 fen4dou4 yu3　 zheng1zha2 de5
　 'Beijing' 'people' 'at' 'New York' 'strive'　 'and' 'struggle'　 AD

　 生存　　　　故事
　 sheng1cun2 gu4shi5
　 'survival'　 'story'

　 'The striving and struggling survival story of people who come from Beijing'

b 美　　　　全国　　　　　步枪　　 协会　　　　　提出
　 mei3　　 quan2guo2　　 bu4qiang1 xie2hui4　　　 ti2chu1
　 'America' 'whole-nation' 'rifle'　 'association' 'propose'

　 [在 学校]　　部署　　 武装　　　　警察
　 zai4 xue2xiao4 bu4shu3 wu3zhuang1 jing3cha2
　 'at'　 'school'　 'deploy' 'armed'　　 'police'

　 'America's National Rifle Association calls for armed police officers in schools.'

Like the English preposition *at*, 在 can be used to refer to a particular location (New York as in Example 22a) or general places (schools as in Example 22b). Also like *at*, 在 can be used to indicate a particular time, as the two expressions in Example 23 show:

Example 23

a 有   许多   名人   ［在 7月   29   日］ 出生
   you3 xu3duo1 ming2ren2 zai4 qi1yue4 er4shi2jiu3 ri4 chu1sheng1
   'have' 'many' 'name-   'at' 'seven- '29'   'day' 'exit-
                   person'   month'   produce'
   'There are many famous people born on July 29.'

b 小偷   一般   ［在 夜里   三点   到   五点］
   xiao3tou1 yi4ban1   zai4 ye4li3   san1dian3 dao4 wu3dian3
   'thief'   'generally' 'at' 'night-inside' '3 o'clock' 'to' '5 o'clock'

   偷   东西
   tou1   dong1xi1
   'steal' 'stuff'

   'Thieves normally steal things between 3:00 and 5:00 in the night.'

In Example 23a, 在 takes a specific date as the object to form a prepositional phrase, and in Example 23b the object is a period of time. In both cases, 在 helps to signpost a particular point or period in time when something happens − babies being born in Example 23a or theft being carried out in Example 23b.

In the beginning of this section, we mentioned the Chinese preposition being able to act as a verb or other parts of speech. This is also true for the morpheme 在. Apart from being a preposition as already mentioned, 在 can also be a verb-like morpheme, or an aspect marker showing the current state of an action. When 在 acts like a verb, it can constitute the sole predicate without any further support. This is shown in Example 24:

Example 24

a 我   思   故   我   ［在］
   wo3 si1   gu4   wo3 zai4
   'I'   'think' 'therefore' 'I'   'exist'
   'I think, therefore I am.'

b 父母   ［在］，   不   远游
   fu4mu3 zai4   bu4   yuan3you2
   'parents' 'around' 'not' 'far-travel'
   'When parents are still alive, one should not travel far.'

c 管理员   ［在 不   在］？
   guan3li3yuan2 zai4 bu2 zai4
   'administrator' 'at' 'not' 'at'
   'Is the supervisor around?'

Example 24a is the Chinese version of Descartes' famous Latin philosophical statement *Cogito ergo sum* (or 'I think, therefore I am'). The 5 Chinese characters in Example 24a correspond exactly to the English translation word-by-word (illustrating again that English and Chinese share the same basic word order). In other words, the last character, 在, corresponds to the meaning and function of *am* in the English translation. A more accurate English translation for 在 in this context would be *exist*, a stronger predicate than *am*. In Example 24b, 在 is the sole predicate for the conditional clause 'when parents are still alive', again positing an existential sense. Finally, in Example 24c, 在 is used in the familiar A-not-A construction to pose a question; in this case, asking if someone is within hearing distance.

Apart from being a preposition and a main verb, 在 can also take on the role of an aspect marker.

Example 25

a 你 ［**在** 想］ 甚么？
　ni3　zai4　xiang3　shen2mo5
　'you' AM 'think' 'what'
　'What are you thinking?'

b 有 人 ［**在** 等 我］
　you3　ren2　zai4　deng3　wo3
　'have' 'person' AM 'wait' 'me'
　'Someone is waiting for me.'

Both sentences in Example 25 contain a 在 acting as the aspect marker whose function is to show the state of the verb as continuing.

2.3.6 Conjunctions

As in English, two kinds of conjunctions can be identified in Chinese: *coordinating* and *subordinating* conjunctions. Primary coordinating conjunctions in English are *and*, *but* and *or*, which connect two words or expressions with the second part being an addition, contrast or alternative to the first portion. Subordinating conjunctions are words like *because*, *when*, *if*, *although* and so on, which explain logical relations between two statements.

And is one of the most frequently used words in English, probably next only to the words *the* and *of. And* is a versatile conjunction as it provides connection between words, phrases and entire sentences. In Chinese, there is no single conjunction to match *and* in its broad functionality. Instead, there are several different conjunctions in Chinese sharing the functions solely performed by *and* in English. We may look at a set of examples showing how *and* works in English.

Example 26

a   [Thomas] *and* [friends]
b   Someone [hit my car today] *and* [drove off]!
c   [Give somebody an inch] *and* [they'll take a mile].

Example 26 shows how the word *and* connects two words (Example 26a), two verb phrases (Example 26b) and two sentences (Example 26c) respectively. This is how the conjunction *and* typically works in English. Now if we translate the sentences in Example 26 into Chinese, *and* will have to be replaced by a different morpheme, word, or machinery in each case depending on what level of linguistic structures it connects, as examples in Example 27 show.

Example 27

a   ［汤玛士］   **和**   ［朋友   们］
    tang1ma3shi4 he2   peng2you3 men5
    'Thomas'   'and' 'friend'   PM
    'Thomas and friends'

b   今天   有   人   ［撞   了   我的   车］ **然后**
    jin1tian1 you3 ren2   zhuang4 le5 wo3de5 che1 ran2hou4
    'today'   'have' 'person' 'hit'   AM 'my'   'car' 'then'
    'Today somebody hit my car then

    ［悄悄   开走   了］！
    qiao3qiao3 kai1zou3 le5
    'quietly'   'drive-go' AM
    quietly drove away.'

c   ［给 他 一   寸］，［他 进   一   尺］
    gei3 ta1 yi2 cun4   ta1 jin4   yi4 chi3
    'give' 'he' 'one' 'inch' 'he' 'advance' 'one' 'foot'
    'Give him an inch, he takes a foot.'

The morpheme 和 in Example 27a is probably the most similar Chinese conjunction to *and* in English. However, 和 tends to work more on the individual word level and rarely connects larger structures. Thus, the *and* which connects two verb phrases in Example 26b is replaced by a temporal conjunction, **然后**, in Example 27b, which is appropriate as the two bits of information happen to be sequential in time. Moreover, the *and* in Example 26c which connects two sentences is replaced by a punctuation mark in Example 27c. This is the 'null conjunction' situation prevalent in Chinese, where a conjunction of some sort can be inferred from two juxtaposed sentences if the logical relation between them and the context are clear (recall a similar type of structure discussed in section 2.2.4 – the VPVP four-character idiom). There are other copulative conjunctions in Chinese whose functions are either similar or complementary to 和. These include 与 'and', 跟 'with', (以)及 'as well as', 而且 'moreover' and so on.

While there is no Chinese word which can be taken as an exact match for *and*, there is indeed a word which translates *but* quite well as a conjunction. This is 但是 'but' (the second syllable can be omitted to become 但 without a change of meaning or syntactic functionality). Again, we can see some examples in English which use *but* as a conjunction.

Example 28

a　[Stylish] *but* [illegal] monkey found roaming Toronto IKEA
b　Firefox [is already running] *but* [is not responding].
c　[You can lead a horse to water], *but* [you can't make it drink].

In Example 28, the English conjunction *but* connects two words (Example 28a), two verb phrases (Example 28b) and two sentences (Example 28c) respectively. The Chinese word 但是, or its simplified form 但, can translate *but* competently in all three settings, as shown in Example 29:

Example 29

a　[时尚]　　　但　　[非法]　　的　猴子　　　漫游　　　多伦多　　　　IKEA
　　shi2shang4　dan4　fei1fa3　de5　hou2zi5　man4you2　duo1lun2duo1　Ikea
　　'fashionable' 'but' 'illegal'　AD 'monkey' 'roam'　　'Toronto'　　'IKEA'
　　'Stylish but illegal monkey roaming Toronto IKEA.'

b　Firefox　[已经　　在　运行]　　　　但　　[不　回应]
　　Firefox　yi3jing1　zai4　yun4xing2　dan4　bu4　hui2ying4
　　'Firefox' 'already' AM 'in motion' 'but' 'not' 'respond'
　　'Firefox (browser) is already running but is not responding.'

c　[你　可以　把　马　　牵　　到　　水边]　，
　　ni3　ke3yi3　ba3　ma3　qian1　dao4　shui3bian1
　　'you' 'may' OB 'horse' 'drag' 'up to' 'water-side'
　　'You can lead a horse to the water,

　　但是　　[你　不能　　　强迫　　　它　喝水]
　　dan4shi4　ni3　bu4neng2　qiang2po4　ta1　he1shui3
　　'but'　　'you' 'cannot' 'force'　　'it' 'drink-water'
　　but you cannot force it to drink water.'

As can be seen, all instances of *but* in Example 28 can be fully translated by 但(是) in the corresponding Chinese sentences in Example 29. Other contrastive conjunctions similar to 但是 include 可是 'however', 不过 'nevertheless', 然而 'even so', although 但是 is by far the most frequently used and universally applicable one.

The final type of coordinating conjunction to be discussed here is 'alternative conjunctions', such as *or* in English. In Chinese, this function is normally carried out by 或(者) or 还是. Some examples follow:

Example 30

a 1   天   1   杯   ［绿茶］   **或者**   ［咖啡］，
  yi4   tian1 yi4 bei1 lv4cha2   huo4zhe3 ka1fei1
  'one' 'day' 'one' 'cup' 'green-tea' 'or'   'coffee'
  'A cup of green tea or coffee a day

  可   降低   患   中风   机率。
  ke3 jiang4di1 huan4   zhong4feng1 ji1lv4
  'can' 'reduce' 'suffer' 'stroke'   'probability'
  can help reduce the risk of a stroke.'

b 您的   电脑   上   是否   安装   了
  nin2de5 dian4nao3 shang4 shi4fou3 an1zhuang1 le5
  'your' 'computer' ' up' 'yes-no' 'install'   AM
  'Has your computer been installed with

  ［Adware］ **或**   ［Spyware］?
  adware   huo4 spyware
  'adware'   'or'   'spyware'
  adware or spyware?'

c ［先   有   鸡］   **还是**   ［先   有   蛋］？
  xian1 you3 ji1   hai2shi4 xian1 you3 dan4
  'ahead' 'have' 'chicken' 'or'   'ahead' 'have' 'egg'
  'Which came first, the chicken or the egg?'

As the phrases in Example 30 show, 或(者) makes connections between words, while 还是 offers connections between sentences. However, it is also possible for 或者 to connect between sentences and for 还是 to do so between words and phrases.

In English, subordinating conjunctions are words like *if*, *when*, and *because* which express conditional, chronological or causal relationships between two statements. In Chinese, we find equivalent items to express the same logical relations. However, unlike the single-word English conjunctions, Chinese conjunctions for this kind of function often come in two parts; for example, 因为···所以 'because... therefore', 如果···那么 'if...then', 虽然···可是 'although...but'. The three sentences in Example 31 show how they work:

Example 31

a **因为**　　［无能为力］，　　　　**所以**　　　［顺其自然］。
　　yin1wei4　wu2neng2wei2li4　　　suo3yi3　　shun4qi2zi4ran2
　　'because' 'not-able-do-strength'　'therefore' 'obey-its-nature'
　　'Because (one) cannot do anything, (therefore) just go with the flow.'

b **如果**　［泰坦尼克号　　　最后　　　没有　　　撞　　　冰山］，
　　ru2guo3 tai4tan3ni2ke4hao4 zui4hou4　mei2you3 zhuang4 bing1shan1
　　'if'　　'Titanic'　　　　　'eventually' 'not'　　'hit'　　'iceberg'
　　'If the Titanic had not ended up hitting an iceberg,

　　那么　［结局　会　是　怎样］？
　　na4mo5　jie2ju2　hui4 shi4 zen3yang4
　　'then'　'ending' 'will' 'be' 'how'
　　then what would the ending be like?'

c **虽然**　［我　不懂　　　　　你　在　说　什么］，
　　sui1ran2　wo3　bu4dong3　　　ni3　zai4 shuo1 shen2mo5
　　'although' 'I'　'not-understand' 'you' AM 'say'　'what'
　　'Although I don't understand what you are saying,

　　可是　［好像　　　　很　有　道理］。
　　ke3shi4　hao3xiang4　　hen3 you3 dao4li3
　　'but'　'good-resemble' 'very' 'have' 'sense'
　　you seem to make sense.'

In Example 31a, the conjunctive pair 因为···所以 connects between a cause ('unable to do anything') and a result ('do nothing'). In English, using the word *because* would have been adequate. In fact, using *because... so* in English would have been ungrammatical, which is a 'mistake' the Chinese learner of English often makes. In English, we also see pairs like *if... then* and *although... yet*, which would have been similar to the conjunction pairs shown in Examples 31b and 31c. However, in Chinese the second element of the pair is more necessary if not exactly compulsory.

2.3.7 Adverbial elements

In this section, we discuss some frequently used monosyllabic adverbs with somewhat broader functionalities than common adverbs. First, we take a closer look at 很, whose function and usage are very similar to the English word *very*. Example 32 illustrates its usage.

Example 32

a   我   [很   快乐]
     wo3 hen3 kuai4le4
     'I'   'very' 'happy'
     'I am happy.'

b   小沈阳   演戏   [很   用心]
     xiao3shen3yang2 yan3xi4   hen3 yong4xin1
     'little-Shenyang' 'perform' 'very' 'use-heart'
     'Little Shenyang is a dedicated performer.'

The monosyllabic adverb 很 intensifies the degree of happiness in Example 32a by modifying the adjective 'happy'. The AP 'very happy' then serves as the predicate for the subject 'I'. In Example 32b, 很 modifies an adverbial unit 'perform'.

Unlike the adverb *very* in English, which only modifies adjectives or adverbs, 很 can also modify some categories of verbs, and even nouns at times! Some examples where 很 modifies verbs are shown in Example 33.

Example 33

a   我   真的   [很   喜欢]   你
     wo3 zhen1de5 hen3 xi3huan1 ni3
     'I'   'really'   'very' 'like'   'you'
     'I really like you.'

b   抽烟   的 女生   [很   讨厌]
     chou1yan1 de5 nv3sheng1 hen3 tao3yan4
     'smoke'   AD 'girl'   'very' 'disagreeable'
     'Girls who smoke are repugnant.'

In Example 33a, 很 modifies the static verb 喜欢 'like', emphasizing the degree of fondness. In Example 33b, 很 again modifies a static verb 讨厌 'dislike', which is an antonym of 喜欢. This usage of 很 seems applicable to verbs denoting mental states only; for example, 很羡慕 'very-admire', 很生气 'very-anger', 很在乎 'very-care', 很痛恨 'very-despise', 很爱惜 'very-cherish' and so on. Structures like these are so prevalent in Chinese that some Chinese speakers beginning to learn English would say things like *very like*, *very hate* and so on.

In relatively rare cases, 很 can be used to modify a noun. The construction [很 N] then comes to be understood as an adjective phrase. In other words, with the addition of 很, the noun acquires an 'adjectiveship' of some sort. This is not a very productive process. It usually takes a while for a new usage like this to catch on among native speakers. Some examples of this type of construction are shown in Example 34:

Example 34

a 我家 的 外劳 [很 油条]
 wo3jia1 de5 wai4lao2 hen3 you2tiao2
 'my home' PD 'outside-labor' 'very' 'oil-stick'
 'The foreign worker at my home is very cunning.'

b 张绍刚   坦言 对 海归 女
 zhang1shao4gang1 tan3yan2 dui4 hai3gui1 nv3
 'Zhang Shaogang' 'frank-speak' 'toward' 'sea-return' 'female'

 [很 "感冒"]
 hen3 gan3mao4
 'very' 'common cold'

 'Zhang Shaogang admitted that he found female returnees from overseas distasteful.'

c 后宫 其实 [很 八卦]
 hou4gong1 qi2shi2 hen3 ba1gua4
 'harem' 'actually' 'very' 'Eight Trigrams'
 'The harem is in fact a rather gossipy place.'

d 班导 [很 机车] 怎么办?
 ban1dao3 hen3 ji1che1 zen3mo5ban4
 'class-guide' 'very' 'motorcycle' 'how-do'
 'Our class tutor is very fastidious. What can I do?'

Each sentence in Example 34 demonstrates a [很 N] construction which serves as an adjective in the context given. For example, in Example 34a, 油条 is a kind of food but when combined with 很 the unit becomes an adjective phrase which describes a person as cunning and slippery. In Example 34b, the word 感冒 acquires adjective status when combined with 很. The new unit, 很感冒, is used to show one's loathing toward something or someone. Likewise, the noun 八卦 in Example 34c originally meant 'Eight Trigrams' but it can also mean 'gossip'. When emphasized by 很, the unit 很八卦 comes to mean a nosy person or a gossipy situation. Example 34d shows an even more interesting example, where the noun 机车 turns into an adjective, when sanctioned by 很, to describe a person as being fussy and irritating. (Note: 机车 is possibly a euphemism for 鸡巴 *ji1ba1* 'dick' which can also couple with 很 to mean roughly the same thing.)

Monosyllabic adverbs similar to 很 include 更 'more', 最 'most', 太 'too', 真 'really' and so on. In most cases, the item 很 can be replaced by any one of them to shift the quantity of the property being described toward the meaning of the new adverb. For example, 很难 'very difficult' can become 太难 'too difficult', 更难 'more difficult' or 最难 'the most difficult' and so on. Some disyllabic adverbs which can replace 很 and vary the degree of emphasis are 非常 'unusually', 比较 'comparatively', 特别 'especially', 相当 'rather', 极端 'extremely' and so on. Their functionalities are largely the same as 很, differing only in degree.

We turn now to some frequently used adverbial elements which can precede a verb to provide more information about the action or situation. The first item we look at is 就. When preceding a verb, 就 can act as a logical connector, showing the predicate marked by 就 to be an obvious consequence of a previous happening. Two examples of this kind of use of 就 are shown in Example 35.

Example 35

a 想   唱   **就**   唱
   xiang3 chang4 jiu4   chang4
   'think' 'sing' 'then' 'sing'
   'You want to sing – then sing.'

b 百度   一下，你 **就**   知道
   bai3du4   yi2xia4 ni3 jiu4   zhi1dao4
   'hundred-times' 'once' 'you' 'then' 'know'
   'Use Baidu (to search) once, you will know (the answer) right away.'

Example 35a says that 'when one feels like singing, one should sing'. The attachment of 就 to the second verb gives it a sense of immediacy and legitimacy – your desire to sing is reason enough for you to start singing. Although 就 is not a conjunction per se, it is a connector at the conceptual level, facilitating the inference process between two propositions. Example 35b is another sentence which uses 就 for its logical connotation. That is, by using the search engine Baidu a little, the user will become knowledgeable immediately.

Another usage of 就 is to keep its sense of immediacy without invoking the causal relationship between two propositions. This kind of 就 often pairs with the particle 了 to denote the immediacy of an action or a change of state.

Example 36

a 屏幕　　　用　　一　　天　　**就**　碎　　　了
　 ping2mu4 yong4 yi4 tian1 jiu4 sui4 le5
　 'screen'　'use'　'one'　'day'　'then'　'shatter'　SFP
　 'The monitor was used for only a day before it was shattered.'

b 我　挂　　掉　　电话　　　**就**　后悔　　了
　 wo3 gua4 diao4 dian4hua4 jiu4 hou4hui3 le5
　 'I'　'hang'　'drop'　'telephone'　'then'　'regret'　SFP
　 'After hanging up the phone, I immediately regret.'

In Example 36a, 就 clearly signals the very short time (one day) between the purchase of a computer screen and its being shattered. The supporting particle, 了, on the other hand, indicates the change of state of the monitor from being intact to being broken. The [就···了] construction like this often provides a sense of contrast, from being intact to being broken in Example 36a, and from being angry to being regretful in Example 36b.

A third usage of 就 is to emphasize the 'exactness' of a proposition. Some examples in this thread are listed in Example 37. The English translation of this kind of 就 is no longer 'then' but something like 'just' or 'exactly'.

Example 37

a 人生　　　**就**　像　　一　　次　　　旅行
　 ren2sheng1 jiu4 xiang4 yi2 ci4 lv3xing2
　 'human-life'　'just'　'like'　'one'　'round'　'trip'
　 'Life is just like a travel experience.'

b 我们　　**就**　喜欢　　折腾　　　男朋友
　 wo3men5 jiu4 xi3huan1 zhe1teng5 nan2peng2you3
　 'we'　'just'　'like'　'torment'　'boyfriend'
　 'We just like to torment our boyfriends.'

就 in Example 37a helps authenticate the simile that life is like a journey. And, in 37b, it lends power to the somewhat paranoid hobby of 'torturing the boyfriend', creating a sense of humor.

Another adverbial element, 才 'only then', seems to work in the same way as 就 but with somewhat different connotations. They are both capable of being integrated into the [if... then] argumentation. While 就 introduces a sense of immediacy and fluency to the transition from the premise to the conclusion, 才 emphasizes the existence of some 'false steps' before arriving at the correct solution. Two examples are provided in Example 38 to show how 才 works.

Example 38

a 开始　　　我　还　以为　　是　跳舞　　　呢，
   kai1shi3   wo3 hai2 yi3wei2 shi4 tiao4wu3 ne5
   'beginning' 'I' 'still' 'assume' 'be' 'dancing' SFP
   'In the beginning I thought they were dancing;

   后来　　才　　　　知道　　　是　打架
   hou4lai2 cai2   zhi1dao4 shi4 da3jia4
   'later' 'only then' 'know' 'be' 'fighting'
   only later did I know it was a fight.'

b 怎样　　　反腐　　　　才　有效?
   zen3yang4 fan3fu3   cai2 you3xiao4
   'how'   'contrary-rotten' 'only' 'effective'
   'What is an effective way to fight against corruption?'

First, Example 38a clearly shows two contrasting suppositions − one assuming the commotion alluded to was an act of dancing, the other that it was actually a fight. The role 才 'only then' plays in this text is to help bring out the contrast between contesting suppositions, and to mark the final resolution as being arrived at through some kind of misconception. In Example 38b, someone is asking the question 'How can we best fight against corruption?' The use of 才 before the keyword 'effective' implies the existence of other futile steps beforehand and the difficulty of arriving at a workable solution.

   Another set of frequently used adverbial elements associated with verbs are 再 'once more', 又 'again' and 还 'in addition', which are used to mark the repetitive nature of the verb or to help achieve an augmentative effect.

Example 39

a 再　　吻　　我　一　　次
   zai4   wen3 wo3 yi2   ci4
   'again' 'kiss' 'me' 'one' Cla
   'Kiss me one more time.'

b 我的　　老婆　　又　　大肚
   wo3de5 lao3po2 you4   da4du4
   'my'   'wife' 'again' 'big-tummy'
   'My wife is pregnant again.'

c 他们　　结婚　　了　还　　　有　很　多　　孩子
   ta1men5 jie2hun1 le5 hai2   you3 hen3 duo1 hai2zi5
   'they' 'marry' AM 'moreover' 'have' 'very' 'many' 'child'
   'They got married and have many children.'

In Example 39a, 再 points to the future and expresses a wish for the repetition of an action. The next morpheme, 又, can also mean 'again' but it focuses more on the effect of an already completed event; such as in 39b, where the use of 又 clearly identifies the woman's pregnancy as being a (probably undesirable) repeated event. The item 还 'in addition' in 39c also marks the augmentative nature of an event, although 还 can also mean 'still, yet' in other contexts.

2.3.8 Verb accessories

Three categories of functional items associated with the use of verbs are discussed in this section. The first category marks the aspects of the verb specifying how the speaker wants the verb to be understood, i.e. whether it is an ongoing event or a completed action and so on. The second category marks the verb as being used in the passive voice; that is, the subject of the sentence is now understood as the object of the verb. The third category is a unique morpheme in Chinese, 把, which marks a noun phrase as the object of a verb.

Among the first category of verb accessory (aspect markers), 在 'at' has been discussed in section 2.3.5, focusing on its capacity as a preposition. When acting as an aspect marker, 在 indicates the action denoted by the verb to be continuing at the time of speaking, as the sentences in Example 25 showed. Another 'duration marker', as it is sometimes called, 着, also marks a verb as continuing but it differs from 在 in word order relative to the verb: 在 always comes before the verb; 着 invariably comes after the verb. This contrast is shown in Example 40:

Example 40

a 你　[在　看]　我　吗?
　ni3　zai4 kan4　wo3　ma5
　'you' AM 'look' 'me' QM
　'Are you looking at me?'

b [哭　着]　说　　再见
　ku1 zhe5 shuo1 zai4jian4
　'cry' AM 'say'　'goodbye'
　'Saying goodbye while weeping'

When 在 marks a verb as continuing, it means the speaker finds a consecutive movement at the time of speech. That is, the movement has been occurring for some time and is still happening when it is mentioned (hence 在 is also called a progressive aspect marker, for example, in Xiao and McEnery 2004). Thus, the speaker asking 'Are you looking at me?' in Example 40a implies that the listener has been looking at the speaker for at least a very brief time before the latter notices it. While 在 emphasizes the impact of the action at the moment of speaking, the other marker of continuation, 着, is more concerned with the duration aspect of the verb. That is, it focuses on the continuing state of the action, rather than emphasizing what the speaker finds at the time of speaking. For that reason, 着 often marks a 'background state' of things against which something happens, as in Example 40b.

The second type of aspect marker is the marker of completion (referred to as a marker for the perfective aspect by Xiao and McEnery 2004, in contrast to 在 and 着, which mark imperfective aspects). This includes the morpheme 了 and 过. The item 了 marks the action represented by the verb as having been completed at the time of speaking, as opposed to a continuing action. Two examples are offered in Example 41:

Example 41

a 我们　　［结婚　　了］
   wo3men5 jie2hun1 le5
   'we'　　　'marry'　AM
   'We have got married.'

b ［感冒　　了］怎么办?
   gan3mao4 le5　zen3mo5ban4
   'catch cold' AM 'what to do'
   'What to do when you have got a cold?'

The expression 我们结婚 'we get married' can be a statement or a proposal without any marker. Once it is marked by 了, as in Example 41a, however, it becomes a completed action ('We have got married!'). In 41b, 感冒 is a verb and 了 helps mark it as a process having been completed (i.e. the person has caught a cold).

Another marker of completion is the experiential marker 过, which marks an action or process as having been experienced by the party in question. The experiential marker 过 differs from the other perfective marker 了 in that, while 了 emphasizes the impact of the completed action or process upon the present, 过 focuses more on the past dimension, emphasizing the significance of the past experience itself or the memory of it. Some examples of the usage of 过 follow:

Example 42

a 我们　　　一起　　［唱　过］　的　歌
　 wo3men5 yi4qi3　　chang4 guo4 de5 ge1
　 'we'　　　'together''sing'　AM　AD 'song'
　 'The song(s) we used to sing together'

b 那些　　年　　我们　　［玩　过］　的　游戏
　 na4xie1 nian2 wo3men5 wan2 guo4 de5 you2xi4
　 'those' 'year' 'we'　　'play' AM　AD 'game'
　 'The games we used to play in those years'

The expression in Example 42a demonstrates a typical use of 过: to shift the perspective of the discourse to a time in the past, here to invoke the memory of the songs once sung together by the discourse participants. Understandably, this usage will often be co-marked by some adverbial elements referring to the past. This is the case with Example 42b where the adverbial phrase 那些年 'those years' clearly points to the past, highlighting the games that used to be played by the participants of the discourse when they were much younger. Apart from a difference in focus (i.e. 了 focuses on the present, while 过 focuses on the past), structurally, a verb marked by 过 can be negated to show the lack of a certain experience, while a verb marked by 了 cannot be used to deny the completion of an action. The contrast is shown in Example 43:

Example 43

a 没　［离开　过］　　　　　b *没　［离开　了］
　 mei2 li2kai1 guo4　　　　　　 mei2 li2kai1 le5
　 'not' 'leave' AM　　　　　　　'not' 'leave' AM
　 'Have never left'　　　　　　 '*Did not have left'

c 还　没　［离开］
　 hai2 mei2 li2kai1
　 'still' 'not' 'leave'
　 'Have not left yet'

The expression in Example 43a shows that the person has not left someone or a place. The same expression, with the experiential marker 过 replaced by the perfective marker 了, in Example 43b, however, is illegitimate. To indicate the incomplete state of an act, the perfective marker 了 cannot be used. Instead, some other adverbial element, like 还, coupled with the negative element 没, are used to mark the bare verb, as in Example 43c, to achieve the 'incomplete action' effect.

We now move on to the second category of verb accessory included in this section, which involves the marking of a verb used in the passive voice. The primary passive marker in Chinese is 被 which, like all the markers discussed above, can serve other grammatical functions, such as a verb or a noun. The sentences in Example 44 show how the morpheme is used as a passive marker.

Example 44

a 居民　　阻止　　强制　　　施工　　[**被** 碾　　　死]
　ju1min2 zu3zhi3 qiang2zhi4 shi1gong1 bei4 nian3　si3
　'resident' 'intervene' 'enforce'　'work'　PB 'run over' 'dead'
　'A resident was run over and killed while trying to stop enforced construction work.'

b 多愁善感　　　　　的 人　　更　　　需要　[**被** 夸奖]
　duo1chou2shan4gan3　de5 ren2　geng4　xu1yao4 bei4 kua1jiang3
　'much-sorrow-good-feel' AD 'person' 'even more' 'need' PB 'praise'
　'Emotional people need to be complimented even more.'

The passive structure in Chinese marked by 被 is predominantly used to encode adverse conditions, such as unfortunate happenings or undesirable outcomes. This is true for Example 44a where a protesting resident was maliciously killed by a demolition team. However, perhaps due to the influence of English, where passive structures are not subject to semantic preferences, it is becoming more acceptable for the Chinese passive to be used in neutral or even positive situations. For example, in Example 44b, 被 is used to mark a positive verb 'praise'.

It can further be observed in the Example 44 sentences that 被 is used in the frame [被 (NP) VP] where, like in English, the NP (the agent who does the action) can be omitted if they are deemed unimportant or cannot be identified.

There are other passive markers in Chinese such as 受 *shou4* 'endure', 遭 *zao1* 'undergo', 经 *jing1* 'experience' etc., but these are much less common and are more restricted in the linguistic environments where they can appear.

The third category of verb accessory to be discussed in this section is 把. Note that some writers consider 把 a preposition (e.g. Bai 2009). However, since its function is fairly restricted and different from the normal functions of prepositions, we treat it as an object marker here. As a direct object marker, 把

is used in a fixed frame of [把 NP V] where NP is the object of the verb V. Like other monosyllabic items explained in this chapter, 把 can serve other grammatical functions, such as verb (meaning 'grasp'), noun (meaning 'handle') or even classifier (to mark 'a chair', 'a fire' and so on). The sentences in Example 45 below demonstrate the use of 把 as direct object marker.

Example 45

a 请   ［把］ ［衣服］ ［穿上］
   qing3 ba3 yi1fu2 chuan1shang4
   'please' OB 'clothes' 'wear-up'
   'Please put clothes on.'

b 乖乖   ［把］ ［功课］   ［作完］
   guai1guai1 ba3 gong1ke4 zuo4wan2
   'obediently' OB 'homework' 'do-finish'
   'Be good and finish the homework.'

In Chinese there is a large category of verb units consisting of a verb morpheme followed by an adverbial element (called a 'resultative complement' in Yip and Rimmington 2004) which denotes the result of the action, such as 吃光 'eat-empty', 打开 'hit-open (unpack)', 说完 'speak-complete (finish speaking)', 吹干 'blow-dry', 看错 'see-wrong', 听懂 'listen-understand', 笑死 'laugh-dead (laugh to death)' and so on. This kind of structure seems to be a preferred candidate for the object marker 把, as Examples 45a–b show, where 穿好 'dress-good' and 作完 'do-complete' are verb units including resultant complements. The [把 NP V] structure is sometimes interchangeable with an ordinary V NP structure. If we use X to represent everything else that goes before *ba3* in a [把 NP V] construction, then both example sentences in Example 45 can be expressed by the formula [X 把 NP V]. In some cases, 把 can be removed from the structure, in which case the NP and the V involved have to change places; that is, for sentences like Example 45a and Example 45b:

[X 把 NP V] = [X V NP]

In other words, it is equally legitimate to say Example 46b, which has the same semantic content as 45a, reproduced below as 46a. The same procedure can be applied to Example 46c to produce a sentence of the same meaning in 46d.

Example 46

a   请   ［把］［衣服］［穿上］
    qing3   ba3   yi1fu2   chuan1shang4
    'please' OB   'clothes' 'wear-up'
    'Please put clothes on.'

b   请   ［穿上］   ［衣服］
    qing3   chuan1shang4 yi1fu2
    'please' 'wear-up'   'clothes'
    'Please put clothes on.'

c   不   小心   ［把］［门牙］   ［撞歪   了］
    bu4 xiao3xin1 ba3   men2ya2   zhuang4wai1 le5
    'not' 'careful' OB   'door-tooth' 'collide-askew' AM
    '(Someone) unintentionally collided (with something) and distorted
    the front teeth.'

d   不   小心   ［撞歪   了］［门牙］
    bu4 xiao3xin1 zhuang4wai1 le5   men2ya2
    'not' 'careful'   'collide-askew' AM   'door-tooth'
    '(Someone) unintentionally collided (with something) and distorted
    the front teeth.'

Sometimes the verb in a [把 NP V] may be followed by a longer adverbial
structure like that in Example 47a and Example 47c below. We will use the
symbol AP (for 'Adverb Phrase') to represent structures like 到大陆 'to-Mainland'
in Example 47a and 回家 'back-home' in Example 47c. Like Examples 45a and
45b, the *ba3*-sentences in Examples 47a and 47c can also be replaced by a
ba3-less structure, with a different formula:

[X 把 NP V AP] = [X V NP AP]

In other words, when the VP in a *ba3*-structure contains an AP, only the V
changes place with the NP when transforming into a *ba3*-less sentence. The
AP stays behind and makes room for the NP which now stands between the
V and the AP. The results of the application of this rule to Examples 47a and
47c are shown respectively in Examples 47b and 47d.

Example 47

a 怎么　　［把］［车子］［运］　　［到　大陆］？
   zen3mo5 ba3　che1zi5 yun4　　dao4 da4lu4
   'how'　OB　'vehicle' 'transport' 'to' 'mainland'
   'How can one transport a car to the mainland?'

b 怎么　　［运］　　［车子］［到　大陆］？
   zen3mo5 yun4　　che1zi5 dao4 da4lu4
   'how'　'transport' 'vehicle' 'to' 'mainland'
   'How can one transport a car to the mainland?'

c 不要　　随便　　［把］［流浪　狗］［带］［回　家］
   bu2yao4 sui2bian4 ba3　liu2lang4 gou3 dai4　hui2 jia1
   'no''want' 'at will'　OB　'stray'　'dog' 'bring' 'back' 'home'
   'Do not take a stray dog home without thinking.'

d 不要　　随便　　［带］［流浪　狗］［回　家］
   bu2yao4 sui2bian4 dai4　liu2lang4 gou3 hui2 jia1
   'no''want' 'at will'　'bring' 'stray'　'dog' 'back' 'home'
   'Do not take a stray dog home without thinking.'

There is a subcategory of *ba3*-structure which cannot be transformed in the ways described above. This is the *ba3*-structure where two noun phrases are involved and one is the complement of the other, much like the two noun phrases in the English sentence 'Officials call the pilot a hero' (where 'the pilot' is the first NP and 'a hero' is the second NP, the second NP being the complement of the first NP). The range of verbs usable in this type of structure is fairly restricted. The most frequently used one is 当(作) 'take as'. Moreover, the *ba3*-structure is obligatory for this kind of expression. There is no equivalent structure without *ba3* in this subcategory. An example of this type of *ba3*-sentence is illustrated in Example 48a below.

Example 48

a 男子   酒   后   ［**把**］［妻子］［**当**］ ［ " 小姐 " ］
  nan2zi3 jiu3 hou4 ba3   qi1zi5 dang1   xiao3jie3
  'man'   'wine' 'after' OB 'wife' 'take as' 'miss'
  'A drunken man mistook his wife for a sex worker.'

b *男子   酒   后   ［**当**］   ［妻子］ ［ " 小姐 " ］
  nan2zi3 jiu3 hou4 dang1 qi1zi5 xiao3jie3
  'man'   'wine' 'after' 'take as' 'wife' 'miss'
  '(uninterpretable)'

c 男子   酒   后   ［**当**］ ［妻子］ **是** ［ " 小姐 " ］
  nan2zi3 jiu3 hou4 dang1   qi1zi5 shi4 xiao3jie3
  'man'   'wine' 'after' 'take as' 'wife' 'be' 'miss'
  'A drunken man mistook his wife for a sex worker.'

Example 48a is the original sentence from a news headline, where a drunkard mistook his wife, on her way to collect him from the street, as a sex worker. If we attempt to transform the sentence in the way in which Example 47a is transformed into 47b, we get the ungrammatical result of Example 48b. However, if we add a copula verb 是 between 妻子 and " 小姐 " , as in Example 48c, then the sentence becomes grammatical again. The meaning of sentence Example 48c is the same as 48a, although this kind of structure is relatively less used than the *ba3*-structure.

2.4 SUMMARY AND CONCLUSION

In this chapter, we have examined Chinese meaning-making units of various lengths (in terms of the number of syllables). We noted that the concept of 'word' is difficult to define in Chinese. However, if we define it as a habitually used unit of meaning that expresses a self-contained concept, then we are able to meaningfully distinguish between the content units of various lengths. For example, we noted that some monosyllabic items can function independently in a sentence and may qualify as 'words'. Others are best called morphemes, because they are normally subsumed in some kind of multisyllabic unit in actual usage. The best candidate for 'prototypical word' is the disyllabic unit, which is frequently used in contemporary Chinese to express a self-contained concept. The majority of items listed as words in Xiao *et al.* (2009), for example, are disyllabic units. We also found that, for trisyllabic units, idiomaticity seems a good indication of wordhood. As for quadrisyllabic units, or the four-character idioms, they demonstrate a lot of syntactic properties and can be treated as 'mini sentences' or phrases in Chinese.

We have also explored a wide range of functional items in Chinese, including pronouns, classifiers, modal auxiliaries, conjunctions, intensifiers, aspect and experiential markers and so on. Some of these are common grammatical categories (such as pronouns, modal auxiliaries, and conjunctions) which also exist in other languages. However, despite the similarities in function, the forms these grammatical categories take in each language may be dramatically different. For example, we noted the different ways of representing pronouns in Chinese from English, and the different ways of saying the days of the week, months of the year and so on. Some grammatical categories may represent entirely new concepts for English native speakers, such as the noun classifier, which is obligatory when referring to a noun. Some frequently used adverbial morphemes, such as 就 and 才, are also particular to Chinese, which we have discussed in some detail. Knowledge of all these grammatical items is useful for exploring Chinese sentences further.

CHAPTER 3

Chinese sentences

In this chapter, we study Chinese sentences in some detail. Where available, comparisons are made between Chinese and English sentences in terms of type and structure. Based on the syntactic properties of the Chinese language, sentences are classified into simple sentences, subjectless sentences, ergative sentences, existential sentences, emphatic sentences, coordinated sentences, complex sentences and extended sentences.

3.1 INTRODUCTION

As previously noted in Chapter 2, and as will gradually transpire in this chapter, 'sentence' may not be an ideal term for conceptualizing the Chinese language. However, it is a good starting point as a readily understood concept to readers who are familiar with English. Many of the properties associated with the concept of 'sentence' are useful in understanding how Chinese text works.

The Oxford Advanced Learner's Dictionary defines 'sentence' as

> a set of words expressing a statement, a question or an order, usually containing a subject and a verb.

In linguistics terms, the second part of the definition means a sentence usually contains a noun phrase (NP) and a verb phrase (VP), since the subject is normally a noun, and both the noun and the verb often attract modifiers such as adjectives and adverbs around them to form a larger unit – usually called a phrase. In this chapter, we adhere to the principle that a typical sentence consists of an NP and a VP. Depending on the requirements of the speaker, a subject NP may contain some descriptive elements such as an adjective phrase (AP) to modify the head noun (N). Depending on the type of verb used, the VP may contain obligatory elements such as an object NP and optional elements such as an adverb phrase (also abbreviated as AP). In this chapter, a syntactic marking convention is used to explain the structure of Chinese sentences. The convention is explained below using the English sentence *The exceptionally cold weather in March damaged business activity* as an example.

S [NP [The ₐᵣₜ AP [exceptionally ₐdᵥ cold ₐdⱼ] weather ₙ PP [in ₚᵣₑₚ March ₙ]]

'The' is an article   'exceptionally cold' is an   'weather' is a noun   'in March' is a prepositional
                        adjective phrase (AP)   phrase (PP)

'The exceptionally cold weather in March' is a noun phrase (NP)

VP [damaged ᵥ NP [business ₙ activity ₙ]]]

'damaged' is a verb   'business activity' is a noun phrase

'damaged business activity' is a verb phrase (VP)

'The exceptionally cold weather in March damaged business activity' is a sentence (S)

Thus, some example sentences in this chapter will be structurally marked in the above fashion, but the level of marking will vary for each sentence depending on the point of explanation and the space available.

A sentence does not necessarily have only one NP and one corresponding VP serving as its predicate. A sentence may have two or more subject NPs sharing a predicate:

S [NP [The Lion] and NP [the Unicorn] VP [are symbols of the United Kingdom]] .

A sentence may also have two or more VPs; that is, a subject NP doing multiple tasks or having multiple properties:

S [NP [We] 've VP [worked together], VP [argued together], VP [cried together] and VP [laughed together]] .

A sentence can also have more than one NP which are predicated by a set of VPs:

S [NP [Tammy] and NP [her lover] VP [got married at Lakeland] and VP [had four children]] .

However, the above sentences must be distinguished from a compound unit formed by two sentences, each having a distinct set of NP-VP configurations, like so:

S [NP [China] VP [sneezes]] and S [NP [the world] VP [catches a cold]] .

In this chapter, we will follow the convention illustrated above with English and explore various kinds of Chinese sentences. First, we sample some texts from

Chinese online newspapers with a view to understanding what a Chinese sentence may involve and what may be the best way to approach it. Then we move on to explore the possible range of Chinese sentences and consider both the basic facts and the salient features associated with them.

Example 1

a ₛ[NP [宅男 N　　　女神 N]　VP [开球 V]]
　　zhai2nan2　　nv3shen2　　kai1qiu2
　　'resident-man' 'female-god'　'open-ball'
　　'Goddess of housebound men (or otaku) kicks off the game.'

b ₛ[NP [北韩 N　　　万门 N　　　　火炮 N]
　　bei3han2　　wan4men2　　　huo3pao4
　　'North-Korea' 'ten-thousand' Cla 'fire-canon'

　　VP [瞄准 V　　首尔 N]]
　　miao2zhun3 shou3er3
　　'aim at'　　'Seoul'

　　'Ten thousand artillery in North Korea are targeting Seoul.'

c ₛ[NP [安全 N] VP [是 V NP [最好 A 的 礼物 N]]]
　　an1quan2　　shi4　　zui4hao3 de5 li3wu4
　　'safety's'　'be'　'the best' AD 'gift'
　　'Safety is the best present.'

d ₛ[NP [美貌 N]　　　VP [不 Adv 是 V NP [婚姻 N 保证卡 N]]]
　　mei3mao4　　　　bu2　shi4　hun1yin1 bao3zheng4 ka3
　　'beautiful-look'　'not'　'be'　'marriage' 'guarantee-card'
　　'A pretty face is not a guarantee for (long-term) marriage.'

e ₛ[NP [枇杷膏 N] AP [太 Adv 甜 Adj]] !
　　pi2pa2gao1　　tai4　　tian2
　　'loquat paste'　'too'　'sweet'
　　'The loquat paste is too sweet!'

f ₛ[NP [H7N9 N　　致死率 N]　　　AP [高于 Adj　　SARS N]]
　　h-qi1-n-jiu3 zhi4si3lv4　　　gao1yu2　　sars
　　'H7N9'　　'cause-death-rate'　'higher than' 'SARS'
　　'The mortality rate of H7N9 is higher than SARS.'

All five sentences in Example 1 include a subject NP and a predicate consisting of a VP or an AP. Note that the verb in Example 1a, 开球 'open-ball', cannot be analyzed as a VP consisting of a verb ('open') and a noun ('ball'). For one thing, the combined meaning 'open ball' does not make any sense, at least not in the current context. On the sports field, on the other hand, the disyllabic unit

开球 does have a special meaning, which is 'to kick off (a ball game)'. Therefore, the disyllabic unit should be analyzed as an intransitive verb taking no objects in the sentence rather than as a V+N verb phrase itself. In other words, for sentence 1a, the VP consists of a verb only, or VP → V. The verb phrase in 1b, on the other hand, does consist of a verb ('aim at') followed by its object ('Seoul'), that is, VP → V NP where V is a transitive verb.

Another kind of verb, a linking verb 是 appears in both Examples 1c and 1d. This verb acts like an equal sign (=) giving the subject NP a different identity to show how the speaker would like the term to be conceptualized. For example, the sentence in Example 1c asks the reader to understand 'safety' as 'the best gift of all', thus strengthening its importance in our daily life. The sentence in 1d, on the other hand, diminishes the importance of a beautiful face by theorizing that it is no guarantee of a long-term marriage.

A further different kind of internal structure of a sentence is shown in Examples 1e and 1f. There is no main verb in this kind of sentence, only an adjective phrase (AP) serving the role of predicate; that is, S → NP AP. In 1e, the predicative AP consists of an adverb ('excessively') and an adjective ('sweet'). In 1f, the AP is made of an adjective in comparative form ('higher than') and the noun being compared with (the SARS disease).

To summarize, Chinese shares the basic word order of SVO with English when creating a standard sentence. In the case of Chinese, the predicate can sometimes be an AP (or even an NP as we will later see) rather than a VP.

Before moving on to more complicated sentence structures, it is worth noting the dramatic difference between Chinese and English in contriving more complex NPs. Sentence Example 1b, for example, shows three disyllabic nouns 'stacked together' to form a longer NP – 'North Korea', 'ten-thousand units' and 'artillery'. In English, the order of the nouns inside the NP would have been different and there would have been some grammatical items added; for example, 'ten-thousand units of artillery in North Korea'. In Chinese, it is just a matter of stacking more peripheral units on to the outside layers of an existing core (i.e. the so-called head noun) usually to its front (i.e. the left side) disregarding which type of modifier is in question. This is different from English, where word-level modifiers are to the left of the head noun and phrasal and clausal modifiers are to its right. For example, the structure of the NP *the wartime cooperation between the Soviet Union and the US* can be analyzed as in Example 2 below, where the head noun *cooperation* is surrounded by the adjective modifier *wartime* to the left and the prepositional phrase *between the Soviet Union and the US* to the right.

Example 2

NP [the Art wartime N cooperation N PP [between the Soviet Union and the US]]

If we were to translate the English phrase in Example 2 into Chinese, it would become Example 3, where both the word-level and the phrasal modifiers are stacked together to one side (i.e. the left) of the head noun.

Example 3

NP [PP [苏联　　　　与　美国　　之间]　的　战时 N　合作 N]
　　su1lian2　　yu3　mei3guo2 zhi1jian1 de5 zhan4shi2 he2zuo4
　　'Soviet Union' 'and' 'US'　　'between' AD 'wartime' 'cooperation'

Thus, it is important that in forming a complex Chinese NP, we need to stack all the descriptors to the left side of the head noun, no matter whether they are single-word modifiers or phrasal or even clausal modifiers. In the case of phrasal or clausal modifiers, the functional item 的 is necessary to mark the entire phrase or clause as a descriptor of the noun (see Figure 2.9 in Chapter 2 and the related explanations). This is what happens to the prepositional phrase (PP) in Example 3, where 的 is added to the end of the PP. The same procedure applies to the NP 婚姻保证卡 'marriage-guarantee-card' in Example 1d, which, when translated into English, would become *a guarantee card for marriage*, that is, the prepositional phrase *for marriage* is moved to the right side of the head noun *card*, leaving the word-level modifier 'guarantee' to the left side of the head noun. In the Chinese version, as 婚姻 is a word-level modifier, the descriptive marker 的 is optional in this case.

Returning to the structural issue of Chinese sentences, we noted earlier that Chinese and English both follow the basic SVO order in forming a sentence, but this seems to be where the similarity ends. We have just observed the different strategies between English and Chinese for building up longer noun phrases, especially the Chinese method of stacking up noun modifiers to the front of the noun. We also know by now that a Chinese sentence can be 'verb-less', like Examples 1e and 1f, where adjectives serve the predicative function without the support of a copula verb. In general, the Chinese language is more tolerant about the *well-formedness* of a sentence. That is, there is no rigorous definition as to what a sentence *must have* in Chinese, even though we are following the English convention to explore the concept of 'sentence' in Chinese. The sentence in Example 4a below, for example, features two verb phrases in a sentence without a conjunction linking them (which would have been the case in English). The same is true with sentence 4b, where a succession of two VPs and an AP constitute a long predicate. In Example 4c, there are as many as four VPs telling the story of what happened to the subject NP.

Example 4

a s [NP [消防员]   VP [开 V 灵骨塔 N   门 N] VP [移走 V 蜂巢 N]]
      xiao1fang2yuan2   kai1 ling2gu3ta3 men2   yi2zou3 feng1chao2
      'fire fighter'   'open' 'mausoleum' 'door'   'remove' 'beehive'
      'Fire fighters opened the door to the mausoleum and removed the
      beehive.'

b s [NP [阿汤哥]   VP [花 V   四亿 N]]
      a1tang1ge1   hua1   si4yi4
      'Brother A-Tang'   'spend' '4-hundred-million'

      VP [买 V 房 N] AP [不 Adv 手软 Adj]]
      mai3 fang2   bu4   shou3ruan3
      'buy' 'house'   'not'   'hand-soft'

      'Tom Cruise spent four hundred million buying a house without
      blinking an eye.'

c s [NP [父子]   VP [车祸]   VP [就医]
      fu4zi3   che1huo4   jiu4yi1
      'father and son'   'car accident'   'sent to hospital'

      VP [等 V 红灯 N] VP [又 Adv 被 撞 V]]
      deng3 hong2deng1 you4 bei4 zhuang4
      'wait' 'red light'   'further' PB 'hit'

      'Father and son on way to hospital after car accident were hit again
      while waiting for red light.'

The syntactic structure of Example 4b is very different indeed from a conventional English sentence. A grammatical English sentence would have only one VP headed by a finite verb (or the main verb). If there are two or more finite verbs, they must be properly connected by conjunctions, as in *I fought two lions <u>and</u> won*. In a Chinese sentence, as there is no such thing as inflection, all verbs appear to be of equal status within a sentence, and a conjunction is not needed (although you can use one if you want) to connect the verbs which are supposedly in the same sentence. It is quite normal in Chinese, as shown in Example 4, for a sentence-like unit to include an NP predicated by a succession of verb and adjective phrases without the intervention of any conjunction.

We have seen how a Chinese sentence can include an NP which is predicated by a succession of VPs, and possibly also by other types of predicates (like an AP). Another significant fact about this kind of sentence is that the subject can 'hop about' within the sentence and attach itself to almost any predicative phrase the user wishes. Example 5a is an example where an NP is predicated by three VPs. Example 5b is another news headline reporting on the same incident, where the subject NP is placed before the second, rather than the first VP as in Example 5a.

Example 5

a ₛ[₍ₙₚ[女 ₐ 高中 ₙ   生 ₙ] ᵥₚ[坐 ᵥ 云霄飞车 ₙ]
     nv3   gao1zhong1 sheng1   zuo4 yun2xiao1fei1che1
     'female' 'high school' 'student' 'sit' 'roller coaster'

     ᵥₚ[送医]   ᵥₚ[不治]]
     song4yi1   bu2zhi4
     'sent to hospital' 'not cured'

     'A female high school student riding a roller coaster was sent to hospital and died there.'

b ₛ[ᵥₚ[搭 ᵥ   云霄飞车 ₙ]   [ₙₚ[少女 ₙ] ᵥₚ[猝死 ᵥ]]
     da1   yun2xiao1fei1che1   shao4nv3   cu4si3
     'travel by' 'roller coaster'   'young-girl' 'sudden-die'
     'Riding roller coaster, young girl died a sudden death.'

It would have been equally legitimate for the NP of Example 5b to be moved to the front of the first VP, just like that of 5a. Conversely, we can also take the NP in Example 5a out of its canonical position and relocate it in front of either of the other two VPs rather than the first one. The same is true with 4c, which contains a series of four VPs. Apart from the first VP, the subject NP can also be placed in front of any of the other three VPs, as illustrated in Example 6 below:

Example 6

ₛ[ₙₚ[父子] ᵥₚ₁[车祸] ᵥₚ₂[就医] ᵥₚ₃[等ᵥ 红灯 ₙ] ᵥₚ₄[又 ₐ 被 ₚ 撞ᵥ]]

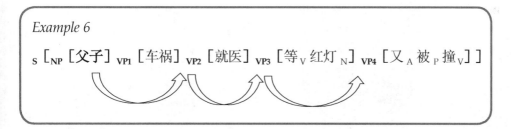

Although the position of 父子 can be moved to the front of VP2, VP3 or VP4, in practice some kind of punctuation (e.g. a Chinese comma) may be needed to separate the NP from the preceding VP(s) to facilitate reading.

We have been sampling isolated sentences from news headlines. Now, let us consider a text which presumably contains more than one sentence to see how it fits into the profile we have built for Chinese sentences so far. What follows is a continuous text running as the first paragraph of a news report on the web:

旅美棒球名将王建民今天身穿中华队 40 号球衣，在澄清湖球场登板，
对义大犀牛投 2 局无失分，最快球速 146 公里。

Note that the text is divided by three commas into four sections and is terminated by a Chinese-style period (。). The analysis offered in Example 7 below divides the text into six portions based on structural boundaries. As we shall see after the analysis, Chinese punctuation often does not correspond to structural delineations, probably due to the flexible nature of Chinese syntax. The commas and the period in the original text have been kept in Example 7 and highlighted with brackets so we can see how the language user's structural awareness corresponds to the linguistic analysis.

Example 7

a ₛ [NP [旅美 ᵥ   棒球 N   名将 N   王建民 N]
        lv3mei3   bang4qiu2 ming2jiang4   wang2jian4min2
        'travel-US' 'baseball' 'famous-player' 'Wang Chien-Ming'
        'US-resident baseball legend Wang Chien-Ming'

b VP [今天 ₐ 身穿 ᵥ   NP [中华队 N   40号 N   球衣 N]] [，]
        jin1tian1 shen1chuan1   zhong1hua2dui4 si4shi2hao4 qiu2yi1
        'today' 'body-wear'   'Chinese Taipei' 'No. 40' 'ball-clothes'
        'today wearing Chinese Taipei No. 40 sports shirt'

c VP [PP [在 Prep NP [澄清湖 N   球场 N]] 登板 ᵥ]   [，]
        zai4   cheng2qing1hu2 qiu2chang3 deng1ban3
        'at'   'Chengcing Lake' 'ball-field' 'mount-board'
        'at Chengcing Lake sports field mounting the pitcher's plate'

d VP [PP [对 Prep NP [义大 N   犀牛 N]] 投 ᵥ   2局 N]
        dui4   yi4da4   xi1niu2   tou2 er4ju2
        'against'   'Yi-University' 'rhino'   'pitch' '2-innings'
        'against I-Shou University Rhinos (he) pitches for two innings'

e VP [无 Adv 失分 ᵥ]] [，]
        wu2   shi1fen1
        'no'   'lose-score'
        'without losing any score.'

f ₛ [NP [最快 ₐ 球速 N]   VP [[]ᵥ NP [146   公里]]] [。]
        zui4kuai4 qiu2su4   yi4bai3si4shi2liu4 gong1li3
        'fastest' 'ball-speed'   '146-km'
        'The fastest ball speed (is) 146 kilometers (per hour).'

A rough examination of Example 7 shows the text to consist of two sentences based on the structural marking provided. The first sentence, 7a–e, is very long and has four VPs. This is reminiscent of Example 6a which also consists of one NP and four VPs. The second sentence, 7f, is a short one whose structure we will explain later. At this point, we will note first, that the Chinese period (。) given by the original author does not seem to correspond well to a sentential boundary. For one thing, 7f is obviously a separate sentence with its own subject NP. If the period mark should be used to conclude a sentence, an extra period should have been provided at the end of 7e, allowing 7f to begin as a fresh sentence. This is not the case in the original text. Therefore, it might be fair to say that the Chinese period mark does not offer much help in analyzing the syntactic structures of Chinese, since it gives no clear information as to where a sentence begins and where it ends.

What about the Chinese commas (，)? Again, from our structural analysis in Example 7, commas do not seem to provide clear and consistent information for identifying the boundaries between phrases or sentences. There are three commas altogether in the original text, two of which appear at the ends of 7b and 7c respectively. This seems reasonable as they each conclude a VP, so a comma may be a good punctuation mark to separate a VP from a neighboring VP or from another structure. However, this consistency is broken by the lack of a comma toward the end of 7d, to separate it from the next VP, 7e. Overall, Chinese punctuation marks are not reliable in defining what a sentence is in Chinese, be they commas or periods.

A detailed look at each line in Example 7 shows that the phrase structures fall largely in line with the range of structures discussed so far. For example, 7a is a complex NP serving as the subject of the sentence starting from 7a and ending at 7e. The head noun of this NP is 王建民, the baseball player's name. Conforming to the pattern previously explained, several modifiers come before this head noun, including the two nouns 棒球 'baseball' and 名将 'famous-player' and a verb unit 旅美 'travel-US' acting as an adjective (which can be understood as a present participle in English, such as *residing in the US*).

Next, the four VPs appearing in 7b–e also fall within the pattern explained before where a sentence can consist of an NP predicated by several VPs. A noticeable digression from the previous model is the generally longer VPs in comparison to the previous sentences. This is why we started to see commas separating the longer VPs, which otherwise may cause reading difficulty due to their sheer length. Note that the length of the VP is contributed to by a prepositional phrase (PP) in 7c and 7d. The default position in English for a prepositional phrase modifying a verb is to the right of the verb (e.g. *sing along in the car*). The default position for such a prepositional phrase in Chinese is to the left of the verb (e.g. 在车上跟着唱 'at-car-up-follow-AM-sing').

Finally, the short concluding sentence in 7f mentioned earlier illustrates a phenomenon we have not seen so far. This is the omission of the copula verb when the predicate is a noun phrase (imagine *is* being removed from the sentence *His brother is a doctor*, becoming *His brother a doctor*, which nonetheless is still used as a sentence). The omission of 是 is acceptable here, although it can also be kept.

Another thing we notice from Example 7 is that there are very few functional items in the text overall. In particular, there are no conjunctive devices between the various VPs or the sentences. There are only two prepositions (在 and 对) and one negative item (无) in the entire text. This illustrates an important fact about the Chinese language – that the understanding of Chinese discourse is often quite intuitive and dependent on context, as there is relatively little guidance from the grammatical department.

It would be wrong to assume that we have covered the most complicated situation in analyzing the Chinese sentence. For example, although Example 7 includes a relatively long sentence consisting of four VPs, at least all of them share the same subject NP. In those cases, it is easy to understand who did what as the subject is always the same person even though there is more than one action stretching over a range of structures. A more complicated situation would involve a series of structures consisting only of VPs, but where the omitted NPs do not refer to the same entity! This is the case in another newspaper text:

> 2011 年 12 月 5 日，独居的刘先生接到辽阳市一位熟人王某的电话，称其家里有一位非洲女孩儿，想在中国找个丈夫。

To facilitate understanding of the above text and help with its linguistic analysis, the text is broken down into five sections in Example 8 below.

Example 8

a   ₛ [_AP_ [2011   年   12   月   5   日] [，]
er4ling2yi1yi1 nian2 shi2er4 yue4   wu3 ri4
'2011'   'year' '12'   'month' '5'   'day'
'On December 5th, 2011

b   _NP_ [独居 _V_   的 _AD_ 刘   先生 _N_]
du2ju1   de5   liu2 xian1sheng5
'alone-living' AD   'Liu' 'Mr'
a Mr Liu who lives by himself

c   _VP_ [接到 _V_   辽阳市 _N_   一位 _Art_   熟人 _N_
jie1dao4 liao2yang2 shi4 yi2wei4   shou2ren2
'received' 'Liaoyang-city' 'one'-Cla 'familiar-person'

王某 _N_   的   电话 _N_]] [，]
wang2mou3 de5 dian4hua4
'Wang-sth' AD 'telephone'

received a phone call from Mr Wang, an acquaintance from Liaoyang city.

d   ₛ [_NP_ []] _VP_ [称 _V_   其 _Pos_ 家 _N_ 里 _Prep_   有 _V_   一位 _Art_   非洲 _N_
cheng1 qi2   jia1li3   you3 yi2wei4   fei1zhou1
'claim' 'his' 'home-inside' 'have' 'one'-Cla 'Africa'

女孩儿 _N_]] [，]
nv3hai2er5
'girl'

(He) reported that he had an African girl in his home.

e   ₛ [_NP_ []] _VP_ [想 _V_ 在 _Prep_ 中国 _N_   找 _V_ 个 _Cla_ 丈夫 _N_]] [。]
xiang3 zai4   zhong1guo2 zhao3 ge5   zhang4fu1
'think' 'at'   'China'   'find' Cla 'husband'
(She) wants to find a husband in China.'

Example 8 looks different to Example 7 at a glance. However, if we get rid of the AP (here Adverb Phrase) in 8a and the initial S and NP symbols in both 8d and 8e, it actually looks very similar to the first sentence of Example 7 which consists of an initial NP, followed by several VPs. Unfortunately, the similarity on the surface is deceptive in this case. This is because in

Example 8, among the three VPs in 8c–e, only the first in 8c predicates the subject NP in 8b. The 'hidden subject' of 8d is, in fact, another entity embedded in the VP of 8c – a 'Mr Wang'. Likewise, the hidden subject of Example 8e is another NP ('an African girl') that comes within the previous VP in Example 8d. The situation quickly gets confusing for a novice Chinese language learner as there is no way of telling who is doing what when confronted by a succession of VPs in a long sentence. All the VPs could claim the same subject NP, as in Example 7 or all could have different subject NPs, as is the case in Example 8. In appearance, both structures look exactly the same. Again, syntax is at the mercy of semantics and pragmatics in Chinese. A lot of aids are required from the meaning and the context to help disambiguate the sentence. Unsuspecting language learners will not be able to know that the empty NP slots in both 8d and 8e each represents a different entity than the first NP of the sentence in 8b.

To summarize, we have seen so far that the Chinese language can be analyzed using the English-based syntactic model, even though there are many radical differences. For example, the Chinese complex NP is formed by stacking up modifiers before the noun; whereas in English, word modifiers come before the noun and phrasal and clausal modifiers come after it. In English, a series of VPs predicating a subject NP must be properly coordinated by punctuation and conjunctions. In Chinese, punctuation marks are more loosely used and the interpretation of multiple VPs in a sentence is largely based on intuition rather than grammatical rules. Moreover, an English sentence must have at least one main verb in order to be seen as a proper sentence, but a Chinese sentence can be verbless so long as it has a predicative AP (adjective/adverb phrase) or an NP (noun phrase).

Bearing in mind the flexibility of Chinese syntactic properties, we will examine some typical Chinese sentence types and look into some distinct structures within the sentence.

3.2 SIMPLE SENTENCES

By 'simple sentence' I mean an expression which consists of an NP–VP configuration without any embedded sentence in the NP or VP. Both the NP and the VP can also contain a reasonable number of coordinated same-category units (e.g. 'the dog and the cat' or 'lay down and went to sleep'). This is in line with Loar's (2011) definition of a simple sentence as 'one that comprises a single independent clause' ('clause' is in turn defined as 'minimally consisting of a predicate of various forms') (p. 15).

In Chinese, the VP serving as the predicate to a sentence can be replaced by an AP, as discussed next in 3.3. The sentences in Example 9 are both simple sentences, each with a subject NP and a predicate VP.

Example 9

a ₛ[_{NP}[飞机 _N] _{VP}[降落 _V   了 _{AM}]]。
   fei1ji1   jiang4luo4   le5
   'aircraft'   'decent-drop' AM
   'The airplane has landed.'

b ₛ[_{NP}[我 _{Pro}] _{VP}[昨天 _{Adv}   刚 _{Adv} 从 _{Prep} 日本 _N 回来 _V]]。
   wo3   zuo2tian1 gang1 cong2 ri4ben3 hui2lai2
   'I'   'yesterday' 'just' 'from' 'Japan' 'return'
   'I only came back from Japan yesterday.'

Both of the sentences in Example 9 have an intransitive verb ('land' and 'return' respectively) as their main verb. Sentence 9a is short because all that it contains are an unmodified noun ('aircraft') and an unmodified verb ('land'), plus a functional item *le5*. Sentence 9b is slightly longer as it includes three adverbial elements − 'yesterday', 'just' and the prepositional phrase 'from Japan' − on top of the N V ('I-return') configuration. Nevertheless, the sentence is still as short as nine characters long. The relatively short length of both sentences in Example 9 is typical for a simple Chinese sentence. According to Shei (2010), a good Chinese sentence is around 12 syllables/characters (e.g. sentence 10b below), as it expresses adequate information within a pleasant reading span.

Next we look at sentences whose main verbs are transitive; that is, verbs that take object NPs.

Example 10

a ₛ[_{NP}[我 _{Pro}] _{VP}[爱 _V 死 _{Adv} 北京 _N   了 _{SFP}]]。
   wo3   ai4   si3   bei3jing1 le5
   'I'   'love' 'dead' 'Beijing' SFP
   'I love Beijing to death.'

b ₛ[_{NP}[一个   老外]   _{VP}[娶 _V 了 _{AM} _{NP}[一 _{Num} 个 _{Cla}
   yi2 ge5 lao3wai4   qu3   le5   yi2   ge5
   'one' Cla 'old-external'   'marry' AM   'one'   Cla

   中国 _N   媳妇 _N]]]。
   zhong1guo2 xi2fu4
   'Chinese'   'wife'

   'A foreigner married a Chinese woman.'

The sentence in Example 10a consists of a pronoun ('I') occupying the NP slot and a VP consisting of a verb ('love'), a complement ('dead') and a noun object ('Beijing'). The particle 了 is not an aspect marker but a sentence-final particle, which is a discourse marker expressing the speaker's current mental state (see section 5.12 in Chapter 5).

Example 10b consists of two NPs, one serving as the subject ('a foreigner') the other as the object ('a Chinese wife') of the verb 'marry'. The head noun in the first NP, 老外, meaning 'foreigner,' is an interesting word. It inherits a sense of familiarity from the prefix 老 'old', often attached to a surname, to address or refer to a person in a congenial way (e.g. 老王 'old-Wang'). However, the word 老外 also gives a sense of strangeness or even hostility because of the second morpheme 外 'outside, external'. Thus, it can be used and understood in either way (familiar and friendly or strange and hostile) or a bit of both. The head noun in the object NP, 媳妇, can refer to either one's wife (mainly in mainland China) or one's daughter-in-law. In the hosting NP, the head noun 'wife' is modified by another noun 'China' used as an adjective to describe the nationality of the wife. Farther to the left is a numerical morpheme 'one' attached by a general classifier 个 which can be used to count humans or objects. This number-classifier unit also appears to the front of the first noun, 'the foreigner'. Finally, an aspect marker 了 is attached to the main verb 'marry', to indicate the completion of the action.

We have seen examples of two common types of verbs so far: transitive verbs (e.g. 喜欢 'like') and intransitive verbs (e.g. 死亡 'die'). As in English, there is a kind of transitive verb in Chinese that has two object NPs. These are called ditransitive verbs. Some examples of this type of sentence follow:

Example 11

a ₛ[_NP_ [老师 _N_] _VP_ [教 _V_ _NP_ [我 _Pro_] _NP_ [数学 _N_]]] 。
lao3shi1   jiao1   wo3   shu4xue2
'teacher'   'teach'   'me'   'mathematics'
'The teacher teaches me mathematics.'

b ₛ[_NP_ [美女 _N_]   _VP_ [借 _V_ _NP_ [他 _Pro_] _NP_ [信用卡 _N_]]] 。
mei3nv3   jie4   ta1   xin4yong4ka3
'pretty-woman' 'lend'   'him'   'credit-card'
'A pretty woman lent him a credit card.'

Each of the ditransitive verbs in Example 11 takes two NPs as direct and indirect object. In Example 11a, 'math' (direct object) is taught to 'me' (indirect object). In Example 11b, a 'credit card' is lent to 'him'. Both sentences in Example 11 have equivalent verb usages in English as evidenced by their English translations. However, in English, a sentence incorporating a ditransitive verb can usually be expressed in a different way by reversing the order of the two objects and adding a preposition before the indirect object. Thus *She gave me everything* becomes *She gave everything to me*. Not all Chinese sentences involving the use of ditransitive verbs can be converted in the same way. Of the two sentences in Example 11, for example, only 11b can undergo the same kind of transformation as English. The transformed sentence from Example 11b is shown in Example 12 below.

Example 12

ₛ [NP [美女 N]   VP [借 V NP [信用卡 N]   PP [给 Prep NP [他 Pro]]]]。
   mei3nv3   jie4   xin4yong4ka3   gei3   ta1
   'pretty-woman'   'lend'   'credit-card' 'to'   'him'
   'A pretty lady lent a credit card to him.'

As can be seen, for the Chinese ditransitive verb 'borrow' used in Example 11b, the other way of using it is as a transitive verb taking only one object NP, as shown in Example 12, where the original indirect object 'him' has been subsumed in a prepositional phrase instead. Interestingly, the preposition used in this case is 给 'give', which can itself be a ditransitive verb. Again, not all ditransitive verbs in Chinese can be used in both ways.

We have covered three kinds of simple sentence so far, involving the use of intransitive verbs, transitive verbs, and ditransitive verbs respectively. We will now look at simple sentences whose main verb is a linking verb (or copula) – the equivalents of *be*, *become*, *appear* and so on in English. In Chinese, by far the most frequently used copula is the morpheme 是 'be'.

Example 13

a   ₛ [NP [我 Pro]   VP [是 V NP [歌手 N]]]。
      wo3   shi4   ge1shou3
      'I'   'be'   'singer'
      'I am a singer.'

b   ₛ [NP [我 Pro 爸 N]   VP [是 V NP [李刚 N]]]。
      wo3   ba4   shi4   li3gang1
      'my' 'dad'   'be'   'Li Gang'
      'My father is Li Gang (a government official).'

Note that 是 normally only links two NPs – the subject NP and the complement NP which is an equivalent term of the first NP. In English it is correct to say both *I am a singer* and *I am poor* but in Chinese, 是 is used only with an NP complement and not with an adjective one. That is, the translation of *I am poor* is 我穷 'I-poor' (or more commonly 我很穷 'I am quite poor') rather than 我是穷 'I-<u>am</u>-poor' (which is still an acceptable sentence but is an emphasized expression not used in normal circumstances).

Other linking verbs that also take an NP as complement are shown in Example 14 below. There are not many more verbs of this kind.

Example 14

a ₛ [ₙₚ [情侣 ₙ] ᵥₚ [变成 ᵥ   ₙₚ [陌生人 ₙ]]] 。
    qing2lv3   bian4cheng2   mo4sheng1ren2
    'lovers'   'change-into'   'strangers'
    'Lovers have become strangers.'

b ₛ [ₙₚ [我 ₚᵣₒ] ᵥₚ [ₚₚ [在 ₚᵣₑₚ 美国 ₙ] 当 ᵥ   ₙₚ [老师 ₙ]]] 。
    wo3   zai4   mei3guo2 dang1   lao3shi1
    'I'   'at'   'US'   'serve as'   'teacher'
    'I work as a teacher in the US.'

c ₛ [ₙₚ [剑桥 ₙ]   ᵥₚ [成为 ᵥ   ₙₚ ["英国 ₙ   自行车 ₙ
    jian4qiao2   cheng2wei2   ying1guo2 zi4xing2che1
    'Cambridge'   'become'   'UK'   'bicycle'

    之   都 ₙ"]] 。
    zhi1 du1
    PD 'city'

    'Cambridge has become "City of the Bicycle" in the UK.'

d ₛ [ₙₚ [这 ₇ₑₘ 家 ₇ₗₐ 酒店 ₙ] ᵥₚ [号称 ᵥ   ₙₚ [世界 ₙ 最大 ₐ₇ⱼ
    zhe4   jia1   jiu3dian4   hao4cheng1   shi4jie4 zui4da4
    'this'   Cla   'hotel'   'purport'   'world' 'biggest'

    规模 ₙ]]] 。
    gui1mo2
    'scale'

    'This hotel claims to be the world's biggest in scale.'

e ₛ [ₙₚ [这 ₇ₑₘ 种 ₇ₗₐ   纸牌 ₙ   的 玩法 ₙ]   ᵥₚ [类似 ᵥ
    zhe4   zhong3 zhi3pai2 de5 wan2fa3   lei4si4
    'this'   Cla   'card'   PD 'play-method'   'resemble'

    ₙₚ [麻将 ₙ]]] 。
    ma2jiang4
    'mah-jong'

    'The playing method of this card game is similar to mah-jong.'

Most English linking verbs can take either an NP or an AP as a complement. For example, *He seems nice* and *He seems a nice guy* are both legitimate. In Chinese, it is rare for a linking verb to be able to take both an NP and an AP as a complement. The sentences in both Example 13 and Example 14 all include linking verbs that only take NPs as a complement. One frequently used linking verb, 好像 'as if', is a notable exception, which does take both NPs and APs as complements, as Example 15 shows.

Example 15

a ₛ [NP [人生 N] VP [好像 V   NP [一 Num 场 Cla   梦 N]]] 。
　　　　ren2sheng1   hao3xiang4   yi4   chang3 meng4
　　　　'life'   'seem'   'one'   Cla   'dream'
　　　　'Life is like a dream.'

b ₛ [NP [她 Pro] VP [最近 Adv 好像 V   AP [很 Adv 忙 Adj]]] 。
　　　　ta1   zui4jin4 hao3xiang4   hen3   mang2
　　　　'she'   'recently' 'seem'   'very'   'busy'
　　　　'She seems quite busy recently.'

As can be seen, in Example 15a 好像 takes an NP ('a dream') as a complement; while in 15b it takes an AP ('very busy'). However, this is a notable exception. Most Chinese linking verbs take either a VP or an AP as a complement. The linking verbs in Example 16 below all take APs exclusively as complements.

Example 16

a ₛ [NP [她 Pro] VP [看起来 V   AP [很 Adv 年轻 Adj]]] 。
　　　　ta1   kan4qi3lai2   hen3   nian2qing1
　　　　'she'   'look'   'very'   'young'
　　　　'She looks very young.'

b ₛ [NP [战争 N]   VP [似乎 V AP [很 Adv 遥远 Adj]]] 。
　　　　zhan4zheng1   si4hu1   hen3   yao2yuan3
　　　　'war'   'seem'   'very'   'far'
　　　　'War seems quite far away.'

c ₛ [NP [官方 N   媒体 N] VP [保持 V   AP [沉默 Adj]]] 。
　　　　guan1fang1 mei2ti3   bao3chi2   chen2mo4
　　　　'official'   'media'   'maintain'   'silent'
　　　　'Official media remain silent.'

d ₛ [PP [在 Prep 爸爸 N 怀 N   里 Prep] NP [我] VP [显得 V   AP [好小 Adj]]] 。
　　　　zai4   ba4ba5 huai2 li3   wo3   xian3de5   hao3 xiao3
　　　　'at'   'father' 'bosom' 'inside'   'I'   'appear'   'so small'
　　　　'I looked so small on my father's lap.'

The last group of sentences further illustrates an important aspect of Chinese syntax. That is, the linking verb in some sentences can be omitted, especially when the complement is an AP and when the AP contains a degree adverb such as 很 and 好, as are the cases in Examples 16a, 16b and 16d. In other words, the three sentences in Example 17 are all legitimate.

Example 17

a ₛ [NP [她 Pro] AP [很 Adv 年轻 Adj]] 。
      ta1   hen3   nian2qing1
      'she'   'very'   'young'
      'She (is) very young.'

b ₛ [NP [战争 N]   AP [很 Adv 遥远 Adj]] 。
      zhan4zheng1   hen3   yao2yuan3
      'war'   'very'   'far'
      'War (is) quite far away.'

c ₛ [PP [在 Prep 爸爸 N 怀 N   里 Prep]，NP [我] AP [好 Adv 小 Adj]]。
      zai4   ba4ba5 huai2 li3   wo3   hao3   xiao3
      'at'   'father' 'bosom' 'inside'   'I'   'so'   'small'
      'I (am) so small on my father's lap.'

The contrived sentences in Example 17 are acceptable and differ from their corresponding original sentences in Example 16 only in the absence of a linking verb. As a result, their meanings are slightly different because the linking verb represents a reduction in truth value (i.e. 'looks', 'seems'). Once the linking verb is gone, the sentences in Example 17 appear to be 'truer' than the original (i.e. 'She is young' rather than 'She looks young').

3.3 VERBLESS SENTENCES

We have seen in the previous section that a Chinese sentence can be without a verb. Instead, an adjective or adverb phrase (AP) can be the sole predicate of a sentence, like those in Example 17. Although these sentences can each take a suitable linking verb to become a normal sentence with a VP, as in Example 16, we saw that their truth value can be compromised when a linking verb is added. Thus, a sentence with an AP as predicate exists in its own right and is not necessarily the result of a transformation from a sentence with a linking verb. More examples of this kind of verbless sentence follow.

Example 18

a ₛ[₍NP₎ [这 ₍Dem₎ 个 ₍Cla₎ 话题 ₍N₎] ₍AP₎ [很 ₍Adv₎ **热** ₍Adj₎]]。
　　zhe4　　ge5　　hua4ti2　　　hen3　　re4
　　'this'　　Cla　　'topic'　　　'very'　　'hot'
　　'This topic (is) very hot.'

b ₛ[₍NP₎ [今年 ₍N₎　的　冬天 ₍N₎] ₍AP₎ [特别 ₍Adv₎　**冷** ₍Adj₎]]]。
　　jin1nian2 de5　dong1tian1　　te4bie2　　leng3
　　'this year' PD　'winter'　　　'especially' 'cold'
　　'Winter this year (is) especially cold.'

c ₛ[₍NP₎ [朱令 ₍N₎　　的　双手 ₍N₎] ₍AP₎ [**细长** ₍Adj₎　**而** ₍Conj₎　**灵活** ₍Adj₎]]]。
　　zhu1ling4 de5 shuang1shou3　　xi4chang2 er2　　ling2huo2
　　'Zhu Ling' PD 'pair-hand'　　　'thin-long' 'and'　'nimble'
　　'Zhu Ling's hands (are) thin and long and nimble.'

The first two sentences in Example 18 each have an AP as predicate. Moreover, both APs consist of a head adjective ('hot' or 'cold') each modified by an adverb ('very' or 'especially'). We have noted before this is the common trait of a predicative AP – as if an intensifier is enlisted to fill the vacancy of a verb. Example 18c, however, does not come with an intensifier (or degree adverb). There is an important difference between Example 18c and Examples 18a and b. The AP in Example 18c consists of two adjectives joined together by a conjunctive morpheme and there is no intensifier preceding the adjectives. Perhaps the requirement of a degree adverb is waived because of the relatively long and complicated AP.

An adjective phrase is the primary kind of predicate for verbless sentences but it is not the only kind. Other candidates to fill the predicate slot of a verbless sentence are a locational phrase, a time phrase or some kind of numerical phrase. They are normally in the form of a noun phrase or a prepositional phrase. Some examples are shown in Example 19:

Example 19

a ₅[$_{NP}$［台湾 $_N$］ $_{PP}$［在 $_{Prep}$ 太平洋 $_N$ 西方 $_N$］］。
tai2wan1   zai4   tai4ping2yang2 xi1fang1
'Taiwan'   'at'   'Pacific'   'west-side'
'Taiwan (is located) at the west side of the Pacific Ocean.'

b ₅[$_{NP}$［我的 $_{Pro}$ 生日 $_N$］ $_{NP}$［1997   年   6   月
wo3de5   sheng1ri4   yi1jiu3jiu3qi1 nian2 liu4 yue4
'my'   'birthday'   '1997'   'year' '6' 'month'

30   日］］］。
san1shi2 ri4
'30'   'day'

'My birthdate (is) June 30, 1997.'

c ₅[$_{NP}$［交通 $_N$ 事故 $_N$ 死亡 $_N$ 人数 $_N$］
jiao1tong1 shi4gu4   si3wang2 ren2shu4
'traffic'   'accident' 'death'   'person-number'

$_{NP}$［一百七十二 $_{Num}$ 人 $_N$］］］。
yi4bai3qi1shi2er4 ren2
'172'   'person'

'The number of people who have died in traffic accidents (is) 172.'

In Example 19a, a prepositional phrase introduced by 在 serves as the predicate for the sentence, explaining the whereabouts of the noun subject. For the rest of the sentences in Example 19, the predicate is an NP – a specific date for Example 19b and a number of headcounts in 19c. To some extent, Examples 19b–c resemble the sentences in Example 13 as they involve the use of the linking verb 是 and an NP complement. Indeed, it is possible to add 是 to both Examples 19b and 19c and keep the same meaning (while adding 是 to 19a would turn it into an emphasized clause with very restricted usage, such as in contrasting two different views). However, 是 is not always removable from a sentence involving a subject NP and a complement NP. In most cases, getting rid of 是 (where 是 should really be) will create either ambiguity or difficulty in comprehension.

The final kind of verbless sentence we will mention is one with a nominal predicate and without a subject or a verb, like those shown in Example 20:

Example 20

a ₛ[**NP** [冬天 **N**]   了 **SFP**] 。
        dong1tian1 le5
        'winter'   SFP
        '(It is) winter already.'

b ₛ[**NP** [九 **Num** 点 **Mea**]   了 **SFP**] 。
        jiu3   dian3   le5
        'nine'   'o'clock' SFP
        '(It is) nine o'clock already.'

c ₛ[**NP** [一百万 **Num**]   了 **SFP**] 。
        yi4 bai3 wan4 le5
        'one-million'   SFP
        '(We have) one million already.'

The sentences in Example 20 manifest a [NP 了] pattern which can be understood by the Chinese native speaker as a complete sentence of some sort. This kind of sentence typically comes with the sentence-final particle 了 to mark a transition of state; for example, the speaker of Example 20a comments on the change of season from autumn to winter. Example 20b draws the listener's attention to the current point of time as a result of the inexorable movement of the clock. As for 20c, it may refer to the amount of money collected up to the point of speech (e.g. in a charity event). Apparently, not all nouns can be subsumed in this [NP 了] frame to express a change of state. As can be gathered from Example 20, nouns that belong to a set of circular entities (e.g. seasons, months, days, units of time) or objects that can be counted in an accumulative sense (e.g. money, scores, distance) are possible candidates to fit in this scheme.

3.4 SUBJECTLESS SENTENCES

By 'subjectless sentence' I mean a normal sentence with a sound VP, AP or complement-NP structure as discussed in sections 3.2 and 3.3 but without a subject NP. A subjectless sentence in English is normally an imperative sentence (e.g. *Listen to me!*) whose subject is understood to be the second person pronoun (i.e. *you*). In Chinese, however, it is possible for any person to be the hidden subject of a subjectless sentence – whether it is the second person 'you', the first person pronoun 'I; we', or even the third person 'they'. First, in Example 21, we will see what Chinese imperative sentences are like.

Example 21

a ₛ[꜀NP [ ] ꜀VP [走 ᵥ 开 ꜀Adv]] !
    zou3 kai1
    'walk' 'broad'
    'Go away!'

b ₛ[请 ꜀Hon ꜀NP [ ] ꜀VP [等 ᵥ 一下 ꜀Adv]] !
    qing3   deng3 yi2xia4
    'please'   'wait' 'once'
    'Just a moment please!'

c ₛ[꜀NP [ ] ꜀VP [别 ꜀Neg 伤心 ᵥ]]] !
    bie2   shang1xin1
    'don't' 'hurt-heart'
    'Don't be sad!'

d ₛ[꜀NP [ ] ꜀VP [不要 ꜀Neg 说话 ᵥ]] !
    bu2yao4   shuo1hua4
    'not-want' 'say-words'
    'Do not speak!'

All of the sentences in Example 21 are subjectless and the omitted subjects are the listeners of the sentence ('you'). The sentences would still be sound and mean the same if a second person pronoun 你 were reintroduced into the sentence to fill in the empty NP slot. Example 21a is the simplest among them, consisting only of a VP ('Get away!'). Example 21b comes with an honorific element 请 'please' whose usage here is roughly the same as its English equivalent *please*. Examples 21c and 21d are both negative imperatives – advising the hearer against certain actions. The negative morpheme 别 and the disyllabic unit 不要 both mean 'do not' in this context. As a negative element, 别 can only be used in an imperative sentence like Example 21c, while 不要 can also be used literally to mean 'not want'; for example, 我不要死 'I-not-want-die' means 'I do not want to die'. This is different from its imperative use in 不要死 which means 'Do not die!'

There is a kind of imperative sentence which suggests actions not only to the listener but also for the speaker. In English, this is equal to a sentence starting with *Let's* or *Let us*. Two examples are given in Example 22. Example 22a is a fixed expression suggesting a joint toast together with the listeners. Example 22b involves a serial verb construction 'go-travel'. Both are invitations for hearers to join the speaker in performing some kind of action. If we were to fill in the empty NP slots of Example 22, we would use the first person plural pronoun 我们.

Example 22

a ₛ[_{NP} [ ] _{VP}[干杯 _V]] !
     gan1 bei1
     'dry-glass'
     'Bottoms up!'

b ₛ[_{NP} [ ] _{VP}[一起 _{Adv} 去 _V 旅行 _V]] !
     yi4qi3 qu4 lv3xing2
     'together' 'go' 'travel'
     'Let's go travel together!'

The aforementioned sentences correspond to the English imperatives with the omitted subjects being either 'you' or 'we'. There is another kind of subjectless sentence in Chinese which omits the first person singular 'I'. This is similar to an informal English sentence like *Have been to London today*. While this is a rather informal usage in English, it is a regular type of sentence in Chinese. Some examples are offered in Example 23:

Example 23

a ₛ[_{NP} [ ] _{VP}[好 _{Adv} 久 _{Adv} 没 _{Neg} 来 _V 了 _{SFP}]] 。
    hao3 jiu3 mei2 lai2 le5
    'very-long' 'not' 'come' SFP
    '(I) have not come (here) for a long time.'

b ₛ[_{NP} [ ] _{VP}[小时候 _{Adv} 常 _{Adv} _{PP}[在 _{Prep} 河 _N 里 _{Prep}] 游泳 _V]] 。
    xiao3shi2hou4 chang2 zai4 he2 li3 you2yong3
    'small-time' 'often' 'at' 'river' 'inside' 'swim'
    'When young, (I) often swam in the river.'

c ₛ[_{NP} [ ] _{VP}[从来 _{Adv} 没有 _{Neg} 离 _V 死亡 _N 这么 _{Adv} 近 _{Adv} 过 _{AM}]] 。
    cong2lai2 mei2you3 li2 si3wang2 zhe4mo5 jin4 guo4
    'all along' 'not' 'away from' 'death' 'so' 'near' AM
    '(I) have never been so close to death before.'

d ₛ[_{NP} [ ] _{VP}[今天 _{Adv} 无意中 _{Adv} 逛 _V 了 _{AM} 古玩 _N 市场 _N]] 。
    jin1tian1 wu2yi4zhong1 guang4 le5 gu3wan4 shi4chang3
    'today' 'unintentionally' 'roam' AM 'antique' 'market'
    'Today unintentionally (I) wandered through the antique market.'

All of the sentences in Example 23 are the first sentence of a paragraph in their original texts and are not followed by a sentence with a clear subject. Therefore, they can be construed to mean something related to the writers themselves, often subsumed in a kind of 'expressive text' (Reiss 1981). Note the thematic positions (the beginning word or phrase of a sentence) of all four sentences in Example 23 are occupied by time adverbs ('for a long time', 'when young', 'up to now', 'today'). This is a reasonable arrangement as it gives clear background information for interpreting the verb, which is especially important when the subject is missing (i.e. the semantic processing of the adverb-verb combination may quickly reveal who the subject is).

Still another kind of subjectless sentence involves the omission of a 'generic subject' or an unspecified entity.

Example 24

a   ₛ [꜀NP [ ] ꜀VP [在 ꜀Prep 中国 ꜀N   可以 ꜀Aux 购买 ꜀V   美国 ꜀N
     zai4   zhong1guo2 ke3yi3 gou4mai3 mei3guo2
     'at'   'China'   'can'   'purchase' 'USA'

     的 股票 ꜀N   吗]]] ?
     de5 gu3piao4 ma5
     PD 'stocks' QM

     'Can (one) purchase American stocks in China?'

b   ₛ [꜀NP [ ] ꜀VP [在 ꜀Prep 非洲 ꜀N   发现 ꜀V   一 ꜀Num 个 ꜀Cla 新 ꜀Adj 古 ꜀Adj
     zai4   fei1zhou1 fa1xian4 yi2   ge5   xin1   gu3
     'at'   'Africa' 'discover' 'one' Cla   'new' 'ancient'

     人种 ꜀N]]]。
     ren2zhong3
     'human-kind'

     '(Someone) discovered a new ancient human species
     in Africa.'

c   ₛ [꜀NP [ ] ꜀VP [年轻 ꜀Adj 时 ꜀Conj]] ₛ [꜀NP [ ] ꜀VP [总 ꜀Adv 会 ꜀Aux 认为 ꜀V
     nian2qing1 shi2   zong3 hui4 ren4wei2
     'young'   'when'   'always' 'will' 'believe'
     'When young, (people) always think

     ₛ [꜀NP [ ] ꜀VP [还 ꜀Adv 能 ꜀Aux 找到 ꜀V   更 ꜀Adv   好 ꜀Adj 的]]]]
     hai2   neng2 zhao3dao4 geng4   hao3   de5
     'still' 'can' 'find'   'even more' 'good' AD
     (they) can find an even better one.'

Example 24a is a question asked by someone in an online forum about whether a person living in China can buy US stocks or not. The sentence is subjectless and the thematic position is occupied by a locational phrase ('in China'). Because of the nature of the question – the broad reference to China and the generic action of buying US stocks – it is easy to construe the subject of the sentence to be a member of the general public residing in China. Example 24b is similar to 24a in the respect of the thematic position being occupied by a prepositional phrase. In this case, the background given is 'Africa', where an unknown ancient human species is found. The subject of this sentence would have been a specific group of scientists or archaeologists but this is common knowledge and is fine to be omitted. The more important information is the location and the discovery. Example 24c presents a more complicated situation, where three NPs appear to have been omitted from the subject position of their respective clauses or sentences, representing the same generic person.

In the most extreme cases, a text can start with a series of subjectless sentences and the omitted subjects may not all refer to the same entity. Example 25 consists of two sentences connected by a coordinative conjunction 'but'. The subjects of both sentences have been omitted.

Example 25

s [NP [XY] VP [分开 V 了 AM]], 但 Conj s [NP [X] VP [忘 V 不 Neg 了 AM],
　　　　fen1kai1 le5　　dan4　　　　　　wang4 bu4　liao3
　　　　'part'　AM　　'but'　　　　　　'forget' 'not'　AM
　　　　'(We) have parted but (I) still cannot forget,

VP [有时候 Adv　还是 Adv 会 Aux 很 Adv 难过 Adj]]] 。
you3shi2hou4 hai2shi4 hui4　hen3　nan2guo4
'sometimes' 'still'　'will' 'very' 'sad'
sometimes (I) still feel miserable.'

The first sentence in Example 25, based on the meaning of the predicate and the context (i.e. a love and relationship discussion forum), means that a couple have parted from each other. The first missing NP thus stands for 'my lover' (Y) and 'I' (X) or, most likely, 我们 'we' in Chinese. The second sentence comprises an omitted NP and two VPs serving as the predicate. Again, based on the meaning of the VPs ('unable to forget and often sad'), we can infer that the missing NP refers to the writer him- or herself rather than their ex-lover, as the feelings disclosed are quite personal and private.

We conclude this section with a text consisting of a series of sentences with all the subjects withdrawn. The empty NP slots have been marked with symbols X (female speaker), Y (interested males) and XY (X and Y).

Example 26

₅ [NP [X] VP [最近 Adv 遇到 V 一些 QN 男人 N]] ,
zui4jin4　yu4dao4　yi4xie1　nan2ren2
'recently'　'meet'　'some'　'man'
'Recently (I) encountered some men.

₅ [NP [XY] VP [没 Neg 聊 V 几 QN 句 Cla]]
mei2　liao2　ji3　ju4
'not'　'chat'　'several'　'sentences'
(We) have merely exchanged a few words.

₅ [NP [Y] VP [竟然 Adv 说 V 要 V
jing4ran2　shuo1 yao4
'unexpectedly' 'say' 'want'

NP [X] VP [做 V 他 Pro 女朋友 V]]] 。
zuo4 ta1　nv3peng2you3
'be' 'he'　'girlfriend'

Surprisingly, (they) went on and asked (me) to be his (their) girlfriend.'

Example 26 is a short narrative explaining how the female speaker has been approached directly by men suggesting a romance only moments after getting to know each other. The omitted NP of the first sentence stands for the speaker herself (X), the subject of the VP 'having met some men lately'. The omitted subject of the second sentence, however, should be the speaker and a certain man who approached her (XY) judging from the predicate, as it takes at least two people to 'chat only for a while'. There are two omitted NPs in the third sentence. The first NP missing is the man (Y) who suggested romance to the woman, while the second NP is the speaker herself (X) who was asked to be the man's girlfriend. All of these missing NPs are instantly recoverable by a native Chinese human processor but may prove difficult for foreign language learners.

3.5 EXISTENTIAL SENTENCES

Chinese existential sentences are like the English sentences that start with *There is/are* which point out the existence of certain concrete or abstract objects at a certain location. The most frequently used device for pointing out existence in Chinese is the morpheme 有 'have'. The easiest way of using 有 to report the existence of something is the construction [有 NP], as Example 27 shows:

Example 27

a ₛ[ᵥₚ[有 ᵥ 人 ₙ]] !   b ₛ[ᵥₚ[有 ᵥ 老鼠 ₙ]] !
　　you3 ren2   you3 lao3shu3
　　'have' 'person'   'have' 'mouse'
　　'There is someone here!'   'There is a mouse here!'

The exclamation marks in both sentences of Example 27 reveal the warning nature of the sentence. For example, Example 27a could be used by a husband to warn his wife when they return home to find an unexpected 'guest' upstairs. A girl may shout Example 27b when a mouse suddenly runs across the living room. Sometimes the aspect marker 了 can be used with [有 NP] to express a sense of completion and to emphasize the transition from zero to something.

Example 28

a ₛ[ᵥₚ[有 ᵥ 结果 ₙ 了]] 。 b ₛ[ᵥₚ[有 ᵥ 麻烦 ₙ 了]] 。
　　you3 jie2guo3 le5   you3 ma2fan2 le5
　　'have' 'result' SFP   'have' 'trouble' SFP
　　'The result is available now.' 'There is a sign of trouble.'

Example 28a assumes that there has been a period of waiting which is terminated when the result of something (e.g. a singing competition) is known. Example 28b, on the other hand, means an uneventful period of time is about to end as the speaker senses trouble.

An initial adverb unit is often added to the [有 NP] structure to indicate where the highlighted object is. For example, the prepositional phrase, 屋内 'inside the house', in Example 29a points to the source of the smell. Another PP in Example 29b, 湖里 'in the lake', indicates where the trout are.

Example 29

a ₛ[ᵥₚ[屋 ₙ 内 ₚᵣₑₚ 有 ᵥ 臭味 ₙ]] 。
　　wu1   nei4   you3 chou4wei4
　　'house' 'inside' 'have' 'foul-smell'
　　'There is a bad smell inside the house.'

b ₛ[ᵥₚ[湖 ₙ 里 ₚᵣₑₚ 有 ᵥ 很多 ₐ𝒹ⱼ   鳟鱼 ₙ]] 。
　　hu2 li3   you3 hen3duo1 zun1yu2
　　'lake' 'inside' 'have' 'many'   'trout'
　　'There are many trout in the lake.'

Apart from locality, the initial adverb (frequently in the form of a prepositional phrase) can also be related to time or other properties of action. The initial adverb in both sentences of Example 30 below indicates the time spent or to be spent in waiting for the outcome.

Example 30

a s [VP [终于 Adv 有 V] NP [答案 N 了]] 。
    zhong1yu2 you3   da2an4 le5
    'eventually' 'have'   'answer' SFP
    'Finally (we) have the answer.'

b s [VP [等会儿 Adv   就 Adv 会 Aux 有 V] NP [ ]] 。
    deng3hui3er5 jiu4   hui4 you3
    'wait-a while' 'then' 'will' 'have'
    '(Something) will appear after a while.'

The negative form of 有 is 没有 'not-have', which can be used to indicate the non-existence of something, as Example 31 shows. Both Examples 31a and 31b are introduced by an adverb unit ('in the world' and 'here' respectively). Next comes 没有 in Example 31a to announce the non-existence of something ('free lunch'). In Example 31b a second adverb precedes 没有 to emphasize the extent of non-existence ('total').

Example 31

a s [VP [世上 Adv 没有 V] NP [免费 Adj   午餐 N]] 。
    shi4shang4 mei2you3   mian3fei4   wu3can1
    'world-up' 'no-have'   'exempt-fee' 'lunch'
    'There is no free lunch in the world.'

b s [VP [这里 Adv 完全 Adv 没有 V] NP [噪音 N]] 。
    zhe4li3 wan2quan2 mei2you3   zao4yin1
    'here'   'totally' 'no-exist'   'noise'
    'There is absolutely no noise here.'

A more complicated structure than [有 NP] is [有 NP VP]; that is, the entity whose existence has been highlighted can also be engaged in some kind of activity at the time of mention.

Example 32

a ₛ [ᵥₚ [微薄 ₙ 也 ₐdᵥ 会 ₐᵤₓ 有 ᵥ] ₙₚ [人 ₙ] ᵥₚ [骂 ᵥ]] 。
wei2bo2 ye3 hui4 you3 ren2 ma4
'Weibo' 'also' 'will' 'have' 'person' 'swear'
'On Weibo blog there will also be people using abusive
language (against you).'

b ₛ [ᵥₚ [应该 ₐᵤₓ 也 ₐdᵥ 有 ᵥ] ₙₚ [一些 QN 老 作家 ₙ]
ying1gai1 ye3 you3 yi4xie1 lao3 zuo4jia1
'should' 'also' 'have' 'some' 'old' 'writer'

   ᵥₚ [戳 ᵥ 你 Pro 啊]] !
chuo1 ni3 a5
'poke' 'you' SFP

   'There should be some old writers poking you
   (on Facebook) too.'

In Example 32a, the celebrity speaker says there will be people using abusive language against her on the Weibo social network if they dislike something she posts. In Example 32b, a TV chat show host advises an older writer using Facebook that she will also have friends who use the 'poke' command to get her attention. In both cases, the [有 NP] construction is followed by a verb describing what the NP does (i.e. 'curse' and 'poke' respectively).

When a quantifier (QN) is inserted between 有 and an NP to create a [有 QN NP] construction, the NP can be placed at the front to become [NP 有 QN]. So, for example, it is equally legitimate to say 有很多钱 'have-very-much-money' or 钱有很多 'money-have-very-much'. Moreover, the structure [NP 有 QN] can be further simplified to become [NP QN] (i.e. 有 is omitted), especially if the quantifier involves the use of an intensifier like 很. That is, 钱很多 'money-very-much' is also legitimate. Thus, the three sentences in Example 33 all mean the same thing, although their frequencies of use by native speakers will vary (Google hits show 33a > 33c > 33b).

Example 33

a ₛ[vp[打ᵥ 麻将ɴ] vp[有ᵥ] np[很 多Adj 好处ɴ]]。
da3 ma2jiang4   you3   hen3 duo1 hao3chu4
'play' 'mah-jong' 'have'   'very' 'many' 'advantage'
'There are many advantages to playing mah-jong.'

b ₛ[vp[打ᵥ 麻将ɴ] np[好处ɴ] vp[有ᵥ] np[很 多ɴ]]。
da3 ma2jiang4   hao3chu4   you3   hen3 duo1
'play' 'mah-jong' 'advantage' 'have' 'very' 'many'
'There are many advantages to playing mah-jong.'

c ₛ[vp[打ᵥ 麻将ɴ] np[好处ɴ] ap[很 多Adj]]。
da3 ma2jiang4   hao3chu4   hen3 duo1
'play' 'mah-jong' 'advantage' 'very' 'many'
'There are many advantages to playing mah-jong.'

Although 有 is the predominant device for encoding existential sentences, there are other means of doing so. The Chinese copula 是 can also carry out such a function. Compare, for example, Example 34a and Example 34b.

Example 34

a ₛ[np[这Dem] vp[是ᵥ np[一Num 张Cla 中国ɴ   地图ɴ]]]。
zhe4   shi4   yi4   zhang1 zhong1guo2 di4tu2
'this'   'be'   'one' Cla   'China'   'map'
'This is a map of China.'

b ₛ[vp[pp[墙ɴ 上Prep] 是ᵥ] np[一Num 张Cla 中国ɴ   地图ɴ]。
qiang2 shang4 shi4   yi4   zhang1 zhong1guo2 di4tu2
'wall' 'up' 'be'   'one' Cla   'China'   'map'
'There is a map of China on the wall.'

The two sentences in Example 34 differ only in their thematic elements – 'this' for Example 34a and 'on the wall' for Example 34b. While Example 34a is a standard sentence, complete with a subject NP and a VP, Example 34b is an existential sentence, where 有 is substituted by 是. In other words, while 是 is a linking verb in Example 34a, where the subject NP ('this') is equal to the complement ('a map of China'), we cannot say the same thing about Example 34b, where the adverb unit ('on the wall') cannot be equal to 'a map of China'. Example 34b is, in fact, an existential sentence which gives more emphasis to the highlighted NP than the 有 existential sentence. In other words, 是 retains some of its copula function and implies, in Example 34b, that the map is the sole object, or at least should be the sole object of attention, regarding what is on the wall. If 是 were replaced by 有, then the map would be just one of the many possible objects on the wall. More examples of existential sentences involving 是 can be found in Example 35:

Example 35

a ₛ[VP [PP [皮包 ₙ 内 Prep 是 ᵥ] NP [一 Num 本 Cla 厚厚 Adj
   pi2bao1   nei4   shi4   yi4   ben3   hou4hou4
   'handbag' 'inside' 'be'   'one'   Cla   'thick-thick'

   的 名册 ₙ]] 。
   de5 ming2ce4
   AD 'name-book'

   'There is a thick volume of names inside the handbag.'

b ₛ[VP [PP [房 ₙ 内 Prep] 全 Adv 是 ᵥ] NP [木制 Adj 家具 ₙ]] 。
   fang2 nei4   quan2 shi4   mu4zhi4   jia1ju4
   'house' 'inside' 'all' 'be'   'wood-made' 'furniture'
   'All that is inside the house is wooden furniture.'

c ₛ[VP [PP [脑 ₙ 中 Prep] 都 Adv 是 ᵥ] NP [母亲 ₙ 笑容 ₙ]] 。
   nao3 zhong1 dou1 shi4   mu3qin1 xiao4rong2
   'brain' 'middle' 'all' 'be' 'mother' 'smile'
   'All that is inside the brain is mother's smiles.'

d ₛ[NP [百姓 ₙ] VP [饿 ᵥ 死 Adv]] 时 Conj,
   bai3xing4   er4   si3   shi2
   'civilians' 'hunger' 'die'   'when'
   'When civilians starved to death'

e ₛ[VP [PP [中南海 ₙ 桌 ₙ 上 Prep] 是 ᵥ] NP [燕窝 ₙ 鱼翅 ₙ]。
   zhong1nan2hai3 zhuo1 shang4 shi4   yan4wo1   yu2chi4
   'Zhongnanhai' 'table' 'up' 'be'   'swallow-nest' 'fish-fin'
   'Zhongnanhai's (dinner) table is (full of) swallow's nests and
   shark's fins.'

In Example 35a, the NP 'a thick booklet of names' is probably an unexpected and the most important finding for anyone examining the handbag. Hence 是 '(exactly) is' is used in this existential sentence rather than the standard and neutral 有. In Examples 35b and 35c, the emphatic value of 是 is further strengthened by the co-occurring adverbial elements 全 'whole' and 都 'all' respectively, which cannot co-occur with 有 in this context. Finally, in Example 35d, 是 helps produce a sharp contrast between people starved to death and the expensive foods enjoyed by communist officials in Mao Zedong's times. It would have been less effective if 有 were used to bring about the contrast.

In addition to sentences containing 有 or 是, there are other types of existential sentences in Chinese. One of them uses the continual aspect marker 着 coupled with a verb which can semantically connect an object to a locational phrase – some sentences in this strand are shown in Example 36 below:

Example 36

a ₛ [ᵥₚ [ₚₚ [桌 ₙ 上 ₚᵣₑₚ] 放ᵥ 着 ₐₘ] ₙₚ [一 ₙᵤₘ 把 ₖₗₐ 刀 ₙ]] 。
    zhuo1 shang4 fang4 zhe5   yi4   ba3   dao1
    'table' 'up' 'set' AM   'one'   Cla   'knife'
    'On the table a knife (is) placed.'

b ₛ [ᵥₚ [ₚₚ [病床 ₙ   前 ₚᵣₑₚ] 站ᵥ 着 ₐₘ] ₙₚ [一 ₙᵤₘ 位 ₖₗₐ 神父 ₙ]] 。
    bing4chuang2 qian2 zhan4 zhe5   yi2   wei4   shen2fu4
    'sick-bed'   'front' 'stand' AM   'one'   Cla   'priest'
    'In front of the sickbed stands a priest.'

c ₛ [ᵥₚ [ₚₚ [房产证 ₙ   上 ₚᵣₑₚ] 写ᵥ 着 ₐₘ]
    fang2chan2zheng4 shang4 xie3 zhe5
    'property-certificate' 'up' 'write' AM

    ₙₚ [女友 ₙ   的 名字 ₙ]] 。
    nv3you3   de5 ming2zi4
    'girl-friend' PD 'name'

    'On the deeds of the property (is) written the girlfriend's name.'

d ₛ [ᵥₚ [ₚₚ [天 ₙ 上 ₚᵣₑₚ] 飘ᵥ 着 ₐₘ] ₙₚ [雪 ₙ]] 。
    tian1 shang4 piao1 zhe5   xue3
    'sky' 'up' 'drift' AM   'snow'
    'In the sky the snowflakes drift.'

All of the sentences in Example 36 start with either a PP or an NP serving the adverbial function of identifying a place. The VP then describes what happens in the place. In most cases, it describes a static situation such as a knife being placed on a table (Example 36a), a priest standing in front of a sickbed (Example 36b), or a girlfriend's name written on the property deeds (Example 36c). However, the pattern can also be used in a dynamic situation when referring to the working of the elements, such as snow falling in Example 36d.

A small number of verbs can also be used in existential sentences with or without the support of an aspect marker. This is similar to sentences starting with *There appeared*, *There occurred* and so on in English. Some examples along this line are provided in Example 37 below:

Example 37

a ₛ [_{VP} [人生 _{N(Adv)} **充满**_V]   _{NP} [矛盾 _N]] 。
   ren2sheng1 chong1man3   mao2dun4
   'life'   'full of'   'spear-shield'
   'Life (is) full of contradictions.'

b ₛ [_{VP} [_{PP} [草原 _N   上 _{Prep}] 开_V   满 _{Adv} 了 _{AM}] _{NP} [野花 _N]] 。
   cao3yuan2 shang4 kai1   man3 le5   ye3hua1
   'prairie' 'up'   'open' 'full' AM   'wild-flower'
   'On the prairie wild flowers fully blossom.'

c ₛ [_{VP} [_{PP} [脑海 _N   里 _{Prep}] **浮现**_V]   _{NP} [你的 _{Pos} 背影 _N]] 。
   nao3hai3 li3   fu2xian4   ni3de5   bei4ying3
   'brain-sea' 'inside' 'float-appear' 'your'   'back-shadow'
   'In (my) mind's eye emerges the silhouette of your back.'

d ₛ [_{VP} [_{PP} [北京 _N 地铁 _N   里 _{Prep}] **出现**_V]   _{NP} [一 _{Num} 只 _{Cla} 熊猫 _N]] 。
   bei3jing1 di4tie3 li3   chu1xian4   yi4   zhi1 xiong2mao1
   'Beijing' 'subway' 'inside' 'appear' 'one' Cla 'panda'
   'A panda appeared at the Beijing subway.'

The structures of the sentences in Example 37 largely fall in line with those of Example 36 and manifest the S → VP NP pattern for Chinese existential sentences. The theme of Example 37a is a noun ('human life'), which may seem incongruent with Examples 37b–d as the latter all start with an adverbial structure (i.e. a prepositional phrase). However, a noun phrase denoting a location is as good as an adverbial phrase in an existential sentence. The two usages (i.e. NP or PP) are often interchangeable; that is, we can substitute 人生 'life' (N) with 人生中 'in life' (PP) in Example 37a and obtain the same meaning. We can also remove the prepositions 上 from Example 37b and 里 from Example 37c–d without changing the meaning.

3.6 ERGATIVE SENTENCES

An ergative verb allows either the *performer* or the *receiver* of an action to be the subject of an active sentence involving the verb. For example, in English, it is equally legitimate to say *Someone opened the door* or *The door opened*. By ergative sentence I mean a sentence whose subject can be the object of the same verb in another form of the sentence. Thus, *The door opens* is an ergative sentence as the subject *the door* can become the object in *John opens the door*. In English, an ergative sentence (*The fish is cooking*) is structurally different from a passive sentence (*The fish is being cooked*) which should also imply some semantic and/or pragmatic differences. Bear in mind, though, that not all transitive verbs can be used in the 'ergative way'. For example,

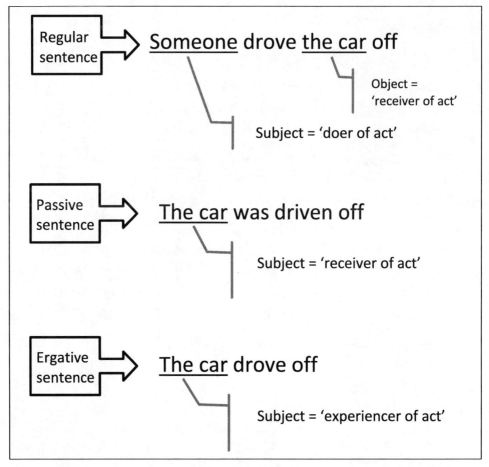

Figure 3.1 English active, passive and ergative sentences

Someone is writing a letter cannot be transformed into *A letter is writing* (ergative), but *A letter is being written* (passive) is fine. Figure 3.1 offers a comparison between the three kinds of sentences.

Practically all ergative sentences frequently seen in English can be translated into equivalent Chinese ergative sentences, as the sentences in Example 38 show.

Example 38

a   The condom broke!
保险套   破   了！
bao3xian3tao4   po4   le5
'insurance-sheath' 'break apart' AM
'The condom burst!'

b   All the ice melted.
所有   的 冰   都   融化   了。
suo3you3 de5 bing1 dou1   rong2hua4 le5
'all'   AD 'ice' 'unanimously' 'melt'   AM
'All the ice has melted.'

c   The house is shaking.
房子   在   摇。
fang2zi5 zai4 yao2
'house' AM 'shake'
'The house is shaking.'

d   The turkey is roasting.
火鸡   正在   烤。
huo3ji1   zheng4zai4 kao3
'fire-chicken' 'just' AM 'roast'
'Turkey is currently roasting.'

e   The film shoots in New York.
电影   在   纽约   拍摄。
dian4ying3 zai4 niu3yue1 pai1she4
'movie'   'at' 'New York' 'pat-absorb'
'The movie shoots at New York.'

It seems that Chinese ergative sentences can also be readily translated into their English counterparts, as Example 39 shows:

Example 39

a 杯子　**摔破**　　了。
bei1zi5　shuai1po4　le5
'glass'　'fall-break'　AM
'The glass fell and broke.'

b 汤　　正在　　　**沸腾**。
tang1　zheng4zai4　fei4teng2
'soup'　AM　　　'boil'
'The soup is boiling.'

c 飞机　**降落**　　在　公路　　上。
fei1ji1　jiang4luo4　zai4　gong1lu4　shang4
'airplane'　'land'　　'at'　'highway'　'up'
'The airplane landed on the highway.'

d 车　正在　　　修　突然　**烧**　起来。
che1　zheng4zai4　xiu1　tu2ran2　shao1　qi3lai2
'car'　AM　　　'fix'　'suddenly'　'burn'　'rise'
'The car suddenly burned while being fixed.'

Example 39 shows four Chinese ergative sentences which can be translated into their equivalent English sentences – 'glass breaks', 'soup boils', 'airplane lands' and 'car burns'. Example 39d contains another verb, 'fix', which is normally not used in the 'ergative way' in English so we cannot translate it into *The car is fixing* (although Google does return some hits for this expression). It is interesting that in Chinese, 'fix' is used in the same predicate structure as a generally recognized ergative verb 'burn'. This could mean that another type of VP shares the same sentence structure with Chinese ergative verbs. In fact, there are plenty of Chinese sentences which look like ergative sentences in that their subject can be the object within a different type of sentence with the same meaning. Most of them cannot be directly translated into English without structural adjustment.

Example 40

a 我的   钱   丢   了。
   wo3de5 qian2 diu1 le5
   'my'   'money' 'lose' SFP
   'My money (is) lost.'

b 早饭   吃   了   吗?
   zao3fan4 chi1 le5 ma5
   'breakfast' 'eat' AM QM
   'Breakfast has (been) eaten?'

c 寒假   作业   写   完   了。
   han2jia4   zuo4ye4   xie3 wan2 le5
   'winter break' 'homework' 'write' 'finish' AM
   'The homework for the winter holiday (is) finished.'

d 紧急   电话   打 6 次   才   通。
   jin3ji2   dian4hua4 da3 liu4 ci4 cai2 tong1
   'emergency' 'telephone' 'hit' 'six' 'times' 'only' 'through'
   'The emergency phone call (was) made six times before
   it got through.'

One of the main differences between the sentences in Example 40 and Example 39 lies in a certain semantic property of the verb involved. Due to the nature of the verbs involved, it is relatively easy to conceptualize the role of the subjects in the Example 39 sentences in relation to their verbs as either a passive receiver or a voluntary experiencer of an action. For example, a house can be passively shaken by an earthquake, but a house may also shake on its own for some reason. Conversely, it is difficult to imagine the money 'losing itself' as in Example 40a, or breakfast 'eating' (40b), homework 'writing' (40c) or telephone 'calling' (40d) for the same reason. Thus, such sentences should be analyzed as consisting of an object as the topic of the sentence followed by the transitive verb which takes the topic as its object. The sentence structures in Example 40 are thus indistinguishable from ergative sentences in appearance, as both start with an object followed by its governing verb. I shall call the kind of sentence in Example 40 'object-fronted sentence'. Figure 3.2 illustrates the differences between a Chinese active sentence, ergative sentence and object-fronted sentence.

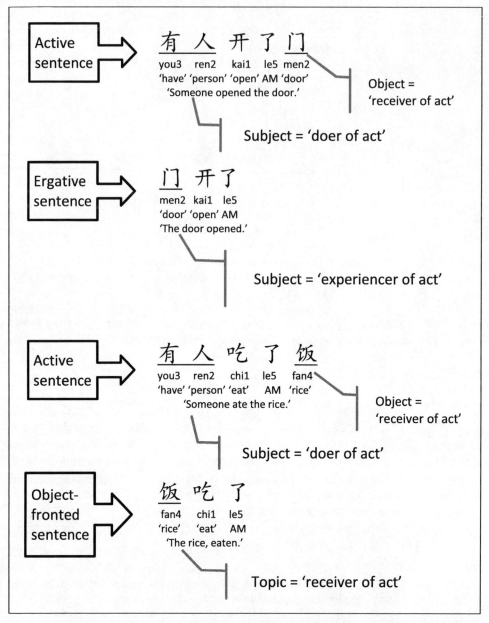

Figure 3.2 Chinese active, ergative and object-fronted sentences

The first sentence in Figure 3.2, 有人开了门 'someone opens the door' can be transformed into an ergative sentence 门开了 'the door opens', which is also an object-fronted sentence as 'the door' can either be construed as the subject of an ergative sentence or the object of an active sentence which is transposed to the front to become the topic of the sentence. The third sentence in Figure 3.2, 有人吃了饭 'someone ate the rice' cannot be transformed into an ergative sentence as 'the rice has eaten' does not make any sense (or, rather, the sentence 饭吃了 cannot be interpreted in this way). But it can indeed be transformed into an object-fronted sentence 'The rice, eaten'. The latter is comparable to the passive sentence 饭被吃了 'The rice was eaten' but is not necessarily a derivation of it. The object-fronted sentence is a special means of emphasizing the object in the topic position without the passive connotation. In fact, many object-fronted sentences do not have highly acceptable passive counterparts, such as Examples 40c and 40d – both 作业被写完 'homework is written' and 电话被打通 'phone call is put through' – are rather unusual expressions.

3.7 PASSIVE SENTENCES

The most common (but not the only) marker of passive structure in Chinese is the functional item 被 *bei4*. The standard way to create a Chinese passive sentence is to add 被 in front of the N-V configuration transposed from the original active sentence. For example, 鸟吃虫 'bird-eat-worm' is transformed into 虫被鸟吃 'worm-*by*-bird-eat'; that is, from the active scheme [N₁ V N₂] to the passive scheme of [N₂ *bei4* N₁ V]. It may be useful to conceptualize the morpheme 被 as the preposition *by* in English as used in a passive sentence which marks the agent of the action. A schematic representation of how to transform an active sentence into a standard passive sentence in Chinese is shown in Figure 3.3.

Sometimes the subject of the verb (鸟) in the active sentence (鸟吃虫) can be omitted in the passive sentence, so only the original object and the verb are present (虫被吃). Like English passives, this often happens when the focus is on the entity who takes the consequences of an action and it is relatively obvious (or unimportant or unknown) who carries out the action (e.g. *A dog involved in an attack on a 12-year-old child in Dundee has been destroyed* – it

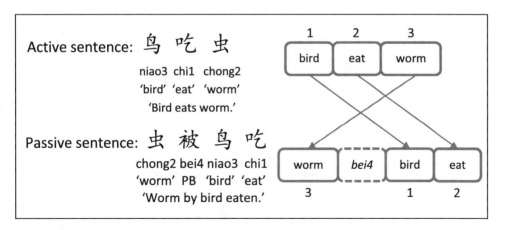

Figure 3.3 Transforming an active sentence into a passive sentence

does not matter very much to the reader who actually destroyed the dog). The two passive sentences in Example 41 below have not specified the agents who carry out the action of 'abandoning' or 'overthrowing' respectively.

Example 41

a 一　　名　　婴儿　　**被**　　**遗弃**。
　yi4　ming2　ying1er2　bei4　yi2qi4
　'one' Cla　'infant'　PB　'desert'
　'An infant was abandoned.'

b 进化论　　　　　　**被**　　**推翻**　　　了。
　jin4hua4lun4　　　bei4　tui1fan1　　le5
　'evolution-theory' PB　'overthrow'　AM
　'The theory of evolution has been overthrown.'

With Example 41a, it is obvious that the baby has been abandoned by its parents and it is not a priority to mention the fact in the sentence. For Example 41b, it is more important to include evolution theory and the word 'overthrow' in the punchy statement and leave other details for later elaboration. Consequently, in both cases, the original subject is omitted and the passive marker 被 is attached directly to the verb.

　　The next pair of passive sentences makes a point of showing who the agents are that perform the action.

Example 42

a 笔记本电脑　　　　　**被**　**室友**　　　**偷**　了。
　bi3ji4ben3dian4nao3　bei4　shi4you3　　tou1　le5
　'notebook-computer' PB　'roommate' 'steal' AM
　'(My) laptop computer was stolen by (my) roommate.'

b 习近平　　演讲　　　数次　　　　**被**　**掌声**　　　　**打断**。
　xi2jin4ping2　yan3jiang3　shu4ci4　　　bei4　zhang3sheng1　da3duan4
　'Xi Jinping'　'speech'　'several-times' PB　'applause'　　'interrupt'
　'Xi Jinping's speech was interrupted by applause several times.'

In Example 42a it is important to specify who the alleged culprit is that stole the computer. It is also crucial to emphasize, in 42b, that the chairman's speech was interrupted by enthusiastic applause and not by a flying shoe! Thus, in both sentences 被 precedes the NP-V combination to give information about 'who-did-what' rather than just the info of 'what happened' as in Example 41.

Like active sentences, passive structures can also come in a series as we saw in Examples 4 and 5, without the presence of conjunctive devices. Each of the two sentences in Example 43 below consists of two passive structures in sequence.

Example 43

a 清朝　　　　　官员　　　古墓　　　　**被　盗，**
　　qing1chao2　　guan1yuan2 gu3mu4　　bei4 dao4
　　'Ching Dynasty' 'officials'　'ancient-tomb' PB　'raid'
　　'The tomb of a Ching Dynasty official was raided and

　　尸体　**被　丢弃**。
　　shi1ti3　bei4 diu1qi4
　　'corpse' PB　'discard'
　　the body was discarded.'

b 三　　　男子　　黄河　　　　游泳，
　　san1　nan2zi3 huang2he2　you2yong3
　　'three' 'man'　'Yellow River' 'swim'
　　'Three men swam in Yellow River.

　　一　　人　　**被　冲走，**　　两　　人　　**被　救起。**
　　yi4　ren2　bei4 chong1zou3 liang3 ren2　bei4 jiu4qi3
　　'one' 'person' PB　'wash-away' 'two'　'person' PB　'save-up'
　　One was carried away by water; the other two were saved.'

Examples 43a and 43b are online news headlines which come without any punctuation marks. The ending periods and the commas within the two sentences are added by the author to facilitate understanding in the current context. The three commas in Example 43 actually mark sentential boundaries rather than define constituents within the sentence. That is, there are in fact two sentences in Example 43a and three in Example 43b, each of which comes with a standard NP-VP sentence structure. In this book I use the term Extended Sentence to refer to the kind of elaborated structure like Example 43a or Example 43b which 'tells a short story' and is made up of several short sentences (see 3.12 for more detail).

Thus, the extended sentence in Example 43b consists of three simple sentences, each comprising an NP and a VP. Each NP is made up of a number morpheme ('three', 'one', 'two' respectively) and a noun meaning 'man' or 'person'. The VP of S_1 starts with a noun 'Yellow River' which serves the adverbial function of naming the place of the action. S_1 is an active sentence whereas S_2 and S_3 are both passive sentences. Both passive structures consist of the simplified [被 V] scheme rather than the full [被 NP V] configuration. The omitted NP in

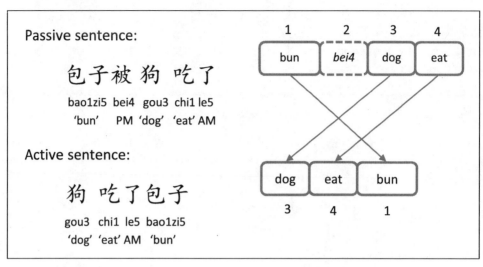

Figure 3.4 Transforming a passive sentence back into an active sentence

the passive structure of S_2 is 'water' (which carried a person away). The omitted NP in S_3 is 'rescuers' (who saved the other two men).

In normal circumstances, the passive sentence can be easily reverted back to an active sentence if both the subject and object are present. For example, 包子被狗吃了 'bun-*bei4*-dog-eat' [N1 被 N2 V] can be changed back to 狗吃了包子 'dog eat bun'. The process is illustrated more fully in Figure 3.4.

However, some passive structures involving the use of a certain type of verb do not allow a straightforward reversion from the passive structure back to the active form. This refers to the verb that is composed of a verb morpheme and a noun morpheme as the verb's object, i.e. [VN]$_V$, such as 打球 'hit-ball (play ball)', 开枪 'open-gun (fire a gun)', 借钱 'borrow-money' and so on. Since this kind of verb already consists of a VN structure, they normally do not take another object in a direct manner. Although some of them can take a notional object (e.g. 'fire a gun at someone' or 'borrow money from someone'), this indirect object has to be connected by a preposition; for example, 她对他开枪 'she-*at*-him-open-gun', 他向我借钱 'he-*toward*-me-borrow-money'. Consequently, when these verbs are used in a passive structure, their reversion back to active structure is not straightforward (i.e. a preposition has to be added before the notional object). Two examples of this type of passive sentence are shown in Example 44:

Example 44

a 糟糕，   我 被 退学   了！
   zao1gao1   wo3 bei4 tui4xue2   le5
   'rotten-cake' 'I' PB 'withdraw-study' AM
   'How terrible! I was dismissed from school.'

b 波士顿   爆炸   案   伤者   被   截肢。
   bo1shi4dun4 bao4zha4 an4 shang1zhe3   bei4 jie2zhi1
   'Boston'   'explosion' 'case' 'injured person' PB   'amputate'
   'The (leg of) the person injured in the Boston explosion
   incident was amputated.'

Both sentences in Example 44 contain a VN type of verb following 被 to form a passive structure. Both verbs denote negative meanings ('kick out of school' and 'amputate leg') which coincide with the general impression that Chinese passive structures are mostly used to encode adverse circumstances. Also, neither of the sentences in Example 44 shows the agent of the action (presumably 'school' and 'doctor' respectively). When attempting to change these sentences back to active ones, it is not a straightforward procedure as Figure 3.4 shows. Instead, a preposition-like morpheme needs to be added in front of the notional object, which is then inserted between the subject and the verb to form an active sentence. One example set of sentences illustrating this point is shown in Example 45, which is based on Example 44a, now resurfacing as 45a.

Example 45

a 糟糕，   我 被 退学   了！
   zao1gao1   wo3 bei4 tui4xue2   le5
   'rotten-cake' 'I' PB 'withdraw-study' AM
   'How terrible! I was dismissed from school!'

b *糟糕,   学校   退学   我 了！
   zao1gao1   xue2xiao4 tui4xue2   wo3 le5
   'rotten-cake' 'school'   'withdraw-study' 'me' AM
   'How terrible! The school kicked out me!'

c 糟糕,   学校   把 我 退学   了！
   zao1gao1   xue2xiao4 ba3 wo3 tui4xue2   le5
   'rotten-cake' 'school'   OB 'me' withdraw-study' AM
   'How terrible! The school kicked me out!'

Example 45a is a passive sentence encoded with 被 where the agent of the action (i.e. the school authority responsible for dismissing the student) is hidden. Example 45b shows the result of a normal passive-to-active conversion which is not acceptable in this instance. Example 45c shows the correctly transformed sentence, where the functional item 把 is added to mark the receiver of the action (i.e. the student).

An interesting recent development regarding the kinds of verbs compatible with 被 involves a group of intransitive verbs with negative senses. Theoretically, an intransitive verb should never engender a passive sentence. For example, the sentence *John cried* involves only a predicate (CRY) and an argument (JOHN) and it is not possible to transform the sentence into a passive one because no entity is involved in doing something to someone. However, a passive sentence involving the use of an intransitive verb is now possible (in Chinese). As of now, there seemed to be two primary categories of usage for this kind of 'intransitive passive' structure:

- The person involved is a victim within an alleged conspiracy theory, for example:

湘籍	工运	领袖	李旺阳	"被 自杀"
xiang1 ji2	gong1yun4	ling3xiu4	li3wang4yang2	bei4 zi4sha1
'Hunan-resident'	'work-activity'	'leader'	'Li Wangyang'	PB 'self-kill'

  'The blue-collar leading activist from Hunan, Li Wangyang, "was committed suicide".'

- The person is the victim of some kind of rumor, for example:

明星	频频	被 结婚	回应	皆	称	没空
ming2xing1	pin2pin2	bei4 jie2hun1	hui2ying4	jie1	cheng1	mei2kong4
'celebrity'	'repeatedly'	PB 'get married'	'respond'	'all'	'claim'	'no-leisure'

  'Celebrities "are repeatedly got married" and claim to be too busy to do so when asked.'

Thus, 被自杀, literally 'was committed suicide', actually means 'was claimed to have committed suicide'; while 被结婚 'was got married' really means 'was rumored to have gotten married'. Similar usages include 被消失 'was disappeared' → 'was made to disappear', 被退休 'was retired' → 'was made to retire' and so on. The first usage usually embodies the public's suspicion of foul play by the government or some other sort of vicious group. The second usage is primarily associated with media and celebrities but it also applies to groups of relatives or friends.

The aforementioned new generative process for [被 V] (where V is an intransitive verb) even goes so far as to include *nouns* into the framework; for example, 被车祸 'was car-accidented' → 'was rumored to be involved in a car accident', 被精神病 'was mental-illnessed' → 'was forced into a mental hospital', 被生日 'was birthdayed' → 'was given a (surprise) birthday party' and so on. The process now seems to come back around full circle to allow the [被 V] structure to take on any previously impossible verbs simply to mean 'being forced to do something'. For example, 被签字 means 'was made to sign one's name (to agree to something involuntarily)'.

Not all passive sentences in Chinese are encoded with the standard passive marker 被. There are other functional items which can also help form a passive structure but their use is more restricted and less frequent in comparison to 被. A miscellaneous collection of passive sentences created by other markers than 被 is presented in Example 46.

Example 46

a 松花江　　　　水　　**受到**　　**污染**。
　song1hua1jiang1 shui3 shou4dao4 wu1ran3
　'Songhuajiang' 'water' 'receive' 'pollute'
　'The water of the Songhua River has been polluted.'

b 我的　　账户　　**遭到**　　**封锁**。
　wo3de5 zhang4hu4 zao1dao4 feng1suo3
　'my' 'account' 'subject to' 'seal-lock'
　'My account was blocked.'

c 母亲节　　　礼物　现金　最　**受**　　**欢迎**。
　mu3qin1jie2 li3wu4 xian4jin1 zui4 shou4 huan1ying2
　'Mother's day' 'gift' 'cash' 'most' 'receive' 'welcome'
　'Among Mother's Day gifts, cash is the most popular.'

d 台湾　　渔船　　**遭**　　菲律宾　　军舰　　**扫射**。
　tai2wan1 yu2chuan2 zao1 fei1lv4bin1 jun1jian4 sao3she4
　'Taiwan' 'fish-boat' 'encounter' 'Philippines' 'warship' 'sweep-shoot'
　'A Taiwanese fishing boat was machine-gunned by a Philippine warship.'

e 那个　　小偷　　已经　**给**　警察　　**捉住**　　了。
　na4ge5 xiao3tou1 yi3jing1 gei3 jing3cha2 zhuo1zhu4 le5
　'that' 'thief' 'already' 'give' 'police' 'catch-stay' AM
　'That thief has already been caught by the police.'

f 完　　了，天大　　的　秘密　**让**　老婆　**发现**　　了！
　wan2 le5 tian1da4 de5 mi4mi4 rang4 lao3po2 fa1xian4 le5
　'finish' SFP 'heaven-big' AD 'secret' 'let' 'wife' 'discover' AM
　'I'm finished! A huge secret was discovered by my wife!'

The two passive markers 受到 and 遭到 in Examples 46a and 46b are disyllabic units whose functions are very close to 被 and can in fact be replaced by it.

The differences between the three are mostly prosodic, although 遭到 is mostly used in written language and is rarely heard in spontaneous speech. Both 受到 and 遭到 share the same morpheme 到 'reach' which can be omitted from both disyllabic units without affecting their passive marking functionality. Example 46c, for example, retains only 受 as the passive marker, while Example 46d retains only 遭. When 受 appears alone as a passive marker it forms habitual combinations (i.e. collocations) with the ensuing verb. For example, the passive structure 受欢迎 'enjoy popularity' in Example 46c is a very common usage.

The morpheme 给 means 'give' when used as a verb. However, in Example 46d it serves the purpose of passive marking in a way similar to 被. The same is true of the verb 让 'let' which, when serving the passive marker function as in Example 46e, is also equivalent to 被. The use of these two variants of 被 seems quite region-specific.

3.8 EMPHATIC SENTENCES

The beginning of a sentence is sometimes called the 'theme' of the sentence in functional linguistics (e.g. Baker 1992). The rest of the sentence is called the 'rheme'. The first unit of the sentence receives the initial attention of the reader and triggers the necessary reference framework in the mind to help process the rheme. In a normal sentence having the standard NP-VP structure, the theme is usually the subject of the sentence. However, sometimes a non-subject NP or something else is fronted to become the theme (see object-fronted sentences in example 40). Again, this is in order for the structure to act as the 'attention catcher' so the reader or listener knows what the sentence is about and can process the rest of the sentence accordingly.

Example 47

a 这个　　问题　　我　也　想　　问。
   zhe4ge5 wen4ti2　wo3 ye3　xiang3 wen4
   'this'　'question' 'I'　'also' 'think' 'ask'
   'I also want to ask this question.'

b 二手　　　　奔驰　　便宜　　卖。
   er4shou3　　ben1chi2 pian2yi2 mai4
   'second-hand' 'Benz'　'cheap'　'sell'
   'Second hand Benz-Mercedes to be sold cheap!'

c 五种　　　食物　　千万　　　别　　趁　　新鲜　　吃
   wu3zhong3 shi2wu4 qian1wan4 bie2　chen4 xin1xian1 chi1
   'five-kind'　'food'　'ten million' 'do not' 'while' 'fresh'　'eat'
   'Five kinds of foods you must not eat fresh.'

In both Examples 47a and 47b, the object ('this question', 'Mercedes') has been fronted to receive the initial emphasis allocated to the beginning of a sentence. Example 47b is a commercial headline and it is obvious why the commodity being advertised is placed at the strategic position of the theme. In fact, the subject of the sentence ('the vendor') is also omitted to make the sentence more compact and punchy. Like passive sentences, the subjects of object-fronted sentences are often omitted when it is obvious or relatively unimportant who they are. Such is the case for 47c, where the warning of 'not eating these five foods fresh' is obviously meant to apply to everybody.

In Chinese, a unit outside a regular sentence can be placed at the front of the sentence to serve as the 'topic' of the sentence. Example 46c is a good example, where 'Mother's day present' is the sentence-external topic, which is followed by a complete sentence 'cash is the most popular option'. In English, this topic would have been packaged in an adverbial unit like *In terms of a Mother's day present,...* but in Chinese, it is common to use an NP to serve the topic function. More examples are shown in Example 48 below:

Example 48

a　星座　　　我　最　　喜欢　　双鱼。
　　xing1zuo4 wo3 zui4　xi3huan1 shuang1yu2
　　'zodiac'　'I'　'most' 'like'　　'Pisces'
　　'Among the zodiac signs I like Pisces most.'

b　12　　岁　女孩　半边　　　脸　被　烫伤。
　　shi2er4 sui4　nv3hai2 ban4bian1 lian3 bei4 tang4shang1
　　'12'　'year' 'girl'　'half-side' 'face' PB　'scald-hurt'
　　'Half of the face of a 12-year-old girl was scalded.'

c　减肥　　　最　有效　　的　方法　　是　运动。
　　jian3fei2　zui4　you3xiao4 de5 fang1fa3 shi4 yun4dong4
　　'reduce-fat' 'most' 'effective' AD 'method' 'be' 'sport'
　　'The most effective way to lose weight is taking exercise.'

d　房子　千万　　　不要　　这样　　　装修。
　　fang2zi5 qian1wan4　bu2yao4　zhe4yang4 zhuang1xiu1
　　'house' 'ten million' 'not-want' 'this way' 'install-repair'
　　'Property decoration and repair must not be done this way.'

e　人生　　　一定　要　活　得　有　意义。
　　ren2sheng1 yi2ding4 yao4 huo2 de5 you3 yi4yi4
　　'human life' 'surely'　'want' 'live' Com 'have' 'meaning'
　　'(We) must live life in a meaningful way.'

All the sentences in Example 48 start with a topic NP ('zodiac signs', '12-year-old girl', 'losing weight', 'house', 'life') which is external to the NP-VP structure of a simple sentence. Each sentence in Example 48 has a separate subject NP ('I', 'half of the face', 'the most effective way' for 48a–c and a hidden 'you' for both 48d and 48e respectively) immediately following the topic, which becomes less significant due to its secondary position. Topicalization is thus a way for an NP to gain extra emphasis in a Chinese sentence. Sometimes a longer topic is physically separated from the sentence by a punctuation mark such as a comma, like those in Example 49.

Example 49

a 新 二十四孝, 你 做到 了 几 条?
xin1 er4shi2si4xiao4 ni3 zuo4dao4 le5 ji3 tiao2
'new' '24 filial exemplars' 'you' 'do-arrive' AM 'how many' Cla
'Among the new 24 filial exemplars, how many have you achieved?'

b 男女 之间 送 礼物, 你 懂 多少?
nan2nv3 zhi1jian1 song4 li3wu4 ni3 dong3 duo1shao3
'man-woman' 'between' 'give' 'present' 'you' 'know' 'how much'
'How much do you know about sending gifts between men and women?'

Both sentences in Example 49 are questions asking the reader about their commitment to, or knowledge about, the topic. The topic in Example 49a is an NP ('new 24 exemplars of filial piety'), while the topic in Example 49b is a VP-like structure ('sending gifts between men and women'). Both structures are set apart from the main sentence by a comma and are apparently not involved in the process of sentence formation beyond the punctuation point. The topic structure, like a fronted object NP, brings more emphasis to that first element of a sentence than a sentence starting with a subject NP or an adverbial structure.

There are other ways to emphasize a certain constituent of a sentence than transposing it to the front of a sentence. One of them is to place the emphasized element in a certain frame. The most frequently used type of emphatic sentence involves the use of 是 and 的 in various configurations. Some examples are shown in Example 50:

Example 50

a　我　是　非常　　专一　　　　的。
wo3　shi4　fei1chang2　zhuan1yi1　　de5
'I'　'be'　'extremely'　'engrossed-one'　ED
'I am extremely single-minded (i.e. I am a very devoted lover).'

b　其实　我　是　很　活泼　　的。
qi2shi2　wo3　shi4　hen3　huo2po1　de5
'in fact'　'I'　'be'　'very'　'lively'　ED
'Actually, I am a very lively person.'

c　鱼　与　熊掌　　　是　不可　　兼得　　　　　的。
yu2　yu3　xiong2zhang3　shi4　bu4ke3　jian1de2　　de5
'fish'　'and'　'bear-palm'　'be'　'not-can'　'concurrent-obtain'　ED
'It is not possible to obtain fish and bear-palm at the same time.'

The three sentences in Example 50 use the [X 是 Y 的] frame where Y is claimed to be a strong property of X. For Example 50a, the emphasis is placed on the speaker's merit of being 'dedicated to one (lover) only' in dealing with romance. In 50b, the speaker emphasizes her being a lively person by nature, possibly in contrast to her serene appearance. Example 50c emphasizes the impossibility of obtaining both the fish and the bear palm.

Note that if we take 是 and 的 away from the above sentences, so the pattern [X 是 Y 的] becomes [X Y] only; what remain are still legitimate sentences, only minus the emphasis. For example, if we take 是 and 的 away from Example 50b, the remnant is still a good sentence. Both the emphasized and de-emphasized sentences are shown in Example 51:

Example 51

a　其实　我　是　很　活泼　的。
qi2shi2　wo3　shi4　hen3　huo2po1　de5
'in fact'　'I'　'be'　'very'　'lively'　ED
'Actually, I am very lively.'

b　其实　我　很　活泼。
qi2shi2　wo3　hen3　huo2po1
'in fact'　'I'　'very'　'lively'
'Actually, I am lively.'

The elements that get emphasized by the [X 是 Y 的] structure in Example 50 are adjective units, or APs, which are used to emphasize the attributes of certain entities (i.e. nouns). Attributes of verbs can also be emphasized in this frame, for example, when verbs are accompanied by modal auxiliaries, adverbs or prepositional phrases. Some examples along this line are presented in Example 52:

Example 52

a 癌症　　　　是　可以　　避免　　　的。
　ai2zheng4　shi4　ke3yi3　bi4mian3　de5
　'cancer'　　'be'　'may'　'avoid'　ED
　'Cancer can indeed be avoided.'

b 这　本　小说　　　是　根据　　事实　　而　　　　写　　的。
　zhe4　ben3　xiao3shuo1　shi4　gen1ju4　shi4shi2　er2　　　xie3　de5
　'this'　Cla　'novel'　　'be'　'base on'　'fact'　　'and then'　'write'　ED
　'This novel is written on the basis of fact.'

c 我　不是　　故意　　　　要　拿　你　帽子　　的。
　wo3　bu2shi4　gu4yi4　　　yao4　na2　ni3　mao4zi5　de5
　'I'　'not-be'　'intentionally'　'want'　'take'　'you'　'hat'　　ED
　'I did not mean to grab your hat.'

In the [X 是 Y 的] structure demonstrated by the sentences in Example 52, X is an NP ('cancer', 'this novel' or 'I'). The Y part – the constituent that gets emphasized – is a VP with a modal auxiliary or an adverb taking the front. In Example 52a, the leading element of the VP ('can be avoided') is a modal auxiliary ('can'). This is the portion of the VP that gets emphasized. In Example 52b, on the other hand, the foremost portion of the NP is a preposi-tional phrase ('according to fact'). The prepositional phrase is what the speaker means to emphasize with the [X 是 Y 的] frame here. Finally, in Example 52c, it is an adverb ('intentionally') modifying the action of 'taking the hat' that gets emphasized. Note that Example 52c also exemplifies the negative form of [X 是 Y 的], that is [X 不是 Y 的].

We have seen that auxiliaries or different adjuncts of a VP can be empha-sized by the [X 是 Y 的] frame. If there is more than one peripheral element like these in or around a VP, any one of them can receive emphasis by being placed immediately after 是. The set of sentences in Example 53 show how various portions of a sentence can be emphasized.

Example 53

a ₛ [NP [同事 N] VP [昨天 Adv PP [为 Prep 我 Pro] 庆生 V]] 。
    tong2shi4   zuo2tian1   wei4   wo3   qing4sheng1
    'colleagues'   'yesterday'   'for'   'me'   'celebrate-birth'
    'Colleagues celebrated my birthday yesterday.'

b 同事   是 [昨天 Adv] 为 我 庆生   的。
    tong2shi4 shi4 zuo2tian1 wei4 wo3 qing4sheng1 de5
    'colleagues' 'be' 'yesterday' 'for' 'me' 'celebrate-birth' ED
    'It was yesterday that colleagues celebrated my birthday.'

c 同事   昨天   是 [为 Prep 我 Pro] 庆生   的。
    tong2shi4 zuo2tian1 shi4 wei4   wo3   qing4sheng1   de5
    'colleagues' 'yesterday' 'be' 'for'   'me'   'celebrate-birth' ED
    'It was for me that colleagues celebrated a birthday yesterday.'

d 是 [同事 N] 昨天   为 我 庆生   的。
    shi4 tong2shi4 zuo2tian1 wei4 wo3 qing4sheng1   de5
    'be' 'colleagues' 'yesterday' 'for' 'me' 'celebrate-birth' ED
    'It was colleagues that celebrated a birthday for me yesterday.'

Example 53a is the original sentence where no particular emphasis is placed on any portion of the sentence. Among the three hypothetical sentences that follow, Example 53b emphasizes the time of the celebration ('yesterday'), while the objective of the celebration ('for me'), and the people who held the celebration ('colleagues') are emphasized in Example 53c and d respectively. Note that in the last sentence of the set, the entire sentence is inserted between 是 and 的 in the [X 是 Y 的] frame as Y. This sentence, Example 53d, where an NP is emphasized rather than a verb auxiliary, can be expressed in another way, as Example 54a shows:

Example 54

a 昨天　　　为　我　庆生　　　　　**的　是**　[同事 _N]。
  zuo2tian1 wei4 wo3 qing4sheng1　de5 shi4 tong2shi4
  'yesterday' 'for' 'me' 'celebrate-birth' AD 'be' 'colleagues'
  'It was colleagues that celebrated a birthday for me yesterday.'

b 最先　　　　发明　　火药　　　　**的　是**　中国人。
  zui4xian1　fa1ming2 huo3yao4　de5 shi4 zhong1guo2ren2
  'most-ahead' 'invent'　'gunpowder' AD 'be' 'China-person.'
  'It was the Chinese who first invented gunpowder.'

c 我　担心　　**的　是**　你的　　健康。
  wo3 dan1xin1 de5 shi4 ni3de5 jian4kang1
  'I'　'worry'　AD 'be' 'your'　'health'
  'What worries me is your health.'

d 林书豪　　　实现　　**的　是**　"美国梦"。
  lin2shu1hao2 shi2xian4 de5 shi4 mei3guo2meng4
  'Lin Shuhao' 'realize'　AD 'be' 'America-dream'
  'What Jeremy Shu-How Lin achieves is the American dream.'

The sentences in Example 54 all follow the emphatic pattern of [Y 的是 X], which is a reverse of [X 是 Y 的]. That is, if in general X = NP and Y = VP or AP, earlier in the [X 是 Y 的] structure, the verb or adverb element in the predicate portion receives the emphasis. For the [Y 的是 X] pattern, it is the NP portion of a sentence that gets emphasized. Thus, in Examples 54a and 54b it is the subject NP ('colleagues' or 'Chinese') that is emphasized. Examples 54c and 54d, on the other hand, show that an object NP ('your health', 'American dream') residing in a VP can also receive emphasis within the pattern.

Note again that if such added elements as 的 and 是 are omitted from the sentence, the resultant sentence differs from the original sentence only in the loss of emphasis. If the emphasized portion is the subject NP, like in Examples 54a and 54b, the NP has to be reintroduced to the beginning of the sentence following the omission of 的 and 是. In the case of object NP being emphasized such as Examples 54c and 54d, there is no change of word order when 的 and 是 are removed. The resultant de-emphasized sentences are offered in Example 55 for comparison with their original emphasized counterparts in Example 54.

Example 55

a 昨天　　　同事　　　　为　　我　　庆生。
　 zuo2tian1 tong2shi4　wei4 wo3 qing4sheng1
　 'yesterday' 'colleagues' 'for' 'me' 'celebrate-birth'
　 'Colleagues celebrated my birthday yesterday.'

b 中国人　　　　　　最先　　　　发明　　　火药。
　 zhong1guo2ren2 zui4xian1　　fa1ming2 huo3yao4
　 'China-person' 'most-ahead' 'invent' 'gunpowder'
　 'The Chinese were the first to invent gunpowder.'

c 我　担心　　你的　　健康。
　 wo3 dan1xin1 ni3de5 jian4kang1
　 'I' 'worry' 'your' 'health'
　 'I worry about your health.'

d 林书豪　　　　实现　　　"美国梦"。
　 lin2shu1hao2 shi2xian4 mei3guo2meng4
　 'Lin Shuhao' 'realize' 'America-dream'
　 'Jeremy Shu-How Lin achieves the American dream.'

The set of sentences in Example 55 are de-emphasized versions of the sentences in Example 54. As previously mentioned, because the emphasized portions in Example 54c and d are the object NPs, the process of de-emphasizing involves only the removal of the redundant morphemes 的 and 是 without having to adjust the word order. For Examples 54a and b, however, since the emphasized portions are the subject NPs, they should be returned to the beginning of the sentence (or after the time adverb as in 55a when no longer emphasized by the 的-是 combination).

Within the emphatic structure [Y 的是 X], the two morphemes 的 and 是 are not glued together but can be separated by an adverb of some sort to create even more emphasis. Some examples of intervening adverbs between 的 and 是 are shown in Example 56:

Example 56

a　虐猫　　**的**　一定　　**是**　坏蛋。
nue4mao1　de5　yi2ding4　hi4　huai4dan4
'abuse-cat' AD 'certainly'' be' 'bad-egg'
'Those who abuse cats are surely the bad guys.'

b　射手　　　最　　在乎　　**的**　绝对　　　**是**　家人。
she4shou3　zui4　zai4hu1　de5　jue2dui4　shi4　jia1ren2
'Sagittarian' 'most' 'care'　AD 'absolute' 'be' 'home-person'
'What the Sagittarian cares most about are definitely the
family members.'

In each sentence of Example 56, an adverb is inserted between 的 and 是
to add more emphasis – 'certainly' and 'absolutely' respectively. To increase the
emphasis even more, complicated patterns are used involving a repetition of the
的-是 combination or 是 alone in some ways. Example 57 illustrates a more
complicated variety of the [Y 的是 X] pattern.

Example 57

a　疲惫　　**的**　不　**是**　脚步，　　而　**是**　心情！
pi2bei4　de5　bu2　shi4　jiao3bu4　er2　shi4　xin1qing2
'exhausted' AD 'not' 'be' 'footsteps' 'but' 'be' 'mood'
'What is exhausted is not the footstep but the mood.'

b　这　里面　　坐　**的**，不是　大官　　　就　**是**　明星。
zhe4　li3mian4　zuo4　de5　bu2shi4　da4guan1　jiu4　shi4　ming2xing1
'this' 'inside' 'sit' AD 'not-be' 'big-official' 'just' 'be' 'bright-star'
'Those who sit inside are either top officials or celebrities.'

Example 57a involves the use of a negative morpheme 不 to deny a statement
which would have been established by 是 – 'footsteps are exhausted'. The
contrastive structure of this sentence is used to deny the allegation of 'exhausted
footsteps' and to emphasize the truthfulness of a 'feeling of tiredness'. Note
that the use of 而 'but' before the second instance of 是 helps highlight
the contrast (between true and false). Conversely, the 不是…就是 'if not…
then' structure in Example 57b carries out an additive rather than contrastive
function. That is, not only 'top officials' but also 'celebrities' sit in the venue
in question. Again, the additive meaning results from an adverbial element –
the morpheme 就 'exactly' which collocates with the verb 是 to form a habitual
disyllabic unit.

There are also more complicated versions for the [X 是 Y 的] pattern discussed earlier. Two examples are offered below, both of which involve the use of the negative morpheme 不.

Example 58

a 我   是   来   工作   的, 不是   来   休息   的!
   wo3 shi4 lai2   gong1zuo4 de5 bu2shi4 lai2   xiu1xi2 de5
   'I' 'be' 'come' 'work'   ED   'not-be' 'come' 'rest' ED
   'I come here to work, not to rest!'

b 权利   不是   等来   的, 而是   争取   来   的!
   quan2li4 bu2shi4 deng3lai2   de5 er2shi4 zheng1qu3 lai2   de5
   'right' 'not-be' 'wait-come' ED   'but-be' 'strive for' 'come' ED
   'The right is not gained by waiting but is obtained through endeavor.'

As previously mentioned, the [X 是 Y 的] structure emphasizes the Y portion, i.e. the predicate part. In both Examples 58a and 58b, the sentence-initial NP ('I' and 'right' respectively) is predicated by two VPs, one of which is positive and the other is negative. This difference in polarity creates the contrast required to maximally emphasize the speaker's belief (i.e. 'to work' rather than 'to rest'; 'to strive for' rather than 'to wait (for something to happen)').

There are other kinds of emphatic sentences in Chinese, but by far the most frequently used ones are those which involve the use of 是 and 的 in ways that are similar to, but not limited to, those discussed in this section.

3.9 SERIAL VERBS CONSTRUCTION

In English, we often see two verbs used together in one expression such as *Go get* the ball, I *want* to *volunteer*, She *quit smoking*, I *saw* you *smile* and so on. In English, only one verb (the main verb, usually the first one) will get grammatical marking such as tense, person and number. This is called a 'finite verb' and the other verb(s) are said to be 'non-finite'. In Chinese, such serial verb constructions also exist but, as usual, there is no inflectional marking to any of the verbs in the series.

Some types of Chinese serial verb construction are similar to English and can be directly translated into corresponding English expressions. One of them is the pattern [V_1 V_2] where V_1 is often cognitive ('consider', 'decide', 'learn'), interactive ('agree', 'refuse', 'promise') or involving future actions ('begin', 'plan', 'avoid'). Some examples follow:

Example 59

a 我 **决定**$_{V1}$ **参加**$_{V2}$ 歌唱 比赛。
 wo3 jue2ding4 can1jia1 ge1chang4 bi3sai4
 'I' 'decide' 'participate' 'song-sing' 'context'
 'I decide to participate in a singing contest.'

b 飞机 **准备**$_{V1}$ **降落**$_{V2}$ 桃园 机场。
 fei1ji1 zhun3bei4 jiang4luo4 tao2yuan2 ji1chang3
 'airplane' 'prepare' 'land' 'Taoyuan' 'airport'
 'Airplane prepares to land at Taiwan Taoyuan International Airport.'

In both sentences of Example 59, the [V$_1$ V$_2$] combination can be translated directly into English, although in English there is a distinction between V$_1$ and V$_2$ in terms of inflection (i.e. only V$_1$ is inflected; V$_2$ is non-finite, surfacing as a gerund or an infinitive). Again, in Chinese, there is no inflection at any level and all verbs appear in base form (which is the only form they have) in all contexts.

There are some Chinese verbs of this type for which there is no corresponding English [V$_1$ V$_2$] structure. In some cases, the second verb is more naturally expressed by a noun in English, as Example 60 shows.

Example 60

a 日本 学生 **取消**$_{V1}$ **访华**$_{V2}$。
 ri4ben3 xue2sheng1 qu3xiao1 fang3hua2
 'Japan' 'student' 'cancel' 'visit-China'
 'Japanese students cancel their visit to China.'

b 中年 女性 应 **注意**$_{V1}$ **防癌**$_{V2}$。
 zhong1nian2 nv3xing4 ying1 zhu4yi4 fang2ai2
 'middle-year' 'female' 'should' 'pay attention' 'guard against-cancer'
 'Middle-aged women should pay attention to the prevention of cancer.'

The kind of verbs that fit into the [V$_1$ V$_2$] frame discussed above can often appear in succession to form a larger structure such as [V$_1$ V$_2$ V$_3$] or [V$_1$ V$_2$ V$_3$ V$_4$]. However, the verb that plays a pivotal role in this kind of construction (that is, V$_2$ or V$_2$ and V$_3$ respectively) must be similar to the original V$_1$ in nature in order to warrant the entrance of the next verb. That is, they should be verbs which are cognitive ('consider') or interactive ('refuse') in nature or involved in future actions ('begin'). Some examples are shown in Example 61:

Example 61

a 今天　　开始 _{V1}　学习 _{V2}　做菜 _{V3}。
   jin1tian1　kai1shi3　xue2xi2　zuo4cai4
   'today'　　'begin'　'learn'　'make-vegetable'
   'Today (we) start learning to cook.'

b 我　考虑 _{V1}　　放弃 _{V2}　订阅 _{V3}。
   wo3　kao3lv4　　fang4qi4　ding4yue4
   'I'　'consider'　'give up'　'subscribe'
   'I consider giving up the subscription.'

c 阿公　　　也　开始 _{V1}　帮忙 _{V2}　　注意 _{V3}　　　挑选 _{V4}。
   a1gong1　　ye3　kai1shi3　bang1mang2　zhu4yi4　　　tiao1xuan3
   'grandfather' 'also' 'start'　'help'　　　'pay attention' 'pick-choose'
   'Grandpa also starts to help pay attention to picking up (likely candidates).'

Examples 61a and b illustrate the [V₁ V₂ V₃] structure and Example 61c the [V₁ V₂ V₃ V₄] structure. Note that all the instances of V₂ in Example 61 and the V₃ in Example 61c are of the type that can initiate a [V₁ V₂] construction. This is why 3 or 4 verbs can appear in succession in these examples. The serial verb construction stops where the last one is not a verb related to cognitive activity, interpersonal relation or future action that can habitually start a [V₁ V₂] structure.

Another prevalent structure in both Chinese and English involving the use of a series of verbs is the [V₁ NP V₂] construction. This differs from the [V₁ V₂] structure in the insertion of an NP between V₁ and V₂ which is the object of V₁ but is the 'subject' of V₂ (e.g. Police *told* residents to *stay* indoors). Again, inflection is where English and Chinese differ. In English, V₁ is normally the main verb which carries inflectional marking (*told*) and V₂ is reduced to the infinitive (*to stay*). In Chinese, there is no morphological difference between V₁ and V₂ (警察 *告诉*居民 *留*在室内). Some Chinese sentences of this type are presented in Example 62 below.

Example 62

a 医生　　劝告 _{V1}　我　休息 _{V2}　几天。
   yi1sheng1 quan4gao4 wo3 xiu1xi2 ji3tian1
   'doctor'　'advise'　'me' 'rest'　'few-day'
   'The doctor advised me to rest for a few days.'

b 请　　帮助 _{V1}　我们　完成 _{V2}　这　个　梦想。
   qing3　bang1zhu4 wo3men5 wan2cheng2 zhe4 ge5 meng4xiang3
   'please' 'help'　　'we'　'accomplish' 'this' Cla 'dream-think'
   'Please help us realize this dream.'

Both sentences in Example 62 illustrate the $[V_1\ NP\ V_2]$ structure where V_1 is a certain type of verb (mostly denoting interpersonal interactions) and V_2 is a common verb. However, if V_2 is the kind of verb that can itself initiate a $[V_1\ V_2]$ or $[V_1\ NP\ V_2]$ construction, then larger structures built upon these two basic forms are possible; for example, $[V_1\ NP\ V_2\ V_3]$, $[V_1\ NP\ V_2\ NP\ V_3]$, $[V_1\ V_2\ NP\ V_3]$ and so on. Some examples are shown in Example 63:

Example 63

a   我   **鼓励**$_{V1}$ 大家   **尝试**$_{V2}$ **写作**$_{V3}$。
    wo3   gu3li4   da4jia1   chang2shi4 xie3zuo4
    'I'   'encourage' 'everybody' 'taste-try'   'write'
    'I encourage everybody to try writing.'

b   日本   大使   **要求**$_{V1}$ 美国   **协助**$_{V2}$ 日本
    ri4ben3 da4shi3   yao1qiu2 mei3guo2 xie2zhu4 ri4ben3
    'Japan' 'ambassador' 'request' 'USA'   'assist'   'Japan'
    'Japanese Ambassador asks the United States to help Japan

    防卫$_{V3}$ 钓鱼岛。
    fang2wei4 diao4yu2dao3
    'defend'   'fishing-island'
    defend the Pinnacle Islands.'

c   不少   市民   **反对**$_{V1}$ **准许**$_{V2}$ 内地   妇女
    bu4shao3 shi4min2 fan3dui4 zhun3xu3 nei4di4   fu4nv3
    'not-few' 'citizen' 'oppose' 'allow'   'mainland' 'women'
    'A large number of citizens oppose allowing mainland women

    来港   **产子**$_{V3}$。
    lai2gang3   chan3zi3
    'come-Hong Kong' 'deliver-child'
    to come to Hong Kong to give birth.'

The three sentences in Example 63 represent the construction $[V_1\ NP\ V_2\ V_3]$, $[V_1\ NP\ V_2\ NP\ V_3]$ and $[V_1\ V_2\ NP\ V_3]$ respectively. In general, they work in the same way as the corresponding English verbs with exactly the same word order and V-NP configurations. Due to the absence of verb inflection in Chinese, the patterns may be less easy to discover (and interpret) than their English counterparts.

So far we have seen serial verb constructions associated with certain types of verbs (cognitive, interactional and those involving future actions). This is, of course, not the only way for verbs to appear together in a Chinese sentence. Another method of verb combination is through some kind of conjunctive relation. Again, this kind of structure is difficult to recognize in Chinese, due to the absence of surface conjunctions. Let us look at some examples.

Example 64

a 13　　岁　女孩　VP1 [离家]　　VP2 [出走] 。
shi2san1 sui4 nv3hai2　li2jia1　　chu1zou3
'13'　'year' 'girl'　'leave-home'　'exit-walk'
'13-year-old girl runs away from home.'

b 曼德拉　　　再次　VP1 [住院]　　VP2 [接受　治疗] 。
man4de2la1 zai4ci4　zhu4yuan4　jie1shou4 zhi4liao2
'Mandela'　'again'　'hospitalized'　'accept' 'treatment'
'Mandela is readmitted to hospital and undergoes treatment.'

c 日本　首富　　　向　　中国　VP1 [道歉]　VP2 [认错] 。
ri4ben3 shou3fu4　xiang4 zhong1guo2　dao4qian4　ren4cuo4
'Japan' 'primary-rich'　'toward' 'China'　'apologize'　'admit-wrong'
'The richest person in Japan apologizes to China and admits fault.'

In Example 64a, the quadrisyllabic unit 离家出走 'leave-home-exit-walk' meaning 'run away from home' has become a fixed expression (gaining over 11 million Google hits as a phrase at the time of writing). The unit actually consists of two VPs 'leave home' and 'walk-out' which form a coordinative relationship rather than a 'control' one like those seen in Examples 59–63. In practice, this means the two actions 'leave home' and 'walk out' are of equal status and are simultaneously happening, unlike the $[V_1 V_2]$ type of structure where the occurrence of V_2 is somehow dependent on V_1 (e.g. 'promise to come'). This is also true for Example 64b, 'being hospitalized' and 'receiving treatment', and Example 64c, 'apologizing' and 'admitting fault', where both actions in the same pair happen simultaneously.

Some pairs of serial VPs appearing in the same sentence do not represent simultaneous movements but denote consecutive actions. In Example 65a, the pilot first ejected and then was saved. In Example 65b, the victim was killed after the perpetrator broke into her house.

Example 65

a 飞行员   VP1 [跳伞]   VP2 [获救] 。
   fei1xing2yuan2   tiao4san3   huo4jiu4
   'fly-person'   'jump-umbrella' 'obtain-save'
   'The pilot ejected and was saved.'

b 女童   遭   陌生人   VP1 [闯入]   VP2 [杀害] 。
   nv3tong2   zao1   mo4sheng1ren2   chuang3ru4   sha1hai4
   'female-child' 'encounter' 'strange-person'   'intrude-into'   'kill-harm'
   'A girl child was killed by a stranger who broke into (the house).'

Another type of serial verb/VP construction demonstrates a facilitative or causal relation. That is, the first action somehow warrants or causes the happening of the next action. Some examples are shown in Example 66:

Example 66

a 我   想   VP1 [回家]   VP2 [吃 晚餐] 。
   wo3 xiang3   hui2jia1   chi1 wan3can1
   'I' 'think'   'return-home'   'eat' 'night-meal'
   'I would like to go home and eat supper.'

b 78 岁   老 医生   VP1 [意外   落水]   VP2 [死亡] 。
   qi1shi2ba1 sui4 lao3 yi1sheng1   yi4wai4 luo4shui3   si3wang2
   '78-year'   'old' 'doctor'   'accident' 'fall-water'   'die'
   'A 78-year-old doctor fell into water and died.'

Example 66a shows someone performing a certain action ('go home') to facilitate a second action ('eat supper'). In Example 66b, on the other hand, someone does something ('falling into water') which triggers another event ('dying'). Note that the serial verb constructions exemplified by Examples 64–66 above are very similar to, and can be called miniature models of, the serial VP/AP structures discussed earlier in Examples 4 and 5. Whatever their size, they all exemplify sentences with multiple-VP structures.

3.10 EMBEDDED SENTENCES

Just as in English, there are three kinds of dependent clause in Chinese: the noun clause, the adjective (or relative) clause, and the adverbial clause. As with other shared structures between English and Chinese, it is harder to detect a subordinate clause in Chinese due to the absence or different styles of grammatical marking. In English, for example, a noun clause is frequently marked with *that*, a relative clause with a *wh-* word (called 'relative pronoun'), and an adverbial clause with subordinate conjunctions like *although*, *because*, *when*, *if* and so on. In Chinese, there is no special marking for nominal clauses, and the adjective clauses are marked by an ending particle 的 rather than by anything at the beginning. For adverbial clauses, although subordinate conjunctions exist, their use is not compulsory. In this book, the term 'complex sentence' is adopted to refer to a sentence consisting of an independent clause (i.e. a simple sentence) and one or more embedded sentences.

Noun clauses serving as the object of an epistemic verb (such as *know*, *think*, *suspect*) may be the most prevalent kind of nominal clauses. Two Chinese sentences subsuming a noun clause as object are presented in Example 67:

Example 67

a ₛ[NP [我] VP [觉得 ₛ[明天 会 下雨]]]。
    wo3   jue2de5   ming2tian1 hui4 xia4yu3
    'I'   'feel'   'tomorrow' 'will' 'rain'
    'I feel it will rain tomorrow.'

b ₛ[NP [我] VP [发现 ₛ[他 有 一根 白 头发]]]。
    wo3   fa1xian4   ta1 you3 yi4gen1 bai2 tou2fa3
    'I'   'find'   'he' 'has' 'one' Cla 'white' 'head-hair'
    'I find that he has a white hair.'

As can be seen, the epistemic verbs in Example 67 are followed by a complete sentence functioning as the object of the verb. Unlike in English, there is no so-called 'complementizer' (i.e. *that*) attached to the noun clause.

Nominal clauses can also serve as the subject of a sentence, like those in English (e.g. *That he was gay* had no effect on the quality of his work).

Example 68

a ₛ[ₛ[宝宝 生病] VP [是 家长 最 头疼 的 事情]]。
    bao3bao5 sheng1bing4   shi4 jia1zhang3 zui4 tou2teng2 de5 shi4qing2
    'baby'   'fall ill'   'be' 'parent' 'most' 'head-sore' AD 'matter'
    'That the baby falls ill is the thing that worries parents most.'

b ₛ[ₛ[蜜蜂 出现 了] VP [表示 春天 也 来 了]]。
    mi4feng1 chu1xian4 le5   biao3shi4 chun1tian1 ye3 lai2 le5
    'bee'   'appear' AM   'indicate' 'spring' 'also' 'come' AM
    'That the bees appear indicates spring has also come.'

Both sentences in Example 68 contain a smaller sentence functioning as the subject of the larger sentence. Note that when the Chinese sentences are translated into English, a complementizer, *that*, has to be added to the beginning of the nominal clause in order to maintain the grammaticality of the English sentence. In Chinese, it is much more difficult to identify the nominal structure as there is no surface marking of any kind.

We will examine Chinese adjective clauses next. The main departure from English here is that whereas an English relative clause comes after the noun being described (Children *who cannot swim well* should remain in shallow water), the Chinese relative clause always comes before the noun (泳技不佳的儿童 应该待在浅水区 'swim-technique not-good *de5* children should stay-at shallow-water-zone'). Furthermore, while an English relative clause is characterized by a relative pronoun (*who, which* etc.), in Chinese there is no relative pronoun but there is a functional item 的 which serves to 'wrap up' the relative clause and mark the unit as an adjective phrase (AP). An AP of this kind thus consists of a full sentence and a functional item 的. The descriptor 的 is attached to a Chinese adjective phrase/clause just like a relative pronoun leads an English relative clause. This analogy is illustrated by Example 69. In particular, Example 69b is a hybrid sentence with English words arranged in Chinese syntactic fashion where the relative clause is concerned.

Example 69

a   You can't beat the person [*who* never gives up]. (English)
b   You can't beat the [never give up *de5*] person. (Chinese-style English)

Example 69a shows an English sentence with a relative clause (*who never gives up*) enclosed by brackets. A crucial element to this relative clause is the relative pronoun *who*, which semantically represents the *person* in the main clause and grammatically signals the beginning of the clause. The entire clause follows the noun it describes (i.e. *person*). This is not how a Chinese adjective clause works, though. As explained elsewhere in this book, the Chinese adjective clause comes *before* the noun it describes. A comparison of the bracketed elements between Example 69a and Example 69b further reveals two differences: first, there is no identifying device such as a relative pronoun at the beginning of a Chinese adjective clause; second, there is indeed a grammatical item *de5* attached to the end of the Chinese adjective clause.

We will further analyze the internal structure of a Chinese sentence which contains an adjective clause. The Chinese sentence in Example 70 corresponds to the English sentence *The person <u>who stole the stuff</u> has been caught* (relative clause emphasized). As can be seen in Example 70, the adjective clause has been moved to the front of the object it describes (i.e. *person*), the relative pronoun *who* is non-existent, and a new item 的 is added to the end of the clause.

Example 70

s [NP [AP [s [NP [ ] vp [偷　东西]] 的] 人 N]　vp [被　抓　了]]。
　　　　　　　　　tou1 dong1xi1 de5 ren2 　　bei4 zhua1 le5
　　　　　　　　　'steal' 'thing'　AD　'person'　PB　'seize' AM
　　　　　　　　　'The person who stole the stuff has been caught.'

The structural notation given in Example 70 seems a bit complex at first glance. The key point is the embedded S which represents a complete sentence and thus contains an NP and a VP. The NP, however, is not filled in by any linguistic device in this instance. The empty slot created by the two brackets following the second NP notation is meant to show something that should have been here (i.e. a subject NP if the dependent clause were to stand alone). In English this empty slot would have been filled in by a relative pronoun (i.e. *who*). Whether it is the relative pronoun in English, or the empty slot in Chinese, the position should have been occupied by the entity that the adjective clause describes (i.e. 'person' in this sentence). Another special notation added in Example 70 is the AP (standing for Adjective Phrase) which, in this instance, includes a sentence and an 'adjective marker' *de5* (AD). Together the sentence and the finalizing 的 form a descriptive unit just like situations where word level (聪明的 'intelligent') or phrase level (大眼睛的 'big-eyed') adjectives both end with 的. A graphic representation of Example 70 with structural analysis is given in Figure 3.5.

Figure 3.5 shows how a sentence combines with a descriptive marker 的 to form an adjective unit which is then used to describe the subject of the sentence. Note that the subject of the embedded sentence is non-existent and is represented by an empty square in the chart. A dotted line connecting this empty slot to the subject noun means the noun is also the 'notional subject' of the embedded sentence even though it is not realized in that particular slot. In contrast, Example 71 shows the subject noun ('dish') to be the 'notional object' of the verb ('cook') in the embedded sentence.

Example 71

s [NP [AP [s [NP [我　妈]　　vp [煮 V [ ] N]] 的] 菜 N]
　　　　　　　　　wo3 ma1 　　zhu3 　　　de5 cai4
　　　　　　　　　'I'　'mother'　'cook'　　AD 'vegetable'

　vp [很　好吃]]。
　　hen3 hao3chi1
　　'very' 'delicious'

　'The dishes my mother cooks are very delicious.'

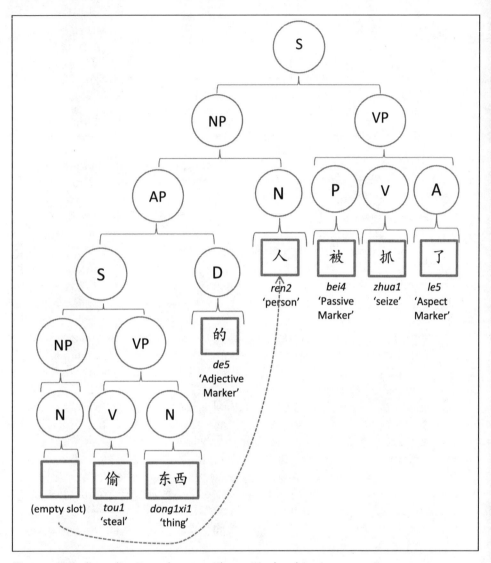

Figure 3.5 An adjective clause with omitted subject

Just like the English relative clause, a Chinese adjective clause can offer additional information about time, place, reason and so on. In English, this would be a clause marked by *where, when, how* or *why* (e.g. *This is the place where stars are born*). Again, in this kind of Chinese adjective clause, the *wh-* word is non-existent, but the embedded sentence itself is relatively complete, in the sense that it is not short of an essential element like the subject or the object of a verb. Two example sentences are shown in Example 72:

Example 72

a s [NP [学校] VP [是 NP [AP [s [儿童 N 生活 V] 的] 地方 N]]] 。
    xue2xiao4   shi4   er2tong2 sheng1huo2 de5 di4fang1
    'school'   'be'   'children' 'live'   AD 'place'
    'School is a place where children live their lives.'

b s [NP [AP [s [宿舍 N 关门 V]   的] 时间] VP [是 V 11   点 N]] 。
    su4she4   guan1men2 de5 shi2jian1   shi4 shi2yi1 dian3
    'dormitory' 'close-door' AD 'time'   'be' '11' 'point'
    'The time when the dorm shuts the door is 11 o'clock.'

In Example 72a, the sentence 'Children live their lives' combines with the descriptive marker *de5* to form an adjective unit to modify the noun 'place'. In Example 72b, the sentence 'Dorm closes', after being tagged by *de5*, is used to describe the subject NP 'time'.

The third and final type of embedded sentence that we will look at is the adverbial clause. Adverbial clauses are normally not said to be 'embedded' as they are more clearly set apart from the main clause (e.g. She fainted *when she saw blood*) instead of being integrated with it in some way. In Chinese, however, they also frequently appear *within* the main clause, usually cutting between the NP and the VP. An adverbial clause of this kind appears in Example 73a. A different version appears in Example 73b, which is equivalent to an English participial phrase.

Example 73

a s [NP [我] 曾经 Adv AP [因为 s [他 N 受伤 V]] 而 VP [流泪]] 。
    wo3 ceng2jing1   yin1wei4 ta1 shou4shang1 er2 liu2lei4
    'I' 'ever'   'because' 'he' 'get hurt' 'so' 'shed tear'
    'I once shed tears because he got hurt.'

b s [NP [一 艘 渡轮] AP [因为 s [[] N 超载 V]]
    yi4 sao1 du4lun2 yin1wei4   chao1zai4
    'one' Cla 'ferry' 'because'   'overload'

   VP [触礁 沉没]] 。
    chu4jiao1 chen2mo4
    'touch-reef' 'sink-drown'

   'A ferry hits the reef and sinks because it is overloaded.'

Example 73a shows the main clause 'I cried once' being split into two halves by an adverbial clause 'because he got hurt'. The adverbial clause consists of a complete sentence 'He got hurt' led by a conjunctive element 'because' followed by a trailing 'so'. Subordinate conjunctions like 'because', 'although', 'if' etc. often come with a second element in Chinese which mediates between the adverbial clause and the main clause (similar to the pair *If . . . then . . .* in English). The subordinate conjunction pair in Example 73a is 因为-而 where the first element introduces the cause and the second part brings out the consequence. The second element 而 is optional for this set of conjunctions and can only be followed by a VP (as opposed to a full main clause). Example 73b shows a simplified kind of adverbial clause where the subject of the embedded sentence is omitted. This is a frequently used structure in Chinese. Example 74 consists of two more sentences of this type.

Example 74

a $_S$[$_{NP}$[两   人] $_{AP}$[为 $_S$[节省   旅费]] 而
    liang3 ren2   wei4 jie2sheng3 lv3fei4   er2
    'two' 'person' 'for' 'economize' 'travel-fee' 'so'

    $_{VP}$[同   睡   一   床]]。
    tong2   shui4 yi4 chuang2
    'together' 'sleep' 'one' 'bed'

    'In order to cut back on the travel budget they both sleep on the same bed.'

b $_S$[$_{NP}$[我] $_{AP}$[戴 着   口罩] $_{VP}$[比较   漂亮]]。
    wo3   dai4 zhe5 kou3zhao4   bi3jiao4 piao4liang4
    'I'   'wear' AM 'mask'   'compare' 'pretty'
    'I am relatively better-looking wearing a mask.'

Another pair of subordinate conjunction appears in Example 74a, 为-而, which functions in the same way as 因为-而 in Example 73a. Like Example 73b though, the embedded sentence in Example 74a is without a subject NP. This is, then, like an infinite phrase or a prepositional phrase in English. In 74b, the subordinate conjunctions disappear altogether. The embedded sentence 'wearing a mask' is an adverb phrase (AP) of some sort, specifying the circumstances when the claim of the main clause 'I look prettier' is true.

    To conclude this section, let us look at a longer sentence which seems to consist of all three kinds of embedded sentence.

Example 75

_S [_{NP} [卡麦隆　　首相]　　　　_{AP} [_S [不顾　　中国　　　的
ka3mai4long2 shou3xiang4　　　　bu2gu4　zhong1guo2 de5
'Cameron'　'Prime Minister'　　　'disregard' 'China'　　AD
'Prime Minister Cameron disregards China's

强力　　　　反对]]，_{VP} [坚持　　_S [会见
qiang2li4　　fan3dui4　　jian1chi2　hui4jian4
'strong-power' 'objection'　'insist'　'meet'
strong objection and insisted on meeting with

_{AP} [_S [到访　　伦敦]　　的] 达赖　喇嘛]]]。
dao4fang3 lun2dun1 de5 da2lai4 la3ma5
'arrive-visit' 'London' AD 'Dalai-Lama'
the Dalai Lama who came to London to visit.'

The main clause of Example 75 is 'Cameron insisted (on something)'. The main verb then takes a noun clause '(Cameron) met with the Dalai Lama' as its object. The noun clause itself includes an embedded adjective clause '(the Dalai Lama) visited London'. Finally, adding to this already complex sentence is an adverbial clause '(Cameron) disregarded China's strong opposition' which gives some background information about the main event. All three subjects in the dependent clauses are omitted.

3.11 COORDINATED SENTENCES

Coordination involves two or more sentences being strung together by a coordinating conjunction in a unit of expression, such as *He cried but no one listened*. In Chinese, coordinating conjunctions such as 'and', 'but', 'or', 'so' are not so prevalently or consistently used. In many cases, two or more sentences produced in a particular order are coordination enough and no superficial device is needed to connect them into a larger structure. The logical relationships between the series of sentences will be evident from the context if no conjunctive device is given. First we consider a few coordinated sentences connected by some commonly used conjunctions. Then we look at pairs or groups of sentences in a coordinative relationship without the help of surface connectors.

Example 76

a ₛ[ₛ[比萨饼 不错]， **但是** ₛ[我 更 喜欢 面条]]。
  bi3sa4bing3 bu2cuo4 dan4shi4 wo3 geng4 xi3huan1 mian4tiao2
  'pizza-cake' 'not-wrong' 'but' 'I' 'even more' 'like' 'noodle'
  'Pizza is alright, *but* I like noodles even more.'

b ₛ[ₛ[你 还 年轻]， **而且** ₛ[你 会 继续 成长]]。
  ni3 hai2 nian2qing1 er2qie3 ni3 hui4 ji4xu4 cheng2zhang3
  'you' 'still' 'young' 'moreover' 'you' 'will' 'continue' 'grow'
  'You are still young *and* you will continue to grow.'

c ₛ[ₛ[我 女朋友 今天 出院]，
  wo3 nv3peng2you3 jin1tian1 chu1yuan4
  'I' 'girlfriend' 'today' 'exit-yard'
  'My girlfriend is discharged from hospital today,

  所以 ₛ[我 来 接 她]]。
  suo3yi3 wo3 lai2 jie1 ta1
  'therefore' 'I' 'come' 'collect' 'her'
  so I come to collect her.'

The three sentences in Example 76 each consist of two independent clauses which are connected by a coordinating conjunction – 'but', 'and' and 'so' respectively. The structural and semantic relationships between the pairs of independent clauses joined together by their particular connector are very similar to their counterparts in English. In Chinese, however, the three kinds of logical relationships – contrastive, additive and causal – can be correctly interpreted by a native speaker when no superficial connectors are used. Some examples of coordination without conjunctions can be seen in Example 77:

Example 77

a ₛ[ₛ[饭　烧焦　　　　　了]，ₛ[菜　也　炒　坏　了]]。
　fan4 shao1jiao1　　　　le5　　cai4 ye3 chao3 huai4 le5
　'rice' 'burn-scorched' AM　　'veg' 'also' 'fry' 'bad' AM
　'The rice is burnt. The dish is also ruined.'

b ₛ[ₛ[夜市　　　　人潮　　　　依旧]，
　ye4shi4　　　ren2chao2　yi1jiu4
　'night market' 'human-tide' 'as usual'
　'At the night market, crowds still flow.

　ₛ[肉羹　店　生意　惨]]。
　rou4geng1 dian4 sheng1yi4 can3
　'meat soup' 'shop' 'business' 'pathetic'
　Business for thick meat soup shops is tough.'

c ₛ[ₛ[宿舍　　停水]，　ₛ[学生　　用　消防栓
　su4she4 ting2shui3　　xue2sheng1 yong4 xiao1fang2shuan1
　'dormitory' 'stop-water'　'student'　'use'　'fire hydrant'
　'Water supply is interrupted in the dorm. Students use fire hydrant

　的　水龙头　　　洗澡]]。
　de5 shui3long2tou2 xi3zao3
　AD 'faucet'　　　'bathe'
　taps to shower.'

Example 77a consists of two independent clauses demonstrating an additive relationship ('rice burned' + 'dish ruined') but there is no conjunctive device to string the two together except for a Chinese-style comma. The inter-sentential relationship is arrived at through consecutively processing the two sentences and building up the semantic connection in an intuitive fashion. Likewise, Example 77b demonstrates a contrastive relationship between the two clauses ('a night market full of crowds' but 'no one patronizing the meat soup stalls') without using an overt conjunction. Likewise, the two clauses in Example 77c are causally related ('no water in the dorm' → 'student using fire hydrant to shower) and there is no overt conjunction to show the relationship. Obviously, such a connection is made intuitively by Chinese native speakers reading the sentence, but it may be less easy for non-native speakers and may take them longer to work out the logical relationship.

　　Not only coordinated sentences but also subordinated sentences can come without superficial conjunctions. Structurally, both types of connected sentences would then look exactly the same, being deprived of leading or intervening conjunctions. For example, in Example 78a, the first clause states the reason ('climate warms up') with the main clause stating the outcome ('plants blossom early'). In Example 78b, the first clause gives the background information ('heavy rain causes flooding') with the main clause stating the highlighted information ('The Czech Republic is in a state of emergency').

Example 78

a ₛ[ₛ[气候　暖化]，　ₛ[高山　　　植物　　提早　　开花]]。
　　qi4hou4 nuan3hua4　gao1shan1　　zhi2wu4 ti2zao3　kai1hua1
　　'climate' 'warming'　'high-mountain' 'plant'　'lift-early' 'open-flower'
　　'Climate warms up. High mountain plants blossom early.'

b ₛ[ₛ[中欧　　　大雨　　成灾]，
　　zhong1ou1　　da4yu3　cheng2zai1
　　'middle-Europe' 'big-rain' 'become-calamity'
　　'Heavy rain causes flooding in central Europe.

　ₛ[捷克　陷　　　紧急　　状态]]。
　　jie2ke4 xian4　jin3ji2　zhuang4tai4
　　'Czech' 'cave in' 'emergency' 'condition'
　　The Czech Republic declares state of emergency.'

When coordinated sentences are not connected by conjunctions, in many cases they can still be identified by certain adverbial elements which show the relationship. Example 77a is a case in point, where the adverbial element 也 'also' appears at the second clause to give the additive connotation. More examples like this follow in Example 79:

Example 79

a ₛ[ₛ[爸爸　因　　　车祸　　　去世]，
　　ba4ba5 yin1　che1huo4　qu4shi4
　　'father' 'because' 'car accident' 'pass away'
　　'Father died as a result of car accident.

　ₛ[妈妈　又　　　得　了　癌症]]。
　　ma1ma5 you4　de2 le5 ai2zheng4
　　'mother' 'moreover' 'get' AM 'cancer'
　　Moreover, mother contracted cancer.'

b ₛ[ₛ[买方　付　了　订金]，ₛ[卖方　却　　　反悔]]。
　　mai3fang1 fu4 le5 ding4jin1　mai4fang1 que4　fan3hui3
　　'buyer' 'pay' AM 'deposit'　'seller' 'conversely' 'retract'
　　'The buyer paid the deposit. The seller however backed out.'

c ₛ[ₛ[电梯　坏　了]，ₛ[我 只好　　　爬　楼梯]]。
　　dian4ti1 huai4 le5　wo3 zhi3hao3　pa2 lou2ti1
　　'lift' 'bad' AM　'I' 'only-good' 'climb' 'stairs'
　　'The elevator is out of order. I can only climb the stairs.'

All three sentences in Example 79 consist of two coordinated clauses without overt conjunctions mediating between the two. However, each of the complicated sentences has an adverbial element usefully embedded in the second installment to relate it to the previous clause. In Example 79a, for example, the morpheme 又 helps mark 'mother has cancer' as additional information to 'father died of car accident'. In Example 79b, the morpheme 却 helps develop a quick contrast between 'buyer paid deposit' and 'seller backed out'. In Example 79c, the disyllabic unit 只好 'cannot but' also implies a kind of semantic relation between two propositions. In this case, it helps point out its host sentence ('I climb stairs') as an inevitable consequence of the previous sentence ('Elevator broke down').

Other means are also used to help facilitate the interpretation of coordination between two sentences. Cohesion, for examples, plays a role in linking the two independent clauses together in Example 77b, where 'meat soup stall' and 'night market' demonstrate a 'part-whole' relationship. In Example 77c, 'water' appears in both clauses, forming a lexical cohesive tie (Halliday and Hasan 1976). Two more examples of coordinated sentences connected by cohesive devices are shown in Example 80:

Example 80

a ₛ[ₛ[台大　校园　　　电线　　　　　走火]，
　　tai2da4 xiao4yuan2 dian4xian4　zou3huo3
　　'NTU'　'campus'　'electric-wire' 'walk-fire'
　　'Fire occurred in National Taiwan University due to short circuit.

　　ₛ[松鼠　　　遭　　　电　　死]]。
　　song1shu3 zao1　　dian4　si3
　　'squirrel'　'encounter' 'electrify' 'dead'
　　Squirrels were electrocuted and died.'

b ₛ[ₛ[新北市　　　　出现　　冷气　　　　大盗]，
　　xin1bei3shi4　chu1xian4 leng3qi4　　da4dao4
　　'New Taipei City' 'appear'　'air conditioner' 'bandit'
　　'Air-conditioner theft appeared at New Taipei.

　　ₛ[民众　　半夜　　被　热　醒]]。
　　min2zhong4 ban4ye4　bei4 re4 xing3
　　'citizens'　'midnight' PB　'hot' 'wake'
　　People were awakened by heat in the night.'

In Example 80a, the same morpheme 电 'electricity' appears in both independent clauses, making a connection between the two (i.e. lexical cohesion). In Example 80b, 冷 'cold' and 热 'hot' are antonyms, constituting a cohesive tie of the 'collocation' kind (Halliday and Hasan 1976). This kind of cohesion no doubt helps language users realize the semantic relationships between the coordinated sentences without the explicit guidance of a conjunction.

A symmetrical structure between the two independent clauses is also a means for forming coordinative relationships. Earlier we saw an example in Example 77a, where 'rice is burnt' and 'dish is ruined' are structurally symmetrical, making it easier to see the connection between the two sentences. Two more examples of this kind are shown in Example 81:

Example 81

a $_s$ [$_s$ [北韩　　　　释　　　善意]，$_s$ [南韩　　　表　　　欢迎]]。
　　bei3han2　　shi4　　shan4yi4　　nan2han2　　biao3　　huan1ying2
　　'North Korea' 'release' 'good-will'　'South Korea' 'express' 'welcome'
　　'North Korea offers good-will. South Korea expresses welcome.'

b $_s$ [$_s$ [经济　　成长　　　　衰退]，$_s$ [银行　　呆账　　增加]]。
　　jing1ji4　cheng2zhang3 shuai1tui4　yin2hang2 dai1zhang4 zeng1jia1
　　'economy' 'grow'　　　'decline'　'bank'　'bad debt' 'increase'
　　'Economic growth declines. Bank bad debts increase.'

Example 81a shows a perfect structural symmetry between the two independent clauses – 'North Korea' against 'South Korea', 'release' versus 'express' and 'good will' contrasting with 'welcome'. Symmetrical couplets like these are frequently seen in Chinese poetry and other genres such as newspaper headlines. Structural similarity is an invitation for readers to interpret each sentence in relation to the other to arrive at the intended meaning. Example 81b follows the same routine in contrasting 'economy' with 'bank', 'growth' with 'bad debt' and 'decline' with 'increase'. The causal relationship between the two propositions can be better arrived at if the reader realizes the two sentences are related through a perception of structural symmetry.

3.12 EXTENDED SENTENCES

Extended sentence (ES) is a term I use in this book to refer to a Chinese text consisting of two or more sentences which are not appropriately coordinated and the entire unit is marked by a terminating Chinese-style period (。). As noted earlier in this chapter, while discussing the extended sentence in Example 7, a Chinese period does not really mark the boundary of a sentence, or any precisely defined unit, but is often loosely used to mark the combination of a series of related sentences or a very long and complicated sentence. It may be useful, therefore, to invent another term to refer to this kind of long structure which must correspond to some kind of conceptual unit in the Chinese native speaker's mind. An example of the extended sentence thus defined is shown in Example 82:

Example 82

台铁	基隆	火车站	月台	天桥	今天	坍塌,
tai2tie3	ji1long2	huo3che1zhan4	yue4tai2	tian1qiao2	jin1tian1	tan1ta1
'Taiwan Railways'	'Keelung'	'train station'	'platform'	'overpass'	'today'	'collapse'

'A platform overpass at Taiwan Railways Keelung Train Station collapsed today.

一	名	行走	桥	上	的	詹	姓	女子
yi4	ming2	xing2zou3	qiao2	shang4	de5	zhan1	xing4	nv3zi3
'one'	Cla	'walk'	'bridge'	'up'	AD	Zhan	'surname'	'woman'

A woman walking on the footbridge

坠落	到	月台,
zhui4luo4	dao4	yue4tai2
'fall'	'reach'	'platform'

dropped down to the platform.

消防局	将	她	送往	基隆医院	急救。
xiao1fang2ju2	jiang1	ta1	song4wang3	ji1long2 yi1yuan4	ji2jiu4
'fire station'	OM	'her'	'send to'	'Keelung Hospital'	'first aid'

The fire department sent her to Keelung Hospital for emergency treatment.'

Example 82 clearly consists of three sentences which together complete a mini-story: 1. Footbridge collapsed, 2. Woman fell off bridge, and 3. Firemen sent her to hospital. In this case, the Chinese style comma (,) usefully marks the boundaries between sentences. In many cases, however, the use of a comma within an extended sentence is more confusing than helpful in terms of structural delineation. Example 83 is a case in point.

Example 83

a 屏荣高中   昨天 举办 毕业典礼，
 ping2rong2gao1zhong1 zuo2tian1 ju3ban4 bi4ye4 dian3li3
 'Ping Rong High School' 'yesterday' 'hold' 'graduation-ceremony'
 'A graduation ceremony was held at Ping Rong High School yesterday.

b 泰国 交换学生   陈琳 来台   1 年，
 tai4guo2 jiao1huan4xue2sheng1 chen2lin2 lai2 tai2 yi4 nian2
 'Thailand' 'exchange student' 'Chen Lin' 'come to Taiwan' 'one' 'year'
 An exchange student, Chen Lin from Thailand, has come to Taiwan for
 one year;

c 从 完全   不会 中文，
 cong2 wan2quan2 bu2hui4 zhong1wen2
 'from' 'total'   'not''able' 'Chinese'
 from being totally unable to speak Chinese

 到 现在 国、 台语 都 会 通，
 dao4 xian4zai4 guo2 tai2yu3 dou1 hui4 tong1
 'to' 'now' 'Nation' 'Taiwanese' 'all' 'able' 'through'
 to now being familiar with both Mandarin and Taiwanese.

d 昨天 她 在 毕业典礼   上 致词，
 zuo2tian1 ta1 zai4 bi4ye4dian3li3   shang4 zhi4ci2
 'yesterday' 'she' 'at' 'graduation-ceremony' 'up' 'make speech'
 Yesterday she delivered a speech at the graduation ceremony

 博 得 满堂彩，
 bo2 de2 man3tang2cai3
 'gain' 'obtain' 'house down'
 and brought the house down.

e 她 跟 同学 约定， 有 机会 还 要 来 台
 ta1 gen1 tong2xue2 yue1ding4 you3 ji1hui4 hai2 yao4 lai2 tai2
 'she' 'with' 'classmate' 'agree on' 'have' 'chance' 'still' 'want' 'come' 'Taiwan'

 念 大学。
 nian4 da4xue2
 'read' 'university'

 She promised classmates she would come back to Taiwan to attend
 university if there is a chance.'

Example 83 is the beginning paragraph of an online news report. It is also an extended sentence as defined in this section, consisting of more than one sentence and concluding with an ending Chinese-style period. The division of Example 83 into five sections is based on the permitted number of comma-marked units on each line space, which in this case happens to coincide with five distinguishable structures from the paragraph. The first line, 83a, is a simple sentence with a clear NP-Adv-VP structure. It gives the background of the story that follows. The next line, 83b, is also a simple sentence having the structure of NP-VP which introduces the student in question. 84c is a coordinated sentence of some sort comprising two independent clauses ('She did not know Chinese' and 'She is good at both Mandarin and Taiwanese'). However, the subject ('Chen Lin') of both sentences is omitted so their sentential status may be questionable. Next, 83d is a sentence consisting of one NP ('she') and two VPs – 'delivered a speech' and 'brought the house down'. The second VP is separated from the main sentence by a comma and no further conjunction is present (in English a conjunctive device like *and* would have been obligatory). Finally, 83e consists of a main clause 'She promised her classmates' and a noun clause 'She would return to Taiwan to attend university' serving as the content of the promise.

Thus, the extended sentence shown as Example 83 consists of three simple sentences (83a, 83b and 83d), a possible coordinated sentence (83c) and a complex sentence (83e). Because of the intervention of Chinese-style commas, sentential boundaries are neutralized (i.e. commas are used to mark not only sentences but also structures within sentences) and can only be recovered through in-depth structural analysis. This is why 'extended sentence' seems a more practical term to use in Chinese running text than simply 'sentence'. The comma, on the other hand, can delineate anything from a phrase, to a sentence, to a structure longer than a sentence. It is useful in terms of semantic grouping and the segmentation of particularly lengthy structures (bearing in mind that a favorable reading span in Chinese is about 12 syllables), but it also releases confusing information that may be unhelpful to structural processing. To make this point clearer, in the next example, we examine another extended sentence by looking at comma-delineated units one at a time.

Example 84

a　日本　　　茨城县　　　　　　的　一　　所　　小学，
　　ri4ben3 ci4cheng2xian4　　de5 yi4　suo3　xiao3xue2
　　'Japan' 'Ibaraki Prefecture' AD 'one' Cla　'primary school'
　　'At an elementary school in Ibaraki prefecture in Japan

b　今天　　　白天　　举办　　校园　　　　运动会　　　　的　时候，
　　jin1tian1 bai2tian1 ju3ban4 xiao4yuan2 yun4dong4hui4 de5 shi2hou4
　　'today'　'daytime' 'hold'　'campus'　'sporting event' AD 'moment'
　　during the day, when a sporting event was held on campus,

c　操场　　　　上　　突然　　　出现　　　龙卷风，
　　cao1chang3 shang4 tu1ran2　chu1xian4 long2juan3feng1
　　'playground' 'up'　'suddenly' 'appear'　'hurricane'
　　a hurricane suddenly appeared above the playground.'

d　龙卷风　　　　威力　　强劲，
　　long2juan3feng1 wei1li4 qiang2jin4
　　'hurricane'　　　'power' 'strong'
　　'The hurricane was very powerful.'

e　把　操场　　　边　　的　帐棚　　　都　给　吹　翻　　　　了，
　　ba3 cao1chang3 bian1 de5 zhang4peng2 dou1 gei3 chui1 fan1　　le5
　　OB 'playground' 'side' AD 'tent'　　　'all' 'give' 'blow' 'overturn' AM
　　'(It) turned the canopy at the side of the playground upside down.'

f　小朋友　　　　们　吓　　得　四处　　　奔逃，
　　xiao3peng2you3 men5 xia4　de5 si4chu4　ben1tao2
　　'little-friend'　PM 'frighten' Com 'four-place' 'run-escape'
　　'Little children were scared into running in all directions.'

g　六　名　　学生　　　走避　　　不及，
　　liu4 ming2 xue2sheng1 zou3bi4　bu4ji2
　　'six' Cla　'student'　'walk-avoid' 'too late'
　　'Six students did not run away in time.'

h　受到　　　　轻伤。
　　shou4dao4　　qing1shang1
　　'endure-reach' 'light-wound'
　　'(They) received minor injuries.'

As can be seen from Example 84, the extended sentence is divided by seven commas into eight sections. Each section is either a sentence, a clause or an additional portion of a sentence, as shown in the structural analysis below:

a   NP (as a location phrase of c)
b   AP (adverbial clause to c)
c   S (main clause of a complex sentence)
d   S (simple sentence)
e   VP (additional predicate for d)
f   S (simple sentence)
g   S (simple sentence)
h   VP (additional predicate for g)

Chinese-style commas are therefore not very consistent in labeling structures since they are habitually used to mark miscellaneous units. The Chinese-style period, on the other hand, is more helpful, but it does not correspond to a sentence boundary in the way an English period does. Rather, as Examples 82–84 show, the Chinese-style period seems to mark the conclusion of a mini-story, a section of a longer narration, which normally consists of more than one sentence.

It may be tempting to equate the Chinese period to a paragraph marker based on the above demonstration, but, in many cases, two or more periods can appear in the same paragraph, splitting the paragraph into two or more conceptual units. In fact, the Chinese-style period is used to mark the end of a paragraph, an extended sentence, or even a simple sentence. The following example will illustrate this point. Example 85 is a Chinese text appearing as the third paragraph of a news report, extracted in original form for the reader to observe the three Chinese-style periods scattered about in this paragraph in addition to the period which concludes the paragraph. The text is further analyzed in Examples 86–89.

Example 85

据悉，安德森进入朋友家的前院时正在吃食物，几条狗扑上来抢食。可能她不肯给，导致疯狗向她发起进攻。目前尚不知悉狗主人的身份，经辨认其中两条为斗牛獒犬，另外两条为斯坦福斗牛㹴。它们均属于好斗犬类。

Example 85 consists of four units defined by the four Chinese-style periods. Each unit includes at least one sentence, as analyzed below:

Unit 1: one complex sentence, one simple sentence
Unit 2: a coordinated sentence
Unit 3: three simple sentences
Unit 4: one simple sentence

The first unit marked by a Chinese-style period is annotated in Example 86:

Example 86

a 据悉， 安德森 进入 朋友 家
 ju4xi1 an1de2sen1 jin4ru4 peng2you3 jia1
 'as reported' 'Anderson' 'enter' 'friend' 'home'

 的 前院 时 正在 吃 食物，
 de5 qian2yuan4 shi2 zheng4zai4 chi1 shi2wu4
 AD 'front yard' 'time' AM 'eat' 'food'

 'According to a report, Anderson was eating when she entered
 the front yard of a friend's home.

b 几 条 狗 扑 上来 抢食。
 ji3 tiao2 gou3 pu1 shang4lai2 qiang3shi2
 'a few' Cla 'dog' 'spring at' 'up-come' 'snatch-eat'
 A few dogs jumped forward to grab a bite.'

Example 86 is an extended sentence as defined in this book since it consists
of two simple sentences connected by a comma and ending with a Chinese-
style period. Semantically and pragmatically, it offers a prologue to the entire
story, paving the way for further development of the story. The next unit is a
coordinated sentence consisting of two simple sentences.

Example 87

a 可能 她 不肯 给，
 ke3neng2 ta1 bu4ken3 gei3
 'possible' 'she' 'not-willing' 'give'
 'Possibly she was unwilling to give (food to the dogs).

b 导致 疯狗 向 她 发起 进攻。
 dao3zhi4 feng1gou3 xiang4 ta1 fa1qi3 jin4gong1
 'result in' 'crazy-dog' 'toward' 'her' 'launch' 'attack'
 (This) caused the crazy dogs to launch an attack on her.'

The second unit of Example 85, shown above as Example 87, consists of two
sentences coordinated by a conjunctive device 'leading to'. By definition this is
a pair of well-coordinated sentences and is not an extended sentence. However,
the fact that it is demarcated by a Chinese-style period means it is a stand-alone
section of a story, a legitimate conceptual unit. In this case, the unit gives the main

theme of the story – that the girl was attacked by voracious dogs due to her unwillingness to share the food. The next unit consists of three simple sentences.

Example 88

a 目前　　尚　　不　知悉　狗　主人　　的　身份，
mu4qian2　shang4　bu4　zhi1xi1　gou3　zhu3ren2　de5　shen1fen4
'at present' 'yet'　'not' 'know' 'dog' 'host'　PB 'identity'
'So far the name of the dog owner is still unknown.

b 经　　　辨认　　　　其中　　两　　条　为　斗牛獒犬，
jing1　bian4ren4　　qi2zhong1　liang3　tiao2　wei2　dou4niu2ao2quan3
'through' 'identification' 'within'　'two' Cla 'be' 'bull mastiff'
Two of the dogs were identified to be the bull mastiff breed.

c 另外　　两　　条　为　斯坦福　斗牛㹴。
ling4wai4　liang3　tiao2　wei2　si1tan3fu2　dou4niu2 geng3
'the other' 'two' Cla 'be' 'Staffordshire bull terrier'
The other two (dogs) are Staffordshire bull terriers.'

By definition, Example 88 is an extended sentence as it consists of at least two stand-alone sentences. Although Examples 88b and 88c look like a pair of coordinated sentences, there is no overt conjunctive device. A cohesive device ('two of . . . , the other two . . .') does exist to reveal the connection between the two. Altogether, this extended sentence serves the pragmatic function of offering background information, implying who were to blame for the unusual event (which resulted in a girl's death).

The fourth and final unit in Example 85 is a short simple sentence which concludes the paragraph and is marked by a Chinese-style period.

Example 89

它们　　均　　属于　　好斗　　犬　　类。
ta1men5　jun1　shu3yu2　hao4dou4　quan3　lei4
'they'　'all' 'belong to' 'like-fight' 'dog' 'type'
'They all belong to the type of dogs which like fighting.'

Example 89 is, in fact, a meta-statement of Examples 88b and 88c, summarizing the traits of the two kinds of dogs involved. As its content resides on a more abstract level than the previous unit, it makes sense that it is separated from the main story by two Chinese-style periods (instead of it being preceded by a comma and subsumed into the previous ES). The 'conceptual demarcation' function and the legitimacy of the ES unit seem well supported by how this text is marked by punctuation.

In this section, we have seen how the term 'extended sentence' is useful for delineating a semantic-pragmatic unit which can span a few sentences. We have noted how the Chinese-style period is consistently used to demarcate an extended sentence, separating one conceptual unit from another in a text. Given that the period is also used to mark the end of a single sentence, we might consider the term of 'conceptual sentence' too, which is essentially what the Chinese period is used to demarcate.

3.13 SUMMARY AND CONCLUSION

In this chapter, we have adopted the concepts and terms habitually used to discuss English grammar to examine types of sentences in Chinese. Many similarities between English and Chinese sentences surfaced during the process. In particular, both languages appear to share the basic sentence structure of NP and VP, in the same order. Both languages also have the same types of independent clauses embedded in a complex sentence – nominal, adjectival and adverbial clauses. Within this largely homogeneous picture, however, there are dissimilarities which reveal the significant traits of Chinese sentences. For example, a simple Chinese sentence can have 'run-on VPs'; that is, several VPs predicating an NP without proper coordination between them. Two coordinated sentences can appear without an overt coordinating conjunction, just like a subordinate sentence can come without a subordinating conjunction. Mechanically, we also found the use of two main punctuation devices – the Chinese-style comma and period – to be very different from their English counterparts. In particular, the Chinese period carries out a more conceptual than grammatical function; it is often used to mark a distinct section of a narration (or argumentation). This offers the inspiration for the term 'extended sentence' used in this book to refer to a series of sentences marked by a Chinese-style period which form a conceptual or pragmatic unit in a text. The Chinese comma, on the other hand, can be used to mark a phrase, a sentence, or a structure longer than a sentence (before a semantic-pragmatic unit is concluded by a period).

CHAPTER 4

Speech acts

When a sentence is spoken in the real world (referred to as an 'utterance'), it carries with it the speaker's intention, the purpose it is supposed to fulfill and the likely effect it is going to have on the listener(s). From this perspective, the speaker is conducting a 'speech act' when they utter a sentence. In this chapter, we consider how native speakers of Chinese use language to do things. First we discuss different kinds of speech acts with authentic examples. Then we focus on how to ask questions in Chinese and how to create negative sentences.

4.1 SPEECH ACT CATEGORIES

Searle (1969) distinguishes five speech act categories:

- Representatives: Speaker asserts something believed to be true.
  - *She was a very good swimmer.*
- Directives: Speaker requests the listener to do something.
  - *Please keep your voice down!*
- Commissives: Speaker commits themself to a future course of action.
  - *We will always be there to support those who need help.*
- Expressives: Speaker reveals their psychological state.
  - *Thank you for the meat!*
- Declaratives: Speaker brings about a new state of affairs.
  - *You are now the registered owner of the property!*

These speech act categories are valid across all languages, including Chinese. Most of the sentences discussed in Chapter 3 are 'representatives', where speakers share something which they believe to be true. These will not be further discussed here. We also touched upon imperative sentences in Chapter 3 when discussing subjectless sentences. In English, an imperative normally starts with a verb (*Come in! Shut up!*); in Chinese many more varieties exist. We will have a closer look at the 'directive' sentences in this chapter. First we revisit the Chinese command starting with a verb, like those in English.

Example 1

a 等　　一下！
  deng3 yi2xia4
  'wait' 'one moment'
  'Wait a moment!'

b 帮　　个　忙　　　吧！
  bang1 ge5 mang2 ba5
  'help' Cla 'busy' SFP
  'Do me a favor!'

c 做　　完　　功课　　　去　睡觉！
  zuo4 wan2 gong1ke4 qu4 shui4jiao4
  'do' 'finish' 'homework' 'go' 'sleep'
  'Finish your homework (then) go to sleep!'

All the Chinese imperative sentences in Example 1 start with a verb, which translates into English sentences in a straightforward manner because of the structural correspondence. A sentence final particle (SFP) 吧 is added to the end of Example 1b to 'soften' the request. Example 1c includes two commands which would require a conjunction like *and* to join them in English.

In Chinese, it is possible to add an adverb in front of the verb in forming an imperative sentence. In English, it would be more acceptable to say *Walk slowly!* than **Slowly walk!*

Example 2

a 慢　　　走。
  man4 zou3
  'slowly' 'walk'
  'Take your time (leaving).'

b 快点　　　滚！
  kuai4dian3 gun3
  'quickly' 'roll'
  'Get out of my sight now!'

c 一定　　　要　　保密　　　哦！
  yi2ding4 yao4 bao3mi4 o2
  'definitely' 'must' 'keep-secret' SFP
  'Be sure to keep the secret!'

Instead of starting the command with a verb, sentences Examples 2a–c each start with an adverb – 'slowly', 'quickly' and 'definitely' respectively.

As in English, an honorific term like 请 'please' can be added to the front of an imperative to make the request more polite. However, this tends to happen only on formal occasions in Chinese where 请 is incorporated in fixed phrases such as that in Example 3a. Otherwise the word 请 is comparatively less heard in daily interactions. As a result, a Chinese person speaking English may sometimes 'forget' to use the word 'please' and may be (mistakenly) perceived to be 'impolite'. Conversely, a foreign language learner using the Chinese 请 too much may well be perceived to be too formal and 'pretentious'.

Example 3

a **请**   进!
   qing3 jin4
   'please' 'enter'
   'Please come in!'

b **麻烦**   填写   一下   问卷!
   ma2fan2 tian2xie3 yi2xia4 wen4juan4
   'trouble' 'fill-write' 'once' 'questionnaire'
   'Please take the trouble to fill in the questionnaire!'

c **拜托**   给   我   水   喝!
   bai4tuo1   gei3 wo3 shui3 he1
   'worship-entrust' 'give' 'me' 'water' 'drink'
   'Please give me (some) water to drink!'

d **求求**   你   再   回   到   我   身边!
   qiu2qiu2 ni3   zai4   hui2   dao4   wo3 shen1bian1
   'beg-beg' 'you' 'again' 'return' 'reach' 'I'   'body-side'
   'I beg you to return to my side again.'

The morpheme 请 in Example 3a coincides with the English *please* in function and meaning when used in a request. However, this is where the similarity ends. The Chinese 请, when used as a verb, means 'to invite', 'to treat with food' and so on (while the English *please* means 'to make happy'). Also different from English, apart from 请, there are other honorific items in Chinese with different degrees of formality, sincerity and urgency. For example, 麻烦, appearing in Example 3b, is at the same level of formality as the English *please*. Another term, 拜托, in Example 3c sounds much more sincere and urgent. The verb with duplicated morphemes, 求求, in Example 3d is the strongest form to be used in a request in terms of degree of urgency and desirability for the listener's action.

Unlike English imperatives, where the subject of the sentence is more frequently omitted, the Chinese imperative often includes the person it is addressed to in the sentence, which in most cases is the second person pronoun.

Example 4

a 你　明天　　早点　　来！
ni3　ming2tian1　zao3dian3　lai2
'you' 'tomorrow' 'early-bit' 'come'
'Come earlier tomorrow!'

b 请　　你　原谅　　　我！
qing3　ni3　yuan2liang4　wo3
'please' 'you' 'forgive'　'me'
'(Would) you please forgive me!'

Example 4a looks different from its appropriate English translation – the subject is omitted in the English imperative and the Chinese verb comes after the adverbs. In Example 4b, the second person pronoun 你 appears *after* 请.

A Chinese imperative sentence can also be a command or suggestion intended for the first person plural ('we'). Some examples follow:

Example 5

a 我们　　走！
wo3men5 zou3
'we'　　'walk'
'Let's go!'

b 大家　　来　打　麻将！
da4jia1　lai2　da3 ma2jiang4
'everyone' 'come' 'hit' 'mah-jong'
'Everyone come and play mah-jong!'

Example 5a starts with the so-called 'inclusive we' – the suggested action is for both the speaker and the listeners. In Example 5b, the term 大家 'big-home (everybody)' is used to address 'everyone within hearing range' and invite them to join in the proposed action.

The subject of an imperative sentence need not always be a pronoun. It can also be a common noun or a descriptive phrase, as the following examples show:

Example 6

a 司机　　们　　要　　注意　　　　　安全　　啊！
si1ji1　men5　yao4　zhu4yi4　　　an1quan2　a5
'driver' PM　'want' 'pay attention' 'safety'　SFP
'Motorists (you) must pay attention to safety!'

b 赞成　　　　的　举手！
zan3cheng2　de5　ju3shou3
'agree'　　AD 'raise-hand'
'Those who agree raise your hands!'

Example 6a addresses motorists as a whole, suggesting they should pay attention to road safety. Example 6b uses an adjective phrase to name the persons to whom the action is proposed.

Sometimes the first element of an imperative sentence is neither a description nor a named person, but is a term that is relevant to the proposed action. Some examples follow:

Example 7

a 头　　抬　　起来！
tou2　tai2　qi3lai2
'head' 'raise' 'get up'
'Raise (your) head!'

b 眼睛　　　看　这边！
yan3jing1　kan4　zhe4bian1
'eye'　　'see' 'this-side'
'Eyes (look) this way!'

c 掌声　　　　给　他　鼓励　　　一下！
zhang3sheng1 gei3　ta1　gu3li4　　yi2xia4
'palm-sound'　'give' 'him' 'encourage' 'one-bit'
'(Let's hear some) applause to give him a bit of encouragement!'

d 屋子　里　　的　灯　可以　关掉　　　了！
wu1zi5 li3　　de5 deng1 ke3yi3 guan1diao4 le5
'house' 'inside' AD 'lamp' 'can' 'turn off'　AM
'Lights in the house (you) can turn off!'

In Examples 7a and 7b, the addressee is told to perform some action related to one of their body parts – the head and the eyes respectively. These body parts appear as the first element of the imperative sentence. In 7c, the 'clapping sound' occupies the thematic position but it is only an 'instrument' in this command (the addressees being the plural 'you' who are invited by the speaker to join in the hand-clapping action). In 7d, 'light in the house' is the first element of the command, which again is the object of an action to be carried out by the hidden subject – the second person pronoun.

Thus, we saw that the first constituent in a Chinese imperative sentence can be a verb (like in English), an adverb, a polite word, a pronoun, a common noun, an adjective phrase, and so on. This is different from English, where an imperative sentence normally allows a verb, the word *please*, or occasionally the second person pronoun *you*, to occupy the thematic position.

While the 'directive' speech act represents the speaker's intention to get the addressee to do something, the 'commissive' represents a commitment made by the speaker to a future action; for example, when giving a promise. In English, this may be done by the overt use of a 'performative' verb such as 'promise' or by using a modal auxiliary like *will* or *shall* to show the determination of the speaker. In Chinese, performative verbs also exist, as well as auxiliaries revealing a speaker's commitment.

Example 8

a　我　**答应**　帮助　　你。
　　wo3　da1ying4　bang1zhu4　ni3
　　'I'　'promise'　'help'　　'you'
　　'I promise to help you.'

b　我　**愿意**　和　你　一起　　慢慢　　变　　老。
　　wo3　yuan4yi4　he2　ni3　yi4qi3　　man4man4　bian4　　lao3
　　'I'　'willing'　'with'　'you'　'together'　'slow-slow'　'transform'　'old'
　　'I am willing to gradually grow old together with you.'

Example 8a shows the use of the performative verb 'promise' which subsumes the speech act in its meaning. The auxiliary 愿意 in 8b, on the other hand, reveals the speaker's commitment to the proposed action.

The 'expressive' kind of speech act is less associated with a particular structure or type of sentence. This speech act can also be realized as a 'joint act' with some other speech act in the same host sentence. For example, *Shut up your big mouth!* not only conducts a 'directive' speech act, it also shows the speaker's strong emotion (i.e. being 'expressive'). A command given to the listener can be with or without personal feelings, as illustrated by the following pair of sentences.

Example 9

a 请   到   旁边   休息。
  qing3 dao4   pang2bian1 xiu1xi2
  'please' 'move to' 'the side'   'rest'
  'Please adjourn to the side to rest.'

b 滚   到   一边   去！
  gun3 dao4   yi4bian1 qu4
  'roll' 'move to' 'one-side' 'go'
  'Get away to the side!'

Both sentences in Example 9 ask the listener(s) to physically get away from the current location; that is, they both carry out a 'directive' function. However, in terms of emotion, Example 9a sounds formal and detached, whereas 9b seems loaded with anger and hatred. Therefore, we can say that Example 9a conducts a 'directive' speech act solely, while 9b carries out both 'directive' and 'expressive' functions. More Chinese sentences which include an 'expressive' speech act are shown in Example 10:

Example 10

a 你   这   个   骗子！
  ni3   zhe4 ge5 pian4zi5
  'you' 'this' Cla 'swindler'
  'You are such a liar!'

b 欢迎   你们   来   高雄   玩。
  huan1ying2 ni3men5 lai2   gao1xiong2 wan2
  'welcome'   'you' PM 'come' 'Kaohsiung' 'play'
  '(I) welcome you to Kaohsiung for a visit.'

c 我   下辈子   一定   要   嫁   给   你。
  wo3 xia4bei4zi5 yi2ding4 yao4 jia4   gei3 ni3
  'I'   'next life'   'certainly' 'want' 'marry' 'give' 'you'
  'I definitely want to marry you in my next life.'

d 打   死   你   这   个   混蛋！
  da3 si3   ni3 zhe4 ge5 hun2dan4
  'hit' 'dead' 'you' 'this' Cla 'mixed-egg'
  'I am beating you to death, asshole!'

Example 10a seems to carry out two speech acts simultaneously: a 'representative' act to convey the speaker's belief about the truthfulness of the statement, and an 'expressive' act to reveal the speaker's emotional state. Example 10b is an invitation ('directive') which also shows the speaker's positive and pleasant attitude ('expressive'). Example 10c shows the speaker's determination ('commissive') as well as revealing her deep affection for the addressee. Example 10d, while incorporating a performative verb 'hit to death' to reflect the action being taken, also shows the speaker's resentment toward the addressee.

The final category of speech act to be considered in Chinese is the 'declarative', where the speaker is said to bring about a new state of affairs, such as the boss saying *You are fired!* to an employee or the minister saying *I now pronounce you husband and wife* to a wedding couple. Some Chinese examples follow:

Example 11

a 我　宣布　　退出　　政坛。
wo3 xuan1bu4 tui4chu1 zheng4tan2
'I' 'announce' 'back-exit' 'politics-altar'
'I announce (my) retirement from politics.'

b 这　房子　　是　你的　了。
zhe4 fang2zi5 shi4 ni3de5 le5
'this' 'house ' 'is' 'your' SFP
'This house is now yours.'

c 你　向　　我　借　　的　钱　　不用　　还　　了。
ni3 xiang4 wo3 jie4 de5 qian2 bu2yong4 huan2 le5
'you' 'toward' 'me' 'borrow' AD 'money' 'not-use' 'return' SFP
'The money you borrowed from me no longer needs to be returned.'

The so-called 'felicity conditions' apply to declarative sentences. For example, for someone to say *You are fired!* they must have the authority to do so and in appropriate circumstances. For Example 11a to be valid, it must be said by a politician who is thinking about retiring or changing profession. The speaker in Example 11b must be a house owner who wishes to pass the ownership to someone else or a lawyer passing the legal documents on to a client. The addressee of Example 11c must really owe the speaker money in order for the statement to be valid.

Some utterances can cause ambiguity in speech act interpretation, like Example 12a below.

Example 12

a 下个   礼拜   我们   去   动物园
   xia4ge5 li3bai4 wo3men5 qu4 dong4wu4yuan2
   'next'   'week' 'we'   'go' 'animal-garden'
b We are scheduled to go to the zoo next week. [representative]
c (I promise) we will go to the zoo next week. [commissive]
d (I declare) we go to the zoo next week. [directive]

There are at least three ways to interpret Example 12a. In Example 12b, the sentence is considered to be a report of fact. The sentence is interpreted as a promise in Example 12c. Alternatively, it can be interpreted as a command ('I give an order for us to go to the zoo next week') as in Example 12d.

4.2 QUESTIONS

Because using questions to request information (i.e. a 'directive' speech act) is a very important function of language, different ways of asking questions in Chinese are discussed separately in this section.

4.2.1 Yes/no questions

There are many ways of asking yes/no questions in Chinese, just as there are in English. In English, a yes/no question is asked using an auxiliary like *be* (Are you ready?), *do* (Did you know?), *have* (Have they survived?), *can*, *may*, *will* and so on. In Chinese, the same questions can be asked but in entirely different ways; for example, by using a sentence-final particle (SFP) or an A-not-A construction. The easiest way of asking a yes/no question in Chinese is to attach the SFP 吗 to the end of a statement, which instantly turns the statement into a question. Two questions as a result of this operation are shown in Example 13:

Example 13

a 日语   好学   吗?
   ri4yu3   hao3xue2   ma5
   'Japanese' 'good-learn' QM
   'Is Japanese easy to learn?'

b 这   个   世界   需要   核能   吗?
   zhe4 ge5 shi4jie4 xu1yao4 he2neng2   ma5
   'this' Cla 'world' 'need'   'nuclear-energy' QM
   'Does this world need nuclear energy?'

Both questions in Example 13 are created by adding 吗 to the end of a declarative sentence. The removal of this SFP instantly turns the question back into a statement. If 吗 is deleted from Example 13a, for example, the question is reverted to a claim that 'Japanese is easy to learn'. The same is true for Example 13b: if 吗 is removed, what remains is a conviction that 'the world needs nuclear energy'.

Another question particle equal to 吗 in function but much less used is 么. This morpheme, used as a question marker, only appears in written Chinese and not in the spoken language. Two examples copied from the web are shown in Example 14:

Example 14

a 你   孤单   么?
  ni3 gu1dan1 mo5
  'you' 'lonesome' QM
  'Are you lonesome?'

b 这   是   传说   中   的 水怪   么?
  zhe4 shi4 chuan2shuo1 zhong1 de5 shui3guai4   mo5
  'this' 'be' 'legend'   'in'   AD 'water-monster' QM
  'Is this the legendary water monster?'

Another way to ask yes/no questions in Chinese is to use the A-not-A construction, where A is (the first syllable of) an auxiliary, a verb, an adjective, and so on. Two examples of A-not-A questions using auxiliaries are presented in Example 15:

Example 15

a 孕妇   能   不 能   吃   芒果?
  yun4fu4   neng2 bu4 neng2 chi1 mang2guo3
  'pregnant-woman' 'can' 'not' 'can' 'eat' 'mango'
  'Can pregnant women eat mango?'

b 英国   该   不 该   退出   欧盟?
  ying1guo2 gai1 bu4 gai1 tui4chu1 ou1meng2
  'UK'   'should' 'not' 'should' 'back out' 'EU'
  'Should Britain get out of the European Union?'

A-not-A questions as shown in Example 15 are essentially a kind of yes/no question because they require either a positive (yes) or a negative (no) answer.

An easier way to conceptualize the Chinese A-not-A construction is to group it into the (A) (not-A) configuration and to understand the question as demanding a choice between (A) or (not-A). For example, Example 15a asks the reader to provide an opinion as to whether a pregnant woman can eat mango or not. The author of Example 15b, on the other hand, probes the question of whether the UK should leave the EU or not.

Two frequently seen A-not-A constructions are the [*shi4* not *shi4*] and the [*you3* not *you3*] constructions. One example of each is provided in Example 16:

Example 16

a 今天　　是　不　是　母亲节？
　 jin1tian1　shi4　bu2　shi4　mu3qin1jie2
　 'today'　'be'　'not'　'be'　'mother-festival'
　 'Is today Mother's day?'

b 世界　　上　　到底　　　有　没　有　鬼？
　 shi4jie4　shang4　dao4di3　　　you3　mei2　you3　gui3
　 'world'　'up'　　'reach-bottom'　'have'　'not'　'have'　'ghost'
　 'Are there ghosts at all in the world?'

Both questions in Example 16 require only a 'yes' or a 'no' answer. While Example 16a asks the reader to confirm the identity of 'today' using the linking verb 是, 16b uses the existential verb 有 to request info about whether there are ghosts in the world. Note that when the 'A' is 有 in the A-not-A construction, the 'not' is represented by 没 rather than the usual 不. This is because 没有 is an established combination, while *不有 is not.

The A-not-A construction also applies to Chinese adjectives and verbs to form yes/no questions in a quick way, as Example 17 shows.

Example 17

a 狗　吃　不　吃　水果？
　 gou3　chi1　bu4　chi1　shui3guo3
　 'dog'　'eat'　'not'　'eat'　'fruit'
　 'Do dogs eat fruit?'

b 你　喜　不　喜欢　　小孩子？
　 ni3　xi3　bu4　xi3huan1　xiao3hai2zi5
　 'you'　'like'　'not'　'like'　'children'
　 'Do you like children?'

Note that when a disyllabic unit is used in an A-not-A construction, only the first syllable is needed in the first A position (while the full two-syllable unit is required for the second A), as in Example 17b.

The A-not-A construction can sometimes be replaced by an X-否 construction where 否 means 'not X'. Therefore [X *fou3*] equals X-not-X in meaning. This usage occurs almost exclusively in written language. Some examples are given in Example 18:

Example 18

a 无糖　　食品　　**是 否**　真的　　无糖？
　 wu2tang2 shi2pin3 shi4 fou3 zhen1de5 wu2tang2
　 'no-sugar' 'food' 　'yes' 'no' 'real' 　'no-sugar'
　 'Is sugar-free food really free from sugar?'

b 中药　　　　　**能 否** 治好　　糖尿病？
　 zhong1yao4　　　neng2 fou3 zhi4hao3　tang2niao4bing4
　 'Chinese medicine' 'can ' 'not' 'treat-well' 'diabetes'
　 'Can traditional Chinese medicine cure diabetes?'

The 是否 in Example 18a equals 是不是 and the 能否 in Example 18b equals 能不能 in both meaning and function. The former normally appears in written documents, the latter primarily in oral communication.

4.2.2 Alternative questions

To answer an alternative question, the hearer or reader only has to choose one from the two or more options provided. In English, alternative questions are made using a coordinating conjunction like *or* (e.g. Deal *or* no deal?). In Chinese, equivalent items exist such as 还是 and 或是, both of which mean 'or'. Two examples are provided in Example 19.

Example 19

a 先　　有　　鸡　　**还是**　先　　有　　蛋？
　 xian1　you3　ji1　　hai2shi4 xian1　you3　dan4
　 'earlier' 'have' 'chicken' 'or'　'earlier' 'have' 'egg'
　 'Which came first, the chicken or the egg?'

b 单身　　　比较　　好　　**或是**　结婚　　比较　　好？
　 dan1shen1 bi3jiao4　hao3　huo4shi4 jie2hun1　bi3jiao4　hao3
　 'single'　'compare' 'good' 'or'　'marriage' 'compare' 'good'
　 'Is being single better or being married better?'

Example 19a shows one of the most frequently used devices for making Chinese alternative questions – 还是. Example 19b shows another one – 或是. The morpheme 或 can also be used alone or in another combination, 或者, to mean the same thing ('or').

There are other ways of making alternative questions, although these are much less frequently seen in comparison to those in Example 19. One of the methods is using 哪个 'which one?' following a list of two or more items. Two examples are given in Example 20:

Example 20

a 石英　　　表　　和　　机械　　　　表　　　**哪个**　　　　好?
　 shi2ying1　biao3　he2　ji1xie4　　　biao3　na3ge5　　　hao3
　 'quartz'　'watch'　'and'　'mechanics'　'watch'　'which one'　'good'
　 'Quartz watch and mechanical watch – which is better?'

b 美国　　　加拿大　　　新加坡　　　和　　澳大利亚,
　 mei3guo2　jia1na2da4　xin1jia1po1　he2　ao4da4li4ya3
　 'USA'　　'Canada'　　'Singapore'　'and'　'Australia'

　 你　　会　　选择　　　**哪个**　　移民?
　 ni3　hui4　xuan3ze2　na3ge5　yi2min2
　 'you'　'will'　'select'　　'which'　'emigrate'

　 'Where will you choose to emigrate to – USA, Canada, Singapore, or Australia?'

Both questions in Example 20 take the form of a list followed by a question. First, a list of usually two items is provided, then the hearer or reader is asked to pick one. This is the case in Example 20a. For Example 20b, however, the list consists of four items and the reader is asked to choose the most preferred option.

4.2.3 'Wh-' questions

Again, all the *wh-* questions that can be asked in English (*Who?, What?, Why?, How?*) can be asked in Chinese. However, there is a fundamental difference in the machinery for generating *wh-* questions between Chinese and English. In English, all the *wh-* questions have to start with a *wh-* word (e.g. *What would you like?*). In Chinese, the *wh-* word remains 'where it should be' in the question. For example, the question 'What would you like?' in Chinese becomes 你喜欢甚么? ('You like *what?*'). Being the object of the verb 'like', the Chinese *wh-* word remains where the object of 'like' would be in the sentence – directly after the verb, whereas in English, *what* is interposed to the front of the question. The difference is captured graphically in Figure 4.1.

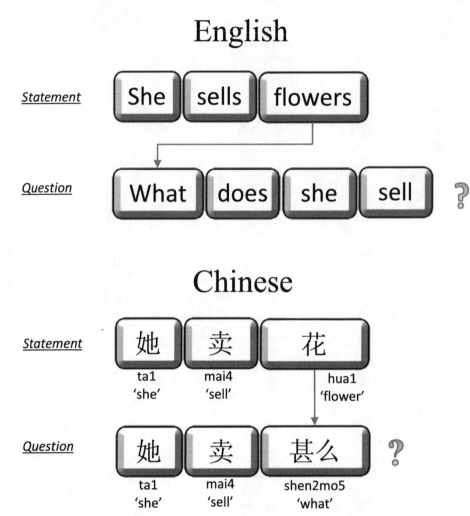

Figure 4.1 The different locations of the *wh-* word in English and Chinese

As Figure 4.1 shows, unlike English where all question words are placed at the front, the Chinese *wh-* word stays where the answer word should be in the corresponding statement. Thus, in terms of 'what', there is a wide range of possible positions for it in a Chinese question, as Example 21 shows.

Example 21

a 你　　想　　说　　**什么**?
　ni3　xiang3　shuo1　shen2mo5
　'you'　'think'　'say'　'what'
　'What would you like to say?'

b 世界　　上　　**什么**　　最　　幸福?
　shi4jie4　shang4　shen2mo5　zui4　xing4fu2
　'world'　'up'　'what'　　'most'　'happy'
　'What is the happiest (thing) in the world?'

c 生命　　　的　目的　　是　**什么**?
　sheng1ming4　de5　mu4di4　shi4　shen2mo5
　'life'　　　AD　'objective'　'be'　'what'
　'What is the purpose of life?'

d 有机　　食品　　是　**什么**　　意思?
　you3ji1　shi2pin3　shi4　shen2mo5　yi4si5
　'organic'　'food'　'be'　'what'　　'meaning'
　'What is the meaning of organic food?'

The word 什么 (sometimes written as 甚么) plays different grammatical roles in the questions of Example 21. In Example 21a, 什么 is the object of the verb 'say'. In Example 21b, it is the subject of the sentence. In Example 21c, 什么 is the complement following the linking verb 是 to explain the subject. In Example 21d, 什么 functions as an adjective to modify 'meaning'. As can be seen, all these instances of 什么 are placed at the slot where the answer would have been if the sentence were a statement rather than a question. This is like saying *He knows what?* rather than *What does he know?* in English.

Like 'what', the *wh*- word representing 'who' in Chinese is a noun and appears in similar positions (except in 21d, where 什么 is used as an adjective). Example 22 offers two questions involving the use of 谁.

Example 22

a **谁**　偷　了　我　的　钱?
　shei2　tou1　le5　wo3　de5　qian2
　'who'　'steal'　AM　'I'　PD　'money'
　'Who stole my money?'

b 请问　　　你　找　**谁**?
　qing3wen4　ni3　zhao3　shei2
　'please-ask'　'you'　'seek'　'who'
　'Please (can I ask) who are you calling on?'

In Example 22a, 谁 is the subject of the sentence that 'stole the money'. In Example 22b, 谁 is the object of the verb 'seek'.

So far we have seen *wh-* words as nouns, i.e. 甚么 and 谁. Undoubtedly, there are also adverbial question words in Chinese equivalent to the English *when* and *where*. Examples of Chinese question words regarding location are given in Example 23.

Example 23

a 风　从　**哪里**　来?
　 feng1 cong2 na3li3 lai2
　 'wind' 'from' 'where' 'come'
　 'Where does the wind come from?'

b 毕业　　后，你　想　　去　**哪**?
　 bi4ye4　 hou4 ni3 xiang3 qu4 na3
　 'graduate' 'after' 'you' 'think' 'go' 'where'
　 'Where would you like to go after graduation?'

c 神　　啊　你　在　**哪儿**?
　 shen2 a5　ni3　zai4 na3er5
　 'God' SFP 'you' 'at' 'where'
　 'Where are you, God?'

d 第一次　　约会　　该　　去　**哪边**?
　 di4yi2ci4　yue1hui4 gai1　 qu4 na3bian1
　 'first-time' 'date'　 'should' 'go' 'where'
　 'Where should one go for a first date?'

First of all, we notice that the Chinese equivalent of *where* behaves more like a noun rather than an adverb. For example, in 23a, the question word 哪里 forms a prepositional phrase with the preceding preposition 从, a characteristic of a noun. The same is true for Example 23c. In Examples 23b and 23d, on the other hand, both 哪 and 哪边 serve as the object of the verb 去 'go' (which is a transitive verb in Chinese), again the regular function of a noun.

The prototypical form of Chinese *where* is 哪里, which appears in Example 23a. However, there are various other forms which all mean the same thing, as shown in Examples 23b–d. Note that all of these variants contain the morpheme 哪, which can also stand alone as in Example 23b.

The morpheme 哪 in Example 23b, when standing alone, can mean 'where'. However, 哪 has a broader meaning somewhat equivalent to 'which' if followed by a classifier; for example, 哪个? 'Which one?', 哪种? 'Which kind?', 哪位? 'Which person?' and so on. The orthographic form of *na3*, represented in Example 13 as 哪, is easily confused with another syllable *na4* 那 'there'. To make the matter worse, some native speakers do not distinguish between the two in writing and use the latter (那) to represent both *na3* and *na4* orthographically. Because of the position of question words in Chinese, a declarative sentence containing 那 and a question using 哪 can look exactly the same apart from the ending punctuation marks. An example is given in Example 24 below to illustrate this point.

Example 24

a 天堂　　　在　那里?
   tian1tang2 zai4 na3li3
   'heaven'　'at'　'where'
   'Where is heaven?'

b 天堂　　　在　那里。
   tian1tang2 zai4 na4li3
   'heaven'　'at'　'there'
   'Heaven is there.'

Example 24a is an actual sentence, used as a question on the web. As already mentioned, many people do not distinguish between 哪 and 那 orthographically and use 那 instead of 哪 for a question. An unambiguous orthographic form for Example 24a is 天堂在哪里. However, when the question is written as 天堂在那里, as in Example 24a, it is indistinguishable from Example 24b, which is a statement. To recognize 24b as a question, the reader will have to rely on the help of the context.

As for the Chinese question words concerning time, there is no predominant form like 哪里 which asks about the location. Several forms are possible for asking about the time. Some examples are provided in Example 25:

Example 25

a 一天　　中　　**哪时**　血压　　　　最　　高?
   yi4 tian1　zhong1　na3shi2　xie3ya1　　　zui4　gao1
   'one-day' 'middle' 'when'　'blood pressure' 'most' 'high'
   'When is the blood pressure highest in a day?'

b 女人　　**几时**　结婚　　最好?
   nv3ren2 ji3shi2 jie2hun1 zui4hao3
   'woman' 'when' 'marry'　'most-good'
   'When is the best time for women to get married?'

c 看　电影　　　**何时**　可　上　　洗手间?
   kan4 dian4ying3　he2shi2 ke3　shang4 xi3shou3jian1
   'see' 'movie'　　'when' 'may' 'up'　'wash-hand-room'
   'When can one go to the lavatory when watching a movie?'

d 你　**什么**　　**时候**　下班?
   ni3　shen2mo5 shi2hou4 xia4ban1
   'you' 'what'　　'moment' 'down-shift'
   'When are you off work?'

Table 4.1 Comparison of the frequency of question words for place and time

Place		Time	
Question word	*Google hits*	*Question word*	*Google hits*
哪里	256,000,000	哪时	1,570,000
哪儿	79,200,000	几时	4,030,000
哪边	2,350,000	何时	20,000,000
		什么时候	46,400,000

Note: As of 1 January 2014

If the locational question word 哪里 behaves like a noun, the temporal question words introduced in Example 25 behave more like adverbs. A typical position for an adverb to appear within a Chinese sentence is between the subject and the verb; for example, 我昨天病了 'I fell ill *yesterday*', 他渐渐变老 'He *gradually* becomes old' and so on. Similarly, the time question word 几时 appears between the subject and the verb in Example 25b. If a location question word like 哪里 is placed in a similar slot, a preposition is normally required, for example, 你在哪里读书 'You-*at*-where-study?'

The question word appearing in Example 25a is the rough equivalent of 哪里 of Example 23a in the dimension of time. However, it is not overwhelmingly popular as a question word about time. There are more popular forms, like 几时 and 何时, but, predominantly, the most common usage is 什么时候, especially in the spoken language. Table 4.1 offers a comparison of frequency of usage among various question words in terms of both place and time.

As suggested by Table 4.1, the most popular item for asking about location is 哪里 and the most frequently used item for asking about time is 什么时候. All the other question words are much less used than these two terms.

Like other question words, there is also more than one Chinese counterpart for the English *wh-* question word *how*, asking about the manner in which something is done. Some possible Chinese equivalents of *how* are shown in Example 26:

Example 26

a 你 怎 知道？
ni3 zen3 zhi1dao4
'you' 'how' 'know'
'How do you know?'

b 螃蟹 怎么 吃？
pang2xie4 zen3mo5 chi1
'crab' 'how' 'eat'
'How do you eat a crab?'

c 怎样 取得 驾驶 执照？
zen3yang4 qu3de2 jia4shi3 zhi2zhao4
'how' 'obtain' 'drive' 'license'
'How do you obtain a driving license?'

d 怎么样 才 能 生 儿子？
zen3mo5yang4 cai2 neng2 sheng1 er2zi5
'how' 'just' 'can' 'bear' 'son'
'What can one do in order to give birth to a son?'

e 中国 领导人 是 如何 产生 的？
zhong1guo2 ling3dao3ren2 shi4 ru2he2 chan3sheng1 de5
'China' 'lead-person' 'be' 'how' 'produce' ED
'How are the leaders of China produced?'

Example 26 first shows a series of questions all using a variant of 怎 'how'. A completely different form of 'how', 如何, then appears in Example 26e, which is more often used in writing than in the spoken language. The morpheme 怎 is the simplest form of 'how' in Chinese and is rarely used alone. It can combine with 么 or 样 or both into three different configurations as shown in Examples 26b–d, all of which have identical meaning and function.

A phrase which Chinese speakers often use as an extension of 怎 is 怎么办, which means 'What can one do?' Two examples illustrating the usage of 怎么办 are given in Example 27:

Example 27

a 电脑 中毒 怎么办？
dian4nao3 zhong4du2 zen3mo5ban4
'computer' 'poisoned' 'how-do'
'What to do when a computer is infected?'

b 我 被 骗 了 怎么办？
wo3 bei4 pian4 le5 zen3mo5ban4
'I' PB 'swindle' AM 'how-do'
'I was swindled, what can I do?'

It can be seen from Example 27 that 怎么办 normally occurs at the end of a sequence (or it may also act as an independent utterance). Usually an event is given as a premise and, in the face of some dire consequences, the speaker solicits advice on what to do next.

The final *wh-* word to tackle is *why*, for which there is a prototypical form: 为什么 'for-what'. There are also variant forms such as 为啥 and 为何. Some examples are given in Example 28:

Example 28

a 人　　　为什么　　　会　变　　老？
　ren2　　wei4shen2mo5　hui4　bian4　lao3
　'person'　'why'　　　　'will'　'become'　'old'
　'Why do people get old?'

b 为什么　　　　二月　　只有　　28　　　天？
　wei4shen2mo5　er4yue4　zhi3you3　er4shi2ba1　tian1
　'why'　　　　'February'　'only'　'28'　　'day'
　'Why are there only 28 days in February?'

c 生病　　　　为什么　　　要　打针？
　sheng1bing4　wei4shen2mo5　yao4　da3zhen1
　'fall ill'　　　'why'　　　　'want'　'strike-needle'
　'Why do we get injections when falling ill?'

d 飞机　　上　　为啥　　禁止　使用　　手机？
　fei1ji1　shang4　wei4sha2　jin4zhi3　shi3yong4　shou3ji1
　'airplane'　'up'　'why'　'forbid'　'use'　'hand-machine'
　'Why do they forbid the use of cell phones on airplanes?'

e 金价　　　为何　暴跌？
　jin1jia4　wei4he2　bao4die2
　'gold-price'　'why'　'violent-fall'
　'Why does the gold price slump?'

In Example 28a, 为什么 as an adverbial question word appears between the subject 'people' and the verb 'can grow old'. In Example 28b, 为什么 appears at the beginning of a question, followed by a full sentence. In Example 28c, a condition is given ('being ill') before a question is asked about the necessity of an injection. Example 28d uses a colloquial form of 为什么, that is, 为啥, which has no place in formal language. On the contrary, 为何, as shown in Example 28e, is mostly used in written language.

Another common question morpheme is 几 'how many', often used to ask about quantities of countable things. It is normally coupled with a classifier. Some examples follow in Example 29.

Example 29

a 你   今年   几   岁？
  ni3 jin1nian2   ji3   sui4
  'you' 'present-year' 'how many' 'year of age'
  'How old are you this year?'

b 你 穿   几   号   鞋？
  ni3 chuan1 ji3   hao4   xie2
  'you' 'wear' 'how many' 'number' 'shoe'
  'What size shoes do you wear?'

c 今天   星期 几？
  jin1tian1   xing1qi2 ji3
  'present-day' 'week' 'how-many'
  'What day is today?'

The quantity question item 几 is normally followed by a classifier specific to a certain category of nouns. In Example 29a, this is 岁, normally used to describe living things which can age. In Example 29b, the classifier is 号, which is widely used to label clothing, sports goods, objects in a series, and so on. In Example 29c, however, 几 appears in an unusual position – it follows a noun 'week' rather than preceding a classifier. This is because days of a week are said in this way in Chinese: 星期一 'week-one' for Monday, 星期二 'week-two' for Tuesday and so on. To question what day of the week it is, the number is replaced by the morpheme 几, which, according to the Chinese *wh*-question formation rule, appears at the same place as the expected answer (i.e. the number). Thus 星期几 'week how-many' means 'What day of the week?' When 几 precedes 星期, however, to become 几星期, then it means 'How many weeks?' instead, as is the normal usage of 几 (i.e. being followed by a unit for counting).

Another frequently used question item concerning quantity is 多 'plenty'. Some example usages involving this morpheme appear in Example 30:

Example 30

a 地球　有　　多　　重?
di4qiu2 you3 duo1 zhong4
'Earth' 'have' 'much' 'heavy'
'How heavy is the Earth?'

b 你　的　智商　　　　有　多　　高?
ni3　de5 zhi4shang1　　you3 duo1 gao1
'you' PD 'wisdom-quotient' 'have' 'much' 'high'
'How high is your IQ?'

c 吸烟　　　的　危害　　　有　多　　大?
xi1yan1　　de5 wei2hai4　　you3 duo1 da4
'inhale-smoke' PD 'danger-harm' 'have' 'much' 'big'
'How great is the danger from smoking?'

d 北京　　到　香港　　　有　多　　远?
bei3jing1 dao4 xiang1gang3 you3 duo1 yuan3
'Beijing' 'reach' 'Hong Kong' 'have' 'much' 'far'
'How far is it from Beijing to Hong Kong?'

e 玉米　　煮　多　久　才　　　　能　熟?
yu4mi3　zhu3 duo1 jiu3 cai2　　　neng2 shou2
'jade-rice' 'cook' 'much' 'long' 'subsequently' 'able' 'ripe'
'How long does sweet corn have to be cooked to be ready to eat?'

Note that in English, when asking about the measurement of something, by default we use words on the 'top end' (How *tall*?) rather than those on the 'bottom end' (How *short*?) The same is true for Chinese. Hence, we have 'How heavy?' in Example 30a, 'How tall?' in 30b, 'How big?' in 30c, 'How far?' in 30d and 'How long?' in 30e, all consisting of the morpheme 多 and a 'top end' measure morpheme like 高, 大 and so on.

A fixed combination involving the use of 多 is 多少 literally 'many-few' but meaning 'How many?' or 'How much?' This is a very frequently used question word to ask about quantities.

Example 31

a 人体　　　正常　　　体温　　　是　多少？
ren2ti3　　　zheng4chang2　ti3wen1　　　shi4　duo1shao3
'human-body'　'normal'　　　'body-warm'　'be'　'how much'
'How many (degrees) is the normal human body temperature?'

b 到　　美国　　上　　大学　　　需要　　多少　　　钱？
dao4　mei3guo2　shang4　da4xue2　xu1yao4　duo1shao3　qian2
'go to'　'USA'　　'up'　'university'　'need'　'how much'　'money'
'How much money do you need to go to a university in USA?'

In Example 31a, 多少 is used to ask about normal human body temperature. Temperature is counted using the measure morpheme 度 'degree' but it can be omitted in the presence of 多少. In Example 31b, 多少 is followed directly by a noun 钱, which normally does not come with a classifier when collocating with 多少 in a question.

A final question phrase to conclude this section is 干嘛 which is an abbreviated form of 干什么, literally 'do-what'. This is a very frequently used colloquial expression. Some examples of its usage follow in Example 32.

Example 32

a 快　暑假　　　　　　了，大家　　要　干嘛？
kuai4　shu3jia4　　　　le5　da4jia1　yao4　gan4ma2
'quick'　'summer-holiday'　SFP　'everybody'　'want'　'do-what'
'Summer holidays are approaching; what will everybody be doing?'

b 要　这样　　　的　环保　　　　署长　　干嘛？
yao4　zhe4yang4　de5　huan2bao3　　　shu3zhang3　gan4ma2
'want'　'this-type'　AD　'environment-protect'　'director'　'do-what'
'What do we want this kind of director of environmental protection for?'

Example 32a is a genuine question asking the addressee what they intend to do in summer. Example 32b is a rhetorical question which does not expect any answer. Both 干嘛 and 干什么 are very frequently used expressions and can stand alone to mean 'What are you doing?', 'What do you want?' and so on, depending on the context. Both expressions are somewhat rude and the more polite form for both is 做甚么 'do-what'.

4.3 NEGATION

All of the five speech act categories mentioned in 4.1 can be negated. For example, one could use the negative form of a 'representative' to assert something which they believe to be false. A negative 'directive' would involve telling someone *not* to do something. In this section, we explore some of the most frequently used negation words or structures.

There is more than one functional item which can be used for negation in Chinese. The most widely used is 不 'not', which can work at many levels of the language to create a sense of negation. First of all, it combines with other morpheme(s) to form established lexical units such as those shown below:

- Disyllabic items

  - 不错 *bu2cuo4* 'not-wrong (not bad; good)'
  - 不行 *bu4xing2* 'not-able (no good; not allowed)'

- Trisyllabic items (不 = 1st syllable)

  - 不舒服 *bu4shu1fu2* 'not-comfortable (unwell)'
  - 不一样 *bu4yi2yang4* 'not-same (different)'

- Trisyllabic items (不 = 2nd syllable)

  - 对不起 *dui4bu4qi3* 'match-not-rise (I am sorry)'
  - 受不了 *shou4bu4liao3* 'receive-not-end (cannot stand)'

- Quadrisyllabic item

  - 不知不觉 *bu4zhi1bu4jue2* 'not-know-not-feel (unaware)'
  - 不好意思 *bu4hao3yi4si5* 'not-good-meaning (embarrassed)'

In English, some antonyms are created by adding a negative prefix such as *un-* to the positive term (e.g. *comfortable* vs. *uncomfortable*). In Chinese, 不 carries out the function of a negative prefix and creates antonyms from existing words, such as 不一样 'different' derived from 一样 'same'.

When 不 occurs in a phrase or sentence, it normally precedes a verb, an adjective, or an auxiliary, for example:

Example 33

a 明天　　　不　会　下雨。
ming2tian1 bu2 hui4 xia4yu3
'tomorrow' 'not' 'will' 'down-rain'
'It will not rain tomorrow.'

b 人民　　　不　应该　　怕　　政府。
ren2min2 bu4 ying1gai1 pa4 zheng4fu3
'civilian' 'not' 'should' 'afraid' 'government'
'People should not be afraid of the government.'

In negating an English auxiliary, *not* is added after the auxiliary (e.g. *will not*); whereas in Chinese, the negative device 不 comes *before* the auxiliary as the negative sentences in Example 33 show.

In modern English, verbs are not directly negated using the negative element *not*; instead, a dummy symbol *do* is added to form a negative structure consisting of two words (i.e. *do not*, *did not* and so on). In Chinese, as happens with the auxiliary, 不 again directly prefixes the verb to form a negative structure, as shown in Example 34:

Example 34

a 我　　不　　喜欢　　　考试。
　　wo3　bu4　xi3huan1　kao3shi4
　　'I'　'not'　'like'　　'exam'
　　'I do not like exams.'

b 人　　　可以　多久　　　　不　吃　东西？
　　ren2　　ke3yi3　duo1jiu3　　bu4　chi1　dong1xi1
　　'person'　'can'　'how long'　'not'　'eat'　'thing'
　　'How long can a person live without eating anything?'

In both sentences above, the negative morpheme 不 directly precedes a verb to negate it. Unlike English, no extra element is needed to perform the negation apart from the negative morpheme 不 itself.

The Chinese verb is often followed by a complement of some sort which describes the result, extent, direction etc. of the action; for example, 坐下 'sit-down', 擦干 'wipe-dry', 饿死 'starve-dead', 跑出去 'run-exit' and so on. For this kind of verb-complement structure, there are two possible locations where the negative morpheme 不 can be placed. If 不 is attached to the front of the entire structure, it denies the whole action-result sequence. If 不 is inserted *between* the verb and the complement, it has no effect on the verb but denies the consequence of the action solely. Thus, for the positive Example 35a, there are two possible ways to negate it, shown in Examples 35b and 35c respectively.

Example 35

a 我们   冲   出去!
   wo3men5 chong1 chu1qu4
   'we'   'dash'   'exit'
   'Let's dash out!'

b 我们   **不** 冲   出去。
   wo3men5 bu4 chong1 chu1qu4
   'we'   'not' 'dash'   'exit'
   'We are not going to dash out.'

c 我们   冲   **不** 出去。
   wo3men5 chong1 'bu4' chu1qu4
   'we'   'dash'   'not' 'exit'
   'There is no way we could dash out.'

Example 35a is a 'directive', which can be a command given by the leader of a group of soldiers trapped in a besieged house, for example. Example 35b is then opposing the proposal of dashing out. Example 35c is a pessimistic evaluation of the proposal. In practice, the [V 不 Com] construction of 35c is much more frequently seen than the [不 V Com] structure in 35b. Two more sentences like Example 35c are shown in Example 36 below.

Example 36

a 降落伞   故障   **打 不 开**。
   jiang4luo4san3 gu4zhang4   da3 bu4 kai1
   'parachute'   'malfunction' 'hit' 'not' 'open'
   'The parachute malfunctions and cannot be opened.'

b 你 说   什么   我 **听**   **不**   **懂**。
   ni3 shuo1 shen2mo5 wo3 ting1 bu4 dong3
   'you' 'say' 'what'   'I'   'listen' 'not' 'understand'
   'I don't understand what you are saying.'

As previously explained, for the basic [V Com] structure 打开, two possible negative forms exist: **不打开** which means 'not trying to open' and **打不开** which means 'try to but fail to open'. Thus, Example 36a shows the more frequently used option: 'fail to open'. Similarly, we have 听不懂 in 36b which means 'have listened but failed to understand'.

     We have seen how a [V Com] unit can be negated using the form [V 不 Com]. In fact, there is a related form, [V 得 Com], which means that the result can indeed be achieved by the proposed action; for example, 打破 means to break something. There are four related expressions, like these, in Example 37.

Example 37

a 打 破 传统 不断 进化。
  da3 po4 chuan2tong3 bu2duan4 jin4hua4
  'hit' 'broken' 'tradition' 'incessantly' 'evolve'
  'Break the tradition and evolve continuously.'

b 不 打 破 传统 就 没有 出路。
  bu4 da3 po4 chuan2tong3 jiu4 mei2you3 chu1lu4
  'not' 'hit' 'broken' 'tradition' 'then' 'none' 'exit-road'
  'Without breaking the tradition there is no future prospect.'

c 这 是 打 不 破 的 传统。
  zhe4 shi4 da3 bu2 po4 de5 chuan2tong3
  'this' 'be' 'hit' 'not' 'broken' AD 'tradition'
  'This is an unbreakable tradition.'

d 我们 打 得 破 这 个 传统 吗?
  wo3men5 da3 de5 po4 zhe4 ge5 chuan2tong3 ma5
  'we' 'hit' 'get' 'broken' 'this' Cla 'tradition' QM
  'Are we able to break this tradition?'

The basic [V Com] form 打破 in Example 37a means causing something to break by hitting − in this case, abstract tradition rather than tangible things. Example 37b, with the negative morpheme 不 external to the entire [V Com] structure, denies both the action of breaking and the resultant state of the tradition being broken. Example 37c, on the other hand, uses the [V 不 Com] construction to deny the possibility of a broken tradition even if the action of breaking is launched. Finally, in Example 37d, the [V 得 Com] structure is embedded in the question to ask whether or not the broken state of tradition could be achieved.

We have seen how Chinese verbs can be negated by directly applying the negative morpheme 不 in front of the verb. The same routine also applies to adjectives and adverbs, as the sentences in Example 38 show.

Example 38

a 这 件 衣服 不 便宜。
  zhe4 jian4 yi1fu2 bu4 pian2yi2
  'this' Cla 'clothes' 'not' 'cheap'
  'This piece of clothing is not cheap.'

b 我 不 小心 吞 了 口香糖。
  wo3 bu4 xiao3xin1 tun1 le5 kou3xiang1tang2
  'I' 'not' 'careful' 'swallow' AM 'mouth-fragrant-sugar'
  'I involuntarily swallowed the chewing gum.'

In Example 38a, the negative morpheme 不 is added to the adjective 'cheap' to create a negative structure 'not cheap'. In 38b, 不小心 is used as a negative adverb 'not carefully' (often meaning 'unintentionally') to describe the action of gum swallowing.

The negative element 不 can also be used to deny a phrase, as in Example 39.

Example 39

a 我　不　ₚₚ[跟 ₚᵣₑₚ 你 ₙ]　玩　　了。
　 wo3　bu4　gen1　ni3　wan2　le5
　 'I'　'not'　'with'　'you'　'play'　SFP
　 'I am no longer playing with you.'

b 家长　　　不　ₚₚ[在 ₚᵣₑₚ 家 ₙ]　孩子　爬　　窗　　　坠　　楼。
　 jia1zhang3　bu2　zai4　jia1　hai2zi5　pa2　chuang1　zhui4　lou2
　 'parent'　'not'　'at'　'home'　'child'　'climb'　'window'　'fall'　'building'
　 'Parents not at home, the child climbed up the window and fell out of the building.'

In Example 39a, the speaker does not want to play 'with you', but they may want to play 'with someone else'. In 39b, the parents are not 'at home' but they may be 'somewhere else'. In each case a prepositional phrase is negated.

The negative morpheme 不 can be modified by a degree adverb to lessen the degree of negativity, as in Example 40:

Example 40

a 我　心情　　不　太　好。
　 wo3　xin1qing2　bu2　tai4　hao3
　 'I'　'mood'　'not'　'too'　'good.'
　 'My mood is not too good.'

b 这　个　世界　不　够　　完美。
　 zhe4　ge5　shi4jie4　bu2　gou4　wan2mei3
　 'this'　Cla　'world'　'not'　'enough'　'perfect'
　 'This world is not adequately perfect.'

c 什么　　时候　戒　　烟　　都　不　算　晚。
　 shen2mo5　shi2hou4　jie4　yan1　dou1　bu2　suan4　wan3
　 'what'　'moment'　'admonish'　'smoke'　'all'　'not'　'count'　'late'
　 'Whenever one (decides to) quit smoking it is not regarded as too late.'

d 你　的　回答　不　完全　　正确。
　 ni3　de5　hui2da2　bu4　wan2quan2　zheng4que4
　 'you'　PM　'answer'　'not'　'total'　'correct'
　 'Your answer is not entirely correct.'

In Example 40a, within the original negative structure 不好, an adverbial element 太 is inserted to mean 'not very good' – a mitigated criticism. Likewise, 不够完美 'not perfect enough' in 40b is somewhat better than 'not perfect' thanks to the addition of the adverb 够. In 40c, the unmodified negative expression is 不晚 'not late', a double negative which actually means 'early enough'. However, since 'quit smoking' is important to one's health and is difficult to accomplish, the speaker would like any potential listener to start quitting immediately. Thus 不算晚 'not regarded as too late' is a compromised term, which anticipates the difficulty of quitting smoking and at the same time encourages the audience to start the process as soon as possible. Finally, in Example 40d, the adverb 完全 'totally' is used to partially deny the correctness of the answer given by the other party. The unmodified negation 不正确 'incorrect' would have meant total denial.

Note that for some adverbial elements in this kind of construction, the order of the two items (i.e. 不 and the mitigating adverb) can be reversed. This will create very different meanings, as illustrated in Example 41 below:

Example 41

a 外表　　　　不　很　　重要。
   wai4biao3　　bu4 hen3 zhong4yao4
   'appearance' 'not' 'very' 'important'
   'Appearance is not very important.'

b 外表　　　　很　不　　重要。
   wai4biao3　　hen3 bu2 zhong4yao4
   'appearance' 'very' 'not' 'important'
   'Appearance is very unimportant.'

Thus, 不很 in Example 41a means 'not very' – a mitigated form of negation. 很不 in Example 41b, on the other hand, means 'very not' – a reinforced negative form. The two meanings differ dramatically.

Apart from 不, there are other negative items in Chinese which work in similar or slightly different ways. The next item we examine is 没有 'none', sometimes partially rendered as 没. The differences between 不 and 没有 are contrasted in Example 42:

Example 42

a 政府　　　　不　告诉　你　的　事
zheng4fu3　　bu2　gao4su4　ni3　de5　shi4
'government' 'not' 'tell'　　'you' AD 'matter'
'Things that the government does not want to tell you.'

b 政府　　　　没有　　　告诉　你　的　事
zheng4fu3　　mei2you3　gao4su4　ni3　de5　shi4
'government' 'have not' 'tell'　　'you' AD 'matter'
'Things that the government has not told you.'

The negation of the verb 'tell' by 不 in Example 42a implies intention, determination and future action. If negated by 没有, as in 42b, the focus is on the non-occurrence of the action, involving deliberation or deception. More examples of 没有 referring to non-occurrence of things are shown in Example 43:

Example 43

a 那些　老师　没有　　　教　　我　的　事
na4xie1 lao3shi1 mei2you3 jiao1　wo3 de5 shi4
'those' 'teacher' 'have not' 'teach' 'I'　AD 'matter'
'Those things that the teacher did not teach me.'

b 我们　　没有　　　要　　偷　　东西。
wo3men5 mei2you3 yao4　tou1　dong1xi1
'we'　　'not-have' 'want' 'steal' 'thing'
'We do not want to steal anything.'

The complex NP in Example 43a is similar to Example 42b in structure and connotation. In both cases, the negative item 没有 helps focus on the non-occurrence of an action and its implication. In 43b, 没有 emphasizes the speaker's lack of intention to steal things.

Although 没有 can be used to mean the non-occurrence of action, its primary usage is to refer to the non-existence of objects, as shown in Example 44:

Example 44

a 世　　上　　**没有**　　　免费　　　午餐。
　shi4　shang4　mei2you3　mian3fei4　wu3can1
　'world' 'up'　'not-have'　'free'　　　'lunch'
　'There is no "free lunch" in the world.'

b 20　　年　后　中国　　　将　　　**没有**
　er4shi2　nian2　hou4　zhong1guo2　jiang1　mei2you3
　'20'　　'year' 'after' 'China'　　　'about to' 'not-have'

　水　　资源。
　shui3　zi1yuan2
　'water' 'resource'

　'After 20 years water resources will be exhausted in China.'

Thus, 没有 precedes a noun when denying the existence of an object. In Example 44a, the idea of a 'free lunch' is dismissed. In 44b, 没有 helps point out the non-existence of water resource in 20 years' time, in the speaker's opinion.

In addition to denying verbs and nouns, 没有 is also used to negate adjectives in limited circumstances, as shown in Example 45.

Example 45

a 我　**没有**　　　醉。
　wo3　mei2you3　zui4
　'I'　'not-have' 'drunk'
　'I am not drunk.'

b 生　　　孩子　**没有**　　那么　　可怕。
　sheng1　hai2zi5　mei2you3　na4mo5　ke3pa4
　'give birth' 'child' 'not-have' 'such'　'terrible'
　'Giving birth to a child is not so horrible.'

In Example 45a, 没有 negates a monosyllabic adjective 'drunk' to mean 'not drunk'. Not all adjectives can collocate with 没有 in this way. For example, expressions like *没有高 'not-have tall', *没有热 'not-have hot', *没有舒服 'not-have comfortable', *没有快乐 'not-have happy' are not highly acceptable expressions by themselves. However, if a degree adverb like 那么 'to such a degree' is added, then the entire negative expression becomes acceptable, like that in Example 45b.

Another frequently used Chinese negative morpheme is 别, normally used in 'directive' speech acts, as in Example 46:

Example 46

a   别   乱   讲！
    bie2   luan4   jiang3
    'do not' 'disorderly' 'talk'
    'Do not talk irresponsibly!'

b   你   别   过来！
    ni3 bie2   guo4lai2
    'you' 'do not' 'cross-come'
    '(You) Do not come over!'

c   中国人   别   丢   了   自己   的   文化！
    zhong1guo2ren2 bie2   diu1 le5 zi4ji3 de5 wen2hua4
    'China-person'   'do not' 'lose' AM 'self' PD 'culture'
    'Chinese (people) do not throw away your own culture!'

The negative morpheme 别 is used as the first element in the imperative Example 46a. This is identical in structure to a negative English imperative starting with *Do not.* Example 46b, however, differs from this pattern by introducing a second person pronoun at the beginning of the sentence. In Example 46c, 'you' is replaced by a common noun, 'the Chinese' (i.e. offering a suggestion to all Chinese persons in general).

Apart from the three main negative markers mentioned above, there are some less well-used negative items with very restricted usages. The first one we look at is 无 'without'.

Example 47

a   老人   患   癌   无   钱   医治。
    lao3ren2 huan4 ai2   wu2   qian2 yi1zhi4
    'old-person' 'contract' 'cancer' 'without' 'money' 'cure-treat'
    'An old person suffers from cancer and has no money to treat it.'

b   打造   安全   无   毒   的   居家   环境。
    da3zao4 an1quan2 wu2   du2   de5 ju1jia1   huan2jing4
    'hit-build' 'safe'   'without' 'poison' AD 'live-home' 'environment'
    '(Let's) build a safe and poison-free residential environment.'

The negative morpheme 无 is primarily used in written language, often surfacing as part of an idiom or other fixed unit. In Example 47a, 无 replaces 没(有) to make the news headline less colloquial, giving it a formal touch. In Example 47b,

无 combines with a negative word 毒 ('poison') to cancel out the negativity. This is a word-formation rule based on 无. Other examples include 无害 'harmless', 无臭 'not smelly', 无污染 'pollution-free', 无障碍 'obstacle-free (accessible)' and so on, all very formal usages.

Another negative item mainly used in formal settings is 非 'not'. Some examples are offered in Example 48:

Example 48

a 对不起，　　那　是　非卖品！
dui4bu4qi3　　na4　shi4 fei1mai4pin3
'sorry'　　　　'that' 'be' 'non-sell-article'
'I am sorry but that article is not for sale.'

b 被　鳄鱼　　　咬到，　　　非死即伤。
bei4 e4yu2　　yao3dao4　　fei1si3ji2shang1
PB　'crocodile' 'bite-reach' 'not-die-then-injure'
'Bitten by a crocodile, one either dies or sustains injury.'

c 美国　　非法　移民　　　可能　　获得　　绿卡。
mei3guo2 fei1fa3 yi2min2　　ke3neng2 huo4de2 lv4ka3
'USA'　　'illegal' 'immigrant' 'possible' 'obtain' 'green-card'
'Illegal immigrants in the US can probably obtain the green card.'

Like 无, contemporary usage of 非 is for it to be subsumed in a lexicalized unit or an idiomatic expression rather than participating in syntactic formulation as a free morpheme. In 48a, 非 is part of a lexical item, 非卖品 'not-for-sale article'. In Example 48b, 非 appears in a quadrisyllabic fixed term, 非死即伤 'dead or injured', which can only be used as a whole and normally in writing. In 48c, 非 occurs within a technical term, 非法移民 'illegal immigrants'. However, in this case, 非法 is a moveable item and often combines with other items to form a phrase; for example, 非法手段 'illegal means', 非法捕鱼 'illegal fishing', and so on.

A final negative item to be looked at is 未 'not (yet)', which is also usually confined to written language.

Example 49

a 未　　　　満　　　十八　　　岁　　　　　　禁止　　进入。
wei4　　man3　shi2ba1　sui4　　　　　jin4zhi3　jin4ru4
'not yet' 'full'　'18'　　'year of age'　'forbid'　'enter'
'Entry is forbidden for persons less than 18 years of age.'

b 加强　　　　未　　　成年　　　人　　　思想
jia1qiang2　wei4　cheng2nian2　ren2　si1xiang3
'strengthen' 'not yet' 'grown up'　'person' 'thought'

道德　　　建设。
dao4de2　jian4she4
'moral'　'construct'

'Strengthen the ideational moral construction for minors.'

c 男童　　　疑　　　未　　扣　　安全带　　　　飞出
nan2tong2　yi2　　wei4　kou4　an1quan2dai4　fei1chu1
'male-child' 'suspect' 'not' 'buckle' 'safe-belt'　　'fly-exit'

车外　　　惨死。
che1wai4　can3si3
'car-outside' 'tragic-die'

'The boy child suspected of not fastening seat belt flew out of the car and died a tragic death.'

The negative morpheme 未 means 'not' or 'not yet' depending on context. In Example 49a, 未 combines with 満 to mean 'not yet fully (18 years of age)'. Similarly, in 49b, 未 negates 成年 not in an absolute sense (i.e. 'not fully grown yet'). In 49c, however, 未 does negate the action of 'seat belt fastening' in an absolute sense. Like 无 and 非, the morpheme 未 is predominantly used in formal, written language.

4.4 CONCLUSION

In this chapter, we explored how the Chinese language is used to express opinions, to give commands, to offer promises, to express feelings and to bring about changes of state. We found that the linguistic patterns used by Chinese and English to carry out the same speech act may be structurally different. Some critical differences have been highlighted in the relevant discussions within this chapter.

We also examined different ways of asking questions and creating negative sentences in Chinese. For example, we saw how differently the *wh-* words behave in Chinese from those in English. We also examined a variety of negating devices in Chinese, which again is different from English where similar words like *no*, *not*, *none* and *never* seem to dominate the functionality of negation.

To sum up, with speech act categories explored and interrogative and negative structures explained, we now know how the language is equipped to carry out basic functions in daily life. In the next chapter, we explore Chinese conversations in depth, focusing on a key ingredient – the Chinese sentence-final particles.

CHAPTER 5

Sentence-final particles

In this chapter, we explore a range of Chinese particles primarily used in the spoken language. Most of these particles are monosyllabic and they are mostly discourse functional in nature. Our main focus is on sentence-final particles (SFPs) but I also call some of them constituent-final particles (CFPs) when they appear at the end of a constituent rather than at the end of a full sentence. A further category in this is the independent particle (IP); these mostly appear before the start of a sentence. We will treat the various Chinese particles as discourse markers (DMs) and explain their meanings and functions with plenty of examples, as used in authentic contexts.

5.1 INTRODUCTION

The sentence-final particle is a language device which is not seen in a Western language like English. It is mainly used in spoken language and is attached to a short sentence or phrase to provide more information on top of the lexical and structural meaning. The SFP is a special category of functional items that a foreigner learning the Chinese language must acquire separately, in real-life settings, in order to understand their meanings and usage.

An SFP is outside the canonical structure of a sentence. It plays no part in sentence formation and is not subsumed in regular grammatical frameworks. A good way to understand the SFP is through existing discussions on discourse markers. Schiffrin's (1987) book, for example, proposes a model for analysing discourse which consists of five components:

- Idea Structure
- Exchange Structure
- Action Structure
- Participation Framework
- Information State

In English, according to Schiffrin, discourse markers are words and phrases like *oh*, *well*, *I mean*, *you know*, and so on, which help organize a speaker's ideas in their speech (Idea Structure), reveal the speech acts performed in their utterances (Action Structure), show their awareness of the amount and kinds of information currently available to participants in conversation (Information State), reflect their perception of role relationships in discourse (Participation Framework) and show the influence of conversation structure on speaker contributions (Exchange Structure).

Chinese SFPs can potentially be analysed using Schiffrin's framework. Some SFPs are indeed used to mark the idea structure of an utterance by highlighting the saliency of a contribution, contrasting notions or entities, or sidelining a piece of information. Some SFPs are used to indicate the speaker's awareness of their participatory role. Others appear at certain junctures in the conversation to help *staple* the utterance into a certain position so it can be interpreted in relation to other utterances in the vicinity. Still other SFPs help manage the knowledge pool and information flow in discourse, by marking a piece of information as already shared or as newly introduced information.

Fung and Carter (2007) propose a 'functional paradigm' for analyzing pedagogical discourse which distinguishes four groups of functions associated with discourse markers.

- Interpersonal: marking shared knowledge; indicating attitudes; showing responses.
- Referential: cause; contrast; coordination; disjunction; consequence; digression; comparison.
- Structural: opening and closing of topics; sequence; topic shifts; summarizing opinions; continuation of topics.
- Cognitive: denoting thinking process; reformulation/self-correction; elaboration; hesitation; assessment of the listener's knowledge about the utterances.

Both Schiffrin's and Fung and Carter's models are useful for comprehending the functions of discourse markers as a whole and at a conceptual level. However, the functions of Chinese SFPs are so versatile and complicated it is difficult to assign an SFP to any individual or collection of modules proposed by these models. As will become evident in the ensuing discussion, individual and in-depth examinations of the SFPs are highly desirable for understanding their particular meanings and usages.

In the following sections, around a dozen of the most commonly used Mandarin SFPs will be examined on an individual basis. The data are collected from contemporary Chinese reality TV shows broadcast in China or Taiwan. Table 5.1 lists the primary Mandarin SFPs that can be heard on Chinese and Taiwanese television. Some SFPs listed in Table 5.1 have phonetic variants which are not shown in the table. Although 吗 is an SFP, it is already covered in Chapter 4 as a question marker and so will not be further treated here.

For sentence-final particles, the spoken forms are primary. That is, the Pinyin notations are better approximations to their identities than the characters chosen to represent them. Some SFPs recognized in this book have established orthographical representations; for example, 啊 for *a5*, 吧 for *ba5*, 呢 for *ne5*,

啦 for *la5* and so on. Other SFPs are used in spoken Chinese but (as yet) there is no consensus as to how to represent them in writing; for example, *ye5* is variously written as 耶, 哎, 欸 or something else.

Even more troublesome are the SFPs which have no established identities, whether from language users' or researchers' points of view. For example, this book recognizes three variants of *o* – *o2*, *o5* and *ou5* – and orthographically represents them as 哦, 喔 and 噢 respectively. However, this is far from an established practice. As will be explained later, some researchers only recognize one kind of *o* in their publications. Moreover, the third *o* identified in this chapter (i.e. *ou5*) is in fact identical to the second *o* (i.e. *o5*) in spoken form. The representation of it as *ou5* is only to avoid the confusion of having two SFPs represented in exactly the same Pinyin notation.

Chinese language learners should bear in mind that most SFPs can only be observed and reliably learned from the spoken language. This book may offer a relatively complete model for understanding and identifying currently active Chinese SFPs. However, for certain SFPs such as *ye5* and the different *o*'s, no consistent evidence of usage may be found in the written language. Learners should associate the properties of these particles explained in this chapter with their spoken forms (i.e. Pinyin) rather than tying them to the characters used here.

Table 5.1 also shows the Google hits for each orthographically represented SFP at the time of writing. These numbers offer a very rough impression of SFP usage scales and rough comparisons between different SFPs and do not reflect the real usage of SFPs in spoken language. Also, for some SFPs like 哦, 喔, 噢 and 耶, there is no consensus among Chinese speakers regarding their orthographical representations. Some researchers avoid the orthographical

Table 5.1 The primary Mandarin SFPs currently in use

Pinyin	Grapheme	Google Frequency (December 25, 2013)	Primary Function
a5	啊	401,000,000	showing emotion/conviction
ba5	吧	633,000,000	marker of uncertainly
bei5	呗	11,800,000	marker of light-heartedness
ne5	呢	364,000,000	marker of contrast
o2	哦	179,000,000	giving warning
o5	喔	66,000,000	wondering/admiring
ou5	噢	16,600,000	seeking agreement
ma5	嘛	75,400,000	assuming shared information
ye5	耶	N/A	expressing surprise
la5	啦	273,000,000	dismissing
le5	了	1,480,000,000	aspect marker change of state

issue altogether by using only Pinyin to present their work (e.g. Wu 2004). The frequency of 耶 is not shown because the character is also used as a content element and most of the Google hits reflect the content usage rather than the SFP function.

We now turn to examine each of the SFPs in Table 5.1, using examples to illustrate their usage in Chinese conversations.

5.2 SFP *A5*

啊 *a5* is one of the most frequently used Mandarin SFPs; it is often heard in spoken Chinese and is very versatile in discourse functions. First of all, like the other SFP 吗, *a5* can be used to turn a statement into a question.

Marker of question

Example 1

孟非:	你	高中		念	四	年,
meng4fei1	ni3	gao1zhong1		nian4	si4	nian2
'Meng Fei'	'you'	'high-middle'		'read'	'four'	'year'

'Host: You spent four years finishing high-school,

你	父母	不	知道	**啊**?
ni3	fu4mu3	bu4	zhi1dao4	a5
'you'	'parents'	'not'	'know'	SFP

and your parents did not know?'

(fcwr 20130810)

When used as a question marker, 啊 participates in the process of question formation, turning a declarative sentence into a yes/no question. A question marked with *a5* displays a mildly inquisitive, somewhat caring, attitude. This is different from a question marked by 吗, which is either completely neutral or used to challenge as a rhetorical question. If 啊 is replaced by 吗 in Example 1, for example, the question could sound somewhat more impolite, almost as if the speaker is condemning the situation or is demanding an explanation.

The SFP 啊, when used in a question, differs from the default question marker 吗 in one important aspect: *a5* can be attached to a question which is already made a question by other means (e.g. by containing a *wh-* word), but *ma5* cannot do so (i.e. it must be attached to a declarative sentence). Example 2 shows *a5* attached to a sentence which is already a question without the addition of *a5*.

Example 2

邱启明： 　　　五号　　吴文英
qiu1qi3ming2　wu3hao4　wu2wen2ying1
'Qiu Qiming'　'No. 5'　　'Wu Wengying'
'Host: No. 5 Wu Wengying,

为什么　　　　　灭灯　　　　　　**啊**？
wei4shen2mo5　mie4deng1　　　　a5
'why'　　　　　'extinguish-light'　SFP
why did you turn off the light?'

(wmyhb 20130115)

The difference between Example 1 and Example 2 will be self-evident if we strip 啊 off both questions. The result is shown in Example 3 below.

Example 3

a　你　高中　　　念　四　年，你　父母　不　知道。
　　ni3　gao1zhong1　nian4　si4　nian2　ni3　fu4mu3　bu4　zhi1dao4
　　'you'　'high-middle'　'read'　'four'　'year'　'you'　'parents'　'not'　'know'
　　'You spent four years finishing high-school, and your parents did not know.'

b　五号　　　吴文英　　　　为什么　　　　灭灯？
　　wu3hao4　wu2wen2ying1　wei4shen2mo5　mie4deng1
　　'No. 5'　'Wu Wengying'　'why'　　　　'extinguish-light'
　　'No. 5 Wu Wengying, why do you turn off the light?'

Having been stripped of 啊, Example 3a is no longer a question. On the other hand, Example 3b is still a question even without *a5*. This is, of course, because Example 3b contains a question word 为什么. The issue then boils down to what extra information *a5* adds to the question in a situation like Example 2. It would seem that whether *a5* creates a question or is attached to a question, it expresses the speaker's curiosity and their attitude of concern. Without *a5*, Example 3b sounds formal and nonchalant. With the addition of *a5*, the same question expressed in Example 2 sounds informal, showing the speaker to be interested and probably caring too.

Marker of engagement

The SFP 啊 used in both Example 1 and Example 2 is pronounced with a low pitch, with a relatively weak accent. This low-pitch *a5* can also be used to express a generally friendly and engaging attitude toward the audience. Example 4 illustrates this usage of *a5*.

Example 4

a 谭苗：　　　希望　　　主持人　　　多　　　帮帮　　　　我　　啊。
    tan2miao2　xi1wang4　zhu3chi2ren2　duo1　bang1bang1　wo3　a5
    'Tan Miao'　'hope'　'host'　　　　'much'　'help-help'　'me'　SFP
    'Male Guest: I hope the host of the show will help me out a little bit.'
    　　　　　　　　　　　　　　　　　　　　　　　　(wmyhb 20130129)

b 李进云：　　可能　　　稍微　　　有点　　　慢　　啊。
    li3jin4yun2　ke3neng2　shao1wei2　you3dian3　man4　a5
    'Li Jinyun'　'possible'　'slightly'　'a bit'　　'slow'　SFP
    'Male Guest: It may take some time to happen.

    稍微　　　等　　一下　　啊。
    shao1wei2　deng3　yi2xia4　a5
    'slightly'　'wait'　'one bit'　SFP
    Please wait a moment.'
    　　　　　　　　　　　　　　　　　　　　　　　(fcwr 20130810)

The male candidate in Example 4a is asking the host of the show to help him with his courtship session on TV. The addition of 啊 seems to make the request more engaging and worthy of consideration. The male in Example 4b, on the other hand, is asking the audience to bear with him while he is trying to memorize all the numbers the 24 female guests have written on their individual pieces of paper, so that he can accurately match person to number later on when asked to demonstrate his extraordinary powers of memory. The speaker is foreseeing the inconvenience caused by his delay and is trying to make peace with the audience using the *a5*-accompanied statement ('It will be slow in coming') and the suggestion ('Please wait patiently'). In both cases, *a5* signals the speaker's continued interest in participating in the discourse and that the hearer's appreciation of this attitude is valued.

The low-key 啊 in Example 4 seems to show a relatively humble attitude in a relatively unexcited manner. When *a5* is said with somewhat more stress and in a higher pitch, however, it can reveal the speaker's emotional commitment to the utterance, thereby giving it a degree of emphasis.

Marker of emotion

Example 5

a 仲伟冬：　　　　男　　嘉宾　　　多　　接　　　地气　　　**啊**！
zhong4wei3dong1 nan2　jia1bin1　　duo1　jie1　　di4qi4　　　a5
'Zhong Weidong'　'male'　'good-guest'　'much'　'connect'　'ground-air'　SFP
'Female Guest: The male guest is so well grounded!'

(wmyhb 20130725)

b 王紫藤：　　　　你的　　共鸣腔　　　　　好低　　　**啊**！
wang2zi3teng2 ni3de5 gong4ming2qiang1 hao3di1　　a5
'Wang Ziteng'　'your'　'resonance-cavity'　'good-low'　SFP
'Female Guest: Your resonant cavity is so low!'

(wmyhb 20130226)

In Example 5a, the SFP 啊 is attached to praise – the female guests commenting on a positive aspect of the male candidate. The addition of *a5* makes the comments 'alive' with feelings, revealing the speakers' emotional state. The emotion shown in Example 5b, on the other hand, is that of surprise.

Apart from revealing emotions that the speaker feels at a certain junction in the conversation, 啊 also often helps express feelings generated by the other speaker's contribution. That is, *a5* may carry out the interpersonal function of 'showing response'.

Marker of Response

Example 6

邱启明：　　　　你　　不是　　东北　　　纯　　爷们　　　　吗？
qiu1qi3ming2 ni3　bu2shi4 dong1bei3 chun2 ye2men5　　ma5
'Qiu Qiming'　'you'　'not-be'　'east-north'　'pure'　'grandpa'　PM　QM
'Host: Are you not a pure-breed Dongbei macho man?'

王禹鹏：　　　　对　　**啊**！
wang2yu3peng2 dui4　a5
'Wang Yupeng'　'correct'　SFP
'Male Guest: Exactly right!'

(wmyhb 20130115)

In Example 6, the host of the dating show asks the male candidate an easy question – whether he is the macho person he earlier claimed to be. The answer is obvious for the man so he says 对 'correct' with the marking of 啊 to indicate the appropriateness of the answer to the question. That is, the SFP *a5* adds an extra dimension in this case – not regarding attitude or emotion but in the structural domain, marking the current contribution as an obvious response and a perfect reply to a question or a situation. The *a5* used to make a response in this way is pronounced with a higher pitch, possibly with a stronger stress and lasting somewhat longer.

Example 7

蔡旸：　你　是　从　　哪儿　见　过　我　的？
cai4yang2 ni3　shi4 cong2 na3er5 jian4 guo4 wo3 de5
'Cai Yang' 'you' 'be' 'from' 'where' 'see' AM 'me' ED
'Female Guest: Where did you see me from?

我　特别　　好奇。
wo3 te4bie2　　hao4qi2
'I' 'especially' 'curious'
I am most curious.'

田宇辰：　　从… 节目　　里　　　**啊**。
tian2yu3chen2 cong2 jie2mu4 li3　　a5
'Tian Yuchen'　'from' 'program' 'inside' SFP
'Male Guest: From the TV program!'　　　　(wmyhb 20130710)

The male guest in Example 7 marks his answer to the female's question with 啊. In this particular example, *a5* seems to be saying 'Where else?' since its presence has made the answer overwhelmingly self-evident. This makes sense as the female has become famous for her witty remarks on that particular dating show. Anyone interested enough to come to the show could be reasonably expected to know her as a celebrity.

Example 8

孙天文：　　你　能　刻意　　　为　我　不　接　　吻戏　　吗？
sun1tian1wen2 ni3　neng2 ke4yi4　　wei4 wo3 bu4 jie1　wen3xi4　ma5
'Sun Tianwen' 'you' 'can' 'intentionally' 'for' 'me' 'not' 'accept' 'kiss-show' QM
'Male Guest: Can you make an effort not to accept a role in a show that involves kissing?'

金铭：　我　吻戏　　本来　　就　　不　多　**啊**！
jin1ming2 wo3 wen3xi4　ben3lai2 jiu4　bu4 duo1 a5
'Jin Ming' 'I' 'kiss-show' 'originally' 'exactly' 'not' 'much' SFP
'Female Guest: I did not act in kissing scenes a lot, to begin with.'

　　　　　　　　　　　　　　　　　　　　　(zsydt 20130706)

Like the previous two examples, the adjacency pair shown in Example 8 consists of a question and an answer, and the answer is again marked with 啊. Unlike the previous examples, however, this answer is not particularly obvious to the male asking the question. Nevertheless, the *a5* still functions to make the answer seem obvious so that the listener can appreciate the underlying logic (that is, she seldom acts in kissing scenes so she does not have to avoid the scenes suggested by the male candidate).

Example 9

王若飞:　　　她　说　我　是　大叔。　我　想　问　她　一下。
wang2ruo4fei1 ta1　shuo1 wo3 shi4 da4shu2　wo3 xiang3　wen4 ta1　yi2xia4
'Wang Ruofei' 'she' 'say' 'I' 'be' 'big-uncle' 'I' 'think' 'ask ' 'her' 'one bit'
'Male Guest: She calls me an uncle. I would like to question her about that.'

孟非:　　　就是!　凭　　甚么　说　人　　大叔　　**啊**?
meng4fei1 jiu4shi4 ping2　　shen2mo5 shuo1 ren2　da4shu2　a5
'Meng Fei' 'exactly' 'based on' 'what'　'say' 'person' 'big-uncle' SFP
'Host: Exactly! On what basis can she call you an old guy?'　　(fcwr 20130811)

In Example 9, the SFP 啊 is integrated into an utterance where the host of the show 'attacks' a female guest in fake anger. The utterance involved is a rhetorical question and *a5* is used to mark it as a response to the situation. Specifically, the female calling the male an old man is thought to be ungrounded and the host's condemnation of that claim is a justified response to that situation.

Example 10

李莉娜:　我　爸爸　是　逢　人　　就　夸　　我,
li3li4na4　wo3 ba4ba5 shi4 feng2 ren2　jiu4　kua1　wo3
'Li Lina' 'I'　'father' 'be' 'meet' 'person' 'then' 'praise' 'me'
'Female Guest: What my father does is praise me in front of everybody.

我　在　　　的　时候　　他　也　是　夸　　我,
wo3 zai4　　de5 shi2hou4 ta1 ye3　shi4 kua1　wo3
'I'　'present' AD 'moment' 'he' 'also' 'is' 'praise' 'me'
He even praises me (in front of people) when I am present.

每次　　　我　都　非常　　　不好意思,
mei3ci4　　wo3 dou1 fei1chang2 bu4hao3yi4si5
'every time' 'I'　'all'　'extremely' 'not-good-meaning'
I feel extremely embarrassed every time.

我　就　　觉得　我　没有　　那么　好　**啊**!
wo3 jiu4　　jue2de5 wo3 mei2you3 na4mo5 hao3　a5
'I'　'exactly' 'feel'　'I'　'none'　'such'　'good' SFP
I just feel I am not really that good!'　　(fcwr 20130810)

Example 10 is a longer speech consisting of four sentences, where Li complains about her father's overindulgence of her. The last sentence is marked by 啊, whose function in this instance is to respond to her own narrative (i.e. the previous three sentences). The attachment of *a5* seems to enable the final sentence to 'step aside' and comment on the story, thanks to its normal function of making responses. The SFP *a5* also maintains its interpersonal function of showing a self-righteous attitude to endorse the claim that 'I am not so good!'

Example 11

吴诗婷：　　从来　　都　　没有　　女朋友？
wu2shi1ting2 cong2lai2 dou1 mei2you3 nv3peng2you3
'Wu Shiting' 'all along' 'all' 'none' 'female-friend'
'Female Guest: (You) have never had any girlfriend?'

张强：　　　　对！
zhang1qiang2 dui4
'Zhang Qiang' 'correct'
'Male Guest: You are right!'

吴诗婷：　　三十　　岁？
wu2shi1ting2 san1shi2 sui4
'Wu Shiting' '30' 'years (of age)'
'Female Guest: You are 30 years old?'

张强：　　　　对，　挺　尴尬　　　的。
zhang1qiang2 dui4 ting3 gan1ga4 de5
'Zhang Qiang' 'correct' 'very' 'embarrassing' ED
'Male Guest: Yes, it is quite embarrassing.

确实……比较　　　罕见。
que4shi2 bi3jiao4 han3jian4
'indeed' 'comparatively' 'rare-see'
This is indeed very rarely seen.'

吴诗婷：　我　觉得　很好　**啊**！(…) 没有　甚么　问题。
wu2shi1ting2 wo3 jue2de5 hen3hao3 a5 mei2you3 shen2mo5 wen4ti2
'Wu Shiting' 'I' 'feel' 'very-good' SFP 'none' 'what' 'question'
'Female Guest: I think this is quite alright! There is no problem with that.'

张强：　　　　谢谢…
zhang1qiang2 xie4xie5
'Zhang Qiang' 'thanks'
'Male Guest: Thank you . . .

(zsydt 201307013)

Example 11 illustrates the 'distant effect' of 啊 in responding to an utterance or situation which occurred not immediately before but a little while ago. The dialogue centers on the male's earlier claim that he has never had a girlfriend in his thirty years of life. From her first turn in Example 11, the female guest starts to seek confirmation about the incredible information she has received. She asks two questions in succession, both of which are answered affirmatively. It is then in her third turn that she uses the expression 'I think it is very good', marked with *a5*, to respond to the topic in question (i.e. a 30-year-old man not having any experience of romance in contemporary society) rather than responding to a recent verbal contribution. The fact that the topic and the female's ultimate evaluation can be connected conceptually is entirely due to the presence of *a5* with its well established discourse function of making responses (i.e. as a DM working in Schiffrin's Exchange Structure).

Marker of a series

When several instances of 啊 appear successively at the end of a series of phrases or sentences, it is serving the function of a 'series marker'. In this case, *a5* does not come with the rich functional interpretations discussed earlier. It is merely a marker of items in a list, signifying the speaker is providing members of a set which are of particular interest at the moment.

Example 12

不	喜欢	猫	啊	狗	啊	小孩子	啊,
bu4	xi3huan1	mao1	a5	gou3	a5	xiao3hai2zi5	a5
'not'	'like'	'cat'	CFP	'dog'	CFP	'kid'	CFP

'If you do not like cats, dogs, kids and the like,

会	被	人	说	没	爱心。
hui4	bei4	ren2	shuo1	mei2	ai4xin1
'will'	PB	'person'	'say'	'not'	'love-heart'

you will be criticized for lack of a loving heart.'

Example 12 comes from the web which illustrates the usage of 啊 as a series marker. Each item marked with *a5* in this case is a lexical unit (cat, dog or child). The intervention of *a5* makes it unnecessary to introduce a short pause between two items on a list when speaking. It also draws the hearer's attention to the fact that the items being marked by *a5* should be treated as members of a set which share some common properties.

Example 13

Mr Right：	你	是	怎么	追	女生	的？
mister right	ni3	shi4	zen3mo5	zhui1	nv3sheng1	de5
'Mr Right'	'you'	'be'	'how'	'chase'	'girl'	AD

'Computer Program: How do you chase girls?'

欧阳铭骏：		就	跟	其他	男生		都	一样	**啊**！
ou1yang2ming2jun4		jiu4	gen1	qi2ta1	nan2sheng1		dou1	yi2yang4	a5
'Ouyang Mingjun'		'just'	'with'	'other'	'boy'		'all'	'the same'	SFP

'Male Guest: Just the same as other boys.

就	陪		她	逛逛		街,	送	一下	礼物	**啊**,
jiu4	pei2		ta1	guang4guang4		jie1	song4	yi2xia4	li3wu4	a5
'just'	'accompany'		'her'	'stroll-stroll'		'street'	'give'	'one-bit'	'gift'	CFP

Just going window-shopping with her, giving presents.

然后	就	煮	她	喜欢	吃	的	东西	**啊**,
ran2hou4	jiu4	zhu3	ta1	xi3huan1	chi1	de5	dong1xi1	a5
'then'	'just'	'cook'	'she'	'like'	'eat'	AD	'thing'	CFP

Then just cook things she likes to eat,

早餐	**啊**	等等	这些。
zao3can1	a5	deng3deng3	zhe4xie1
'breakfast'	CFP	'etc.'	'these'

such as breakfast and things like that.'

(wmyhb 20130723)

There are four instances of 啊 in Example 13. The first one is marking the statement 'Just like other boys' as an obvious answer to the question 'How do you chase girls?'. The other three *a5*'s are all series markers; two of them marking verb phases while the last one marking a lexical item 'breakfast'. The series marker *a5*, like the response marker *a5*, is also pronounced with a higher pitch and carries more stress and length.

Variants of *a5*

There are at least two variants of 啊 which carry out the same discourse functions but are pronounced somewhat differently. One of them is **呀** *ya5* and the other is **哪** *na5*.

Example 14

a 亚丽： 上次   让   你   牵肠挂肚   的
    ya3li4 shang4ci4 rang4 ni3 qian1chang2gua4du4   de5
    'Yali' 'last time' 'let' 'you' 'drag-intestine-suspend-belly' AD

    那个   女神   是   谁   **呀**?
    na4 ge5 nv3 shen2 shi4 shei2 ya5
    'that' 'goddess' 'be' 'who' SFP

    'Host: Who is the goddess that you have been thinking so much
    about since last time?'   (zsydt 20130706)

b 郭胜媛：   您   掏宝   卖   男装   的,
    guo1sheng4yuan2 nin2 tao1bao3 mai4 nan2zhuang1 de5
    'Guo Shengyuan' 'you' 'Tao Bao' 'sell' 'male-clothing' ED
    'Female Guest: You are selling mens clothing at Taobao Marketplace.'

    你   找   那么   多   女孩   干么   **呀**?
    ni3 zhao3 na4mo5 duo1 nv3hai2 gan4ma2 ya5
    'you' 'find' 'such' 'many' 'girl' 'do-what' SFP
    'What do you find so many girls for?'   (wmyhb 20130725)

Example 14 is similar to Example 2 in terms of the function of the SFP involved. The main difference between 呀 and 啊 is in prosodic salience. The slightly more complicated way of pronouncing *ya5* seems to give it more emphasis than that which *a5* receives. In other words, *ya5* seems to show more curiosity and a higher level of engagement than *a5*.

Example 15

a 沈涛：   是   条   汉子   **呀**!
    shen3tao1 shi4 tiao2 han4zi5 ya5
    'Shen Tao' 'be' Cla 'man' SFP
    'Host: You are indeed a man!'   (zsydt 20130706)

b 仲伟冬：   从事   艺术   行业   的   男生
    zhong4wei3dong1 cong2shi4 yi4shu4 hang2ye4   de5 nan2sheng1
    'Zhong Weidong' 'engage in' 'art' 'profession' AD 'boy'

    挺   好   的   **呀**!
    ting3 hao3 de5 ya5
    'very' 'good' ED SFP

    'Female Guest: A man engaged in the art profession is quite alright!'
                                                        (wmyhb 20130806)

Example 15 shows *ya5* to be used as a marker of emotion, just like the *a5* in Example 5. Again, *ya5* and *a5* are interchangeable in this example, except that *ya5* may place a higher degree of emphasis on the host sentence than *a5*.

Example 16

黄菡:　　　这个　　不仅　　要　　很大　　的　决心,
huang2han4 zhe4ge5 bu4jin3　yao4　hen3da4　de5 jue2xin1
'Huang Han' 'this'　'not-only' 'want' 'very-big' AD 'determine'
'Female Specialist: To do so not only requires a lot of determination

操作　　上　　来　　也　　挺——
cao1zuo4 shang4 lai2　ye3　ting3
'operate' 'up'　'come' 'also' 'quite'
in operation it is also rather . . .

不是　你　想　留　就　留　的 **呀**!
bu2shi4 ni3　xiang3 liu2 jiu4　liu2　de5 ya5
'not-is' 'you' 'think' 'stay' 'then' 'stay' ED SFP
It's not like you want to stay (in that year) then you can stay.'

(fcwr 20130810)

In Example 16, the expert on the show is responding to a situation − a male guest claiming that he deliberately managed not to progress to the next level in school in order to stay in the same year as the girl he liked. The use of *ya5* in this example is similar to Example 10 or 11 which illustrates the responding function of *a5*. The use of both SFPs is interchangeable in these examples.

Example 17

孟非:　都　富　到　六　代　　　了, 我的　天　　**哪**!
meng4fei1 dou1 fu4 dao4 liu4 dai4　　le5 wo3de5 tian1　na5
'Meng Fei' 'all' 'rich' 'reach' 'six' 'generation' AM 'my'　'heaven' SFP
'Host: The legacy of fortune has already passed down to the sixth generation. My goodness!'

(fcwr 20130811)

Example 17 illustrates the usage of another relatively rare variant of *a5* − *na5*. This variant seems to occur only when the previous syllable ends with the alveolar nasal [n]. The sound of *na5* is then a coarticulation of [n] and [a]. The usage of *na5* as an SFP is the same as *a5*. In the case of Example 17, it is a marker of emotion.

5.3 SFP *BA5*

The discourse functions of 吧 seem to center around the idea of 'uncertainty'. It can help express the speaker's uncertainty about something. It accompanies requests for confirmation. It expresses sarcasm in an indirect way. It softens a speaker's command and transforms it into a suggestion or an invitation for action.

Marker of uncertainty

While 啊 expresses a confident and self-righteous attitude, 吧 marks a statement as tentative and uncertain.

Example 18

朱淑娟：	可是	为什么		这个	窗户	是	开	着?
zhu1shu2juan1	ke3shi4	wei4shen2mo5		zhe4ge5	chuang1hu4	shi4	kai1	zhe5
'Zhu Shujuan'	'but'	'why'		'this'	'window'	'be'	'open'	AM

'Female Guest: But why is this window open?'

噢,	我	想	说,	也许	可能	是	忘	了	吧。
ou1	wo3	xiang3	shuo1	ye3xu3	ke3neng2	shi4	wang4	le5	ba5
IP	'I'	'think'	'say'	'maybe'	'possible'	'be'	'forget'	AM	SFP

'Right, I thought to myself, perhaps I have forgotten (to close the window).'

(aywdm 20130812)

The guest speaker in Example 18 is recounting a ghost story. She gets to the point where she woke up in the morning and found the window open, contrary to what she believed. She thought at the time that she might have forgotten to close the window before going to sleep. This thought is marked with *ba5* which often collocates with the word 可能 'possible' to mutually strengthen the uncertainty expressed by the host sentence.

Example 19

张宇强：	可能	那	是	因为	你	太	漂亮	了	吧,
zhang1yu3qiang2	ke3neng2	na4	shi4	yin1wei4	ni3	tai4	piao4liang4	le5	ba5
'Zhang Yuqiang'	'possible'	'that'	'be'	'because'	'you'	'too'	'beautiful'		SFP SFP

'Male Guest: I think that is probably because you are too beautiful

所以	想	这样	比较	吸引	你。
suo3yi3	xiang3	zhe4yang4	bi3jiao4	xi1yin3	ni3
'therefore'	'think'	'this way'	'compare'	'attract'	'you'

so that I think you will be more interested (in me) this way.'

(wmyhb 20130725)

The male guest in Example 19 was asked why he behaved in a certain way toward a particular female guest. He answers that it was probably because of the female's stunning beauty. He also marks this answer with *b5* to increase the uncertainty encoded by the word 'possibly'. This has the effect of reducing the directness of the praise which otherwise may seem somewhat cheeky and impolite.

Example 20

李可笛：	你	是	平常	都	喜欢	穿	紧身裤		吗？
li3ke3di2	ni3	shi4	ping2chang2	dou1	xi3huan1	chuan1	jin3shen1ku4		ma5
'Li Kedi'	'you'	'be'	'ordinary'	'all'	'like'	'wear'	'tight-body-pants'		QM

'Female Guest: Do you usually wear tight trousers?'

高魁喆：		呃…	也	没，	就是…	分		场合	**吧**。
gao1kui2zhe2	e5		ye3	mei2	jiu4shi4	fen1		chang3he2	ba5
'Gao Kuizhe'	PF		'also'	'not'	'just-is'	'distinguish'		'occasion'	SFP

'Male Guest: Er . . . not really, just depending on what the occasion is.'

(wmyhb 20130730)

The female guest in Example 20 asks the male guest a question: whether he wears tight trousers all the time. The man denies the allegation and then gives a phrase to tentatively describe the real situation. There is no collocation involving a word like 'possible' in this phrase. It is the SFP 吧 alone which gives the sense of uncertainty. In other words, *ba5* is serving the function of a hedge. The inclusion of *ba5* in an utterance lessens the speaker's commitment to the claim they are making.

Example 21

苏士为：	如果	说	再	有	这么		一种
su1shi4wei2	ru2guo3	shuo1	zai4	you3	zhe4mo5		yi4zhong3
'Su Shiwei'	'if'	'say'	'again'	'have'	'such'		'one' Cla

环境		出现		的话，
huan2jing4		chu1xian4		de5hua4
'environment'		'appear'		'suppose'

'Male Guest: If this kind of environment should appear again,

我	会	让	另外	一个		女孩	管	我	叫	哥哥		**吧**。
wo3	hui4	rang4	ling4wai4	yi2ge5		nv3hai2	guan3	wo3	jiao4	ge1ge5		ba5
'I'	'will'	'let'	'other'	'one' Cla		'girl'	'govern'	'me'	'call'	'older-brother'		SFP

I will let the other girl call me older brother, I guess.'

(wmyhb 20130725)

In Example 21, the male guest is explaining himself by hypothesizing a situation. Since the situation is hypothetical, it warrants the use of 吧 to mark the intrinsic uncertainty of the conclusion (that he would choose to be an older brother to the other girl rather than being her boyfriend – the latter scenario did happen in real life). If ba5 were not present in Example 21, the main clause would sound like a determination rather than an inclination.

Example 22

蔡康永：　　　　（爸爸）有　　特别　　交代　　吗？
cai4kang1yong3　ba4ba5　you3　te4bie2　jiao1dai4　ma5
'Kevin Tsai'　　　'father' 'have' 'special' 'order'　QM
'Host: Did your father give you any special instructions?'

娜娜：　不　应该　　　讲　　出来　　　**吧**。
na4na4　bu4　ying1gai1　jiang3　chu1lai2　ba5
'Na Na' 'not' 'should'　'tell'　'exit-come' SFP
'Female Guest: I think I am not supposed to tell.'

(kxll 20130820)

The juvenile guest in Example 22 is asked by the host of a chat show whether her celebrity father has told her not to disclose any secrets about him. The young girl is in a dilemma. On the one hand, she should answer a respectable adult's question faithfully. On the other hand, she does not want to admit that her father has indeed some closely guarded secrets. Therefore she uses ba5 to mark the uncertain state of her mind – that she might be expected not to answer the question honestly.

Example 23

邱启明：　会　经常　　　想　　他们　　吗？
qiu1qi3ming2　hui4　jing1chang2　xiang3　ta1men5　ma5
'Qiu Qiming' 'will' 'frequently'　'think' 'them'　QM
'Host: Do you often think about them?'

马毅：呃……不敢　　去　想　　**吧**。
ma3yi4 e5　　bu4gan3　qu4 xiang3 ba5
'Ma Yi' PF　'not-dare' 'go' 'think' SFP
'Male Guest: Er...I don't have the heart to think, I guess.'

(wmyhb 20130326)

In Example 23, the male guest has just finished recounting the story of the loss of both his parents. The host of the show asks him whether he misses them. Upon this, Ma answers that he cannot afford to think of them. His reply is marked with *ba5* to show the indecisive nature of his mind rather than the uncertainty of the statement; that is, he presumably wants to think of his parents but is too sad to do so.

Example 24

蔡康永：　　　　不　需要　　告诉　　他？
cai4kang1yong3 bu4 xu1yao4 gao4su4 ta1
'Kevin Tsai'　　　'not' 'need'　'tell'　　'him'
'Host: There is no need for you to tell him?'

王炜宣：　　　　　不用。
wang2wei3xuan1 bu2yong4
'Wang Weixuan' 'not-use'
'Female Guest: There is no need.'

徐熙娣：　他　知道　　之后　　　应该　　　也　不会　　怎么样　　　**吧**。
xu2xi1di4 ta1 zhi1dao4 zhi1hou4 ying1gai1 ye3 bu2hui4 zen3mo5yang4 ba5
'Dee Hsu' 'he' 'know'　'afterward' 'should'　'also' 'not-will' 'do something' SFP
'Hostess: Even if he knows, he is unlikely to do anything about it.'

(kxll 20130820)

In the previous examples, 吧 marks the speaker's cognitive and emotional state with a degree of uncertainty. In Example 24, *ba5* is shown to mark the speaker's judgment about others' behavior. In cases like this, the speaker is not necessarily unsure about their opinions. It is probably a way of showing respect to others, admitting the unlikelihood of knowing other people's thoughts completely.

Example 25

徐熙娣：　她　只是　　想　　要　　看　我们　　摔倒　　　**吧**。
xu2xi1di4 ta1 zhi3shi4 xiang3 yao4 kan4 wo3men5 shuai1dao3 ba5
'Dee Hsu' 'she' 'only'　'think' 'want' 'see' 'we'　　'fall'　　SFP
'Hostess: She only wants to see us slip on the floor, I guess.'

(kxll 20130813)

Example 25 shows *ba5* again used to mark speculation about the thinking of others, this time to create a humorous effect. In this case, Hsu is referring to other guests' supposedly ill-intentioned wish to see the hostess fall on the slippery catwalk. As the remark itself is an accusation of an unfriendly demeanor, it is suitable to add *ba5* to reduce the credibility of the sentence so that it is turned into a joke rather than a serious accusation.

Marker of request for confirmation

Since the basic function of 吧 is to show uncertainty, it is often used to mark a request for confirmation, especially in the form of a tag question. When *ba5* accompanies a statement like that in Examples 18 to 25, it characteristically gives a sense of uncertainty, whether out of sincerity or just being tactful. When *ba5* is used to tag a question, however, the speaker is usually fairly certain about their proposition and only requires a minimum of confirmation from the listener.

Example 26

a   孟非: 看起来   你   是   为   马莹   准备   了
         meng4fei1 kan4qi3lai2 ni3   shi4 wei4 ma3ying2 zhun3bei4 le5
         'Meng Fei' 'look like'   'you' 'be' 'for' 'Ma Ying' 'prepare'   AM

        一段   舞,   是吧?
        yi2duan4 wu3   shi4 ba5
        'one' Cla 'dance' 'be' SFP

        'Host: It looks like you have prepared a dance routine for Ma Ying, right?'
                                               (fcwr 20130818)

b   程大冲: 你   需要   一个   三好   的
         cheng2da4chong1 ni3   xu1yao4 yi2ge5   san1hao3   de5
         'Cheng Dachong' 'you' 'need'   'one' Cla 'three-good' AD

        男人,   对   吧?
        nan2ren2 dui4   ba5
        'man'   'correct' SFP

        'Male Guest: You need a man with three virtues, right?'
                                               (fcwr 20130811)

Example 26 shows two tag questions used on two different occasions to request confirmation from the addressee on the correctness of a certain proposition. When *ba5* is used in a tag question like this, the speaker is usually quite certain about the proposition, and the answer is normally 'yes'. In the case of Example 25a, for example, the host of the show already knows from his script that the male guest is going to perform a dance. In the case of Example 26b, the speaker is reconfirming a piece of information he received earlier from the female guest whom he is now questioning.

Example 27

邱启明：	手心	又	冒汗	了	**吧**？
qiu1qi3ming2	shou3xin1	you4	mao4han4	le5	ba5
'Qiu Qiming'	'hand-heart'	'again'	'emit-sweat'	AM	SFP

'Host: (Your) palm is sweating again, right?'

李志博：	又	冒汗	了。
li3zhi4bo2	you4	mao4han4	le5
'Li Zhibo'	'again'	'emit-sweat'	AM

'Female Guest: It is sweating again.'

(wmyhb 20130725)

In Example 27, the host of the show is referring to a behavioral pattern normally associated with a female candidate on his show – that the palms of her hands will sweat when she sees a male she likes. Li has earlier expressed her fondness for the current male candidate, which means her hands are probably already sweating; hence the host Qiu's request for confirmation that she is already doing so. As in Example 26, a question tagged by *ba5* shows the speaker's confidence in the proposition. The presence of *ba5* only makes the utterance into a request for confirmation, not a real yes/no question that expects either a positive or a negative answer. And the female guest does give the expected confirmation.

Example 28

蔡康永：	黄西田	应该	很	乐意	去	**吧**？
cai4kang1yong3	huang2xi1tian2	ying1gai1	hen3	le4yi4	qu4	ba5
'Kevin Tsai'	'Huang Xitian'	'should'	'very'	'willing'	'go'	SFP

'Host: I presume Huang Xitian will be more than willing to go, right?'

黄露瑶：	他	会	啊！
huang2lu4yao2	ta1	hui4	a5
'Huang Luyao'	'he'	'will'	SFP

'Female Guest: Indeed he will!'

(kxll 20130820)

Example 28 is a typical adjacency pair involving the use of a *ba5*-marked question as the first pair part, and an *a5*-marked answer as the second pair part. Since the request for confirmation issued by *ba5* normally expresses the speaker's strong belief in the proposition (in this case, that the female guest's father would be willing to go to his daughter's graduation ceremony), it makes sense for the listener to attach an *a5* (marking something as an obvious response to a question or situation) to her positive answer. The *a5* helps approve the correctness of the response and endorse the former speaker's judgment about the obviousness of the situation.

Example 29

孟非：　　你　　是　　搞　　　　电脑　　　那　　方面　　　　的　　**吧？**
meng4fei1　ni3　shi4　gao3　　dian4nao3　na4　fang1mian4　de5　ba5
'Meng Fei'　'you'　'be'　'work on'　'computer'　'that'　'aspect'　　　ED　SFP
'Host: You are in the computer profession, right?'

童雷：　　对　　对　　对，　我　　是　　搞　　IT　的。
tong2lei2　dui4　dui4　dui4　wo3　shi4　gao3　i-t　de5
'Tong Lei'　'right'　'right'　'right'　'I'　'be'　'do'　'IT'　ED
'Male Guest: Yes, yes, yes, I am an IT person.'

(fcwr 20130824)

The dialogue in Example 29 takes place after the host of the dating show reads out some computer jargon and messages printed on the male candidate's T-shirt. Having inferred that the young man must be a computer professional, Meng goes on to ask the question 'You work in a computer related occupation, right?' to which the male candidate readily answers with three instances of 'correct' and a paraphrase (changing 'computer' to 'IT'). Thus, a question marked with *ba5* often elicits conforming answers unless it is used to mock or challenge.

Example 30

徐熙娣：　你　在　学校　　应该　　是　受　欢迎
xu2xi1di4　ni3　zai4　xue2xiao4　ying1gai1　shi4　shou4　huan1ying2
'Dee Hsu'　'you'　'at'　'school'　　'should'　'be'　'receive'　'welcome'

的　喜感　　　人物　　　**吧？**
de5　xi3gan3　　ren2wu4　　ba5
AD　'delight-feel'　'person-object'　SFP

'Hostess: You ought to be a popular comic character at school, aren't you?'

王炜宣：　　　算　是　啦。
wang2wei3xuan1　suan4　shi4　la5
'Wang Weixuan'　'count'　'be'　SFP
'Female Guest: Yes, I might be considered one.'

(kxll 20130820)

In Example 30, the hostess of the chat show presupposes that the female guest must be a popular person in school, her father being a legendary singer. The presupposition is subsumed in a *ba5*-marked question to mitigate its force in the conversation. Even so, the request of confirmation is no more than a formality and it is difficult for the addressee to give a negative answer, or to argue against the presupposition. That being said, it is imprudent and impolite for a person to admit their own popularity in school. Therefore, the female guest uses the vague expression 算是 'count as one' as a compromise (see also 5.11 for *la5* as a marker of dismissal). This shows how powerful *ba5* can be in extracting a positive answer in conversation.

In Schiffrin's model, *ba5* would function in multiple domains. For example, in the Exchange Structure, *ba5* is used in the first pair part which demands a certain kind of response. In the Participation Framework, the use of *ba5* may signify the speaker's superior position in knowledge, reasoning ability or authority.

Marker of satire

In some cases, 吧 is used to mark a question that does not require an answer. That is, it is used in a rhetorical way. The purpose is usually to mock the addressee in order to hurt them or to create a humorous effect.

Example 31

亚丽： 你　 看，　后悔　　　了　吧！　怡珍。
ya3li4　ni3　 kan4　hou4hui3 le5　ba5　yi2zhen1
'Ya Li'　'you'　'look'　'regret'　　SFP　SFP　'Yizhen'
'Hostess: See? Do you regret it now, Yizhen?'

(zsydt 20130706)

The dating show involved in Example 31 requires the four female guests to turn around if they like a certain male candidate based on his brief self-introduction and without looking at him. One female did not turn around for a supposedly good-looking male, and the hostess mocks her by issuing the rhetorical question 后悔了吧? 'Surely you regret it now?' The hearer normally need not answer such a question, but is free to construct their reply in whichever way they like (e.g. by offering an explanation).

Example 32

徐熙娣： 你 跟 爸爸 熟 吧？
xu2xi1di4 ni3 gen1 ba4ba5 shou2 ba5
'Dee Hsu' 'you' 'with' 'father' 'familiar' SFP
'Hostess: Are you close to your father?'

黄露瑶： 很 熟。
huang2lu4yao2 hen3 shou2
'Huang Luyao' 'very' 'familiar'
'Female Guest: Very close.

我们 有时候 都 会 一起 睡觉。
wo3men5 you3shi2hou4 dou1 hui4 yi4qi3 shui4jiao4
'we' 'sometimes' 'all' 'will' 'together' 'sleep'
We sometimes sleep together (on the same bed).'

徐熙娣： 那 也 太 熟 了 吧！
xu2xi1di4 na4 ye3 tai4 shou2 le5 ba5
'Dee Hsu' 'that' 'also' 'too' 'familiar' SFP SFP
'Hostess: That seems a bit too close!'

Two instances of *ba5* are involved in Example 32. The first *ba5* marks a request for confirmation, to which the listener does give a positive response. However, the guest's reply that father and daughter often 'sleep together' seems slightly ambiguous. The hostess of the show spots the chance to mock and makes a witty comment marked with the second *ba5*. Given the context, this utterance is quickly perceived by the audience as a satire rather than an uncertain statement or a request for confirmation.

Example 33

仲伟冬： （你们） 这 都 是 最佳 损友。
zhong4wei3dong1 ni3men5 zhe4 dou1 shi4 zui4jia1 sun3you3
'Zhong Weidong' 'you' 'this' 'all' 'be' 'the best' 'damage-friend'
'Female Guest: You are all best bad friends.'

邱启明： 好像 这个 第一 球 是 你 踢 的 吧！
qiu1qi3ming2 hao3xiang4 zhe4ge5 di4yi1 qiu2 shi4 ni3 ti1 de5 ba5
'Qiu Qiming' 'seem' 'this' 'first' 'ball' 'be' 'you' 'kick' ED SFP
'Host: It seems to be you who kicked the first ball, right?'

(wmyhb 20130326)

In Example 33, Zhong jokingly attacks the other female guests by naming them 'the best bad friends' for the male candidate due to their harsh criticism of him.

The host of the show, however, retorts that it was Zhong who launched the first attack. This is a typical satire marked by *ba5*, taking an unexpected or especially poignant perspective of the issue to create a damaging or humorous effect.

Example 34

婉晴：	婚前	跟	婚后，	差	太多	了	**吧**？
wan3qing2	hun1qian2	gen1	hun1hou4	cha1	tai4duo1	le5	ba5
'Wanqing'	'marry-before'	'with'	'marry-after'	'differ'	'too-much'	SFP	SFP

'Wanqing: (You seem to behave) very differently before and after marriage, don't you?'

Example 34 is extracted from the dialogue of a TV drama. It is a *ba5*-marked rhetorical question used by a wife to challenge her estranged husband in a quarrel. Although a rhetorical question marked by *ba5* used to challenge often constitutes a sentence in itself, sometimes it can also be incorporated in a longer sentence, as Example 35 shows.

Example 35

野新新：	如果	那个	女生	换成
ye3xin1xin1	ru2guo3	na4ge5	nv3sheng1	huan4cheng2
'Ye Xinxin'	'if'	'that'	'girl'	'change to'

'Female Guest: If the girl (you mentioned) were to be replaced by

刚才	跟	你	一起	跳舞	的	大妈，
gang1cai2	gen1	ni3	yi4qi3	tiao4wu3	de5	da4ma1
'just now'	'with'	'you'	'together'	'dance'	AD	'big-mother'

the older woman (that we saw) dancing together with you

你	会	跟	她	在一起	吗？	不	会	**吧**！
ni3	hui4	gen1	ta1	zai4yi4qi3	ma5	bu2	hui4	ba5
'you'	'will'	'with'	'she'	'be together'	QM	'not'	'will'	SFP

would you still be with her? I do not think so!'

(wmyhb 20130725)

In Example 35, the female guest is challenging a male guest's outrageous behavior in having two girlfriends simultaneously, on the grounds that one of the girls needs help. She first gives a hypothetical condition – that the extra girl the male took under his wing is replaced by an older, unattractive woman. She then asks whether he would still be with her. She believes that he would certainly not do so and she marks this belief with *ba5* to turn it into a strong rhetorical question.

Marker of invitation

When 吧 is used with an imperative sentence, it has the power to soften the command and turn it into a suggestion or invitation, which is subject to refusal or lack of response.

Example 36

a 肖骁：   赶快   为   我   转身   吧！
   xiao4xiao1 gan3kuai4 wei4 wo3 zhuan3shen1 ba5
   'Xiao Xiao' 'hurry'   'for' 'me' 'turn-body' SFP
   'Male Guest: Please turn around for me quickly!'

(zsydt 20130706)

b 蔡旸：   勇敢   的 承认   吧！
   cai4yang2 yong3gan3 de5 cheng2ren4 ba5
   'Cai Yang' 'brave'   AD 'admit'   SFP
   'Female Guest: Admit it bravely!'

(wmyhb 20130723)

The Chinese sentence in Example 36a does not contain the word 'please' per se. A proper translation without the SFP would be 'Turn around for me quickly!' However, the inclusion of *ba5* in this sentence has mitigated the force of the command, making it sound like a plea. Being soft and non-obligatory are the core features of a *ba5*-marked imperative sentence. This makes it a promising candidate for use in a light-hearted setting where a command is given as a joke rather than with serious intention. An example of this is shown in 36b, where the speaker issues a command to a male candidate (for him to admit that he adores her, contrary to his behavior) in a pretentious way.

Example 37

王宇轩：   你   也   别   难为   人家   姑娘   了。
wang2yu3xuan1 ni3   ye3   bie2   nan2wei2 ren2jia1 gu1niang2 le5
'Wang Yuxuan' 'you' 'also' 'do not' 'embarrass' 'others' 'girl'   SFP
'Female Guest: You might as well not put the girl on the spot.

你   就   放   了 她   吧！
ni3   jiu4 fang4   le5 ta1 ba5
'you' 'just' 'set free' AM 'she' SFP
You might as well let her go!'

(wmyhb 20130719)

The speaker in Example 37 is pleading for the male guest to stop embarrassing a female guest. Both sentences in Example 37 are imperatives starting with the second person pronoun 'you'. The use of *ba5* at the end of a series of commands seems to soften the overall tone of the speech, making it friendlier and less compelling.

Example 38

饶艺： 有   一次 呢， 我   跟   女朋友   路过   车站，
rao2yi4 you3 yi2ci4 ne5 wo3 gen1 nv3peng2you3 lu4guo4   che1zhan4
'Rao Yi' 'have' 'once' CFP 'I' 'with' 'girlfriend'   'road-pass' 'station'
'Male Guest: There was one time, I and my girlfriend passed a (train) station.

我   突然   跟   她   说   「我们   去   旅行   **吧！**」
wo3 tu2ran2   gen1 ta1 shuo1 wo3men5 qu4 lv3xing2 ba5
'I' 'suddenly' 'with' 'her' 'say' 'we'   'go' 'travel' SFP
I suddenly said to her: Let's go on a trip!'

(wmyhb 20130326)

As in English, the subject of an imperative sentence can also be the first person plural (i.e. the inclusive 'we'). This kind of imperative sentence is often marked with *ba5* in Chinese, as is the embedded sentence in Example 38. The sentence is then understood as a warm suggestion, an invitation for a joint venture between friends.

Example 39

邱启明：   找   到   知音   了， 咱   俩   走   **吧！**
qiu1qi3ming2 zhao3 dao4   zhi1yin1   le5 zan2 lia3 zou3 ba5
'Qiu Qiming' 'find' 'reach' 'know-sound' AM 'we' 'both' 'walk' SFP
'Host: I found someone who knows me. Let's both go away together!'

(wmyhb 20130725)

The host of the dating show in Example 39 is pretending to match himself with a male guest due to their common interests and suggesting they leave the stage together as a couple. The colloquial usage 咱 'I; we' or 咱们 'we' is an inclusive kind of 'we' (that is, including the speaker and the hearer or hearers), while the formal usage 我们 'we' can be either inclusive or exclusive (i.e. excluding the hearer or hearers). The expression 咱俩 'we both' in Example 39 refers to both the host and the guest of the show, and the sentence is a suggestion made jokingly, to achieve a funny effect. This kind of imperative sentence is typically accompanied by a gesture or a bodily movement in line with the proposed action.

Example 40

邱启明：　　　大家　　　行行好　　　吧！
qiu1qi3ming2 da4jia1　　xing2xing2hao3 ba5
'Qiu Qiming' 'big-home' 'do-do-good'　SFP
'Host: Everybody, please be kind!'

(wmyhb 20130725)

The speaker in Example 40 is addressing the entire group of 30 female guests, asking them to be kind to the current male candidate − that is, do not turn off all the lights so he has some hope of taking home a date. The subject of this imperative sentence is 大家 'everyone in hearing range'. The addition of *ba5* at the end in this case makes the request more sincere and earnest.

Marker of ending

A distinct usage of 吧 is to mark a contribution which is meant to bring an end to a particular strand of conversation. This would be what Fung and Carter (2007) called the 'structural' function of the discourse marker − opening or ending a topic. The expression which bears the marking of *ba5* may be a word of farewell, a perfunctory remark, a compromised statement, a proposal to leave the current venue, and so on.

Example 41

杨哲：　　　关于　　我　为什么　　　找　　不　到　　女朋友，
yang2zhe2 guan1yu2 wo3 wei4shen2mo5 zhao3 bu2 dao4 nv3peng2you3
'Yang Zhe' 'regarding' 'I' 'why'　　　'find' 'not' 'reach' 'girlfriend'
'Host: As to why I cannot find a girlfriend

可以　看　下段　　　　　VCR。
ke3yi3 kan4 xia4duan4　v-c-r
'may' 'see' 'next-section' 'VCR'
we can see the next video recording.'

孟非：　　　好　吧，来　　看　下一段　　　吧。
meng4fei1 hao3 ba5 lai2　kan4 xia4yi2duan4 ba5
'Meng Fei' 'good' SFP 'come' 'see' 'next clip'　SFP
'Host: All right, let's see the next video clip.'

(fcwr 20130824)

The male guest in Example 41 is answering a previous question about why he does not have a girlfriend now. In his answer, he refers to a routine of playing the male suitor's video. He means to indicate that the answer can be found somewhere in the video. Since there seems nothing more left to say on this topic, the host of the show acts accordingly, using two short *ba5*-marked sentences to conclude this strand of conversation. The first sentence is a short expression 好吧 'OK' which is typically given as a sign of compromise after some sort of argument or confrontation. The second is an imperative sentence with the subject 'we' omitted. The marking of *ba5* not only reduces the command to a polite invitation but also concludes this segment of the conversation.

Example 42

君山：　　好了，　好了，　我　老婆　　一笑　　　　啊，
jun1shan1 hao3le5 hao3le5 wo3 lao3po2 yi2xiao4　　a5
'Junshan'　'OK'　'OK'　'I'　'wife'　'one-smile'　CFP
'Junshan: Alright, alright, my wife has smiled.

乌云　　　　全　　散　　　了。
wu1yun2　quan2 san4　le5
'black-cloud' 'all'　'scatter' AM
All the clouds are dispersed.

走　　吧！ 一块　　吃饭　　去，我　请客。
zou3 ba5 yi2kuai4 chi1fan4 qu4 wo3 qing3ke4
'walk' SFP 'together' 'eat-meal' 'go' 'I' 'treat-guest'
Come on. Let's go eat together. My treat.'

Example 42 is extracted from the dialogue of a TV drama. There has been a quarrel between a husband and wife in front of a group of friends. The husband said something which turned her tears into smiles, whereupon the argument ends. The expression 走吧 'let's go!' marks a critical turning point in the husband's concluding remark. It not only proposes the physical action of walking away from the scene, but also attempts to bring an end to the interaction/confrontation. The first function is clearly made possible by the verb 走. The second function is entirely due to the presence of *ba5*. The speaker's intention to wrap up the whole scene would not be successful if *ba5* were not present or were replaced by other SFPs such as *a5*.

Example 43

明月：   我   曾经   说   过， 你们   走   了
ming2yue4 wo3 ceng2jing1 shuo1 guo4 ni3men5 zou3 le5
'Mingyue' 'I' 'ever'   'say' AM 'you' PM 'go' SFP
'Female Guest: I said before that if the time came for you to leave

我   肯定   会 挨个   送   你们，
wo3 ken3ding4 hui4 ai1ge5   song4 ni3men5
'I' 'definite' 'will' 'one by one' 'see off' 'you' PM
I definitely will see you off one by one,

但 今天   就——你们   送   我 **吧**。
dan4 jin1tian1 jiu4 ni3men5 song4 wo3 ba5
'but' 'today' 'just' 'you' PM 'see off' 'me' SFP
but today, it will have to be you seeing me off.'

(wmyhb 20130326)

The female guest in Example 43, having found her ideal dating partner, is bidding farewell to her colleagues on the show. Since they have appeared on the show together for several months, the bond is strong and it is hard to say goodbye. Nevertheless, she manages to put together a short speech and concludes it with a *ba5*-marked imperative sentence – 'You all see me off, will you?' Again, the presence of *ba5* makes it clear that this is the final remark in the current strand of discourse. No more need be said.

5.4 *BEI5*

The SFP 呗 *bei5* is a variant of *ba5* that is currently heard mainly in China and not in Taiwan. Its usage largely follows *ba5* but it does introduce a more lively tone due to its pronunciation (i.e. being a diphthong ending in a high vowel). Consequently, it is often attached to a light-hearted remark to introduce a cheerful mood. Even if *bei5* accompanies a more serious statement, it shows the speaker's intention to make the content 'easier to digest' for the audience.

Marker of uncertainty

Like *ba5*, one of the functions of *bei5* is to express the speaker's indecisive attitude or to mark something as uncertain. In Example 44, the male guest is answering a question about the current state of his grandfather's illness. His first sentence involves a false start and then a repair. This already shows his uncertain stance about what is coming next. 'Continue with the treatment' is a somewhat vague expression and works well with the uncertainty marker *bei5*. More than its predecessor *ba5*, the SFP *bei5* introduces an even softer and light-hearted tone, thereby making the serious topic sound less gloomy.

Example 44

田宇辰：　　就是　　每天一　　就是　　坚持　　治疗　　**呗**。
tian2yu3chen2　jiu4shi4　mei3tian1　jiu4shi4　jian1chi2　zhi4liao2　bei5
'Tian Yuchen'　'just-is'　'everyday'　'just-is'　'insist'　'treatment'　SFP
'Male Guest: Just everyday – just insist on treatment; that's all.'

因为　　人　　上　　岁数　　　了　嘛，身体　都　　这样。
yin1wei4　ren2　shang4　sui4shu4　　le5　ma5　shen1ti3　dou1　zhe4yang4
'because'　'human'　'up'　'year-number'　AM　SFP　'body'　'all'　'this way'
Because when people get older, their bodies naturally deteriorate.'

(wmyhb 20130723)

Marker of request for confirmation

Example 45 shows a longer discourse consisting of two Q-A adjacency pairs. The first is a *wh-* question asked by the female in the hope of finding out how much dowry is needed to marry the male candidate. When the male answers that there is no definite criterion for evaluating the adequacy of the dowry, the female obviously thinks that no dowry is also possible. Therefore she asks the second question, which is a hypothesis marked with 呗 to request a confirmation. As this is a somewhat cheeky question, it is suitably marked by the *bei5* rather than the relatively serious *ba5*.

Example 45

王艺洁：　　女方　　　多少　　　嫁妆　　　算　　够　　　啊？
wang2yi4jie2　nv3fang1　　duo1shao3　jia4zhuang1　suan4　gou4　　a5
'Wang Yijie'　'female-side'　'how much'　'dowry'　　'count'　'enough'　SFP
'Female Guest: How much dowry is counted as adequate?'

张瑞静：　　　这　　没有　　　标准。
zhang1rui4jing4　zhe4　mei2you3　biao1zhun3
'Zhang Ruijing'　'this'　'no'　　'standard'
'Male Guest: There is no criterion (for this).'

王艺洁：　　不　给　也　行　　**呗**？
wang2yi4jie2　bu4　gei3　ye3　xing2　bei5
'Wang Yijie'　'not'　'give'　'also'　'alright'　SFP
'Female Guest: Is it also fine not to give (the dowry)?'

张瑞静：　　　出　　　个　人　　就　　行　　了。
zhang1rui4jing4　chu1　　ge5　ren2　jiu4　xing2　le5
'Zhang Ruijing'　'produce'　Cla　'person'　'then'　'alright'　SFP
'Male Guest: It will be alright if you offer yourself as a person.'

(wmyhb 20130730)

Marker of satire

In Example 46, the female guest is commenting on the male guest's behavior. She noticed earlier that he pretentiously turned his head to one side and covered his face with both hands, not wanting to see how many girls had turned off the lights (i.e. not wanting to date him). After the girl finishes her description, the host of the show says something like 'He is trying to look innocent' and marks the utterance with *bei5*. The function of 呗 in this instance is to introduce a satirical light-heartedness so that the host's comment can be understood as a good-natured mocking.

Example 46

王婉洁： 大家 灭灯 的 时候，
wang2wan3jie2 da4jia1 mie4deng1 de5 shi2hou4
'Wang Wanjie' 'everybody' 'extinguish-light' AD 'moment'
'Female Guest: When everybody is turning the light off,

他 把 脸 就 这样子—— 就 转 过 去 了。
ta1 ba3 lian3 jiu4 zhe4yang4zi5 jiu4 zhuan3 guo4 qu4 le5
'he' OB 'face' 'just' 'like this' 'just' 'turn' 'over' 'go' AM
he handles his face like this – just turning over to one side.'

孟非： 卖 萌 呗！
meng4fei1 mai4 meng2 bei5
'Meng Fei' 'sell' 'lovely' SFP
'Host: Sounds like he is faking innocence!'

(fcwr 20130824)

In Example 47, the two female guests are ostentatiously fighting over the current male candidate, each accusing the other of using heavy makeup. Liu first dares Cai to remove her eye shadow, while Cai demands that Liu erase her lipstick. The use of *bei5* greatly reduces the aggression that may otherwise be felt in Cai's command, and the whole interaction turns into a fun-making event.

Example 47

刘琳：　有　　本事　　你　能　　把　你的　　眼影　　　　给
liu2lin2　you3　ben3shi4　ni3　neng2　ba3　ni3de5　yan3ying3　gei3
'Liu Lin'　'have'　'abilities'　'you'　'can'　OB　'your'　'eye-shadow'　'give'

我　卸　　　了　吗？
wo3　xie4　　le5　ma5
'me'　'unload'　AM　QM

'Female Guest: If you are so good why don't you remove your eye shadow for me?'

蔡旸：　那　　你　把　你　红唇　　　卸　　了　**呗！**
cai4yang2　na4　ni3　ba3　ni3　hong2chun2　xie4　le5　bei5
'Cai Yang'　'then'　'you'　OB　'you'　'red-lip'　'unload'　AM　SFP

'Female Guest: Then why don't you remove your red lips as well?'

(wmyhb 20130327)

Prior to the dialogue in Example 48, a special event was featured by the reality dating show, where the program was visited by a young couple. The female was once a guest on the show and she is now married to Liu Ru. After a warm welcome, a video recollection of the past events concerning the woman on the show, and some conversations and joking, the host of the show asks what the newly wedded couple intends to do next. Upon that, Liu comes up with the witty remark shown in Example 48: that they will try to present an 'artistic work', which in that context means a baby. This witty reply was marked by *bei5* to reflect the light-heartedness and the pleasant atmosphere.

Example 48

邱启明：　那　接下来　　两位　　有　甚么　　打算　　吗？
qiu1qi3ming2　na4　jie1xia4lai2　liang3wei4　you3　shen2mo5　da3suan4　ma5
'Qiu Qiming'　'then'　'next stage'　'two'　Cla　'have'　'what'　'plan'　QM

'Host: What plan do you both have for the next stage?'

刘儒：　弄　个　作品　　出来　　**呗。**
liu2ru2　nong4　ge5　zuo4pin3　chu1lai2　bei5
'Liu Ru'　'make'　Cla　'creation'　'come out'　SFP

'Special Male Guest: Maybe (we will) create a masterpiece.'

(wmyhb 201308

The dialogue in Example 49 happens in a quick Question and Answer session where each preliminarily matched couple ask each other questions and answer them as best they can in 30 seconds. In this particular exchange, the female intended to ask the male about a moving experience which is most likely a positive one. However, the male ends up sharing a negative experience – a poignant moment for him when he was dumped by his girlfriend. Nevertheless, in the convivial atmosphere of the dating show, it is not suitable to mention such a miserable experience without any modification. This is where *bei5* comes in, which, to some extent, helps lighten up the remark.

Example 49

张蓝心： 你 经历 过 最
zhang1lan2xin1 ni3 jing1li4 guo4 zui4
'Zhang Lanxin' 'you' 'experience' AM 'the most'
'Female Guest: Among the things that you ever experienced

触动 你的 心 的 事情 是 甚么？
chu4dong4 ni3de5 xin1 de5 shi4qing2 shi4 shen2mo5
'touch' 'your' 'heart' AD 'matter' 'be' 'what'
what experience has touched your heart the most?'

张春： 触动 我 心 呀，
zhang1chun1 chu4dong4 wo3 xin1 ya5
'Zhang Chun' 'touch' 'I' 'heart' CFP
'Male Guest: The most heart-touching event?

就是 我 女朋友 把 我 甩 了 呗。
jiu4shi4 wo3 nv3peng2you3 ba3 wo3 shuai3 le5 bei5
'just-be' 'I' 'girlfriend' OB 'me' 'dump' AM SFP
That is when my girlfriend dumped me!'

(zsydt 20130629)

Incidentally, we see a 呀 appearing in Zhang Chun's speech, which is considered here as a CFP rather than an SFP. This is because *ya5* (as a variant of 啊) is not performing a function normally associated with *ya5/a5* at the end of a sentence, but is simply used here as a pause filler, somewhat like a 'list marker' as discussed earlier in the *a5* section.

Marker of invitation

Like its close relative 吧, the SFP 呗 is also used to soften a command, making it more like a suggestion and making the suggested move seem easier to carry out.

Example 50

a 王煊：　　　啟明　　哥　　　　　你　也　来　　一段　　　　**呗**！
　wang2xuan1 qi3ming2 ge1　　　ni3 ye3 lai2　yi2duan4　　bei5
　'Wang Xuan' 'Qiming'　'older brother' 'you' 'also' 'come' 'one-section' SFP
　'Female Guest: Brother Qiming, why don't you also give a performance?'

(wmyhb 20130806)

b 朱斯慧：　　你　喜欢　　我　吗？　你　夸夸　　我　**呗**！
　zhu1si1hui4 ni3　xi3huan1 wo3 ma5　ni3　kua1kua1 wo3 bei5
　'Zhu Sihui'　'you' 'like'　　'me' QM　'you' 'praise'　'me' SFP
　'Female Guest: Do you like me? Why don't you praise me a bit?'

(wmyhb 20130725)

In Example 50a, the female is asking the host to follow the example of a male guest who just performed a talent show. The host of the dating show is a parent figure on this show and is widely respected; hence it is appropriate for the female guest to use *bei5* to soften the somewhat unscrupulous suggestion. In Example 50b, the female makes a cheeky move of asking the male to praise her. This kind of request is also a good candidate for the marking of *bei5*.

Marker of ending

Finally, 呗 also inherits the function of *ba5* to signal the speaker's intention to close the current strand of conversation. In Example 51 below, the female guest becomes interested in a particular male candidate, and advises him to stop the selection process and just take her away. This is an impossible proposal; the marking of *bei5* is therefore appropriate as it makes the proposal seem a joke (which is indeed the case).

Example 51

苏醒宇：　　我　觉得　　我　跟　你　挺　　合适　　的。
su1xing3yu3 wo3 jue2de5 wo3 gen1 ni3 ting3　he2shi4　de5
'Su Xingyu' 'I' 'feel'　'I' 'with' 'you' 'rather' 'suitable' ED
'Female Guest: I feel you and I are quite suitable together.

要不，　　别　　选　　了，我　跟　你　走　**呗**！
yao4bu4　bie2　xuan3　le5　wo3 gen1 ni3 zou3 bei5
'want-not' 'do not' 'choose' SFP 'I'　'with' 'you' 'walk' SFP
I suggest, you do not choose. I will walk away with you!'

(wmyhb 20130806)

In Example 52, the male guest is pre-scheduled to perform a talent show to impress the ladies so that at least one of them will pick him as her date. At some point there was a discussion as to when to perform the show. The man wishes to put it off until later but the host suggests doing it immediately. The man gives up his original position and agrees to perform straightaway. He marks his final sentence ('Let it be now then') with *bei5*, which duly concludes the discussion.

Example 52

邱启明：	所以	我们	不如	现在	就	演。
qiu1qi3ming2	suo3yi3	wo3men5	bu4ru2	xian4zai4	jiu4	yan3
'Qiu Qiming'	'therefore'	'we'	'had better'	'now'	'just'	'perform'

'Host: Therefore we might as well let you perform now.'

杨智豪：	那	就	现在	呗。
yang2zhi4hao2	na4	jiu4	xian4zai4	bei5
'Yang Zhihao'	'then'	'just'	'now'	SFP

'Male Guest: Let it be now then.'

(wmyhb 20130806)

5.5 SFP *NE5*

The main function of 呢 *ne5* is to manage ideas and information in discourse. It works on the basis of contrast – contrasting two opposing views, known and unknown information, real and hypothetical circumstances, and so on.

Marker of contrast

When *ne5* is used to mark contrasts in discourse, it can mark either a question or a statement, a sentence or a phrase. When *ne5* is marking a phrase, we obviously cannot call it a Sentence *Final* Particle. Instead, I will call it a *Constituent* Final Particle (CFP), which means it can be at the end of any constituent of a sentence, be it a word or a phrase.

Example 53

黄菡： 　　你　可以　说　　得　不　好　听　**呢，**
huang2han4 ni3 ke3yi3 shuo1 de5 bu4 hao3 ting1 ne5,
'Huang Han' 'you' 'can' 'say' Com 'not' 'good' 'listen' CFP
'Female Specialist: You can be a little harsh and

叫— 我　没有　　洞察力。　　说　　得　好　听　　一点　　**呢，**
jiao4 wo3 mei2you3 dong4cha2li4 shuo1 de5 hao3 ting1 yi4dian3 ne5
'call' 'I' 'not-have' 'insight' 'say' Com 'good' 'listen' 'one-bit' CFP
say that I do not have insight. (If you) be a little kinder,

我　有　反思　　　能力。
wo3 you3 fan3si1 neng2li4
'I' 'have' 'reverse-think' 'ability'
(you can say) I have the ability to introspect.'

(fcwr 20130818)

The speaker in Example 53 is responding to a criticism of her style of talk on the show. Her contention is whether you like her speech or not depends on how you look at it. On the one hand, you can criticize her for lack of insight; on the other hand, you can praise her for the ability to examine her thoughts carefully before speaking. There are two instances of *ne5* used in her speech, each marking one of two opposite points of view (i.e. good vs bad).

Example 54

吴显标： 　　其实　我　带　了　好　几　双　　皮鞋　过来，
wu2xian3biao1 qi2shi2 wo3 dai4 le5 hao3 ji3 shuang1 pi2xie2 guo4lai2
'Wu Xianbiao' 'in fact' 'I' 'bring' AM 'good' 'some' 'pair' 'shoes' 'come over'
'Male Guest: In fact, I have brought a good many pairs of shoes with me,

但是　我　不　知道　穿　哪　　一双。
dan4shi4 wo3 bu4 zhi1dao4 chuan1 na3 yi4shuang1
'but' 'I' 'not' 'know' 'wear' 'which' 'one-pair'
but I do not know which pair to wear.'

王宇轩： 　　我　没　说　皮鞋！我　说　裤子　**呢！**
wang2yu3xuan1 wo3 mei2 shuo1 pi2xie2 wo3 shuo1 ku4zi5 ne5
'Wang Yuxuan' 'I' 'not' 'say' 'shoes' 'I' 'say' 'trousers' SFP
'Female Guest: I am not talking about shoes. I am talking about trousers!'

(wmyhb 20130710)

The male candidate in Example 54 has just been criticized by the female guest for his look. The man thinks it is his shoes which causes the problem. However, the girl quickly points out that it is not the shoes but the trousers that are causing the problem. The girl uses two parallel structures to express the contrast – 'I did not mean the shoes; I meant the trousers' and marks the second sentence with *ne5* to emphasize the contrast between the two objects.

Example 55

李莉娜：　我　　爸爸　　就　　说，　我　女儿　　长　　这么　　漂亮，
li3li4na4　wo3　ba4ba5　jiu4　shuo1　wo3　nv3er2　　zhang3　zhe4mo5　piao4liang4
'Li Lina'　'I'　'father'　'just'　'say'　'I'　'daughter'　'grow'　'such'　　'pretty'
'Female Guest: My father says, my daughter is so beautiful.

怎么　　　到　　了　舞台　　上，　　电视　　　上　　看　　出来
zen3mo5　dao4　le5　wu3tai2　shang4　dian4shi4　shang4　kan4　chu1lai2
'How'　　'reach'　AM　'stage'　'on'　　'television'　'up'　　'see'　'emerge'
How come (when she is) on the stage of television

这么　　　丑　　了　**呢**？
zhe4mo5　chou3　le5　ne5
'such'　　'ugly'　SFP　SFP
(she) looks so ugly?'

(fcwr 20130810)

In Example 55, there is a contrast between the girl's being beautiful to her father in daily life and being ugly on TV. The second situation is marked by *ne5* to highlight the difference.

Example 56

李烁红：　　　　在　这里　　没有　　　牵手　　　成功　　　　的话，
li3shuo4hong2　zai4　zhe4li3　mei2you3　qian1shou3　cheng2gong1　de5hua4
'Li Shuohong'　'at'　'here'　'none'　　'hold-hand'　'successful'　'if'
'Female Guest: Now that I have not succeeded in securing a date here (on stage).

那　　下面　　　的　观众　　　　有　　没有　　　**呢**？
na4　xia4mian4　de5　guan1zhong4　you3　mei2you3　ne5
'then'　'under'　　AD　'audience'　　'have'　'not-have'　SFP
What about the audience off stage?'

(zsydt 20130817)

In Example 56, the female guest has just been rejected by the male candidate. When she has the chance to speak, she asks the audience if anyone wants to be her date instead. Again, *ne5* is used to mark the contrast between two situations – 'on stage' and 'off stage' in this case.

Example 57

孟非：　　我　　想　　问　　一下，
meng4fei1　wo3　xiang3　wen4　yi2xia4
'Meng Fei'　'I'　'think'　'ask'　'once'
'Host: I would like to ask

哈尔滨　　其他　女生　　是　怎么　　过来　　的？
ha1er3bin1　qi2ta1　nv3sheng1　shi4　zen3mo5　guo4lai2　de5
'Harbin'　'other'　''girl'　'be'　'how'　'come over'　AD
how the other girls in Harbin manage to overcome this (problem).'

薛盼盼：　　啊，是　噢…
xue1pan4pan4　a5　shi4　ou5
'Xue Panpan'　IP　'yes'　SFP
'Female Guest: Oh, indeed . . .'

孟非：　　姑娘，　　我　逗　你　玩　**呢！**
meng4fei1　gu1niang2　wo3　dou4　ni3　wan2　ne5
'Meng Fei'　'girl'　'I'　'tease'　'you'　'play'　SFP
'Host: Girl, I am just messing with you!'

(fcwr 20130811)

At first glance, the *ne5*-marked sentence in Example 57 does not seem to have another expression to contrast with. In fact, the host of the show has just asked a question which is difficult for the female guest to answer (he asked why all the other girls in Harbin city do not accumulate fat as the girl claims to – like herself, due to the cold weather). The girl suddenly realizes her theory is unworkable and has a hard time finding the words to say. The host therefore says he is just teasing her in order to ease the embarrassment. The addition of *ne5* helps highlight the contrast (between being serious and joking) and maximizes the ability of the expression to ease tension.

Marker of incomplete information

Another function of 呢 related to its ability to contrast ideas or circumstances is for it to form a question used for requesting information. The *ne5* used for this function often attaches itself to a constituent of a sentence, and demands that the listener supplies the other constituent(s) loaded with the missing information to complete the sentence. The listener has to work on the basis of contrast to know what information is expected in their reply.

Example 58

马：艾大妈， 妳 还 好 吧？
ma3 ai4da4ma1 ni3 hai2 hao3 ba5
'Ma' 'Madame Ai' 'you' 'still' 'good' SFP
'Ma: Madame Ai, are you OK?

艾大妈： 我 很好， 只是 行动 有点 不 方便。
ai4da4ma1 wo3 hen3hao3 zhi3shi4 xing2dong4 you3dian3 bu4 fang1bian4
'Madame Ai' 'I' 'very-good' 'only-is' 'move' 'somewhat' 'not' 'convenient'
'Ai: I am fine, just slightly crippled.'

马：那 小芬 呢？
ma3 na4 xiao3fen1 ne5
'Ma' 'as for' 'Xiaofen' CFP
'Ma: What about Xiaofen?'

In Example 58, *ne5* is attached to a structure containing a conjunctive adverb (那 'as for') and a noun (小芬 'female name'). Since this is a sentence fragment, it cannot be made a question by adding 吗, which must be attached to a full sentence. In addition, the fragment does not contain a *wh-* word. Therefore, structurally speaking, the reason 那小芬呢 can be understood as a question is entirely due to the presence of *ne5*. In other words, while 吗 attaches to a full sentence to form a yes/no question, 呢 attaches to a sentence fragment to form a *wh-* question (in this case, the function of *ne5* is equal to *how about*).

To take Example 58 further, we want to know how *ne5* works when it helps form a question. At the point of Ma's second turn in Example 58, the information he has at hand and what he is concerned about is as follows:

Subject	Predicate
Madame Ai	fine, slightly crippled
Xiaofen	(unknown)

The function of *ne5* in Ma's second utterance, then, is to mark Xiaofen as a piece of the puzzle waiting to be placed on the board, and to invite the listener to suggest where to put it. In this case, the required information is the whereabouts and condition of Xiaofen.

A sentence fragment marked by *ne5* to form a question is often an NP, such as the case in Example 58, but it need not be so. The following is an example of an adverbial clause tagged by *ne5*.

> *Example 59*
>
> 罗： 没 感情 慢慢 培养 啊！ 还 来得及 啊！
> luo2 mei2 gan3qing2 man4man4 pei2yang3 a5 hai2 lai2de5ji2 a5
> 'Luo' 'no' 'affection' 'slowly' 'foster' SFP 'still' 'in time' SFP
> 'Luo: No affection – affection can be nurtured gradually. Still in time!'
>
> 伊： 可是， 那 万一 觉得 不 适合 呢？
> yi1 ke3shi4 na4 wan4yi1 jue2de5 bu2 shi4he2 ne5
> 'Yi' 'but' 'then' 'in case' 'feel' 'not' 'suitable' CFP
> 'Yi: But what if they feel unsuitable for each other?'

In Example 59, the first speaker, Mr Luo, suggests that the lack of romantic feelings in a parentally arranged marriage can be improved with time. As a response, the second speaker, Miss Yi, asks a question to challenge Luo's position. The question consists of an adverbial clause expressing a condition. What the listener has to do is to supply the result of the condition as the missing information. The contrast between the two ideas is illustrated below.

Condition	Action
No romantic feelings	Improve situation by time
Incompatible couple	(unknown)

In the case of Example 59, the 'unknown' part is actually quite obvious to the speaker – that some sort of disastrous consequence will result from the parentally arranged marriage if the man and woman are not suitable to each other. Thus the question formed with *ne5* in this case is used to challenge, somewhat like a rhetorical question to which the speaker does not expect an answer.

Like other SFPs, a *ne5*-marked expression does not often target a particular utterance in the previous conversation, but is responding to a situation instead.

> *Example 60*
>
> 孟非： 我们 的 呢？
> meng4fei1 wo3men5 de5 ne5
> 'Meng Fei' 'we' PD CFP
> 'Host: Where is ours?'
>
> (fcwr 20130811)

The host of the dating show in Example 60 is responding to a situation where a male guest has just given each of the 24 female guests a small present.

Mr Meng, jokingly or wishfully, asks, 'Where are ours?' meaning the two resident specialists and himself. The relevance of *ne5* in this case needs to be understood against the background of contrast between the 24 gifts for the female guests and no gift for the host of the show and his associates. In appearance, it would seem the speaker is using a *ne5*-marked question to dig out the information about their gifts. However, this is in fact just another joke the host makes at the expense of the male guest.

Subject	Predicate
24 female guests	each receives a present
host and specialists	(unknown)

In the following example, the speaker asks a *ne5*-marked question and goes on to answer the question himself.

Example 61

何军： 咱 处 着 看。 如果 你 感觉 好 **呢**?
he2jun1 zan2 chu3 zhe5 kan4 ru2guo3 ni3 gan3jue2 hao3 ne5
'He Jun' 'we' 'get along' AM 'see' 'if' 'you' 'feel' 'good' CFP
'Male Guest: Let's get along and see. If you feel good,

再 说 下一步。 好 吗?
zai4 shuo1 xia4yi2bu4 hao3 ma5
'again' 'say' 'next step' 'good' QM
we will talk about the next stage. Is that OK?'

(zsydt 20130817)

Prior to the male guest's speech in Example 61, the female guest whom he is wooing expresses concerns over certain men's negative attitudes about marriage. In an effort to comfort her and yet to refrain from making a commitment, the man suggests they get together for a period of time. If they feel good about each other, they will consider further possibilities. Note that the *ne5*-marked adverbial phrase is similar to the one in Example 59. The difference is that in Example 61 the speaker has already prepared the answer, and the 'question' is really just a more emphasized statement of the condition. Also, the situation being contrasted in Example 61 is implied but not spoken; that is, if the man and woman do not get along, then of course there will not be 'a next step'.

The kind of 呢 we saw in Example 61 is an oral rhetorical device we often hear in Chinese discourse, where *ne5* is used to highlight a particular condition for something to happen.

Example 62

孟非：　　最小　　　　 的　时候　　 是，
meng4fei1 zui4xiao3　　 de5 shi2hou4 shi4
'Meng Fei' 'the smallest' AD 'time'　 'be'
'Host: (When I was) very small,

还　 没　 搞　　 明白　　　 就　 说。
hai2 mei2 gao3　 ming2bai2　 jiu4 shuo1
'still' 'not' 'make' 'understand' 'just' 'say'
I talked straight away before I understood fully.

长大　　　 一点儿　　 **呢，**
zhang3da4 yi1dian3er5 ne5
'grow'　　 'one bit'　 CFP
Later when I grew up a little,

知道　　 多少　　　 就　 说　 多少。
zhi1dao4 duo1shao3 jiu4 shuo1 duo1shao3
'know'　 'how much' 'just' 'say'　 'how much'
I said only as much as I knew.'

(fcwr 20130818)

In Example 62, the host of the show is commenting on the art of speaking. Using his own experience, he argues that as we grow older and wiser we should be more careful about our words. Two stages of life are contrasted in relation to the typical amount of talk at each stage, as the table below shows.

Stage	Amount of talk
small	talk without full understanding
older	say only what you know

Thus, the *ne5*-marked expression in Example 62 is not used to request any information, but to highlight the contrast in talking styles between different life stages and emphasize the correctness of the later approach. Note in Example 62 the *ne5* still marks an incomplete piece of information ('Later when I grow up a little') and the speaker can legitimately stop at *ne5* and make the adverbial clause sound like a question ('What about when I grow up a little?'). He can then answer his own question after a brief pause or wait for someone to complete the sentence.

This kind of usage of *ne5* further develops into its function as a kind of 'attention getter', where it is placed at the end of a conjunctive device or a thematic structure to create some kind of suspension and to signal some important message is coming.

Example 63

a   苏士为：   谈到   我的   爱好   **呢**，
      su1shi4wei2 tan2dao4   wo3de5 ai4hao4 ne5
      'Su Shiwei' 'talk-reach' 'my'   'hobby' CFP
      'Male Guest: Speaking about my hobbies,

      那   是   非常   非常   的 多   的。
      na4   shi4 fei1chang2 fei1chang2 de5 duo1   de5
      'that' 'be' 'extremely 'extremely' AD 'much' ED
      I have plenty, plenty of them.'

                                              (wmyhb 20130725)

b   马晓俊   同事：   他   人缘   很好，   而且
      ma3xiao3jun4 tong2shi4 ta1 ren2yuan2   hen3hao3 er2qie3
      'Ma Xiaojun' 'colleague' 'he' 'people relation' 'very good' 'moreover'
      'Colleague of Male Guest: He is quite popular, and

      工作   上   **呢**，也   非常   积极   上进。
      gong1zuo4 shang4 ne5 ye3 fei1chang2 ji1ji2   shang4jin4
      'work'   'up'   CFP 'also' 'extremely' 'constructive' 'make progress'
      in terms of his work, he is also very constructive and constantly making
      progress.'

                                              (fcwr 20130825)

c   程大冲：   三位   女   嘉宾   都   挺   好   的，
      cheng2da4chong1 san1wei4 nv3   jia1bin1   dou1 ting3 hao3 de5
      'Cheng Dachong' 'three' Cla 'female' 'good guest' 'all'   'very' 'good' AD
      'Male Guest: All three female guests are quite good,

      但是   **呢**， 我   更   相信   我的   眼缘。
      dan4shi4ne5 wo3 geng4   xiang1xin4 wo3de5 yan3yuan2
      'but'   CFP 'I' 'even more' 'believe'   'my'   'eye-attraction'
      but I believe in my first impression even more.'

                                              (fcwr 20130811)

In Example 63a, the speaker inserts a *ne5* between the topic of the sentence (i.e. his hobbies) and the comment (i.e. there are plenty). The presence of *ne5* seems to wrap the structure in a significant package that both creates suspense and forecasts the coming of an important message. The same thing happens in Example 63b, where the topic of the sentence (i.e. work) is marked with *ne5* to generate listeners' interest, and the comment on work follows to fulfill the expectations. In Example 63c, the *ne5* is placed after a conjunction instead of a nominal or an adverbial element. By doing so, the speaker leaves in suspense the entire sentence rather than just part of the sentence.

Marker of expectation

Although 呢 can be used to form a question out of a sentence fragment, it is also used to mark an existing question, that is, a question which is already a question without the addition of *ne5*. In these cases, the marking of *ne5* often shows the speaker's expectation or presupposition of some sort (e.g. expectation of a contrary situation).

Example 64

a   Mr Right：你　　身边　　　这么　　　多　　美女，
    Mr Right　　ni3　shen1bian1　zhe4mo5　duo1　mei3nv3
    'Mr Right' 'you' 'body-side' 'such'　　'many' 'pretty-woman'
    'Co-host: There are so many pretty girls by your side.

    为什么　　　　一直　单身　　　呢？
    wei4shen2mo5 yi4zhi2 dan1shen1 ne5
    'why'　　　　'always' 'single'　　SFP
    Why are you single all the time?'

                                      (wmyhb 20130723)

b   Mr Right：为什么　　　　你　放弃　　深圳
    Mr Right　wei4shen2mo5 ni3　fang4qi4 shen1zhen4
    'Mr Right' 'why'　　　　'you' 'give up' 'Shenzhen'
    'Co-host: Why did you give up

    那么　　好　　的　工作　　回　　到　锦洲　　呢？
    na4mo5 hao3 de5 gong1zuo4 hui2　dao4 jin3zhou1 ne5
    'such'　'good' AD 'job'　　　'return' Com 'Jinzhou'　SFP
    such a good job in Shenzhen, and went back to Jinzhou?'

                                      (wmyhb 20130828)

The co-host of the dating show in Example 64a asks the male candidate a question based on the man's personal data. Since he works in show business, a natural assumption is that he will be surrounded by plenty of beautiful girls, and that it is easy for him to 'get one'. However, the fact is that the man is still single, and that he is on a dating show trying to get a date. Therefore, the question Mr Right asks is embedded in the assumption, or the expectation, that the man will already have a girlfriend. The SFP *ne5* is representative of that assumption and expectation. It gives a sense of incredulity to the question. It shows the speaker's desire to find the answer to something which defies their expectation. The same mechanism applies to Example 64b, where *ne5* helps highlight the contrast between giving up a fabulous job in Shenzhen and returning to Jinzhou without a job.

Example 65

沈涛:	妳	愿意	和	叶杰	来	分享	你的	秘密	吗?
shen3tao1	ni3	yuan4yi4	he2	ye4jie2	lai2	fen1xiang3	ni3de5	mi4mi4	ma5
'Shen Tao'	'you'	'willing'	'with'	'Ye Jie'	'come'	'share'	'your'	'secret'	QM

'Host: Would you like to share your secret with Ye Jie?'

一号	女生:	我	不	愿意。
yi2hao4	nv3sheng1	wo3	bu2	yuan4yi4
'No.1'	'girl'	'I'	'not'	'willing'

'Girl No. 1: I am not willing.'

沈涛:	er ...	为什么	呢?
shen3tao1	er	wei4shen2mo5	ne5
'Shen Tao'	PF	'why'	SFP

'Host: Why so?'

(aqllk 20130730)

In Example 65, the host of the show asks a female guest if she would like to share her secret with the current male candidate. The girl's rejection means she is not interested in dating the man. The host then asks 'Why?' which he tags with *ne5*. Likewise, this *ne5* also shows the host's incredulity at the girl's response, since it is the host's duty to match couples successfully. Any rejection is against his expectation and intrinsically disagreeable to him.

The kind of 呢 which is laden with expectations is often used to chide someone for failing to meet the expectations of the speaker.

Example 66

陈婷:	男	嘉宾	你	怎么	一点
chen2ting2	nan2	jia1bin1	ni3	zen3mo5	yi4dian3
'Chen Ting'	'male'	'good guest'	'you'	'how'	'a little'

'Female Guest: Male guest, why do you not have any

原则	都	没有	呢?
yuan2ze2	dou1	mei2you3	ne5
'principle'	'all'	'none'	SFP

principles at all?'

(aqllk 20130806)

The female guest in Example 66 is about to be rejected by the male candidate, who has just taken the resident specialist's advice to choose another girl. She feels disappointed and criticizes the man for 'not having any principles'. The marking of *ne5* reflects her belief that a man should have his own principles and not blindly follow other people's advice. The SFP *ne5* is an agent carrying the girl's expectation, used here to reprimand the man's unacceptable behavior.

Sometimes what is expected need not be the opposite of some current situation. The expectation assumed by the existence of *ne5* can serve as a foundation for further elaboration.

Example 67

许海益: 你 第一次 和 女生 约会，
xu3hai3yi4 ni3 di4yi1ci4 he2 nv3sheng1 yue1hui4
'Xu Haiyi' 'you' 'first time' 'with' 'girl' 'date'
'Female Guest: On your first date with a girl,

你 会 送 她 甚么 礼物 **呢**?
ni3 hui4 song4 ta1 shen2mo5 li3wu4 ne5
'you' 'will' 'give' 'she' 'what' 'gift' SFP
what gift will you give her?'

(zsydt 20130817)

In Example 67, the female speaker is assuming that a man will always give a gift to the girl on their first date. On that basis, the girl asks what present the man will give on his first date with a girl. Like the previous three examples, the question shown in Example 67 is still a question without the presence of *ne5* and is likely to get the same response. However, the addition of *ne5* seems to make the question more pertinent and more demanding, not least because it incorporates the speaker's assumptions and expectations.

Marker of elaboration

Another, related usage of 呢 is to help highlight an elaboration – a statement or a question built upon previously established information and relevant expectations.

Example 68

宁财神:	你	说	你	只有	一个	朋友,
ning4cai2shen2	ni3	shuo1	ni3	zhi3you3	yi2ge5	peng2you3
'Ning Caishen'	'you'	'say'	'you'	'only-have'	'one' Cla	'friend'

'Male Specialist: You said you have only one friend.'

那个	朋友	的	甚么	特质,
na4ge5	peng2you3	de5	shen2mo5	te4zhi2
'that' Cla	'friend'	PD	'what'	'special-quality'

What distinguishing characteristic of that friend

能够	让	你	认同	他	呢?
neng2gou4	rang4	ni3	ren4tong2	ta1	ne5
'can'	'let'	'you'	'identify with'	'him'	SFP

do you identify with?'

(fcwr 20130818)

In Example 68, the specialist on the dating show asks the male candidate a question. The question is built upon the man's earlier claim that he is not a highly sociable person and has only one friend. The specialist wants to know, given such circumstances, what particular merits the unique friend has that attract the male candidate. The presence of *ne5* seems to highlight the relevance of the existing background information to this question. That is, what the speaker seeks to understand will constitute a helpful addition to existing knowledge.

Example 69

胡静一:	我	跟	他	说	到	大观园,
hu2jing4yi1	wo3	gen1	ta1	shuo1	dao4	da4guan1yuan2
'Hu Jingyi'	'I'	'with'	'him'	'say'	Com	'Grand View Garden'

'Female Guest: When I spoke of the Grand View Garden with him,'

他	就	问	我	那	到底	是	甚么	样子,
ta1	jiu4	wen4	wo3	na4	dao4di3	shi4	shen2mo5	yang4zi5
'he'	'then'	'ask'	'me'	'that'	'after all'	'be'	'what'	'form'

he would ask me what on earth the Garden looks like,

为什么	他们	要	住	在	那个	里面	呢?
wei4shen2mo5	ta1men5	yao4	zhu4	zai4	na4ge5	li3mian4	ne5
'why'	'they'	'want'	'live'	'at'	'that' Cla	'inside'	SFP

and why they would want to live in the Garden.'

(fcwr 20130825)

The female guest in Example 69 is complaining about a German friend pestering her about every detail of the famous Chinese novel *Dream of Red Chamber*. The second and third sentences are reported speech, simulating the questions asked by the German. In principle, both indirect questions can be marked by *ne5* although only the second question is actually marked. As in Example 68, the use of *ne5* helps maintain the relevance of the current utterance in relation to what has been established in discourse (i.e. the German friend's annoying questions about the fictional Grand View Garden).

Example 70

邱启明:　　　十二号　　你　说　**呢**?
qiu1qi3ming2 shi2er4hao4 ni3　shuo1　ne5
'Qiu Qiming' 'No. 12'　'you' 'say'　SFP
'Host: No. 12, what is your opinion?'

(wmyhb 20130129)

What happens in Example 70 is that someone has just finished commenting on something, and the host of the dating show wants to hear a second opinion. He uses a very short sentence 'No. 12, you say' to delivery this request. Given the succinctness of the structure, the use of *ne5* is the only way to connect the sentence back to the previous circumstance; that is, to help the listener understand that feedback based on the previous comment is being sought.

Example 71

郑永骏:　　　我　可以　做　很多　　好吃　　的。
zheng4yong3jun4 wo3 ke3yi3 zuo4 hen3duo1 hao3chi1　de5
'Zheng Yongjun' 'I'　'can' 'do' 'many'　'delicious' AD
'Male Guest: I can cook many delicious dishes.'

潘琦静梓:　　你　觉得　我　像　　　哪　　一道　菜　**呢**?
pan1qi2jing4zi3 ni3 jue2de5 wo3 xiang4　　na3　　yi2dao4 cai4 ne5
'Panqi Jingzi'　'you' 'feel'　'I'　'resemble' 'which' 'one' Cla 'dish' SFP
'Female Guest: Which dish do you think I look like?'

(zsydt 20130817)

The man in Example 71 is a chef and reminds the female candidate that he can cook many delicious dishes. On that basis the girl asks the man what dish he thinks she resembles. Again, *ne5* marks the question as being relevant to the previous utterance and is an elaboration to bring further information into the discourse.

Example 72

徐文武：　　我　给　大家　　唱　　一首　　歌。
xu2wen2wu3　wo3　gei3　da4jia1　　chang4　yi4shou3　ge1
'Xu Wenwu'　'I'　'for'　'everybody'　'sing'　'one' Cla　'song'
'Male Guest: I will sing a song for all of you.

歌名　　　叫　甚么　　呢？《热情　　的　沙漠》！
ge1ming2　jiao4　shen2mo5　ne5　re4qing2　de5　sha1mo4
'song-name'　'call'　'what'　　SFP　'passionate'　AD　'desert'
What is the name of the song? Passionate desert!'

(zsydt 20130817)

The male guest in Example 72 first says he is going to sing a song for the audience. In the second sentence, he asks 'What is the name of the song?' and then goes on to give the answer. The rhetorical effect of this question and answer format is different from a statement like 'The name of the song is ...' as the *ne5* not only creates a sense of suspense but also adds to the interest of the audience in finding out more information about the song.

Example 73

何军：　以后　　有　了　孩子，　你　希望
he2jun1　yi3hou4　you3　le5　hai2zi5　ni3　xi1wang4
'He Jun'　'later on'　'have'　AM　'child'　'you'　'hope'
'Male Guest: Later when we have kids, do you wish

这　孩子　以后　　说　相声　　呢，还是　干　主持？
zhe4　hai2zi5　yi3hou4　shuo1　xiang4sheng5　ne5　hai2shi4　gan4　zhu3chi2
'this'　'child'　'later on'　'say'　'cross talk'　SFP　'or'　'do'　'hosting'
the child to perform Chinese comic dialogue or have a television hosting job?'

(zsydt 20130817)

The male guest in Example 73 asks an A-or-B question and the first option is tagged by *ne5*, which helps maintain the attention of the listener for the second option to come, so that they can choose one option from the two as required.

Marker of challenge

Based on its ability to contrast ideas and circumstances, *ne5* is often used to challenge the listener in discourse.

Example 74

杨凡：	你	都	能	把	你的	耐心
yang2fan2	ni3	dou1	neng2	ba3	ni3de5	nai4xin1
'Yang Fan'	'you'	'all'	'can'	OB	'your'	'patience'

'Female Guest: Since you can readily show patience

用到	你的	宠物	狗	上，
yong4dao4	ni3de5	chong3wu4	gou3	shang4
'use' Com	'your'	'pet'	'dog'	'up'

to your pet dog,

为什么	不能	用	在	女朋友	身上	呢？
wei4shen2mo5	bu4neng2	yong4	zai4	nv3peng2you3	shen1shang4	ne5
'why'	'cannot'	'use'	'at'	'girlfriend'	'body-up'	SFP

why can you not have some patience with your girlfriend?'

(wmyhb 20130326)

In Example 74, the female guest is accusing the male candidate of lack of patience with his ex-girlfriends. In order to make the accusation maximally effective, the speaker contrasts his lack of patience toward humans with the abundance of patience he has with dogs. The use of *ne5* shows that the speaker is highlighting the contrast, is imposing the normal expectation that humans are more important than pets, and is demanding an explanation from the listener.

Example 75

丁洪芳：	你	都	说	你	不	喜欢	哈尔滨	的	了，
ding1hong2fang1	ni3	dou1	shuo1	ni3	bu4	xi3huan1	ha1er3bin1	de5	le5
'Ding Hongfang'	'you'	'all'	'say'	'you'	'not'	'like'	'Harbin'	ED	SFP

'Female Guest: You already said you did not like Harbin city.

我	为什么	还要	给	你	留灯	呢？
wo3	wei4shen2mo5	hai2yao4	gei3	ni3	liu2deng1	ne5
'I'	'why'	'still-want'	'give'	'you'	'keep-light'	SFP

Why would I still keep the light on for you?'

(wmyhb 20130528)

Example 75 is very similar to Example 74 in that they both consist of two sentences, the first establishing the premise, the second challenging the listener on that basis. The second sentence in both cases is a rhetorical question used to challenge rather than really expecting an answer.

Example 76

黄菡：	找	个	女朋友		真	不	容易	噢？
huang2han4	zhao3	ge5	nv3peng2you3		zhen1	bu4	rong2yi4	ou5
'Huang Han'	'find'	Cla	'girlfriend'		'really'	'not'	'easy'	SFP

'Female Specialist: Finding a girlfriend is not easy, is it?'

孟非：	谁	叫	他	说	他	记忆力	好	的	**呢！**
meng4fei1	shei2	jiao4	ta1	shuo1	ta1	ji4yi4li4	hao3	de5	ne5
'Meng Fei'	'who'	'call'	'he'	'say'	'he'	'memory-ability'	'good'	ED	SFP

'Host: Who told him to claim that he had great memory capacity!'

他	不	说	这	不	就	没	事儿	了	吗？
ta1	bu4	shuo1	zhe4	bu2	jiu4	mei2	shi4er5	le5	ma5
'he'	'not'	'speak'	'this'	'not'	'then'	'none'	'business'	SFP	QM

'If he had not made that claim, would there have been such a big fuss?'

(fcwr 20130810)

Example 76 shows a conversation between the host of the dating show and the resident specialist. Prior to this conversation, a male suitor was asked to perform a demonstration of his supposedly superior memory capacity. After a good ten minutes of concentration and answering questions correctly, the man finally succeeded in making a good impression on the female guests. As a result, the female specialist voiced her concerns about the formidable task of finding a girlfriend. The male host, in turn, blamed the male suitor for bragging about his memory talent, which brought the grueling test upon himself. The host's first sentence is a rhetorical question marked with *ne5* to contrast the situation of 'his bragging about memory and the subsequent ordeal' with 'his saying nothing and remaining safe' situation expressed by the host's second sentence.

Example 77

亚丽：	生	孩子	和	事业	怎么	就
ya3li4	sheng1	hai2zi5	he2	shi4ye4	zen3mo5	jiu4
'Ya Li'	'produce'	'children'	'and'	'career'	'how'	'just'

'Hostess: Why (do you think) having kids and having a career

不能	同步	**呢？**
bu4neng2	tong2bu4	ne5
'cannot'	'synchronize'	SFP

cannot happen at the same time?'

(zsydt 20130706)

The hostess in Example 77 is challenging a dating candidate's position that a married couple must choose either to have a career without children or to have children without a career. The contrast is on whether having children 'can' or 'cannot' co-exist with having a career, and the position the hostess challenges in Example 77 is the 'cannot' option.

There are a couple of phonological variants of *ne5* pronounced as *le5* or *lei5* etc. These are variously expressed orthographically as 咧, 嘞 etc. as Example 78 shows (where the Pinyin notation associated with each character in the input method has been kept as is, without reflecting the actual spoken forms of the SFP, which are quite evasive in this case). Their functions are basically the same as those discussed above.

Example 78

a 沈涛：　　我　以为　　画　　的　是　我　和　　亚丽　**嘞**！
    shen3tao1 wo3 yi3wei2 hua4 de5 shi4 wo3 he2 ya3li4 le1
    'Shen Tao' 'I' 'assume' 'paint' AD 'be' 'I' 'and' 'Yali' SFP
    'Host: I thought you were drawing me and Yali!'

                                     (zsydt 20130706)

b 蔡康永：　　　　那　　干么　　　不　就　大家
    cai4kang1yong3 na4 gan4ma2 bu2 jiu4 da4jia1
    'Kevin Tsai' 'then' 'how come' 'not' 'just' 'everybody'

    好好　　相处　　**咧**？
    hao3hao3 xiang1chu3 lie5
    'well' 'get on' SFP

    'Host: Then why don't you try to get along with each other?'
                                       (kxll 20130820)

Both SFPs shown in Example 78 are variants of 呢 and can be understood as using the functional categories of *ne5* discussed above. For example, in Example 78a, 嘞 expresses the contrast between the couple of persons painted in the picture and the host-hostess couple the speaker jokingly refers to. This is a typical usage of 呢 – to perform a specific discourse function (in this case, making a joke) on the basis of its ability to contrast. Likewise, in Example 78b, the host of the chat show is challenging a conflict situation using a rhetorical question marked with 咧, which helps contrast an alleged confrontational situation with the proposed peaceful condition.

5.6 SFP *O2*

The primary function of 哦 *o2* is to give warning. It normally marks a message which the speaker considers important to the hearer but may have been neglected. The function of *o2* is to remind the listener of the importance and relevance of the message. It tells the listener to be psychologically prepared to take in the information and perhaps to translate the message into immediate action of some sort.

Marker of warning

Some messages of warning marked by 哦 can be retrieved from the Internet if we use the SFP itself as the query word. These messages are typically short and are normally imperative sentences.

Example 79

a　不要　　　告诉　　妈妈　　　**哦**
　　bu2yao4　gao4su4　ma1ma5　o2
　　'not-want'　'tell'　　　'mother'　SFP
　　'Do not tell your mother!'

b　小心!　车　坏　了　修理　很　贵　　　**哦**!
　　xiao3xin1　che1　huai4　le5　xiu1li3　hen3　gui4　　　o2
　　'careful'　'car'　'bad'　AM　'repair'　'very'　'expensive'　SFP
　　Be careful! The car costs a fortune to repair if it is damaged!

Both sentences in Example 79 can be interpreted as a command or suggestion without the company of *o2*. However, the presence of *o2* adds a sense of warning, an implication that something bad will happen if the advice is not taken. The *o2* is used to catch attention when commanding others to keep a secret, as in Example 79a or to be careful around an expensive car as in Example 79b.

Example 80

a　井川:　　　你　要　听取　　　别人　　　的　意见　　**哦**!
　　jing3chuan1　ni3　yao4　ting1qu3　bie2ren2　de5　yi4jian4　o2
　　'Jing Chuan'　'you'　'want'　'listen-take'　'others'　PD　'opinion'　SFP
　　'Male Guest: Make sure you listen to others' opinions!'

　　　　　　　　　　　　　　　　　　　　　　　　　　　(zsydt 20130629)

b　丁明利:　　　那　你　千万　　别　灭灯　　　　**哦**!
　　ding1ming2li4　na4　ni3　qian1wan4　bie2　mie4deng1　o2
　　'Ding Mingli'　'then'　'you'　'be sure to'　'do not'　'extinguish-light'　SFP
　　'Male Guest: Then be sure not to turn your light off!'

　　　　　　　　　　　　　　　　　　　　　　　　　　(wmyhb 20130410)

In Example 80a, a male suitor is advising another suitor to consider the others' opinions when deciding whether to turn around for a female candidate (whom others can see but not he) or not. Again, *o2* turns the imperative into a warning implying that there will be a consequence if the listener does not follow the instruction. Likewise, in Example 80b, a male candidate asks a female guest not to turn off the light. The implication is that she might miss a good date if she does that.

Marker of unexpected information

Apart from being used to issue warnings of some sort, *o2* can also mark an expression as incorporating some information which is important to, and least expected by, the listener. The function of *o2* here is to hammer in the message swiftly and change the epistemic condition of the listener regarding the current topic in a dramatic fashion.

Example 81

沈玉琳：　　你　　是　　高山峰　　　　的　菜　　哦！
shen3yu4lin2 ni3　shi4 gao1shan1feng1 de5 cai4　o2
'Shen Yulin'　'you'　'be'　'Gao Shanfeng'　PD 'dish' SFP
'Male Guest: (Mind you!) You are the type Gao Shanfeng likes!'

(kxll 20130815)

The speaker in Example 81 is advising a female guest on the chat show on her suitability to become a male celebrity's girlfriend. Since Shen is an acquaintance of Gao, this information is disclosed as insider knowledge. The use of *o2* marks the sentence as incorporating an important and unexpected piece of information.

Example 82

刘保敏：　　我的　　身材　　　也　　练得　　　　　非常　好。
liu2bao3min3 wo3de5 shen1cai2 ye3　lian4de5 fei1chang2 hao3
'Liu Baomin'　'my'　'figure'　'also' 'exercise' Com 'very'　'good'
'Male Guest: I also exercise a lot and am in extremely good shape.

有　　腹肌，　　　　　还有　　　传说　　　中　　　的　人鱼线　　　哦！
you3　fu4ji1　　　　hai2you3 chuan2shuo1 zhong1 de5 ren2yu2xian4 o2
'have' 'abdominal muscle' 'still-have' 'legend'　'middle' AD 'mermaid-line' SFP
(I) have abdominal muscles, and the legendary Apollo's Belt, mind you!'

(fcwr 20130818)

The speaker in Example 82 is a male suitor hoping to attract the female guests' attention in order to get a date. He advertises himself by referring to the muscles and curves on his body, which are covered by clothes. The use of *o2* helps strengthen the sense of 'hidden surprise' waiting to be discovered.

Example 83

段超：	之后	我	又	创办	了
duan4chao1	zhi1hou4	wo3	you4	chuang4ban4	le5
'Duan Chao'	'afterward'	'I'	'moreover'	'found'	AM

'Male Guest: Afterwards I went on to establish

一家	自己	的	舞蹈	工作室	生意	不错	**哦！**
yi4jia1	zi4ji3	de5	wu3dao3	gong1zuo4shi4	sheng1yi4	bu2cuo4	o2
'one' Cla	'self'	PD	'dancing'	'workshop'	'business'	'not-wrong'	SFP

a dancing workshop of my own. Business is not bad, I shall say!'

(aqllk 20130827)

In Example 83, another male suitor, on a different dating show, is trying to impress the female guests in a different way. In Example 82, the secret being revealed is the male charm – abdominal muscles and Apollo's Belt. This time, the hidden attraction being disclosed in Example 83 is the promising business the man owns. What *o2* implies in this case is that 'I am rich' and probably 'All this could be yours if you date me'. As in many other cases, *o2* represents a well-intentioned 'warning' about some hidden benefits to be reaped.

Example 84

吴隐川：	你们	别	看	我	现在	这么	胖，
wu2yin3chuan1	ni3men5	bie2	kan4	wo3	xian4zai4	zhe4mo5	pang4
'Wu Yinchuan'	'you' PM	'do not'	'see'	'I'	'now'	'such'	'fat'

'Male Guest: Although you see me in very fat shape now

其实	我	曾经	也	很	瘦	过	**哦！**
qi2shi2	wo3	ceng2jing1	ye3	hen3	shou4	guo4	o2
'in fact'	'I'	'ever'	'also'	'very'	'thin'	AM	SFP

in fact I used to be very slim, mind you.'

(wmyhb 20130725)

The male suitor in Example 84 also reveals an unexpected piece of information which he marks with *o2*. He claims that he was once a slim guy, i.e. he was not always so fat. With *o2* highlighting the importance of that secret, the implication is that he could be slim and fit again, despite his current bad shape.

Example 85

雷明：	从	今天	起	矮	个子	男生，
lei2ming2	cong2	jin1tian1	qi3	ai3	ge4zi5	nan2sheng1
'Lei Ming'	'from'	'today'	'start'	'short'	'height'	'boy'

'Male Specialist: From today, men of short build,

你们	要	知道，	哪怕	我	只有	一米	六五，
ni3men5	yao4	zhi1dao4	na3pa4	wo3	zhi3you3	yi4mi3	liu4 wu3
'you'	'want'	'know'	'even if'	'I'	'only-have'	'one-meter'	'65'

you should know that even if I am only 165 cm tall,

我	也	有	可能	是	男神	哦！
wo3	ye3	you3	ke3neng2	shi4	nan2shen2	o2
'I'	'also'	'have'	'possible'	'be'	'male-god'	SFP

I can probably be a god-like man (adored by women).'

(aqllk 20130820)

In Example 85, the resident specialist is responding to a girl's claim that she has pursued a man who is only 165 cm for a number of years, contrary to the expectation of a typical Prince Charming who is tall and handsome. The specialist therefore openly advises the short men among the audience that they can also become extremely popular with women despite their short-coming. This news is directly contrary to ordinary people's expectation and the marking of *o2* helps highlight the dramatic nature of this information. The slot occupied by *o2* in Example 85 is reminiscent of *ne5* which is used to contrast two pieces of information, and therefore can also fit into this position. However, the use of *ne5* in this position would turn the speech into an argumentation that focuses on the present, rather than a warning that looks to the future as *o2* does.

The habitual function of *o2* to reveal unexpected information will indeed create some expectations on the part of the listener (i.e. to anticipate something unusual and interesting). Therefore, the *o2*-marked sentence is often used for promotional activities of some sort.

Example 86

a 这个　　　神　　题目，　　　　答对　　　　　　有　　奖励　　**哦**
　　zhe4ge5　shen2　ti2mu4　　　da2dui4　　　　you3　jiang3li4　o2
　　'This' Cla　'god'　'test question'　'answer-correct'　'have'　'reward'　SFP
　　'Whoever answers this tough question correctly will get a reward!'

b 招室友！　　　　　非常　　　靠近　　　OU，
　　zhao1 shi4you3　　fei1chang2 kao4jin4　o-u
　　'recruit''roommate'　'very'　　'near'　'Ottawa University'
　　'Roommate wanted! Very close to Ottawa University.

　　坐车　　　只要　　　一站　　　**哦**
　　zuo4che1　zhi3yao4　yi2zhan4　o2
　　'sit-car'　'only-want'　'one' Cla　SFP
　　Only one bus stop away!'

Example 86a is a web title to catch readers' attention so they can continue to the test question. Without *o2*, Example 86a would be a simple comment without the pragmatic implication. Example 86b is an online advertisement showing a college student looking for a roommate. The advantage of the advertised accommodation is its being near the university. The sentence 'It is only one bus stop away' is marked with *o2* to promote it as the main attraction. The speech act function of *o2* (to suggest, to invite) is evident.

Example 87

文静怡：　　如果　　你　选择　　我，
wen2jing4yi2　ru2guo3　ni3　xuan3ze2　wo3
'Wen Jingyi'　'if'　　'you' 'choose'　'me'
'Female Guest: If you choose me,

我　会　为　你　唱　　首　　歌，
wo3　hui4　wei4　ni3　chang4　shou3　ge1
'I'　'will' 'for' 'you' 'sing'　Cla　'song'
I will sing a song for you.

刚刚　　　现场　　　编　　　的　**哦**！
gang1gang1　xian4chang3　bian1　　de5　o2
'just now'　'the scene'　'compose'　AD　SFP
This was composed just now on the spot!'

(wmyhb 20130723)

In Example 87, the female candidate is trying to impress the male guest by promising to sing him a song if he chooses her. Moreover, she adds that the song will be composed on the spot. By using *o2* the girl hopes to give the impression that her music talent is unusual, enabling her to compose a song at such short notice.

A related SFP, *lo5*, is a relatively infrequent particle which can be seen as a combination of 了 *le5* and 哦 *o2*. Its usage largely coincides with the 'promotional function' of *o2* discussed above. The Pinyin annotation used here (*lo5*) is a phonological approximation of the actual SFP in spoken form. I have used the character 啰 to represent the sound but it is also rendered as 喽 (e.g. Chao 1968) or something else. Some examples are shown in Example 88 below.

Example 88

a 新   爱疯   来   **啰**!
   xin1 ai4feng1   lai2   lo5
   'new' 'love-crazy' 'come' SFP
   'The new iPhone has come out!'

b 三阳   机车   回   娘家   活动   开始   **啰**
   san1yang2 ji1che1   hui2   niang2jia1   huo2dong4 kai1shi3 lo5
   'San Yang' 'motorcycle' 'return' 'mother-home' 'activity' 'begin' SFP
   'The San Yang motorcycle returning to base activity has now begun!'

c 高雄   观音山   渔龙   休闲   池
   gao1xiong2 guan1yin1shan1   yu2long2 xiu1xian2 chi2
   'Kaohsiung' 'Guanyin-Mountain' 'Yulong' 'leisure' 'pool'
   'The Yulong leisure pool at Kaohsiung Guanyin Mountain

   (开放   夜钓   **啰**)
   kai1fang4 ye4diao4   lo5
   'open'   'night-fishing' SFP
   (open for night fishing now!)'

All three examples in Example 88 are advertisement titles on the web. Each *lo5* in Example 88 is preceded by a verb which denotes an approaching, beginning or opening action. For each statement in Example 88, if we look closely at the relations between *lo5* and the other part of the sentence, we will find that it is reasonable to analyze *lo5* in two parts, that is, *lo5* = *le5* + *o5*. Our reasoning is that, for each sentence in Example 88, the verb was initially followed by the aspect marker 了 to signal the completion of the action (i.e. 'have come', 'have begun', 'have opened' respectively). The SFP 哦 is then added to help catch the reader's attention. Finally, 了 and 哦 are combined phonetically to form *lo5*. In fact, the combination of 了哦 can also be used as is, without the sandhi. Many examples of the two particles used together can be retrieved from the web.

As for the three examples of *lo5* in Example 88, 88a announces the arrival of the new iPhone, 88b encourages owners of motorcycles of a certain make to revisit the servicing center, and 88c announces the launch of night fishing at a leisure pool. All these messages are meant to be unusual and exciting news which the reader should pay attention to.

Apart from getting attention and promoting commodity as seen in Example 88, *lo5* can also be used to give a warning, just like its parent, 哦.

Example 89

邱启明:　　　看　你　的　**啰**!
qiu1qi3ming2　kan4　ni3　de5　lo5
'Qiu Qiming'　'see'　'you'　PD　SFP
'Host: All eyes are on you now!'

(wmyhb 20130115)

In Example 89, the host of the dating show is giving a warning to a certain male suitor who is getting ready to perform a talent show. The warning simply means 'You can start now!' but the connotation is that the success or failure of securing a date depends on the man's performance, so he should concentrate fully and do his best. All these implications are embedded in the sentence-final particle.

5.7 SFP *O5*

The *o* that gives warning is a reasonably established particle in terms of both phonological (*o2*) and orthographical (哦) representations. Some sentence-final particles do not (as yet) have a fixed sound-character representation corresponding to their functional paradigm. The *o* that reveals the speaker's emotion, which will be discussed in this section as *o5*, is one of the SFPs that have not been properly identified and given unique orthographical representations. In the previous section, we have consistently used the character 哦 to represent *o2*. In actual written language, native speakers may represent *o2* with a character other than 哦 (for example, 喔). In this chapter, we will consistently use 喔 to represent *o5*. Readers, however, should not assume the consistency of this sound–character correspondence elsewhere in the real world (and this principle applies to other SFPs in different degrees). The two *o*'s are perceptually different in pronunciation and very different in their functions.

While 哦 is mainly used to give warning and recommendations, the primary function of 喔 is to help mark the speaker's strong emotions, whether out of surprise, admiration, longing, sadness, disgust or frustration. The *o5* is almost always used in a fixed pattern of [X 好 Y 喔] (meaning 'X is so Y'), where X is a person, object, event and so on, while Y is a descriptive unit. Note that although we adopt 喔 to represent the particle *o5*, the conventional Pinyin notation for this character is *o1* instead of *o5*. This is because there is no Chinese character corresponding to the *o5* sound. In this chapter, we use *o5* to annotate this character but readers should type *o1* if they want to get the character 喔 using a Pinyin input method.

At the time of Chao's (1968) writing, the existence of *o5* was not identified (or was not separated out from a generic *o*), and the character Chao used to represent *o2* was 呕 instead of the 哦 used here. However, Chao did identify two broad categories of function for *o* – to give warnings (our *o2*) and to utter exclamations (our *o5*). This convention is followed by Sun (2006).

Marker of positive emotion

喔 *o5* can be used to mark all sorts of emotions the speaker feels toward a person, an object, a process or a situation. The function of *o5* is to intensify the feeling of that emotion. First, we see examples where *o5* is used to mark positive emotions.

Example 90

a 亚丽：   好   厉害   喔！
   ya3li4   hao3   li4hai4   o5
   'Yali'   'very' 'formidable' SFP
   'Hostess: Awesome!'

                                              (zsydt 20130706)

b 黄国伦：   我们   好   喜欢   你   老婆   喔！
   huang2guo2lun2   wo3men5   hao3   xi3huan1 ni3   lao3po2   o5
   'Huang Guolun'   'we'   'so'   'like'   'you' 'wife'   SFP
   'Male Guest: We like your wife so much!

   你   老婆   好   漂亮   喔！
   ni3   lao3po2   hao3   piao4liang4   o5
   'you' 'wife'   'so'   'beautiful'   SFP
   Your wife is so beautiful!'

                                              (kxll 20130827)

The hostess in Example 90a uses the [X 好 Y 喔] formula to describe a guest after her impressive performance. The X factor can be omitted if the speaker thinks it is clear to the listener what it refers to. The male celebrity guest in Example 90b is reporting the speech of some ordinary people seeing him in a restaurant and praising his wife. Both of these examples use the [X 好 Y 喔] construction to show their positive emotions toward a person or a situation.

Note that all or most of the sentences tagged with *o5* can also be tagged by *o2* instead and produce a different meaning. For example, the second sentence in Example 90b can be interpreted in two different ways depending on whether the SFP is *o5* or *o2*:

你老婆好漂亮**喔** (*o5*)!
'Your wife is so beautiful! (We really admire her)'

你老婆好漂亮**哦** (*o2*)!
'Your wife is so beautiful! (You need to keep an eye on her)'

The fact that the same sentence can be tagged by two different *os* to generate different pragmatic implications seems to authenticate our two-*o* analysis as opposed to the traditional single-*o* one.

Marker of negative emotion

The [X 好 Y 喔] formula can also be used to describe an unfavorable person or an undesirable situation.

Example 91

a 路怡珍: 好 可惜 **喔**!
　 lu4yi2zhen1 hao3 ke3xi2 o5
　 'Lu Yizhen' 'very' 'pity' SFP
　 'Female Guest: What a pity!'

(zsydt 20130706)

b 安钧璨: 你们 好 令 我 失望 **喔**!
　 an1jun1can4 ni3men5 hao3 ling4 wo3 shi1wang4 o5
　 'An Juncan' 'you' 'so' 'make' 'me' 'disappoint' SFP
　 'Male Guest: I am so disappointed with you all!'

(kxll 20130813)

Like that in Example 90a, the X variable in Example 91a is also absent, but it can be understood to refer to a situation which just happened. The result of the happening is obviously not up to the speaker's expectation, hence the comment of 'what a pity' showing her feeling about the result. In 92b, on the other hand, the X is clearly specified as the plural 'you'. The *o5*-marked sentence shows the male celebrity's ostentatious disappointment at his fellow celebrities on the show who did not support him in the way he wanted.

Marker of neutral emotion

In some cases, *o5* is not used to express personal feelings of a positive or negative kind. Instead, it is used to highlight a person's impression of something, or to express a wish.

Example 92

a 张芯瑜：   好像   万圣节   喔！
    zhang1xin1yu2 hao3xiang4 wan4sheng4jie2 o5
    'Zhang1 Xinyu' 'very-like' 'Halloween'   SFP
    'Female Guest: The atmosphere is really like Halloween!'
                                                (zsydt 20130706)

b 女嘉宾：   他 好 会 卖关子   喔！
    nv3jia1bin1   ta1 hao3 hui4 mai4guan1zi5   o5
    'Female-good-guest' 'he' 'so' 'able' 'keep listeners in suspense' SFP
    'Female Guest: He is so good at keeping people in suspense!'
                                                (zsydt 20130706)

In Example 92a, the female guest is commenting on a magic show performed by a male guest, which reminds her of Halloween. In 92b, an unidentified female guest is commenting on the behavior of another male candidate who does not answer questions in a straightforward manner.

5.8 SFP *OU5*

There is a third member in the *o* SFP family represented as 噢 *ou5* here. The actual pronunciation of the particle is very similar to 喔 (the closest Pinyin notation for both sounds is *o5* – the *o* sound said with a neutral tone). However, there are many more individual variations for this sound than for other SFPs among Chinese speakers, in both spoken and written forms. Taiwanese speakers of Mandarin may use 吼 *hou3* or 厚 *hou4* (or something else) to represent this particle in writing.

The core function of 噢 identified in this chapter is to seek the agreement of the listener. In most cases, a sentence with 噢 represents a thought which the speaker thinks is also agreeable to the listener. The speaker uses *ou5* to check whether it is true that the assumption carried by the *ou5*-marked utterance is shared by both speaker and listener.

Example 93

黄菡:	找	个	女朋友		真	不	容易	**噢?**
huang2han4	zhao3	ge5	nv3peng2you3		zhen1	bu4	rong2yi4	ou5
'Huang Han'	'find'	Cla	'girlfriend'		'really'	'not'	'easy'	SFP

'Female Specialist: Finding a girlfriend is not easy, is it?'

孟非:	谁	叫	他	说	他	记忆力		好	的	呢!
meng4fei1	shei2	jiao4	ta1	shuo1	ta1	ji4yi4li4		hao3	de5	ne5
'Meng Fei'	'who'	'call'	'he'	'say'	'he'	'memory-ability'		'good'	ED	SFP

'Host: Who told him to claim that he had great memory capacity?'

(fcwr 20130810)

In Example 93, the female specialist summarizes a male suitor's strenuous display of his memory talent with the comment 'it is really not easy to find a girlfriend'. The remark would be a declarative sentence without the marking of *ou5*. With *ou5*, however, it is transformed into a question, to which the listener can either simply agree or offer additional information. In this case, the host of the show, Mr Meng, quickly blames the male suitor for bragging about his own talent, which brings the ordeal onto himself. In offering this comment, Meng has in fact confirmed the assumption of Huang, that the talent show is indeed hard work, as his comment must be based upon the truthfulness of Huang's assumption.

Example 94

庹宗康:	最近	很	幸福	**噢?**
tuo3zong1kang1	zui4jin4	hen3	xing4fu2	ou5
'Tuo Zongkang'	'lately'	'very'	'happy'	SFP

'Host: You have been quite happy lately, right?'

王思佳:	没有,	我	还好	啦,	哪能	跟	你	比	啊!
wang2si1jia1	mei2you3	wo3	hai2hao3	la5	na3 neng2	gen1	ni3	bi3	a5
'Wang Sijia'	'no'	'I'	'still-good'	SFP	'how-can'	'with'	'you'	'compare'	SFP

'Female Guest: No, I am just so so. How can I compare with you!'

(aywdm 20130823)

In Example 94, the host of the show asks a female guest whether or not she is currently leading a happy life. He is referring to her being spotted together with her boyfriend by the paparazzi. Since it is already on the news, the host assumes this is common knowledge and uses *ou5* to seek the agreement of the girl. The female celebrity, however, strategically denies the assumption, as is the custom of celebrities on TV.

5.9 SFP *MA5*

The SFP 嘛 *ma5* is easily confused with another similar-sounding particle – the question marker 吗 *ma5* we saw in Chapter 4. Although the Pinyin notations for 嘛 and 吗 are the same, their pronunciations are different. The differences are in tone (i.e. pitch level) and intonational contour which cannot be reflected by the Pinyin system (吗 is higher in tone and 'flatter' in pitch contour; 嘛 is lower and with a falling pitch). The question marker 吗, as seen in Chapter 4, is mainly used for forming yes/no questions. The SFP 嘛, on the other hand, marks the speaker's conceptualization about the status of certain information at the time of speaking and how the speaker intends to use that information in speech.

The fundamental function performed by 嘛 is to mark some information as shared by the speaker and the listener in the current discourse domain. In doing so, *ma5* either accompanies some common knowledge (e.g. 'Dogs bark') or some piece of information recently established in conversation. This basic function of marking shared knowledge is then expanded to carry out further functions like reasoning, clarifying, paraphrasing, and so on.

Marker of allegedly shared information

Roughly speaking, there are two kinds of information that 嘛 marks as shared by the speaker and the listener. One is universally shared common knowledge; the other is recently established knowledge up to the point of speaking in the current conversation.

Example 95

a 邱启明：　　　魔术　　　就是　　　一个　　　障眼法　　　　　　　嘛。
　　qiu1qi3ming2　mo2shu4　jiu4shi4　yi2ge5　　zhang4yan3fa3　　　　ma5
　　'Qiu Qiming'　'magic'　'just-is'　'one' Cla　'barricade-eye-method'　SFP
　　'Host: (We all know) magic is just an eye-barricading method.'

　　　　　　　　　　　　　　　　　　　　　　　　　　　　　　(wmyhb 20130115)

b 朱斯慧：　　　我们　　也　　只是　　为了　　让　　你们
　　zhu1si1hui4　wo3men5　ye3　zhi3shi4　wei4le5　rang4　ni3men5
　　'Zhu Sihui'　'we'　　'also'　'only'　'for'　'let'　'you' PM
　　'Female Guest: We do this only so you can

　　带　　出去　　好看　　　　啊！
　　dai4　chu1qu4　hao3kan4　　a5
　　'bring'　'out'　　'good-looking'　SFP
　　look good when bringing us to a social occasion!

　　大家　　　都　　说　　女　　为　　悦　　己　　者　　容　　　嘛。
　　da4jia1　　dou1　shuo1　nv3　wei4　yue4　ji3　zhe3　rong2　　ma5
　　'everybody' 'all'　'say'　'women' 'for'　'like'　'self' 'those' 'make up'　SFP
　　Everyone says a woman applies cosmetics for those who like her, right?'

　　　　　　　　　　　　　　　　　　　　　　　　　　　　　　(wmyhb 20130723)

In Example 95a, a male guest has just performed a simple magic show. The host of the dating show makes the comment that 'magic is but an eye-cheating method' in the ensuing conversation. The 嘛 in this sentence marks the speaker's assumption that this is commonly shared knowledge, and he is only reminding the listeners of the fact that magic show is nothing more than camouflage. In Example 95b, the female guest is arguing why girls have to put on makeup, one of the reasons being for men's pleasure. She attaches *ma5* to a well-known Chinese saying 'A woman uses makeup to please the man who likes her' to mark it as shared information. In other words, 嘛 signals that her contention, based on this common knowledge, is well supported.

Example 96

靳曼;	男	嘉宾		啊,	你	在	法国	里昂	对		吧?
le4man4	nan2	jia1bin1		a5	ni3	zai4	fa3guo2	li3ang2	dui4		ba5
'Le Man'	'male'	'good-guest'		CFP	'you'	'at'	'France'	'Lyon'	'correct'		SFP

'Female Guest: Male guest, hello, you are currently living in Lyon, France, right?'

侯吉旋:		对!
hou2ji2xuan2		dui4
'Hou Jixuan'		'correct'

'Male Guest: You are right!'

靳曼;	那…	就是	法国人		很	浪漫	**嘛,**
le4man4	na4	jiu4 shi4	fa3guo2ren2		hen3	lang4man4	ma5
'Le Man'	'that'	'just-is'	'France-people'		'very'	'romantic'	SFP

'Female Guest: er . . . that is, (it is a common impression that) the French are very romantic.

那	你	在	那边	有没有		感受	他们的
na4	ni3	zai4	na4bian1	you3mei2you3		gan3shou4	ta1men5de5
'then'	'you'	'at'	'that-side'	'have-not-have'		'perceive'	'their'

浪漫		气息,	而	你	也	变得	很	浪漫		呢?
lang4man4		qi4xi2	er2	ni3	ye3	bian4de5	hen3	lang4man4		ne5
'romantic'		'breath'	'and'	'you'	'also'	'become'	'very'	'romantic'		SFP

'So have you felt the romantic atmosphere while living in that country and turned into a romantic person yourself?'

(wmyhb 20130710)

The girl in Example 96 wants to find out if the male suitor is a romantic person. She bases her question on the common impression that the French are a romantic people. Once this assumption is established as common knowledge, it makes sense to wonder if a person living in France has also become romantic, hence the marking of 嘛 on that assumption. Unless the *ma5*-marked utterance is explicitly challenged, it is established as common ground and can be used in all kinds of ways. In this case, it is meant to support the idea that the environment may have an effect on a person's temperament.

Example 97

a   吴燕华：   看   那个   VCR   你的   那个   庄园
     wu2yan4hua2 kan4 na4ge5 v-c-r ni3de5 na4ge5 zhuang1yuan2
     'Wu Yanhua' 'see' 'that' 'VCR' 'your' 'that' 'manor'

     很   大   **嘛**，   然后   你   每天   的 生活
     hen3 da4 ma5 ran2hou4 ni3 mei3tian1 de5 sheng1huo2
     'very' 'big' SFP 'then' 'you' 'everyday' AD 'living'

     是   甚么   样子   的?
     shi4 shen2mo5 yang4zi5 de5
     'be' 'what' 'form' ED

     'Female Guest: From the VCR (just played) we saw you have a very big farmland. So what kind of daily life are you leading?'

     (fcwr 20130831)

b   朱斯慧：   白马王子，   一路   我 看   你，   好像
     zhu1si1hui4 bai2ma3wang2zi5 yi2lu4 wo3 kan4 ni3 hao3xiang4
     'Zhu Sihui' 'white-horse-prince' 'one-road' 'I' 'see' 'you' 'seem'

     VCR 说   你   这   几   年   变   了 很   多   **嘛**，
     v-c-r shuo1 ni3 zhe4 ji3 nian2 bian4 le5 hen3 duo1 ma5
     VCR 'say' 'you' 'this' 'some' 'year' 'change' AM 'very' 'many' SFP

     那   你   能   不   能   用   一   首   歌   来
     na4 ni3 neng2 bu4 neng2 yong4 yi4 shou3 ge1 lai2
     'then' 'you' 'can' 'not' 'can' 'use' 'one' Cla 'song' 'come'

     描述   一下 你   这   几   年   的 变化   呢?
     miao2shu4 yi2xia4 ni3 zhe4 ji3 nian2 de5 bian4hua4 ne5
     'describe' 'once' 'you' 'this' 'several' 'year' AD 'transformation' SFP

     'Female Guest: Hi, Prince Charming. I see you have come a long way. The VCR seemed to show that you have changed a lot in recent years. I wonder if you could use a song to describe your transformation in recent years.'

     (wmyhb 20130828)

We can see that in both of the examples in Example 97 the 嘛 is used to mark a piece of information gathered from the respective video recordings played on the show to introduce each male candidate prior to the speech. The videos must have included the crucial information referred to in both examples: in Example 97a, the big farm owned by the male suitor and, in Example 97b, the other man's recent history of dramatic change. The female candidates use *ma5* to mark their respective sentences as recently established information, and then go on to ask related questions based on that knowledge.

Marker of reason

One of the most frequently used functions of 嘛 is to mark something as an obvious reason for a certain situation or a premise leading to a certain conclusion. When applying this function, the intermediate steps of reasoning are often omitted, leaving the listener to fill in the gap between the *ma5*-marked expression and the phenomenon it is supposed to explain.

Example 98

a 高梦潞:　　　为什么　　　现在　　　男孩　　都　　爱
   gao1meng4lu4　wei4shen2mo5　xian4zai4　nan2hai2　dou1　ai4
   'Gao Menglu'　'why'　　　　'now'　　'boy'　　'all'　'love'

   穿　　　九分裤?
   chuan1　jiu3fen1ku4
   'wear'　'ankle-length pants'

   'Female Guest: Why do all boys like to wear ankle-length pants nowadays?'

   林伟锋:　　　比较　　　　凉快　　　**嘛**。
   lin2wei3feng1　bi3jiao4　　liang2kuai4　ma5
   'Lin Weifeng'　'comparatively'　'cool'　　SFP
   'Male Guest: Because it is relatively cool.'　　　　(wmyhb 20130725)

b 郝紫薇:　　　特别　　特别　　特别　　的　高兴。
   hao3zi3wei1　te4bie2　te4bie2　te4bie2　de5　gao1xing4
   'Hao Ziwei'　'especially'　'especially'　'especially'　AD　'happy'
   'Female Guest: I am very, very, very happy.'

   邱启明:　　　为什么　　　呢?
   qiu1qi3ming2　wei4shen2mo5　ne5
   'Qiu Qiming'　'why'　　　　SFP
   'Host: Why? (if I may ask)'

   郝紫薇:　　　帅　　　**嘛**。
   hao3zi3wei1　shuai4　　ma5
   'Hao Ziwei'　'handsome'　SFP
   'Female Guest: Well, because he is handsome, that's why!'
   　　　　　　　　　　　　　　　　　　　　　　(wmyhb 20130806)

In both examples in Example 98, 嘛 is used to mark a short utterance as having the explanatory power to resolve a mystery. In Example 98a, the girl wonders loudly why men currently like to wear ankle-length pants. The man simply answers 'comparatively cool' plus the *ma5*. If there had been no *ma5*, the utterance could still be understood as an attempt to answer the question. However, the connection between the answer and the question would be much weaker. The presence of *ma5* highlights the obviousness of the answer to the question and helps bridge the gap of reasoning. Another SFP, 啊, is also possible here, as *a5* is normally used to mark obvious responses. But the use of *a5* seems more 'aggressive' here, incorporating a possibly negative attitude. In Example 98b, the female guest repeats the intensifier 'particularly' three times to emphasize her joy at seeing the male candidate. When questioned why, she only answers with a monosyllabic adjective 帅 'handsome' plus *ma5*. The presence of *ma5* is crucial in helping the listener make the necessary connection between the two propositions (i.e. 'He is handsome' and 'She is happy') to quickly arrive at the correct interpretation (that she is happy because he looks handsome).

Example 99

a 邱启明：　　他　今年　　才　　大二　　**嘛**，
　　qiu1qi3ming2 ta1 jin1nian2 cai2 da4er4 ma5
　　'Qiu Qiming' 'he' 'this-year' 'only' 'big-two' SFP
　　'Host: He is only a sophomore.

　　对他　　的　要求　　也　不要　　太高。
　　dui4 ta1 de5 yao1qiu2 ye3 bu2yao4 tai4gao1
　　'to' 'him' AD 'demand' 'also' 'not-want' 'too-high'
　　Do not be too demanding on him.'

　　　　　　　　　　　　　　　　　　　　　　　(wmyhb 20130828)

b 张欣：　　　人　　**嘛**，没有　　不　犯错　　　　的　时候。
　　zhang1xin1 ren2　ma5 mei2you3 bu2 fan4cuo4　　de5 shi2hou4
　　'Zhang Xin' 'human' SFP 'none'　'not' 'make-mistake' AD 'moment'
　　'Female Guest: As humans, no one can be free from making mistakes.'
　　　　　　　　　　　　　　　　　　　　　　　(wmyhb 20130725)

Example 99 shows 嘛 being used in a reasoning process which happens within a speaker's own turn, as opposed to being used to answer questions like that in Example 98. In Example 99a, *ma5* follows the speaker's first sentence ('He is only a level 2 undergraduate') to mark it as a premise for further reasoning. In the second sentence, the speaker issues a command based on that premise.

Example 99b, like 98a, shows the ability of *ma5* to bring forth an entire set of implications ('To err is human' etc.) to the monosyllabic item it accompanies (人), which leads to the conclusion, elegantly and faultlessly, ('he is bound to make mistakes').

Because of its frequent association with structures expressing a reason, *ma5* often collocates with the word 因为 'because', as Example 100 shows.

Example 100

于冰：	因为	我	自己	有	服装店		嘛,
yu2bing1	yin1wei4	wo3	zi4ji3	you3	fu2zhuang1dian4		ma5
'Yu Bing'	'because'	'I'	'self'	'have'	'clothing-shop'		SFP

'Female Guest: Since I own a clothing shop,

我	可以	雇	服务员,
wo3	ke3yi3	gu4	fu2wu4yuan2
'I'	'can'	'hire'	'service-person'

I can hire salespersons (to mind the shop)

然后	白天	我	来	照顾	奶奶,	你	休息。
ran2hou4	bai2tian1	wo3	lai2	zhao4gu4	nai3nai5	ni3	xiu1xi2
'then'	'day time'	'I'	'come'	'look after'	'granny'	'you'	'rest'

and then I can look after granny for you and you can take a rest.'

(wmyhb 20130710)

The female guest in Example 100 is offering herself to be considered by a male candidate. Since the man has to work the night shift and has to take care of his granny in the day, the girl kindly offers to look after the granny for him if he chooses her. In the first sentence, the statement 'I have my own clothing shop' is marked by the collocation 因为 … 嘛 'because … *ma5*' which expresses the logical relation between the reason and the result in a more strengthened way than if either of the two collocates were to appear alone (which, however, would still be acceptable).

In Examples 99 and 100, all the portions stating the reason appear before the parts giving the result. It is also possible, in a speaker's given turn, to add a reason for a previously mentioned statement or proposal. In this case, *ma5* would be more important and indispensable for the host structure to be understood as a reason for the previous utterance. Example 101 is an example of this kind of usage.

Example 101

董至成：	给	他	吃	一点	让	他	补	一下。
dong3zhi4cheng2	gei3	ta1	chi1	yi4dian3	rang4	ta1	bu3	yi2xia4
'Dong Zhicheng'	'give'	'him'	'eat'	'one-bit'	'let'	'him'	'supplement'	'once'

'Male Guest: Give him some of this to eat; supplement him a little.

我们	说	吃	形	补	形	**嘛**。
wo3men5	shuo1	chi1	xing2	bu3	xing2	ma5
'we'	'say'	'eat'	'shape'	'supplement'	'shape'	SFP

As the saying goes: The thing you eat will supplement your body according to its shape.'

(kxll 20130828)

The male celebrity in Example 101 is talking about some foods whose shapes resemble certain human organs (especially the reproductive ones). In his first sentence, the man urges the assistant of the show to feed some of these to another celebrity. In the second sentence, he reveals the reason for such a proposal – 'Eating food of a certain shape strengthens the body part of the same shape'. This is meant to be a joke and *ma5* is indispensable in the second sentence for it to be construed as a reason for making the suggestion and as the punchline of the joke.

Example 102

Mr Right：	如果	你的	父母	不	喜欢	对方,
mister right	ru2guo3	ni3de5	fu4mu3	bu4	xi3huan1	dui4fang1
'Mr Right'	'if'	'your'	'parents'	'not'	'like'	'the other party'

你	会	停止	交往	吗?
ni3	hui4	ting2zhi3	jiao1wang3	ma5
'you'	'will'	'stop'	'socialize'	QM

'Co-host: Would you end the relationship if your parents did not like the girl?'

于尚臣：	肯定	会	停止	交往	的。
yu2shang4chen2	ken3ding4	hui4	ting2zhi3	jiao1wang3	de5
'Yu Shangchen'	'definitely'	'will'	'stop'	'socialize'	ED

百善孝为先	**嘛**。
bai3shan4xiao4wei2xian1	ma5
'hundred-merits-filial piety-be-first'	SFP

'Male Guest: I would definitely end the relationship. Being good to parents comes before all merits.'

(wmyhb 20130903)

When the male guest in Example 102 is asked whether he will respect his parents' opinion about his relationship with a girl, he quickly answers 'yes', and then he offers a reason for that decision. As the reason comes after the claim, it is important for that sentence to be tagged by *ma5*. Otherwise it would be difficult for the listener to understand it as an explanation of the previous statement.

Marker of rectification

We discussed the functions of 嘛 to mark allegedly shared information and to highlight the reason for making a claim. In the examples discussed above, the speakers assume the *ma5*-marked information to be obviously true and readily acceptable to the listener. However, when the speaker feels there is a conceptual difference between the speaker and the hearer, the speaker can still use *ma5* to mark the information which they want to share, possibly with an intention to correct the hearer's misconception. In cases like this, *ma5* often carries an element of impatience which is not seen in the examples of the previous kind.

Example 103

蔡康永：　　　你　　不是　　要　　拿给　　　我们　　　看　　吗？
cai4kang1yong3 ni3　bu2shi4 yao4　na2gei3　wo3men5 kan4　ma5
'Keven Tsai'　　'you' 'not-is' 'want' 'take-give' 'us'　　'see' QM
'Host: Are you not going to let us see (the photo)?'

寇乃馨：　　我　现在　　正在　　　找　　**嘛**！
kou4nai3xin1 wo3 xian4zai4 zheng4zai4 zhao3 ma5
'Kou Naixin' 'I'　'now'　'right-AM' 'find' SFP
'Female Guest: (Can't you see) I am just looking for it!'

(kxll 20130827)

The host of the chat show in Example 102 is questioning a female celebrity why she is not presenting a photograph of her ideal man as promised. The woman answers, a bit impatiently, that she is trying to find her cell phone (while fumbling in her bag) in which the photo is kept. The marking of 嘛 indicates the speaker's intention to correct Mr Tsai about the misconception that she is not presenting the photo, by emphasizing the current visual information Tsai should pay attention to (i.e. Kou is indeed looking for the desirable photo).

Example 104

黄菡:	她	想	说	的	是，	他	不是	我的	菜。
huang2han4	ta1	xiang3	shuo1	de5	shi4	ta1	bu2shi4	wo3de5	cai4
'Huang Han'	'she'	'think'	'say'	AD	'be'	'he'	'not-is'	'my'	'dish'

'Female Specialist: What she really wants to say is, he is not my type.'

孟非:	你	就	直接	这么	说	**嘛**！
meng4fei1	ni3	jiu4	zhi2jie1	zhe4mo5	shuo1	ma5
'Meng Fei'	'you'	'just'	'direct'	'like this'	'say'	SFP

'Host: You should have said so straightforwardly!'

(fcwr 20130831)

The dialogue in Example 104 centers around a female guest's earlier comment on a male suitor. She said that she had turned her light off because she might not be his type. Mr Meng asked why she thought so. The girl said she was trying to be polite, at which Ms Huang says that what the girl really wants to say is 'He is not my type'. Meng then offers his punchy remark on the girl's tactfulness, which he ostentatiously condemns. The marking of *ma5* signals the speaker's recognition of an incorrect situation and his intention to put it right.

Example 105

谢迪凡:	但是	我	没有	做	过	这样	的	事情。
xie4di2fan2	dan4shi4	wo3	mei2you3	zuo4	zuo4	zhe4yang4	de5	shi4qing2
'Xie Difan'	'but'	'I'	'not'	'do'	AM	'such'	AD	'matter'

'Male Guest: But I have never done a thing like that.'

孟非:	你	来	这里	就是	为了
meng4fei1	ni3	lai2	zhe4li3	jiu4shi4	wei4le5
'Meng Fei'	'you'	'come'	'here'	'just-is'	'for'

'Host: The reason you come here is exactly for

做	这种	事情	才	来	的	**嘛**！
zuo4	zhe4zhong3	shi4qing2	cai2	lai2	de5	ma5
'do'	'this-kind'	'matter'	'still'	'come'	ED	SFP

doing this kind of thing!'

(fcwr 20130901)

In Example 105, an unusually timid male suitor says he has never done the kind of romantic things as suggested by other participants of the show. The host then corrects the boy by saying that he came to the show exactly to do that kind of thing. The marking of *ma5* helps highlight the purpose of the host's comment to clarify a misconception.

Example 106

沈涛： 说 实话， 还 真 没 我 妈
shen3tao1 shuo1 shi2hua4 hai2 zhen1 mei2 wo3 ma1
'Shen Tao' 'say' 'true-words' 'still' 'real' 'no' 'I' 'mother'
'Host: To be honest, her dancing was not as good as my mother

每天 出去 跳 得 好看。
mei3tian1 chu1qu4 tiao4 de5 hao3kan4
'everyday' 'go out' 'jump' Com 'good-look'
who goes out dancing every day.'

黄泓博： 人家 是 美女 嘛。
huang2hong2bo2 ren2jia1 shi4 mei3nv3 ma5
'Huang Hongbo' 'others' 'be' 'pretty-woman' SFP
'Male Guest: (She is alright) as she is a pretty girl.'

(aqllk 20130827)

In Example 106, the host of the dating show is commenting on a girl's dancing performance, saying it was worse than his mother's regular dancing exercise. The male suitor responds to this comment with the sentence 'The person in question is a pretty woman'. On the surface, it looks as though there is no connection between the two utterances. However, the presence of *ma5* clearly suggests an underlying process of information addition and revision which should be drawn upon to help interpret the message. What the male guest means is, since the girl in question is pretty (which is the most desirable quality for a woman in this line of reasoning), she is exempt from the expectation of superior dancing skills, so there is no point in criticizing her for her poor dancing performance. The use of *ma5* bridges a relatively large gap of reasoning in this instance. This function of *ma5* is frequently seen in daily Chinese conversation.

Marker of paraphrase

People often feel it necessary to put things into a different perspective during conversation to better understand a piece of information. One of the ways of doing this is to offer a paraphrase of a previous text or a summary of a recent discussion or happening. Due to its various functions in the information domain, 嘛 is also used to mark this kind of paraphrase or summary in order to endorse, illuminate or justify. Since the previous information is already established, the speaker assumes that the paraphrase is also shared information, which licenses the use of *ma5*.

Example 107

曲楠楠:	而且		我	是	来自	哈尔滨,
qu1nan2nan2	er2qie3		wo3	shi4	lai2zi4	ha1er3bin1
'Qu Nannan'	'moreover'		'I'	'be'	'come from'	'Harbin'

'Female Guest: In addition, I come from Harbin city.

所以	说	在	平时	生活	中	呢,
suo3yi3	shuo1	zai4	ping2shi2	sheng1huo2	zhong1	ne5
'therefore'	'say'	'at'	'ordinarily'	'living'	'middle'	CFP

Therefore, in terms of everyday life,

我	也	是	比较	爷儿们	的	人。
wo3	ye3	shi4	bi3jiao4	ye2er5men5	de5	ren2
'I'	'also'	'be'	'comparatively'	'macho'	AD	'person'

I am also a comparatively dominant person.'

吴征:	比较	悍	**嘛**。
wu2zheng1	bi3jiao4	han4	ma5
'Wu Zheng'	'comparatively'	'rough'	SFP

'Male Guest: Relatively ferocious, so to speak.'

(wmyhb 20130528)

The female guest in Example 107 reveals her own character as a dominant one, just like a macho man. The male suitor shows his understanding of the claim by characterizing the trait with a word – 悍 'tough, combative'. He tags his sentence with *ma5* to trigger listeners' processing of the utterance at the level of information management (recall Schiffrin's Information State as a discourse module). In this case, *ma5* helps mark the information as further explanation or elaboration of the previous message. It shows the speaker's wish for this information to be accepted as common knowledge so as to serve its explanatory function. In other words, what *ma5* marks is a paraphrase of a recently shared piece of information based on the speaker's understanding of the message.

Example 108

周丽珍:	所以	我	觉得	男	嘉宾	特别	好。
zhou1li4zhen1	suo3yi3	wo3	jue2de5	nan2	jia1bin1	te4bie2	hao3
'Zhou Lizhen'	'therefore'	'I'	'feel'	'male'	'good-guest'	'especially'	'good'

'Female Guest: Therefore I find the male guest particularly good.'

邱启明:	叫	勤俭	持家	**嘛**。
qiu1qi3ming2	jiao4	qin2jian3	chi2jia1	ma5
'Qiu Qiming'	'call'	'diligent-frugal'	'hold-home'	SFP

'Host: As I understand, this is called diligent and frugal housekeeping.'

(wmyhb 20130903)

In Example 108, the female guest is referring to a virtue of the current male suitor, who advocates the 'emptying the plate' movement (i.e. not leaving any food on the plate). The girl also used the paucity of food in the poor countryside she came from as an example to support this movement. When it is his turn to speak, the host of the show summarizes the situation with an established Chinese phrase 'to manage the household with diligence and frugality'. This expression is tagged with *ma5* to show the speaker's intention to share the information as common knowledge and to wrap up the information accumulated so far.

Example 109

王婉洁：	然后	因为	当时	我	就	觉得
wang2wan3jie2	ran2hou4	yin1wei4	dang1shi2	wo3	jiu4	jue2de5
'Wang Wanjie'	'then'	'because'	'at that time'	'I'	'just'	'feel'

'Female Guest: Then because at that time I felt

那个	学长—	我	就	给	他	神化	了	**嘛**,
na4ge5	xue2zhang3	wo3	jiu4	gei3	ta1	shen2hua4	le5	ma5
'that'	'senior student'	'I'	'just'	'give'	'him'	'god-transform'	AM	SFP

that senior student . . . I idolized him, so to speak.

我	就	觉得	特别	优秀。
wo3	jiu4	jue2de5	te4bie2	you1xiu4
'I'	'just'	'feel'	'especially'	'outstanding'

I just felt he was so outstanding.'

(fcwr 20130810)

The female guest in Example 109 is discussing her infatuation with a senior student as an undergraduate. She makes a false start in the first sentence, reorganizes herself and decides to describe the situation as 'I idolized him'. This description is tagged with *ma5*. The occurrence of *ma5* after a retrospection process and in a restarted sentence seems to relate *ma5* to a paraphrasing and summarizing function, which coincides with the nature of the expression (an abstraction out of a narrative).

Example 110

王艺洁：	你	这	是	愿意	为	我	改变	吗？
wang2yi4jie2	ni3	zhe4	shi4	yuan4yi4	wei4	wo3	gai3bian4	ma5
'Wang Yijie'	'you'	'this'	'be'	'willing'	'for'	'me'	'change'	QM

'Female Guest: Do you mean that you can change for the sake of me?'

欧阳铭骏：		我	听	你的	建议	**嘛**。
ou1yang2ming2jun4		wo3	ting1	ni3de5	jian4yi4	ma5
'Ouyang Mingjun'		'I'	'listen'	'your'	'suggestion'	SFP

'Male Guest: Let's say I am following your recommendation.'

(wmyhb 20130723)

In Example 110, the female guest wants to make sure if the male suitor's previous comment means he is willing to change himself for her, whereupon the man answers 'I am listening to your suggestion'. The tagging of *ma5* not only shows the speaker's willingness to go along with the suggestion but also helps clarify the speaker's stance to a certain extent. That is, he means the idea of changing is not initiated by him but is suggested by the girl which is probably difficult to refuse in the courtship setting. In other words, he paraphrases the information from 'I am willing to change for you' to 'I am willing to follow your suggestion'. The *ma5* carries out a double function here – to paraphrase information and to rectify a misconception.

Example 111

沈涛：	二十号	侯金雨	你	没	表	过	态。
shen3tao1	er4shi2hao4	hou2jin1yu3	ni3	mei2	biao3	guo4	tai4
'Shen Tao'	'No. 20'	'Hou Jinyu'	'you'	'not'	'express'	AM	'attitude'

'Host: No. 20 Hou Jinyu, you have not revealed your attitude yet.'

侯金雨：	我	表	过	态。
hou2jin1yu3	wo3	biao3	guo4	tai4
'Hou Jinyu'	'I'	'express'	AM	'attitude'

'Female Guest: I did reveal my attitude.

我	说——问	他	爱	她	还是	我	**嘛**。
wo3	shuo1 wen4	ta1	ai4	ta1	hai2shi4	wo3	ma5
'I'	'say' 'ask'	'him'	'love'	'her'	'or'	'me'	SFP

I said – asked him whether he loved her or me, right?'

(aqllk 20130827)

In Example 111, a few girls are competing over a male suitor. The host says to one of them that she has not yet expressed her preference for the boy. There are two sentences in the girl's reply. In the first sentence she corrects the host by saying that she did reveal her attitude. In the second sentence (which involves a false start) she explains how she expressed her fondness for him. The second sentence is a paraphrase of the first and it is marked by *ma5* to show its information status (i.e. it is previously established knowledge). The marking of *ma5* has empowered the second sentence to support the claim made in the first sentence.

Example 112

雷明： 侯金雨 的 秘密 我 知道。
lei2ming2 hou2jin1yu3 de5 mi4mi4 wo3 zhi1dao4
'Lei Ming' 'Hou jinyu' PD 'secret' 'I' 'know'
'Male Specialist: I know about Hou Jinyu's secret.'

沈涛： 甚么？
shen3tao1 shen2mo5
'Shen Tao' 'what'
'Host: What is it?'

雷明： 她 不是 必须 得 抱 着
lei2ming2 ta1 bu2shi4 bi4xu1 dei3 bao4 zhe5
'Lei Ming' 'she' 'not-is' 'necessary' 'must' 'hold' AM
'Male Specialist: As far as I know, she has to hold on to

那件 衣服 才 能 睡 **嘛**。
na4jian4 yi1fu2 cai2 neng2 shui4 ma5
'that' Cla 'clothes' 'just' 'can' 'sleep' SFP
that piece of clothing in order to sleep.'

(aqllk 20130827)

Example 112 happens prior to a routine of the dating show where a female guest's personal secret is revealed so the male can decide whether or not to choose her. The resident specialist, having heard a secret of this girl in a previous episode, says he knows what the girl's secret is about. The host asks him what it might be. Mr Lei then reveals his knowledge. The sentence relaying the secret is marked with *ma5* to show its information status (i.e. as formerly established knowledge). The utterance itself is a paraphrase or elaboration of Lei's earlier claim that he knows about the girl's secret. The *ma5* has carried out the function of supporting an earlier claim by sharing established information.

Example 113

黄菡:	其实	说	长得	是	不	是
huang2han4	qi2shi2	shuo1	zhang3de5	shi4	bu2	shi4
'Huang Han'	'in fact'	'say'	'grow Com'	'be'	'not'	'be'

'Female Specialist: As a matter of fact, saying whether

我	喜欢	的,	同样	也	是	一种	感觉	嘛。
wo3	xi3huan1	de5	tong2yang4	ye3	shi4	yi4zhong3	gan3jue2	ma5
'I'	'like'	AD	'similar'	'also'	'be'	'one-kind'	'feeling'	SFP

I like the look or not is also a kind of feeling.

它	也	不是	一个	理性	的	东西。
ta1	ye3	bu2shi4	yi2ge5	li3xing4	de5	dong1xi1
'it'	'also'	'not-is'	'one' Cla	'rational'	AD	'thing'

It is not a rational thing either.'

(fcwr 20130901)

In Example 113, the female specialist, Ms Huang, is responding to a girl's claim that she rejected the suitor based on rational judgment. Huang objects to her claim that evaluating a person based on their appearance is rational. She would rather view the appearance-based appraisal as emotional rather than rational. She presents this argument in a noun clause and two sentences. In the noun clause, she refers to the idea of basing one's fondness on a person's look. In the following sentence, she labels the situation as an expression of feelings. This sentence is tagged with *ma5* so it can be easily accepted by the audience as common knowledge. In other words, *ma5* helps to extend the argument by declaring the preferred interpretation as a readily acceptable message. The next sentence then gives the conclusion based on that presumably already shared information.

5.10 *YE5*

Similarly to the case of *o2*, *o5* and *ou5*, there is no uniquely established orthographical representation for the SFP *ye5*. It is variously written as 耶, 哎, 欸 and so on. We adopt 耶 as the standard representation in this book, but keep other forms in some examples intact, as they appeared in their original settings. The fifth tone in *ye5* is the 'default tone' for all sentence-final particles discussed in this book with the notable exception of 哦, which is clearly uttered in the second tone (i.e. *o2*). Thus, although the characters 耶, 哎, 欸 etc. are not conventionally annotated in Pinyin as *ye5*, we still use *ye5* to represent the sound of these characters in the examples (as this is the closest approximation to the sounds truly uttered in those circumstances).

The primary function of *ye5* is to mark a speaker's recent discovery as something surprising and probably different from the listener's expectation. In this respect, *ye5* bears some similarity to 哦 whose main function is to give warning. The *ye5* differs from *o2* in that it may assume that the listener will have a different point of view. The *o2*, on the other hand, does not make such an assumption. While *o2* is mainly used to introduce a new perspective, *ye5* marks something as opposite to a known assumption. Also, while *o2* is more oriented toward the listener, *ye5* focuses more on expressing one's thoughts and feelings.

Marker of something opposite to expectation

During the course of a conversation, *ye5* is often used to mark something which the speaker thinks is the opposite of the listener's assumption.

Example 114

蔡康永：	我们	放	在	你	面前	的	鱼
cai4kang1yong3	wo3men5	fang4	zai4	ni3	mian4qian2	de5	yu2
'Kevin Tsai'	'we'	'place'	'at'	'you'	'face-front'	AD	'fish'

'Host: The fish we placed in front of you

可	不	是	甚么	长	得	很	和气	的	鱼	哦。
ke3	bu2	shi4	shen2mo5	zhang3	de5	hen3	he2qi4	de5	yu2	o2
'but'	'not'	'be'	'what'	'grow'	Com	'very'	'friendly'	AD	'fish'	SFP

is not just any fish that looks friendly!'

它	就	是	一	条	典型	的	鱼	耶!
ta1	jiu4	shi4	yi4	tiao2	dian3xing2	de5	yu2	ye5
'it'	'just'	'be'	'one'	Cla	'typical'	AD	'fish'	SFP

'(Surprise!) It is just a typical fish.'

(kxll 20130813)

In Example 114, the host of the chat show first declares the fish they use to scare the female celebrity with a fish phobia is not a 'friendly fish'. The first sentence is tagged with *o2* for it to be used as a warning. The second sentence is then tagged with *ye5* to reveal what the fish really is – a typical fish with the appropriate shape, scales, spikes and fins, rather than a more 'friendly' fish with fewer characteristics of fish (which may then be less scary to the female guest). The fact that both *o2* and *ye5* are used in the same turn with similar functions reveals the similarity in their nature. The fact that *o2* comes first strengthens its main capacity as a warning signal. The use of *ye5* then declares the message as something contradictory to the listener's presumed wish (for a more friendly fish).

Example 115

蔡康永：	你	之前	有	试过	吗？
cai4kang1yong3	ni3	zhi1qian2	you3	shi4guo4	ma5
'Kevin Tsai'	'you'	'before'	'have'	'try'	AM QM

'Host: Have you done this before?'

安钧璨	没有	试过	**耶**！
an1jun1can4	mei2you3	shi4guo4	ye5
'An Juncan'	'not-have'	'try'	AM SFP

'Male Guest: No, I have never tried!'

(kxll 20130813)

In Example 115, the host of the chat show asks the male guest whether he has ever tried a certain spicy hot dish before. As the conversation has been dwelling on the male celebrity's extraordinary ability to endure spicy food, the expected answer might be 'yes'. However, the celebrity has never tried that particular dish so the answer has to be 'no'. Thus he attaches *ye5* to the less-preferred answer to highlight the possible discrepancy between the truth and the listener's expectation.

Example 116

a 金友庄：

你	这样	穿	出去	的话，
jin1you3zhuang1	ni3	zhe4yang4	chuan1	chu1qu4	de5hua4

'Jin Youzhuang' 'you' 'this-form' 'wear' 'exit' 'suppose'

'Female Guest: If you go out dressed like that

那	男生	会	觉得	你	没有	穿	**耶**！
na4	nan2sheng1	hui4	jue2de5	ni3	mei2you3	chuan1	ye5
'then'	'boy'	'will'	'feel'	'you'	'none'	'wear'	SFP

then men will think you wear nothing (underneath).'

(jwsdj 20130905)

b 胡维丽：

刷碗	的	那个	手套	是	塑料	的，
shua1wan3	de5	na4ge5	shou3tao4	shi4	su4liao4	de5
'Hu Weili' 'brush-bowl'	AD	'that' Cla	'glove'	'be'	'plastic'	AD

'Female Guest: The gloves used for washing dishes are made of plastic.

我	是	皮质	的	**耶**！
wo3	shi4	pi2zhi2	de5	ye5
'I'	'be'	'skin-texture'	AD	SFP

But mine are made of leather!'

(wmyhb 20130226)

Both examples in Example 116 involve the speaker saying something which they think is against the listener's expectations. In Example 116a, the woman is repeating her warning to her daughter about the danger of wearing a long T-shirt with very short pants. The speaker thinks her daughter does not realize what she looks like to the men around her (i.e. that she appears not to wear any pants), so she tags her caution with *ye5*, presumably to maximize the difference between hearer expectation and the reality. If *ye5* helps achieve the intended result, her daughter may reconceptualize the issue and correct her code of dress. In Example 116b, the speaker is correcting a wrong observation about the gloves she is wearing. That is, her gloves are made of leather, not of plastic. The correct statement is marked with *ye5* to contrast it with the wrong assumption.

Example 117

孟非:　这　　里边　　还有　　　把　伞。
meng4fei1 zhe4 li3bian1 hai2you3 ba3 san3
'Meng Fei' 'this' 'inside' 'still-have' Cla 'umbrella'
'Host: There is also an umbrella inside here.

这个　　　怎么　　　说　　法?
zhe4ge5 zen3mo5 shuo1 fa3
'this' Cla 'how' 'say' 'method'
What is this for?

我们　　　的　中国　　　　文化　　　里边儿,
wo3men5 de5 zhong1guo2 wen2hua4 li3bian1er5
'we' PD 'China' 'culture' 'inside'
In our Chinese culture,

好像　　　不　兴　　送　伞　　　的　哎。
hao3xiang4 bu4 xing1 song4 san3 de5 ye5
'seem' 'not' 'prevail' 'give' 'umbrella' ED SFP
it does not seem popular to give umbrellas as gifts.'

(fcwr 20130811)

In Example 117, the host of the show is responding to a situation where a male suitor has produced some gifts for participants in the show. There is one more thing in the man's bag which is an umbrella. It looks like the man also intends to give away the umbrella. As the sound of umbrella (伞 *san3*) is identical to that of 'breaking up' (散 *san3*), the Chinese people do not normally give umbrellas as presents for fear of being interpreted as wanting to break up with the receiver of the gift. That is why Mr Meng says the umbrella is not a popular gift. His remark is tagged with *ye5* to mark the statement as contradictory to the male suitor's good will in using the umbrella as a gift.

Example 118

薛盼盼：	他	说	他	这	个	药	如何	如何	好
xue1pan4pan4	ta1	shuo1	ta1	zhe4	ge5	yao4	ru2he2	ru2he2	hao3
'Xue Panpan'	'he'	'say'	'he'	'this'	Cla	'medicine'	'how'	'how'	'good'

'Female Guest: He kept saying how wonderful this medicine was.

能	减肥	甚么	之	类	的。
neng2	jian3fei2	shen2mo5	zhi1	lei4	de5
'can'	'reduce-fat'	'what'	'this'	'kind'	AD

How it can help lose weight and so on.

我	竟然	就	信	了	**哎**！
wo3	jing4ran2	jiu4	xin4	le5	ye5
'I'	'unexpectedly'	'just'	'believe'	AM	SFP

And I actually believed him!'

(fcwr 20130907)

At the time when the girl is speaking in Example 118, the participants of the show are discussing how gullible people can be in the face of contemporary swindlers. Xue uses an example to illustrate how innocent and even stupid she was to believe in the advertisement of certain health products. The sentence 'I actually believed' is tagged with *ye5* to show how contrary it is to common sense.

Marker of new discovery

Often *ye5* is used to accompany a discovery which is either new to the speaker at the time of speaking or is one which the speaker thinks is new to the listener.

Example 119

a

徐熙娣：	几	个	围	着	她	**耶**！
xu2xi1di4	ji3	ge5	wei2	zhe5	ta1	ye5
'Dee Hsu'	'several'	Cla	'surround'	AM	'her'	SFP

'Hostess: There are several (men) surrounding her!'

(kxll 20130827)

b

陈维龄：	我	从来	没有	想	过	这	个	问题	**耶**！
chen2wei2ling2	wo3	cong2lai2	mei2you3	xiang3	guo4	zhe4	ge5	wen4ti2	ye5
'Chen Weiling'	'I'	'ever'	'not'	'think'	AM	'this'	Cla	'question'	SFP

'Female Guest: I have never thought about this question before!'

(qngwzyg 20130822)

The two sentences in Example 119 each reveal something new either to the speaker or to the listener. In Example 119a, the speaker was shown a photo of several good-looking men surrounding a female celebrity. The scene was particularly surprising to her and unthinkable for a married woman. The *ye5*-marked expression reveals the magnitude of this new finding. In Example 119b, the female guest was asked what kind of milk packaging would help her decide on buying the milk. Without answering the question directly, she expresses her surprise at the implication of this question (that packaging could have a bearing on milk quality) with a *ye5*-marked sentence.

Example 120

邱启明：	那	意思	就是	1	米	62	以上
qiu1qi3ming2	na4	yi4si5	jiu4shi4	yi1	mi3	liu4er4	yi3shang4
'Qiu Qiming'	'that'	'meaning'	'just-is'	'one'	'meter'	'62'	'over'

'Host: That means everyone over and above 162 cm

的	都	可以。	蔡旸，	你	可以	的。 ⋯	噢，
de5	dou1	ke3yi3	cai4yang2	ni3	ke3yi3	de5	ou5
AD	'all'	'passable'	'Cai Yang'	'you'	'can'	ED	IP

can be considered (by the male suitor). Cai Yang, you are qualified.

不对	哦，	你	1	米	59	**耶**。
bu2dui4	o2	ni3	yi1	mi3	wu3jiu3	ye5
'not-right'	SFP	'you'	'one'	'meter'	'59'	SFP

Oh, that is not true. You are only 159 cm tall!'

(wmyhb 20130806)

Example 120 clearly shows the thinking process of the host of the dating show. For one moment he thought the girl named Cai Yang could be considered by a male suitor who requires his girlfriend to be over 162 cm in height. Then he realizes, from the back of his mind, that Cai is only 159 cm tall and is not qualified after all. This new discovery is marked with *ye5* to show the scale of his surprise and the implication of the finding.

Example 121

蔡康永:	贺一航	大哥,	你	回头	看	一下
cai4kang1yong3	he4yi1hang2	da4ge1	ni3	hui2tou2	kan4	yi2xia4
'Kevin Tsai'	'He Yihang'	'big-brother'	'you'	'return-head'	'see'	'once'

'Host: Big Brother He Hihang, please turn back and look

后面	那	两个	答案,	有	两个	人	写	你	耶。
hou4mian4	na4	liang3ge5	da2an4	you3	liang3ge5	ren2	xie3	ni3	ye5
'back'	'that'	'two' Cla	'answer'	'have'	'two' Cla	'person'	'write'	'you'	SFP

behind you at the two answers. There are two persons who wrote your name!'

(kxll 20130814)

In Example 121, the host of the chat show is passing on an interesting discovery to a male celebrity. The celebrity had probably been a womanizer when he was young and the voting was about choosing the man most unlikely to have an affair among the ten or so celebrities. The host, Kevin Tsai, must have considered the two votes for He Dage a bit shocking to He since he himself knows best about his own history. Tsai therefore marks his announcement of this discovery with *ye5* to reflect its potential to surprise He Dage.

Example 122

黄小柔:	真的	有点	滑	耶!
huang2xiao3rou2	zhen1de5	you3dian3	hua2	ye5
'Huang Xiaorou'	'really'	'have little'	'slippery'	SFP

'Female Guest: It is really a little bit slippery!'

徐熙娣:	你	们	现在	不是	在	伸展台	上	耶!
xu2xi1di4	ni3	men5	xian4zai4	bu2shi4	zai4	shen1zhan3tai2	shang4	ye5
'Dee Hsu'	'you'	PM	'now'	'not-is'	'at'	'catwalk'	'up'	SFP

'Hostess: Mind you, you are not on the catwalk now!'

(kxll 20130813)

In Example 122, the speaker, Huang, had just made the discovery that the 'catwalk' the show prepared for them was really slippery. The *ye5* helps her put this new discovery into words. Hsu, on the other hand, uses *ye5* in her utterance to caution Huang about the possible misconception that this was a real catwalk (i.e. it was a fake designed to embarrass the guests). Thus the two *ye5*'s are slightly different in function (i.e. making a discovery vs revealing unexpected information).

Since the core function of *ye5* is to announce a new discovery or present something unexpected, it often adds emphasis to an expression when it is used to respond to a statement or a question, whether in a preferred or less-preferred way.

Marker of endorsement

A *ye5*-marked expression is often used to respond favorably to a previous speaker's contribution. This is often just a short endorsement of the previous speaker's idea or proposal. It is as if *ye5* is saying 'you have spoken my mind' in these cases.

Example 123

蔡康永：　　　今天　　聊　　下来　　　你　　觉得
cai4kang1yong3 jin1tian1 liao2 xia4lai2　　　ni3　jue2de5
'Kevin Tsai'　　'today'　'chat' 'down-come' 'you' 'feel'
'Host: Having finished chatting today, in your opinion

最　　　震撼　　你　的　一　件　事情　　是　甚么？
zui4　　zhen4han4 ni3　de5 yi2　jian4 shi4qing2 shi4 shen2mo5
'the most' 'shock'　　'you' AD 'one' Cla　'matter'　'be'　'what'
what is the most shocking thing for you?'

徐熙娣：　我　想　　是　不　牵手　　　的　事。
xu2xi1di4　wo3 xiang3 shi4 bu4 qian1shou3 de5 shi4
'Dee Hsu' 'I'　'think' 'be' 'not' 'hold-hand' AD 'matter'
'Hostess: I think it is the issue about not holding hands (with your spouse).'

蔡康永：　　　我　也　是　欸！
cai4kang1yong3 wo3 ye3　shi4 ye5
'Kevin Tsai'　　'I'　'also' 'be' SFP
'Host: Me too!'

(kxll 20130827)

In Example 123, the host of the chat show asks his co-host what she thinks is the most shocking thing she has learnt from the day's chatting. Hsu says it has to be the unusual thing an older celebrity says about never holding his spouse's hand. Upon that, Tsai quickly agrees with a 'me too' marked with *ye5*, which is an agreement accompanied by genuine surprise (about both hosts coincidentally holding the same opinion).

Example 124

蔡康永：		你	觉得	Julie	如果	跟	艾力克斯
cai4kang1yong3		ni3	jue2de5	Julie	ru2guo3	gen1	ai4li4ke4si1
'Kevin Tsai'		'you'	'feel'	'Julie'	'if'	'with'	'Alex'

在一起	好	吗？
zai4yi4qi3	hao3	ma5
'together'	'good'	QM

'Host: Do you think it is alright if we put Julie and Alex together?'

徐熙娣：	我	觉得	好	**耶**。
xu2xi1di4	wo3	jue2de5	hao3	ye5
'Dee Hsu'	'I'	'think'	'good'	SFP

'Hostess: I think it is great!'

(kxll 20130827)

In Example 124, Mr Tsai asks his co-host how she thinks about putting celebrities Julie and Alex together as a couple on the show. Hsu readily agrees and her reply is tagged with *ye5* to introduce a sense of freshness to the agreed proposal. The newness of the proposal lies in the fact that the spouses of both celebrities are not present on the show, so the idea of the new partnership seems unconventional and thought-provoking.

Marker of retort

On the one hand, *ye5* seems to increase the authenticity and the immediacy of an endorsement as aforementioned; on the other hand, *ye5* can also lend its momentum to a negative response used to counter a claim or reject a proposal.

Example 125

关欣：	你	不	是	我	心	中	的	理想	肌肉	型男。
guan1xin1	ni3	bu2	shi4	wo3	xin1	zhong1	de5	li3xiang3	ji1rou4	xing2nan2
'Guan Xin'	'you'	'not'	'be'	'I'	'heart'	'middle'	AD	'ideal'	'muscle'	'type-man'

'Female Guest: You are not an ideal charismatic muscular man in my mind.'

薛盼盼：	人家	是	教练	**哎**！
xue1pan4pan4	ren2jia1	shi4	jiao4lian4	ye5
'Xue Panpan'	'others'	'be'	'coach'	SFP

'Female Guest: This person is a coach, mind you!'

(fcwr 20130817)

In Example 125, a female guest, Guan, is rejecting a male suitor on the grounds that he is not the ideal muscular man for her. The other female guest, Xue, shouts out a retort reminding Guan that the man is actually a fitness coach. The retort is marked with *ye5* presumably to remind the listener of an important piece of information which has been neglected. Note Example 125 is a dialogue observed on a Chinese TV show. The orthographical representation of *ye5* (here 哎) used by the TV subtitlers in Example 125 is different from the one used more frequently on Taiwanese TV shows (耶). However, it should be noted that other orthographical representations for *ye5* are also present in Taiwanese chat show subtitles, such as the 欸 in Example 123, and mainland chat shows also transcribe *ye5* as 耶 in some cases, such as in Example 120.

Example 126

谢震武：　　　　就　　像　　你　　有　　没　　有　　看　　过
xie4zhen4wu3　jiu4　xiang4　ni3　you3　mei2　you3　kan4　guo4
'Xie Zhenwu'　'just'　'like'　'you'　'have'　'not'　'have'　'see'　AM
'Host: It is like – have you ever seen

人家　　　　　　歌星　　到　　KTV　不　　唱歌？
ren2jia1　　　　ge1xing1　dao4　k-t-v　bu2　chang4ge1
'other people'　'singer'　　'reach'　'KTV'　'not'　'sing-song'
other singers going to KTV but not singing a song?'

曾治豪：　　　　可是　　我　　还是　　会　　唱　　**耶**！
zeng1zhi4hao2　ke3shi4　wo3　hai2shi4　hui4　chang4　ye5
'Zeng Zhihao'　'but'　'I'　'still'　'will '　'sing'　SFP
'Male Guest: But I still do my singing (in KTV)!'

(jwsdj 20130904)

In Example 126, the host of the chat show uses an analogy to show that professionals never do in their leisure time what they do for a living. Just like an actor does not perform at home, so a singer does not sing at KTV. However, the guest of the show, Mr Zeng, quickly points out that he, being a singer, also sings at KTV. This seems to undermine Mr Xie's generalization as the *ye5*-tagged sentence offers an exception to the assumption.

5.11 *LA5*

The primary function of 啦 *la5* is to dismiss an idea or object as unimportant or unworthy of consideration and possibly also to express an attitude of contempt or disapproval. However, it can also be used to express something positive, especially against certain adverse conditions or after some kind of misunderstanding. The *la5* is somewhat more frequently heard in Taiwanese Mandarin than in China, possibly due to the Southern Min influence.

Marker of dismissal

The *la5* often accompanies a derogatory statement with or without an impatient attitude. It is often used to dismiss something or someone as unimportant and unworthy of serious consideration.

Example 127

女人： 你 不 送 我 回家 吗？
nv3ren2 ni3 bu2 song4 wo3 hui2jia1 ma5
'woman' 'you' 'not' 'send' 'me' 'go home' QM
'Video Actress: Are you not going to take me home?'

马剑： 自己 坐 地铁 **啦**！
ma3jian4 zi4ji3 zuo4 di4tie3 la5
'Ma Jian' 'self' 'sit' 'underground' SFP
'Male Guest: Take the subway home by yourself!'

(fcwr 20130818)

Example 127 is a short exchange shown in a video clip introducing a male suitor. A woman in the video tries to get the man to take her home. The man's somewhat rude remark 'Go take the subway home yourself' is tagged by *la5*, which adds a careless and contemptuous attitude to the otherwise neutral command.

Example 128

a 邱启明： 他 不 是 你 那 个 专业 的,
qiu1qi3ming2 ta1 bu2 shi4 ni3 na4 ge5 zhuan1ye4 de5
'Qiu Qiming' 'he' 'not' 'be' 'you' 'that' Cla 'discipline' AD
'Host: He is not from the same discipline as you.

他 不 懂 **啦**！
ta1 bu4 dong3 la5
'he' 'not' 'understand' SFP
He does not understand.'

(wmyhb 20130102)

b 小钟： 乀, 两 百 万 太 离谱 了 **啦**！
xiao3zhong1 ei1 liang3 bai3 wan4 tai4 li2pu3 le5 la5
'Xiao Zhong' IP 'two' 'hundred' '10-thousand' 'too' 'absurd' SFP SFP
'Male Guest: Wow, two million is too ridiculous!

太 多 了 吧！
tai4 duo1 le5 ba5
'too' 'much' SFP SFP
It is too much!'

(kxll 20130903)

Both sentences in Example 128 marked by *la5* are used to counter a claim or proposal. In Example 128a, the host of the dating show is defending the male suitor who has not been trained in the same discipline as the female guest who is criticizing him. The host dismisses the presumption that the man should possess any technical knowledge that is not within his specialty. In Example 128b, the celebrity Zhong is complaining about the amount of money a friend supposedly wants to borrow from him. He condemns the amount of two million as too outrageously large. The tagging of *la5* helps express the speaker's attitude that the proposal is entirely out of the question.

Example 129

吴淡如： 满意 吗？
wu2dan4ru2 man3yi4 ma5
'Wu Danru' 'satisfactory' QM
'Hostess: Are you satisfied?'

王中皇： 一般般 **啦**！
wang2zhong1huang2 yi4ban1ban1 la5
'Wang Zhonghuang' 'ordinary' SFP
'Male Guest: I think it is just so so'

(jwsdj 20130905)

In Example 129, the hostess of the chat show asks a celebrity father what he thinks about his teenage daughter's new look. Mr Wang is not particularly impressed with his young daughter's fashionable outfit so he answers 'so-so' which is tagged with *la5* to show a low degree of satisfaction.

Example 130

王中平： 现在 应该— 她 应该 很 放心
wang2zhong1ping2 xian4zai4 ying1gai1 ta1 ying1gai1 hen3 fang4xin1
'Wang Zhongping' 'now' 'should' 'she' 'should' 'very' 'relaxed'
'Male Guest: Now should – she should be very much at ease now.

了 **啦**， 因为 第一 个 我的 …钱 都 在 她 那边。
le5 la5 yin1wei4 di4yi2 ge5 wo3de5 qian2 dou1 zai4 ta1 na4bian1
SFP SFP 'because' 'first' Cla 'my' 'money' 'all' 'at' 'she' 'that-side'
Because, first of all, all my money is with her.'

(jwsdj 20130909)

In Example 130, the host of the show asks the celebrity guest whether his wife is worried about his having any lady friends outside of the marriage. Wang rejects this suggestion by saying 'She should be very much at ease now' (because she has all the money). This sentence is tagged with *la5* to dismiss the possibility of his wife having to worry about anything.

Marker of clarification

Another function of 啦 related to its marking of dismissal is to help make clarifications. This may be to clarify the truth of information or to clarify one's stance after a possible misunderstanding.

Example 131

邱启明：　　他　没　失色，
qiu1qi3ming2 ta1 mei2 shi1se4
'Qiu Qiming' 'he' 'not' 'lose-color'
'Host: He is not overshadowed. Do you mean

你　意思　是　我　失色　　了　是　吧？
ni3　yi4si5　shi4　wo3　shi1se4　　le5　shi4　ba5
'you' 'mean' 'be' 'I' 'lose-color' AM 'be' SFP
I have been overshadowed?'

张瑾：　　　噢，　那　倒　　　也　没有　　啦！
zhang1jin3　ou5　na4　dao4　　ye3　mei2you3　la5
'Zhang Jin' IP 'that' 'after all' 'also' 'not' SFP
'Female Guest: Oh, I did not really mean that!'

(wmyhb 20130226)

In Example 131, the female guest has just commented positively on the appearance of the male suitor in this session. She said that when they stand side by side, the man did not appear any weaker than the tall and handsome host of the show. Upon that, the host challenges her by saying 'Do you mean I am the one who looks weaker then?' The girl quickly denies the accusation, using a *la5*-marked sentence to clarify herself and diminish the implication.

Example 132

吴淡如：	哎呀，	岁月	催	人	老	啊。
wu2dan4ru2	ai1ya5	sui4yue4	cui1	ren2	lao3	a5
'Wu Danru'	IP	'years'	'push'	'person'	'old'	SFP

'Hostess: I say, time flies and people are getting old.

不	是	说	你	们	**啦**。
bu2	shi4	shuo1	ni3	men5	la5
'not'	'be'	'say'	'you'	PM	SFP

I did not mean you, of course.

我	是	说	小孩	不知不觉	都	亭亭玉立	了。
wo3	shi4	shuo1	xiao3hai2	bu4zhi1bu4jue2	dou1	ting2ting2yu4li4	le5
'I'	'be'	'say'	'children'	'not-know-not-feel'	'all'	'erect-jade-stand'	SFP

I mean children all grow up and stand tall and graceful without our noticing.'

(jwsdj 20130905)

Example 132 occurs at the beginning of the chat show, when the hostess uses, as the ice breaker, a Chinese idiom: 'Time pushes people to grow old'. This is not the most pleasant greeting for the row of middle-aged celebrity guests on the show, who all hate to be referred to as being 'old'. The hostess therefore quickly denies the possibility that she is targeting the celebrities. Instead, she says she is referring to their children who are all young grown-ups now. The sentence used to deny the allegation is marked with *la5* to sideline it.

Example 133

徐熙娣：	他	自己	私生活	太多	事情	要	处理	了。
xu2xi1di4	ta1	zi4ji3	si1sheng1huo2	tai4duo1	shi4qing2	yao4	chu3li3	le5
'Dee Hsu'	'he'	'self'	'private-life'	'too-many'	'matter'	'want'	'handle'	SFP

'Hostess: He has too many things to deal with in his private life.'

陈汉典：	比较	忙	一点	**啦**，	比较	忙。
chen2han4dian3	bi3jiao4	mang2	yi4dian3	la5	bi3jiao4	mang2
'Chen Handian'	'comparatively'	'busy'	'a little'	SFP	'comparatively'	'busy'

'Assistant: He is just a little bit busy, that's all. A bit busy.'

(kxll 20130820)

In Example 133, the hostess of the chat show involves a senior celebrity's son by referring to his trouble-laden private life. This young man has been caught in many awkward situations such as having a dubious girlfriend, being repetitively issued with parking tickets, being out of a job frequently and so on. To help alleviate the situation, the assistant of the show suggests a rephrase – that he is just a bit busy. The use of *la5* to accompany this sentence carries out a clarification function and helps dismiss the negative connotations in the previous speaker's contribution.

Example 134

林吟蔚: 「你 就 是 赢 一些 书呆子 而已,
lin2yin2wei4 ni3 jiu4 shi4 ying2 yi4xie1 shu1dai1zi5 er2yi3
'Lin Yinwei' 'you' 'just' 'be' 'win' 'some' 'bookworm' 'only'
'Female Guest: You only defeated some bookworms.

不 要 太 自满。」就是… 他 就是 希望
bu2 yao4 tai4 zi4man3 jiu4shi4 ta1 jiu4shi4 xi1wang4
'not' 'want' 'too' 'self-full' 'just-is' 'he' 'just-is' 'hope'
Do not be too conceited. That is . . . he just wished for

我们 可以 更 好 啦。
wo3men5 ke3yi3 geng4 hao3 la5
'we' 'may' 'even more' 'good' SFP
us to do even better.'   (kxll 20130820)

Prior to the talk presented in Example 134, Miss Lin has been talking about how stern her father was in bringing her up. For example, whenever she won a competition in a performance art, he would say that it was nothing as she only defeated a bunch of weak opponents. The girl realizes that she is making her father look bad in the show, so she adds a *la5*-marked comment at the end of the story to clarify the situation – 'He only wished for us to do better'. This sentence seems to justify her father's action somewhat and diminishes some of the bad connotations. This is one example of *la5* marking a positive contribution in order to reverse a bad situation.

Example 135

徐熙娣: 可是 这 个 工作 最近 也 刚 结束?
xu2xi1di4 ke3shi4 zhe4 ge5 gong1zuo4 zui4jin4 ye3 gang1 jie2shu4
'Dee Hsu' 'but' 'this' Cla 'job' 'recently' 'also' 'just' 'finish'
'Hostess: But this job was also finished recently, right?'

余祥铨: 其实 也 不 是 刚 结束 啦。
yu2xiang2quan2 qi2shi2 ye3 bu2 shi4 gang1 jie2shu4 la5
'Yu Xiangquan' 'in fact' 'also' 'not' 'be' 'just' 'end' SFP
'Male Guest: As a matter of fact, it is not really a job that just finished.'
                                                         (kxll 20130820)

In Example 135, the hostess of the show asks the male guest about his recently ended job as reported on entertainment news. The young man answers with a *la5*-marked correction, maintaining that it is not an ended job. He then goes on to explain the complicated situation about the company he last served in.

Example 136

朱淑娟：	后来	才	知道	那边	是	乱葬岗	**啦**。
zhu1shu2juan1	hou4lai2	cai2	zhi1dao4	na4bian1	shi4	luan4zang4gang1	la5
'Zhu Shujuan'	'later'	'just'	'know'	'that-side'	'be'	'random-bury-mound'	SFP

'Female Guest: Later we learned that it was an unsupervised burial ground.'

(aywdm 20130812)

The speaker in Example 136 has been recounting a ghost story she personally encountered years ago. She and her girlfriend rented a cheap room from an older lady where they saw a number of apparitions. After they ran away at midnight never to return, they learned from a neighbor that the house was actually located in the vicinity of a cemetery. The final words she gives in Example 136 represent an awakening of some sort, a correction of the previous misconception that it was just an ordinary residential neighborhood.

Marker of digression

Due to its core usage for dismissing a claim or proposal, *la5* is also used in the cognitive domain to mark a digression in thought in the process of reasoning or narration. In other words, *la5* is sometimes used to mark a short side sequence within a person's longer turn.

Example 137

朱淑娟：	我	起来	的	时候	就	好像	有	被	一	种…
zhu1shu2juan1	wo3	qi3lai2	de5	shi2hou4	jiu4	hao3xiang4	you3	bei4	yi4	zhong3
'Zhu Shujuan'	'I'	'rise'	AD	'moment'	'just'	'as if'	'have'	PB	'one'	Cla

'Female Guest: When I got up, I feel a kind of thing . . .

应该	是	布料	的——我	觉得	应该	是	布料	**啦**，	布料
ying1gai1	shi4	bu4liao4	de5	wo3	jue2de5	ying1gai1	shi4	bu4liao4 la5	bu4liao4
'should'	'be'	'fabric'	AD	'I'	'feel'	'should'	'be'	'fabric' SFP	'fabric'

Some kind of fabric – it feels like fabric to me.

的	东西，	就	是	一直	这样	刷，	刷	过	我的	脸。
de5	dong1xi1	jiu4	shi4	yi4zhi2	zhe4yang4	shua1	shua1	guo4	wo3de5	lian3
AD	'thing'	'just'	'be'	'keep on'	'like this'	'brush'	'brush'	'over'	'my'	'face'

Some kind of fabric thing, kept on brushing like that, brushing over my face.'

(aywdm 20130812)

The female guest in Example 137 was telling a ghost story she had personally experienced. Note how the *la5*-marked sentence acts like a footnote in this narrative. The footnote explains her assessment of the material brushing across her face as a result of intellectual thinking. This is a different process from the story-telling process itself, and the *la5* usefully sets the sentence apart from the narrative. Also notice how an unfinished phrase starting with 布料的 'made of fabric' is cut off by the 'footnote' and resumes after the inserted remark, repeating the three beginning morphemes 布料的. (A phrase which is cut off in the middle and later resumed, will resume from the beginning rather than from the point where it was cut off; see Fromkin and Bernstein-Ratner 1998.) This further supports the view that the *la5*-marked portion is an inserted sequence generated from another cognitive process.

Example 138

梁赫群:　　　　他　本来　　　要　　来　　送　　我　　去,
liang2he4qun2 ta1 ben3lai2　yao4　lai2　song4 wo3 qu4
'Liang Hequn' 'he' 'originally' 'want' 'come' 'send' 'me' 'go'
'Male Guest: He originally wanted to take me (to the train station).

可是　　因为　　他　说　　他　在　拍戏,　　　所以　　有
ke3shi4 yin1wei4 ta1 shuo1 ta1 zai4 pai1xi4　　suo3yi3 you3
'but'　'because' 'he' 'say'　'he' AM 'shoot-film' 'so'　'have'
But because he said he was doing a film, then there was

一　　个　演员　　　迟到—　他　给　　我　　的　理由　　**啦**—
yi2　ge5 yan3yuan2 chi2dao4 ta1 gei3　wo3 de5 li3you2 la5
'one' Cla 'actor'　　'late'　　'he' 'give' 'me' AD 'reason' SFP
an actor being late for work. This is the reason he gave me anyway –

所以　　他　没　有　　办法　　赶　　过去　　　这样子。
suo3yi3 ta1 mei2 you3　ban4fa3 gan3　guo4qu4 zhe4yang4zi5
'so'　　'he' 'not' 'have' 'means' 'rush' 'over'　　'like this'
so he could not make it (to the station).'

(jwsdj 20130906)

In Example 138, the speaker is explaining why his father did not see him off at the train station years ago when he was joining the army. As he is recounting the incident, he stops in the middle of the story and inserts a side sequence – 'It was the reason he gave me anyway'. The footnote status of this phrase is marked by *la5* as it shows the speaker stepping away from the historical account and offering an evaluative comment from the current standpoint. Note again that 所以 'therefore', the word which introduces the structure before the side sequence, is repeated straight after the insertion, signifying the speaker picking up a previous point after an interruption.

Marker of concession

Since *la5* normally functions in a domain which involves some kind of adverse condition, it is also used to mark a concession, to express something as a final resort or a compromised stance. In doing so, it seems to embody the attitude of a person able to see both the negative and the positive sides of the issue in question, especially the ability to find certain merits inherent in adverse conditions.

Example 139

张小燕： 其实 这 个 心路历程， 其实 是 很 辛苦。
zhang1xiao3yan4 qi2shi2 zhe4 ge5 xin1lu4li4cheng2 qi2shi2 shi4 hen3 xin1ku3
'Chang Hsiao Yen' 'in fact' 'this' Cla 'heart-road-process' 'in fact' 'be' 'very' 'hard'
'Hostess: In fact, this spiritual path, it is in fact very painstaking.'

黄韵玲： 很 辛苦， 但 就 必须 要 坚持 **啦**。
huang2yun4ling2 hen3 xin1ku3 dan4 jiu4 bi4xu1 yao4 jian1chi2 la5
'Huang Yunling' 'very' 'laborious' 'but' 'just' 'must' 'want' 'insist' SFP
'Female Guest: It does take a lot of effort, but you just need to be persistent.'

(SSxyzy 20130910)

In Example 139, the hostess of the show is referring to a male celebrity's struggle in making his way to the current status of an established singer. The female guest, Huang, responds by saying that it is an arduous journey, but one must persist in order to succeed. The portion of her speech marked by *la5* is one that expresses a compromising attitude – that you have to endure the hardship if you want to be successful.

Example 140

吴淡如： 你 爸爸 说 得 对 **啦**，
wu2dan4ru2 ni3 ba4ba5 shuo1 de5 dui4 la5
'Wu Danru' 'you' 'father' 'say' Com 'correct' SFP
'Hostess: Your father was right after all.

你 们 家 应该 也 没 有 脱 的 条件。
ni3 men5 jia1 ying1gai1 ye3 mei2 you3 tuo1 de5 tiao2jian4
'you' PM 'home' 'should' 'also' 'not' 'have' 'strip' AD 'condition'
(Women in) your house do not have the body to take off their clothes.'

(jwsdj 20130906)

What happened before the speech in Example 140 was a fruitless discussion on whether the girl or her mother should take off their clothes in front of the camera. The hostess of the chat show comes to the conclusion that the girl's father was right in saying that neither of them is equipped to do so. The *la5* marks a good point (i.e. the father was right) as a compromise out of a pointless discussion.

Example 141

谢震武:		不过	我	说	实话	**啦**。	你	真的
xie4zhen4wu3		bu2guo4	wo3	shuo1	shi2hua4	la5	ni3	zhen1de5
'Xie Zhenwu'		'however'	'I'	'say'	'true-words'	SFP	'you'	'really'

'Host: But I will be honest with you. Even if you really

要	借，	你	爸	也	没	有	钱	借	你。
yao4	jie4	ni3	ba4	ye3	mei2	you3	qian2	jie4	ni3
'want'	'borrow'	'you'	'father'	'also'	'not'	'have'	'money'	'lend'	'you'

want to borrow, your father will not have the money to lend you.'

(jwsdj 20130906)

Prior to the occurrence of the speech in Example 141, the show staged a prank phone call. A young singer was asked to call his celebrity father to borrow a large amount of money. The father did not agree to lend the money readily and the call ended without a solid conclusion. Afterwards, the host of the show comments that even if the son really wanted to borrow money from his father, the father would not have the money anyway (based on the host's understanding of the celebrity). The remark 'I will be honest with you' is tagged with *la5* to indicate a compromising attitude, meaning that it was not so bad that the father did not agree to lend money, as he did not have the money anyway.

Marker of desirable or overdue action

When *la5* appears together with an imperative sentence, it often marks an action as highly desirable for the speaker and as probably long overdue. The speaker is therefore showing some impatience when giving the command, suggestion, or request. Two examples retrieved from the web are shown in Example 142 to illustrate this function.

Example 142

a 讨厌、   快点   走开   **啦**！
   tao3yan4   kuai4dian3 zou3kai1   la5
   'disgusting' 'hurry'   'walk away' SFP
   '(You are) disgusting. Go away now!'

b 你   嘴巴   很   臭，   快   去   刷牙   **啦**！
   ni3 zui3ba1 hen3 chou4 kuai4 qu4 shua1ya2   la5
   'you' 'mouth' 'very' 'smelly' 'quick' 'go' 'brush-tooth' SFP
   'Your mouth stinks. Go brush your teeth quickly!'

The speaker in Example 142a tells someone to move away from them speedily. The command is still effective without the *la5* but the presence of *la5* gives a strong sense of impatience, signifying the speaker's desire for the action to happen. Likewise, the speaker in Example 142b orders someone to brush their teeth right away. The *la5* aggravates the undesirable condition and increases the urgency of the desirable action.

Example 143

a 黄西田：   没关系，   不   要   急   **啦**。
   huang2xi1tian2 mei2guan1xi5 bu2 yao4 ji2   la5
   'Huang Xitian'   'no-concern' 'not' 'want' 'hasty' SFP
   'No worries. Take your time.'

                                                      (jwsdj 20130906)

b 侯佩岑：   他   刚   有   劝   你   「赶快   去
   hou2pei4cen2 ta1 gang1 you3 quan4 ni3 gan3kuai4 qu4
   'Patty Hou'   'he' 'just' 'have' 'advise' 'you' 'hurry'   'go'

   当   和尚   **啦**！」
   dang1 he2shang4 la5
   'be' 'monk'   SFP

   'Hostess: He advised you just now to hurry and become a monk!'
                                                      (WOWhmj 20130905)

Example 143 shows *la5* used in TV chat shows to tag commands, giving them a sense of urgency and desirability. The speaker in Example 143a tells his daughter to slow down in reporting a difficult situation over the phone. The *la5* commits the speaker to the message content, urging the listener to do as they are told. The *la5*-tagged command in Example 143b is reported speech, where the listener is advised by the original speaker to become a monk due to his well-endowed Buddhist nature. Some humorous effect is achieved by the impatient attitude created by *la5* in the reported speech on top of the urgency it introduces.

Marker of impatience

Sometimes a speaker uses *la5* simply to express an impatient attitude and nothing more. The usage is impolite and often derogatory. Two examples retrieved from the web are shown below.

Example 144

a 你　放屁　　**啦**！
　 ni3　fang4pi4　la5
　 'you'　'fart'　　SFP
　 'Bullshit!'

b 你　去　死　**啦**！
　 ni3　qu4　si3　la5
　 'you'　'go'　'die'　SFP
　 'Go to hell!'

As can be seen from the English translations of the two sentences in Example 144, the addition of *la5* to certain expressions creates a swearing effect. These expressions are mostly used in confrontational settings.

Sometimes the impatience is 'faked' and the *la5*-marked expression seems to exude some feminine charm instead of sounding impolite. The effect is usually applicable only to relatively close friends, couples or family members.

Example 145

a 我　以后　　不　理　你　了　**啦**！
　 wo3　yi3hou4　bu4　li3　ni3　le5　la5
　 'I'　'hereafter'　'not'　'heed'　'you'　SFP　SFP
　 'I will take no notice of you from now on!'

b 你　看　得　人家　　　　都　不好意思　　　　了　**啦**！
　 ni3　kan4　de5　ren2jia1　　dou1　bu4hao3yi4si5　　le5　la5
　 'you'　'look'　Com　'other person'　'all'　'not-good-meaning'　SFP　SFP
　 'You stare so hard, people are getting embarrassed!'

Example 145a is probably said by a female (or a male acting in a feminine way) when upset by someone close in a mild way. In Example 145b, the 人家 'other person(s)' can refer to the speaker themself or some other person(s) the addressee of the sentence happens to be staring at. If 人家 refers to the speaker, the speaker is normally a woman and the *la5* will exude some feminine charm rather than real impatience.

La5 as a variant of *le5*

There is a homograph of 啦 which is phonologically similar and orthographically identical to the *la5* discussed in the above strands, but is entirely different in 'meaning' and function. In most cases, this particle is a variant of 了 used as a sentence-final particle (not as an aspect marker as seen in Chapter 3 – see 5.11 below). Some examples of this kind of *la5* retrieved from the web are shown below.

Example 146

a 新娘　　　你　太　美　　啦！
  xin1niang2　ni3　tai4　mei3　la5
  'new-mother' 'you' 'too' 'pretty' SFP
  'Bride, you are so pretty!'

b 谁　惹　　　你　生气　　啦？
  shei2　re3　　ni3　sheng1qi4　la5
  'who' 'provoke' 'you' 'angry'　SFP
  'Who made you angry?'

Both instances of 啦 in Example 146 are phonological variants of 了, or are end products of the sandhi process of *le5* + *a5*. Hence, they do not have the usual characteristics of *la5*; that is, they do not function to dismiss, to clarify, to step aside from the main storyline, or simply to show impatience. They are mostly used as 了 serving the function of a sentence-final particle instead. For example, the *la5* in Example 146a comes with a positive evaluation. The *la5* in 146b marks a question – it is probably a combination of *le5* and *a5* (i.e. 啦 = 了 + 啊) in this case, and the question is formed using *a5*'s question marking capacity.

A *la5*-marked sentence, if read orthographically instead of being heard phonologically, can be ambiguous if it appears in a slot where both the 'genuine' 啦 and the 了 disguised as 啦 can fit in. One such example is shown in Example 147.

Example 147

a 我们　　结婚　**啦**！
   wo3men5 jie2hun1 la5
   'we'   'marry' SFP
   'Let's get married, please!'

b 我们　　结婚　**啦**！
   wo3men5 jie2hun1 la5
   'we'   'marry' SFP
   'We have got married!'

If pronounced, the pitch level of the 啦 in Example 147b will be somewhat higher than that in Example 147a and with a flatter pitch contour. The 啦 in Example 147a, pronounced with a stronger initial accent and a falling pitch, is the 'genuine' *la5* which in this instance marks a highly desirable action to the speaker, like Example 142. The 啦 in 147b, on the other hand, is meant to be a *le5* surfacing as *la5* (note the similarity in pronunciation), which essentially marks a completed action in this case as well as a change of marital state for the couple from single to married. While Example 147a could have been said by a woman desperate to get married to her boyfriend, 147b is an announcement made by a couple who have just got married.

5.12 *LE5*

We discussed 了 *le5* as the marker of completion in Chapter 3; that is, it comes after a verb and marks the action as having completed in the real world at the time of speaking or up to a point in a hypothesized situation. Two short sentences including *le5* as an aspect marker are shown below.

Example 148

a 他 交 了 坏　朋友。
   ta1 jiao1 le5 huai4 peng2you3
   'he' 'join' AM 'bad' 'friend'
   'He has made bad friends.'

b 全球　　　电子　　　垃圾　　毁　　了 中国　　　　环境。
   quan2qiu2 dian4zi5 le4se4 hui3 le5 zhong1guo2 huan2jing4
   'globe'   'electronic' 'garbage' 'destroy' AM 'China'   'environment'
   'Electronic garbage from all over the world has destroyed the
   environment of China.'

Both examples in Example 148 have 了 in the middle of the sentence, directly after the verb, which clearly shows its status of being an aspect marker. In this case, they both show the action represented by the verb ('make friends' or 'destroy') as a completed action at the time of speaking. However, the *le5* as aspect marker need not always appear somewhere within the sentence. It can also appear at the end of the sentence, if that is where the verb happens to be. Two examples of *le5* as aspect marker appearing at the end of a sentence follow.

Example 149

a   肇事　　　　　司机　　逃走　　　　了。
    zhao4shi4　　　si1ji1　　tao2zou3　le5
    'begin-matter' 'driver' 'escape'　AM
    'The driver who caused the accident fled.'

b   南京　　　市长　　　　　被　　骂　　　惨　　　　　了。
    nan2jing1 shi4zhang3 bei4　ma4　　can3　　le5
    'Nanjing' 'mayor'　　PB　'reprove' 'miserable' AM
    'The mayor of Nanjing was heavily criticized.'

Both sentences in Example 149 each have a verb ('escape' and 'reprove' respectively) followed by 了 as the aspect marker showing the action to have been completed at the time of speaking. Both instances of *le5* appear at the end of their respective host sentences. In some cases it is not always clear whether the *le5* at the end of a sentence is an aspect marker or a sentence-final particle. An aspect marker *le5* simply marks the verb as representing an action that has already happened at the time of speaking; an SFP *le5* shows the speaker's overall cognitive placing and the pragmatic connotation of the entire expression. Such a *le5* may also serve both functions at the same time. Conversely, some sentences may come with both an aspect marker *le5* and a sentence-final *le5*. Two examples are shown below.

Example 150

a   黎启灏：　已经　　放　　了　酱油　　　　了。
    li2qi3hao4 yi3jing1 fang4 le5　jiang4you2 le5
    'Li Qihao' 'already' 'set'　AM　'soy sauce' SFP
    'Male Guest: (I) have already put in soy sauce.'　　　　　　(wmyhb 20130911)

b   汪姗姗：　　　　去　夜店　　　了　当然　　　要　　喝酒　　　　了。
    wang1shan1shan1 qu4 ye4dian4　le5　dang1ran2 yao4　he1jiu3　　le5
    'Wang Shanshan' 'go' 'night-shop' AM 'certainly' 'want' 'drink-wine' SFP
    'Female Guest: Since you have come to a night club, you should drink wine.'
    　　　　　　　　　　　　　　　　　　　　　　　　　　　　　　　　　(fcwr 20130824)

The first *le5* in Example 150a advises the listener that the action of 'adding the soy sauce' was completed sometime in the past. The second *le5* adds the implications of this action to the present – that the dish is now ready to be served, i.e. it represents the so-called 'currently relevant state' of Li and Thompson (1981). Likewise, Example 150b shows aspect marker *le5* being used in a hypothetical condition – 'going to the night club'. The speaker argues that once one enters a night club, one certainly wants to drink alcoholic beverages. The argument portion is tagged with a sentence-final *le5* to show the speaker's commitment to the proposal.

Thus, when *le5* appears within a sentence, it is definitely an aspect marker marking the completion of an action. When *le5* appears at the end of a sentence, it could be an aspect marker or a sentence-final particle or it may be serving both functions. A sentence can come with both the AM *le5* and the SFP *le5*.

When serving the function of SFP, *le5* can add different meanings or implications to the sentence it attaches to. The core function of *le5* as an SFP, it seems, is for the speaker to express their evaluation of, and attitude toward, the current situation as a result of recent happenings in the surroundings.

Marker of change of state

The SFP 了 is often used by the speaker to indicate a change of state that they become aware of during the course of the conversation. The change could be related to the environment (天黑了 'It is dark'), a personal circumstance (我有钱了 'I am rich!'), an object (电脑坏了 'The computer is broken'), an issue (问题解决了 'The problem is solved') or something else. More examples are shown below.

Example 151

孟非:	会	夸	人	了。	他	开始	有救	了。
meng4fei1	hui4	kua1	ren2	le5	ta1	kai1shi3	you3jiu4	le5
'Meng Fei'	'can'	'praise'	'person'	SFP	'he'	'start'	'have-save'	SFP

'Host: He can praise people now. He starts to become curable!'

(fcwr 20130901)

A sequence of two sentences, both tagged with 了, appears in Example 151. These are spoken by the host of the dating show after he heard the male suitor praise a female guest. The man has been extraordinarily shy and not good at pursuing girls. However, the host has tried to teach him what to do here and there in the show. When he saw the boy praising the girl, Mr Meng recognized this as a sign of improvement, and announces that the boy has changed – he is curable now as he has transformed from a timid boy to a sociable person.

Such an expression of change of state would not have been possible without the presence of *le5*. Moreover, the sense of change is doubly increased with two expressions both tagged by *le5* carrying out the same function.

Example 152

邱启明： 你 看， 你 一 说，
qiu1qi3ming2 ni3 kan4 ni3 yi4 shuo1
'Qiu Qiming' 'you' 'look' 'you' 'one' 'say'
'Host: You see, after you said that,

他 不 知道 怎么 说话 了。
ta1 bu4 zhi1dao4 zen3mo5 shuo1hua4 le5
'he' 'not' 'know' 'how' 'speak' SFP
he no longer knows how to respond.'

(wmyhb 20130528)

In Example 152, a question and answer session has just rendered a male suitor speechless as he does not know how to respond to a girl's questions. The host of the show takes over the floor by commenting on the man's behavioral change (i.e. from being a normal person to someone who does not know how to speak) in order to fill in the silence. The sentence 他不知道怎么说话 'He does not know how to speak', without the accompanying *le5*, could have meant the person cannot normally talk. With the addition of *le5*, the sentence in Example 152 correctly means that the speechlessness is a new state the young man has recently lapsed into.

Example 153

符星玮： 那 你 是 不 是 从 以前 的
fu2xing1wei3 na4 ni3 shi4 bu2 shi4 cong2 yi3qian2 de5
'Fu Xingwei' 'then' 'you' 'be' 'not' 'be' 'from' 'before' AD
'Female Guest: Then have you changed from the previous state of

不 敢 爱， 到 现在 的 不 会 爱 了？
bu4 gan3 ai4 dao4 xian4zai4 de5 bu2 hui4 ai4 le5
'not' 'dare' 'love' 'to' 'now' AD 'not' 'able' 'love' SFP
not daring to love to the current state of not knowing how to love?'

(wmyhb 20130911)

The girl in Example 153 is asking a young man whether his previously failed relationship has made him permanently incapable of pursuing love. The sentence-final 了 in Example 153 is not an aspect marker since it does not refer to the timing or state of completion of the verb 'love' in any way. Instead, the *le5* refers to the entire clause of 'not knowing how to love' and marks it as a new state transformed from a previous state (i.e. from 'not daring to love' to 'not knowing how to love').

Reconceptualization

The function of 了 to mark a change of state enables it to work in the cognitive domain. That is, *le5* is often used to show the epistemic change one's mind goes through before the utterance is made.

Example 154

a 谢震武： 我 知道 他 为什么 不 读
xie4zhen4wu3 wo3 zhi1dao4 ta1 wei4shen2mo5 bu4 du2
'Xie Zhenwu' 'I' 'know' 'he' 'why' 'not' 'read'
'Host: I know now why he chose not to (let his children) go to

美国 学校 了。
mei3guo2 xue2xiao4 le5
'America' 'school' SFP
the American School.' (jwsdj 20130910)

b 邱启明： 蔡旸 知道 甚么 叫 仰视 了 吧？
qiu1qi3ming2 cai4yang2 zhi1dao4 shen2mo5 jiao4 yang3shi4 le5 ba5
'Qiu Qiming' 'Cai Yang' 'know' 'what' 'call' 'upward-look' SFP SFP
'Host: Cai Yang, you should know by now what it means to look up to
someone, right?' (wmyhb 20130911)

Example 154 shows how 了 helps to express a piece of recently acquired knowledge as the result of a process of reconceptualization. In Example 154a, the host of the chat show gradually realized, during the course of the conversation, why a celebrity did not send his children to the Taipei American School. The *le5* helps convey this epistemic change, i.e. from being oblivious to the reason to finally realizing it. If there was no *le5* in Example 154a, then the sentence 我知道他为甚么不读美国学校 'I know why he does not go to the American School' would simply mean the speaker has this knowledge all along. In Example 154b, on the other hand, the speaker is modelling the epistemic transition of another person and articulating the result of his observation. Mr Qiu, the host of the dating show, was introducing a new male suitor who was extremely tall. Knowing Cai Yang to be a petite girl, Qiu teases her by saying 'You know now what it is like to look at someone facing upward, don't you?' The *le5* is essential in adding the extra dimension of assumed conceptual change to the sentence.

The role of another SFP, 吧, in Example 154b is to make the statement into a rhetorical question. We can modify the sentence in three different ways, as shown in Example 155 with Example 154b resurfacing as Example 155a.

Example 155

a 蔡旸　　　知道　　　甚么　　　叫　　仰视　　　　　了　吧?
   cai4yang2 zhi1dao4 shen2mo5 jiao4 yang3shi4　　le5　ba5
   'Cai Yang' 'know'　'what'　　'call' 'upward-look' SFP SFP
   'Cai Yang, you should know what it means to look up to someone now, right?'

b 蔡旸　　　知道　　　甚么　　　叫　　仰视。
   cai4yang2 zhi1dao4 shen2mo5 jiao4 yang3shi4
   'Cai Yang' 'know'　'what'　　'call' 'upward-look'
   'Cai Yang knows what it means to look up to someone.'

c 蔡旸　　　知道　　　甚么　　　叫　　仰视　　　　吧?
   cai4yang2 zhi1dao4 shen2mo5 jiao4 yang3shi4　　ba5
   'Cai Yang' 'know'　'what'　　'call' 'upward-look' SFP
   'Cai Yang, you know what it means to look up to someone, don't you?'

d 蔡旸　　　知道　　　甚么　　　叫　　仰视　　　　　了。
   cai4yang2 zhi1dao4 shen2mo5 jiao4 yang3shi4　　le5
   'Cai Yang' 'know'　'what'　　'call' 'upward-look' SFP
   'Cai Yang knows what it means to look up to someone now.'

First, both 了 and 吧 have been stripped off sentence Example 155b, which simply means 'X knows what Y means' (where X = Cai Yang; Y = 'look up at something'). Example 155c keeps *ba5* but is short of *le5*; therefore it does not imply a conceptual change but is still a question ('X knows what Y means, doesn't she?'). Example 155d loses *ba5* but keeps *le5*, which gives it an entirely different meaning from 155b – 'X now knows Y', i.e. 'X did not know Y before'. Finally, for the sake of comparison, the original sentence reproduced as Example 155a means 'X now knows what Y means, doesn't she?' as compared to other sentences in this paragraph.

The 了吧 combination in Example 155a illustrates the phenomenon of two 'sentence-final' particles making an appearance together, self-contradicting the definition of SFP. In fact, the 'dual SFP' situation happens only when the first SFP is *le5*. It is not possible to say, for example, 啊吧, 啦吗 and so on (but 了呢, 了吗 etc. are perfectly fine). This seems to set *le5* apart as a different and unique category of functional item from all the other 'genuine' SFPs.

Example 156

庚卓：	启明	哥		你	比	电视
geng1zhuo2	qi3ming2	ge1		ni3	bi3	dian4shi4
'Geng Zhuo'	'Qiming'	'older brother'		'you'	'compare'	'television'

上	帅	多	了。
shang4	shuai4	duo1	le5
'up'	'handsome'	'much'	SFP

'Male Guest: Qiming old brother, you are much more handsome than you look on TV.'

(wmyhb 20130911)

In Example 156, the young man apparently has been watching the TV programme hosted by Mr Qiu. He is now on the show and sees the host in person. He compares the real Mr Qiu with the one in his imagination and says that Qiu is more handsome in person. The 了 signifies the transition from being 'less handsome' in memory to 'more handsome' in person to the speaker's mind, which is revealed as a compliment to the TV host. Again, the *le5* in this case is not associated with any action and is clearly an SFP providing additional information in the cognitive and pragmatic domain.

Example 157

邱启明：	这	看	来	就	是
qiu1qi3ming2	zhe4	kan4	lai2	jiu4	shi4
'Qiu Qiming'	'this'	'look'	Com	'just'	'be'

'Host: It now looks like this is

孔雀	的	羽毛	了，	是	吧？
kong3que4	de5	yu3mao2	le5	shi4	ba5
'peacock'	PD	'feather'	SFP	'be'	SFP

the feather of a peacock, isn't it?'

(wmyhb 20130911)

Prior to the host's speech in Example 157, there has been confusion and a discussion about an object sticking out from the pocket of the male suitor's shirt. Seen from a distance, it looked like a stalk of grass to most of the people in the show. However, a video recording was then played which introduced the man as the owner of a peacock farm. After the video, people started to reconsider the grass-like object in the man's pocket. The host of the show finally speaks out for everyone: 'Now we know this is a peacock feather, isn't it?' (indeed it is). If there had been no *le5* in this sentence, it would simply mean 'It looks like this is a peacock feather, doesn't it?' and the original meaning regarding the knowledge reconstruction process would have been lost.

Closing statement

There is a pragmatic function for 了 in conversation, which is to serve as a marker of closing or a pre-closing signal for the current topic. This is not surprising as *le5* is often used to express the speaker's awareness of a change of state or a reconceptualization process. The function of *le5* to help present a closing statement is a natural extension of these capacities.

Example 158

a Mr Right: 那　　我　无能为力　　　　了。
mister right　na4　wo3　wu2neng2wei2li4　　le5
'Mr Right'　'then'　'I'　'no-ability-do-force'　SFP
'Co-host: Then I can no longer do anything.'

(wmyhb 20130911)

b 孟非:　　你　　要　　做　　最后　　的　决定　　了。
meng4fei1　ni3　yao4　zuo4　zui4hou4　de5　jue2ding4　le5
'Meng Fei'　'you'　'want'　'make'　'final'　　AD　'decision'　SFP
'Host: Now you must make the final decision.'

(fcwr 20130901)

Prior to the resident robot's speech in Example 158a, it has tried to introduce several female guests to the male suitor, all of whom he rejected. After these failed attempts, the 'human-disguised' robot concludes the session by saying 'I can no longer help'. If *le5* were not present, the sentence would simply mean 'I cannot help' with no reference to previous endeavors. The existence of *le5* is essential for the sentence to serve as a concluding remark, summing up the situation and showing the speaker's lack of interest in pursuing the topic any further. Example 158b is a routine command given by the host of the dating show when one or more female guests are willing to go away with the male suitor. The command 'You must make a final decision now' signifies that the end point of a process has been reached and a conclusion must be drawn. Similar to Example 158a, if there were no *le5* in Example 158b, the sentence would mean 'You must make the final decision' but it would not mean 'You must make a decision NOW'. Nor would it come with the historical implication – that the decision-making is the result of a relatively long process of interaction and selection.

Example 159

沈玉琳：	最后	这	个	最	精彩，
shen3yu4lin2	zui4hou4	zhe4	ge5	zui4	jing1cai3
'Shen Yulin'	'final'	'this'	Cla	'the most'	'wonderful'

'Male Guest: The last presentation is the most brilliant.

前面	剪	掉，	就	留	这	个	就	好	了！
qian2mian4	jian3	diao4	jiu4	liu2	zhe4	ge5	jiu4	hao3	le5
'front'	'cut'	Com	'just'	'keep'	'this'	Cla	'then'	'good'	SFP

Cut away the previous ones and just keep this one. It will be great!'

(ggbbm 20130822)

The celebrity guest in Example 159 is referring to the performance of an assistant at a warm-up activity to the chat show. He dismisses the first few acts as uninteresting and advises the program to keep only the last act, which he thinks is great. The *le5* in the third sentence is essential in conveying the sense of finality and the speaker's inclination to wrap up the issue.

Example 160

付立强：	为了	我们的	幸福，
fu4li4qiang2	wei4le5	wo3men5de5	xing4fu2
'Fu Liqiang'	'for'	'our'	'happiness'

'Male Guest: For our own happiness,

我们	从此	不	要	再	联系	了。
wo3men5	cong2ci3	bu2	yao4	zai4	lian2xi4	le5
'we'	'from now on'	'not'	'want'	'again'	'liaise'	SFP

we should stop communicating with each other from now on.'

(wmyhb 20130820)

Example 160 is an ultimatum given by someone to their lover in a video recording. The *le5* is important in generating a sense of closure to the proposal. Although the sentence would sound roughly the same without *le5* due to the presence of other functional elements (i.e. 'from now on' and 'no more'), it still relies largely on *le5* to convey the speaker's attitude and determination in wanting to put an end to the relationship.

Example 161

揭国其： 我 希望 的 女生 是 能够
jie1guo2qi2 wo3 xi1wang4 de5 nv3sheng1 shi4 neng2gou4
'Jie Guoji' 'I' 'wish' AD 'girl' 'be' 'capable of'
'Male Guest: The girl I wish for is someone who is

朴实 一点， 善良 一点， 孝顺 一点，
pu2shi2 yi4dian3 shan4liang2 yi4dian3 xiao4shun4 yi4dian3
'plain' 'one-drop' 'kind-hearted' 'one-drop' 'filial piety' 'one-drop'
simple, kind, and good to parents.

差不多 就 是 这些 了。
cha4bu4duo1 jiu4 shi4 zhe4xie1 le5
'roughly' 'just' 'be' 'these' SFP
That is about all.'

(wmyhb 20130911)

The male suitor in Example 161 is sharing a list of characteristics his future girlfriends should have with the 30 female guests on the show. He gives three points and then concludes the list with a *le5*-marked expression. Although the *le5* is not essential for this expression to serve as a concluding statement due to the presence of 'roughly' and 'just is', it is still up to *le5* to create the sense of finality and convey the speaker's intention to end the list.

Evaluation

Apart from the cognitive function of expressing a change of state and the pragmatic function of giving a sense of finality to speech, 了 is also used to accompany an evaluation. That is, *le5* can help tag an expression with the value the speaker wishes to set down for a person, object or situation after a period of observation.

Example 162

a 王紫藤： 你 说话 的 速度 实在 是 太 慢 了！
 wang2zi3teng2 ni3 shuo1hua4 de5 su4du4 shi2zai4 shi4 tai4 man4 le5
 'Wang Ziteng' 'you' 'speak' AD 'speed' 'actually' 'be' 'too' 'slow' SFP
 'Female Guest: The speed of your speech is much too slow!'

(wmyhb 20130528)

b 邱启明： 你 俩 也 太 会 互相 恭维 了 吧！
 qiu1qi3ming2 ni3 lia3 ye3 tai4 hui4 hu4xiang1 gong1wei2 le5 ba5
 'Qiu Qiming' 'you' 'both' 'also' 'too' 'able' 'mutual' 'compliment' SFP SFP
 'Host: The two of you are really good at complimenting each other, aren't you?'

(wmyhb 20130911)

Both examples in Example 162 contain a sentence marked with 了 to express the speaker's evaluation and their stance toward people or things. Both sentences also come with the [太 X 了] structure meaning 'too X (in my opinion)', where X is a descriptive phrase of some sort. The speaker in Example 162a, for example, is rejecting the male suitor on the grounds that he talks too slowly. Although the meaning of the sentence remains largely the same without *le5*, the presence of *le5* does show the speaker's firm commitment to the comment and there seems no way to reverse the judgment. Likewise, the speaker in Example 162b criticizes a male and a female guest for complimenting each other too much. The *le5* strengthens the verdict by giving a sense of finality, as if saying that the case is closed and there is no room for further discussion.

Example 163

a   孟非：   好久   没有   听   到   这么
    meng4fei1 hao3jiu3   mei2you3 ting1 dao4 zhe4mo5
    'Meng Fei' 'very-long' 'not'   'hear' Com 'such'

耿直   的   话   了。
geng3zhi2   de5 hua4   le5
'straightforward' AD 'words' SFP

'Host: I have not heard such frank comment for a long time.'

(fcwr 20130914)

b   孟非：   泥人张   挺   好   的，
    meng4fei1 ni2ren2zhang1   ting3 hao3   de5
    'Meng Fei' 'mud-person-Zhang' 'quite' 'good' AD
    'Host: Clay Figure Zhang is quite good.'

如果   再   带   点   麻花   就   更   好   了。
ru2guo3 zai4   dai4   dian3 ma2hua1   jiu4   geng4   hao3   le5
'if'   'further' 'bring' 'dot' 'hemp-flower' 'then' 'even more' 'good' SFP
'Host: It would be even better if you had brought some fried dough twists.'

(fcwr 20130824)

Prior to Example 163a, someone from the audience has just finished praising the host of the dating show, saying he looks much younger in person than on TV. Mr Meng responds with an evaluation of the guest's comment. The marking of 了 reinforces the sense that the comment is the result of a long period of observation rather than a whim. The same TV host in Example 163b is responding to a male guest who just brought a present for the show – a kind of colorful sculpture made of clay and originating from Tianjin. The same city is also famous for a snack called Ma Hua. Mr Meng apparently prefers something edible, so he says that it would be even better if the guest had brought some Ma Hua as well. This comment is marked with *le5* to enable a 'backward comparison' between the preferred Ma Hua and the previously mentioned clay sculpture. In both cases, the evaluation would seem less contextualized (i.e. short of historical reference) without the tagging of *le5*.

5.13 INDEPENDENT PARTICLES

In addition to sentence-final particles (SFPs) and constituent-final particles (CFPs), Chinese speakers also use what I call, in this book, independent particles (IPs). They most frequently happen at the beginning of an utterance and are normally phonologically separate from the ensuing sentence. In other words, they are not as integrated into the sentence as an SFP is. Although IPs come in different phonological forms, their functions are fairly limited and are decidedly less versatile than SFPs. The independent particles are frequently used to express an emotional surge that the speaker experiences at the time of speaking, emotions such as wonder, shock, happiness, embarrassment, gratitude, sadness and so on. They are alternatively called 'interjections' (e.g. Li and Cheng 2008, Yip 2000) or 'exclamative particles' in Chinese linguistics literature. In this brief section, we will look at a few examples of IPs representing different emotions.

Example 164

a　蒋承辰：　　　　　　**啊**！　有　　蟑螂！
　　jiang3cheng2chen2 a5　you3　zhang1lang2
　　'Jiang Chengchen'　IP　'have'　'cockroach'
　　'Female Guest: Oh my goodness! There are cockroaches!'
　　　　　　　　　　　　　　　　　　(wmyhb 20130129)

b　周韦彤：　　　　　**哇**！　好　　man　　的　北京　　大　男孩！
　　zhou1wei3tong2　wa1　hao3　man　　de5　bei3jing1　da4　nan2hai2
　　'Zhou Weitong'　IP　'very'　'macho'　AD　'Beijing'　'big'　'boy'
　　'Female Guest: Wow! What a macho Beijing big boy you are!'
　　　　　　　　　　　　　　　　　　(zsydt 20130706)

As can be surmised from the meaning of the sentence, both independent particles in Example 164 express the speaker's surprise at the sight of an external stimulus. In Example 164a, it is the cockroaches that cause the girl to scream. In Example 164b, it is the pleasant surprise of seeing a macho man. In both cases, the independent particle helps the speaker 'let off steam', so to speak, and there seems nothing more to it. The two particles in Example 164 can in principle be exchanged as the difference is mainly phonological.

Example 165

a   陈洁：   **哎呦**！ 开心   死   了！
    chen2jie2 ai1yao1 kai1xin1   si3   le5
    'Chen Jie' IP   'open-heart' 'die' SFP
    'Female Guest: Oh my! I am so happy I could die!'

(zsydt 20130706)

b   明月：   就   是… 就   是… **哎呀**， 突然   紧张   了！
    ming2yue4 jiu4 shi4 jiu4 shi4 ai1ya5 tu2ran2   jin3zhang1 le5
    'Mingyue' 'just' 'be' 'just' 'be' IP   'suddenly' 'nervous' SFP
    'Female Guest: It's just, just … Oh no! I suddenly become nervous!'

(wmyhb 20130326)

Similar to Example 164, the three independent particles in Example 165 help the speaker let out the emotional surge at the time of speech. In Example 165a, the IP emanates a feeling of happiness which the girl apparently feels at the compliment of a male guest. In Example 165b, the girl cannot find the right words to say and feels momentarily embarrassed. She uses the IP to lead the involuntary 'explosion' of an emotional surge, explaining why she cannot talk normally (i.e. being too nervous). There may be some differences between 哎呀 and 哎呦 in terms of the nuances of emotion expressed on top of the phonological differences, but in principle these two particles are also interchangeable.

Example 166

a   谭苗：   你   也   挺   漂亮   的。
    tan2miao2 ni3 ye3 ting3 piao4liang4 de5
    'Tan Miao' 'you' 'also' 'rather' 'beautiful' ED
    'Male Guest: You are also quite beautiful.'

b   刘琳：   **哎呀**！ 谢谢！
    liu2lin2 ai1ya5 xie4xie5
    'Liu Lin' IP   'thanks'
    'Female Guest: Wow, thank you!'

(wmyhb 20130129)

Example 166 shows how a female guest uses *ai1ya5* to start her response to a male suitor's compliment. The particle acts like a precursor that both reflects the emotional impact the man's compliment has on the girl and announces the coming of a fuller response.

Example 167

于淼：　　我　　漂亮　　　还是　　丫蛋　　漂亮　　　呢？
yu2miao3 wo3 piao4liang4 hai2shi4 ya1dan4 piao4liang4 ne5
'Yu Miao' 'I' 'pretty' 'or' 'Yadan' 'pretty' SFP
'Female Guest: Who is more beautiful, me or Yadan?'

井川：　　　当然　　您　漂亮　　　啦！
jing3chuan1 dang1ran2 nin2 piao4liang4 la5
'Jing Chuan' 'certainly' 'you' 'pretty' SFP
'Male Guest: No doubt you are more beautiful!'

于淼：　　**哎呦喂，**　我　这　都　不好意思　　了！
yu2miao3 ai1you1wei4 wo3 zhe4 dou1 bu4hao3yi4si5 le5
'Yu Miao' IP 'I' 'this' 'all' 'embarrassed' SFP
'Female Guest: Oh, my goodness me! I feel so embarrassed!'

(zsydt 20130831)

Similar to exmple Example 166, the girl in Example 167 is responding to a compliment. Probably because the compliment is inevitable, since the girl practically asks for it, and because the girl is expecting the compliment, the response is somewhat exaggerated, with a trisyllabic particle leading the turn. The 哎呦喂 does not add much to the shorter versions of 哎呀 or 哎呦 except longer duration of exclamation and perhaps more dramatic effect. An even longer unit in this series is 哎呦喂呀 *ai1you1wei4ya5* – a quadrisyllabic particle which can convey the speaker's feeling of surprise, anger, pain, or sometimes pleasure in a maximally dramatic way.

Example 168

a 王文杰　　　　朋友：　　乁？　怎么　　有　　一　　个　美女？
wang2wen2jie2 peng2you3 ei1 zen3mo5 you3 yi2 ge5 mei3nv3
'Wang Wenjia' 'friend' IP 'how' 'have' 'one' Cla 'pretty girl'
'Friend of Male Guest: Huh? – How come there is a pretty girl here?'

(aywdm 20130812)

b 沈涛：　　四　位，　你　们　还　拥有　　选择　权。
shen3tao1 si4 wei4 ni3 men5 hai2 yong3you3 xuan3ze2 quan2
'Shen Tao' 'four' Cla 'you' PM 'still' 'own' 'choose' 'rights'
'Host: The four of you still have the right to choose (female candidates)'

陈戎柚：　　　乁？　还　有　　啊？
chen2rong2you4 ei1 hai2 you3 a5
'Chen Rongyou' IP 'still' 'have' SFP
'Male Guest: Huh? We can have more?'

(zsydt 20130803)

The highlighted particle in Example 168 is represented by a symbol ㇏ taken from the Zhuyin phonetic system used in Taiwan, which is pronounced as *ei1* with a rising tone, as if asking a question. The Zhuyin symbols normally do not appear in formal writing but are occasionally used in casual writing to represent sounds or replace certain characters for fun or other effects. In this case, since there is no Chinese character corresponding to the pronunciation of *ei1*, I have taken the liberty of representing this particle with ㇏. This IP normally shows the speaker's surprise as it happens; that is, the sound is often uttered at the same time as the surprise is received. In Example 168a, for example, the speaker says ㇏? the moment he sees a pretty woman, who probably should not show up there. In Example 168b, one of the four male suitors, Mr Chen, thought they had used all the opportunities to choose female candidates. Therefore, it comes as a surprise when the host of the show declares that they can continue to choose girls in the next round. Chen utters ㇏? the moment he hears the announcement. This exclamation is then followed by a question which spells out the surprise and the doubt.

Example 169

a 孟非:　　　噢，　我　　明白　　　　了。
　　meng4fei1　ou5　wo3　ming2bai2　le5
　　'Meng Fei'　IP　'I'　'understand'　SFP
　　'Host: Oh, now I understand.'

(fcwr 20130810)

b 胡维丽:　　咱　　在　　这　　场　　　上　　　说　　的　　高端　　　　大气。
　　hu2wei2li4　zan2　zai4　zhe4　chang3　shang4　shuo1　de5　gao1duan1　da4qi4
　　'Hu Weili'　'we'　'at'　'this'　'stage'　'up'　'say'　AD　'high-end'　'big-air'
　　'Female Guest: (What I meant was) the high-end and generous disposition we discussed here.'

　　邱启明:　　　噢，　高端　　　大气。
　　qiu1qi3ming2　ou5　gao1duan1　da4qi4
　　'Qiu Qiming'　IP　'high-end'　'big-air'
　　'Host: Oh, I see, high-end and generous disposition.'

(wmyhb 20130226)

The 噢 particle is rather similar to the *oh* used by English speakers. One of its functions in Chinese discourse is to signal understanding, as both examples in Example 169 show. The character 噢 adopted here for this function is by no means universally established for this function. The corresponding Pinyin annotation used here for this particle (*ou5*) is also approximate. Like many other particles discussed in this chapter, the pronunciations for some particles as well as the written forms may vary from individual to individual and from community to community.

5.14 CONCLUSION

We have discussed a wide range of Chinese SFPs and other particles like CFPs and IPs. The large number of examples in this chapter show how versatile the Chinese SFPs are and how complicated their functions may be, despite their light-weight appearance (i.e. each only one syllable in length). The dozen or so sentence-final particles function in the Chinese discourse to help organize ideas, request information, offer suggestions, give evaluation, issue warnings, reveal emotion, seek agreement, build alliances, close conversations, and so on and so forth. Together they help achieve the most effective conversation by catering to the speaker's cognitive, emotional and interpersonal needs during the course of the conversation.

Some pragmatic functions decisively rely on the presence of the relevant SFPs, such as giving warnings (哦), showing admiration (喔) or surprise (耶), giving a reason (嘛), marking a statement as the result of a process (了) and so on. Other SFPs are only marginally required for carrying out the function associated with the utterance as a whole; for example, the 呢 used to mark a question redundantly, or the 啊 used to give more emphasis to a statement. SFPs are primarily used in spoken language but they also show up in informal writings such as text messages and postings on social networks. All in all, sentence-final particles and the like are an indispensable part of the Chinese language. They work in tandem with sentence-based grammar to make the Chinese language more sensitive and productive.

CHAPTER 6

Chinese neologisms on the web

6.1 INTRODUCTION

In this chapter, we consider Chinese neologisms on the web. In particular, we examine a number of new words currently active on Sina Weibo – the most popular social networking tool among Chinese netizens today, which boasts over 500 million registered accounts at the end of 2012. We divide these words into categories and investigate their meanings and usages. By doing so, we hope to get a glimpse of what the Chinese language looks like in one of the busiest sections of contemporary society today. We also hope to learn about some of the current concerns of the Chinese people and society from the new words sampled and the contexts of their usages.

6.2 CATEGORIES OF NEW WORDS

'Chinese neologisms' are defined here as words that have been created or have acquired new meanings roughly from the late twentieth century (say after the 1990s) up to the present day, especially after the internet became popular in mainland China (despite being heavily censored) in the twenty-first century. Many of the new words selected here are also referred to as neologisms by various online resources such as Chinese Wikipedia, Baidu search engine and miscellaneous webpages.

This chapter divides the selected new words and phrases into six categories:

- those used for online social networking
- those representing newly conceived classes of people
- those invented to represent new concepts
- newly formulated descriptive words
- newly formulated action and interaction words
- new colloquial words and phrases.

Each category of neologism is explored in the following sections, in an item-by-item fashion. The discussion on each item includes its meaning, etymology (where available) and socio-cultural implications (where possible). Items which are obviously generated from the same root word are grouped together in the same space for discussion.

6.2.1 Social networking

This category of new words is used predominantly for online networking purposes. The words selected for discussion below refer to either concepts or behaviors that are prevalent on contemporary Chinese social networking websites.

Group 1
(Network relations)

粉丝 *fen3si1* 'fans'
求粉 *qiu2fen3* 'beg-fans'
互粉 *hu4fen3* 'mutual-fans'
回粉 *hui2fen3* 'return-fans'
涨粉 *zhang4fen3* 'swell-fans'
有粉必回 *you3fen3bi4hui2* 'have-fans-must-return'
脑残粉 *nao3can2fen3* 'brain damaged fans'
关注 *guan1zhu4* 'show concern'
大 V *da4v* 'big V'
艾特 *ai4te4* 'to @ someone; to include as recipient of a message'
拉黑 *la1hei1* 'pull-black'

The first seven words in Group 1 all originated from the first item, 粉丝, which is itself transliterated from the English word *fans*. The meaning of 粉丝 is largely the same as that of *fans* in English (though as with all Chinese nouns, it can be used in either the singular or the plural sense). On the Weibo social network, every user can have admirers who are attracted to them by their postings, their photo, their personality, their reputation and so on and become their 'fans'. The more fans one has, the more respectable one is likely to be in both the virtual world and real society. The number of fans also seems to provide social networkers with feelings of satisfaction and security, and the motivation to continue to take part in social networking.

Because of the importance of fans to Weibo networkers, many new words are created around the concept of fans, as demonstrated in Figure 6.1.

Figure 6.1 shows three kinds of words evolving from the concept of 'fans'. Firstly, there is the group of words denoting network participants' online behavior. 求粉 means to 'beg for fans', a word used in Weibo users' postings to invite other networkers to become their fans. 互粉 means to mutually become each other's fans. 回粉 means to return the act of becoming a fan. 有粉必回 means 'if you become my fan, then I will definitely become your fan as well'. All the terms in this group denote actions centering around the idea of increasing the number of one's fans on Weibo.

The second group, currently only one word that I am aware of, reflects the system's behavior with regard to network participants' number of fans. Thus, 涨粉 refers to the increase of the number of fans affiliated to a person, especially a sudden increase of large numbers of fans.

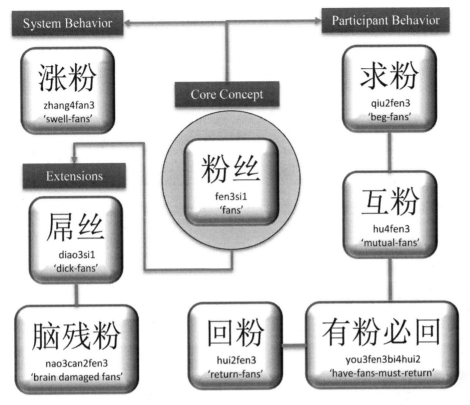

Figure 6.1 New terms evolving from the word 'fans'

Another extension of the core concept is the kinds of fan available on the web. 脑残粉 or the 'brain-damaged fans', can refer to very loyal fans of a celebrity or can be used to accuse some fans of zealous pursuit of worthless celebrities.

The next word in Group 1, 关注 'to express concern', is not a new word, but an old word acquiring new meanings in contemporary society. When used in the Weibo social networking environment, it has the technical meaning of 'adding yourself to the fan list of someone'. When someone has a huge number of fans in their Weibo space, they are called 大 V 'the big V', where V stands for 'verified'; that is, a verified member of Weibo whose phone number has been confirmed and who has a certain number of fans. A 大 V may have millions of fans on Weibo and is very influential in the social network.

The penultimate term, 艾特, is the transliteration of @ 'at'. The symbol is used in Weibo to mark someone as the recipient of a message. The transliteration of the English word 'at' then evolves into a Chinese verb, 艾特, which means to alert someone with a message. The last word in the group, 拉黑, means to add someone to the 'blacklist' of one's networking space, so that this person can no longer get in touch.

Example 1

a 大家　　　帮转　　　　　起来，
da4jia1　　bang1zhuan3　qi3lai2
'everybody' 'help-rotate' 'rise'
'Everybody please help circulate the message.

别　　　忘　　　了　**艾特**　好友　　　　　啊！
bie2　　wang4 le5　ai4te4 hao3you3　　a5
'do not' 'forget' AM 'at'　'good-friend' SFP
Do not forget to alert your friends by messaging!'

b 和　　前任　　　分手　　　必须　　**拉黑**　　　所有
he2　qian2ren4 fen1shou3 bi4xu1 la1hei1　　suo3you3
'with' 'ex'　　'part-hand' 'must' 'pull-black' 'all'
'After parting with your ex, you must add them to the blacklists of all

联系　　　方式
lian2xi4　　fang1shi4
'correspond' 'means'
your communication methods.'

Example 1a shows how a Chinese disyllabic unit 艾特, evolving from the symbol @, is now used as a regular verb on the web. The second sentence illustrates the usage of another newly formulated verb 拉黑, which can only be understood against the social networking background.

Group 2
(Message posting)

顶一下 *ding3yi2xia4* 'butt-once'
帮顶 *bang1ding3* 'help-butt'
帮转 *bang1zhuan3* 'help-forward'
沙发 *sha1fa1* 'sofa'
板凳 *ban3deng4* 'stool'
灌水 *guan4shui3* 'fill with water'
潜水 *qian2shui3* 'diving'
路过 *lu4guo4* 'pass by'
飘过 *piao1guo4* 'drift by'
无语 *wu2yu3* 'no language'
无言 *wu2yan2* 'no words'
枪文 *qiang1wen2* 'gun-article'

Group 2 words are used for responding to messages posted on social networks. The core concept is represented by the character 顶 in this group, which originally means 'to push something upward with the head', like heading in a football game. However, in the context of message responding, 顶 means to push the message upward one notch among the array of postings on a message board so it becomes more noticeable. That is, the message is pushed upward on a vertical stack. Therefore, 顶, 顶一下, or 帮顶 all mean lending support to the message so that the message stays longer on the board. 帮转, on the other hand, means passing the message on to another social networking space to increase the width of the distribution.

The next two terms, 沙发 'sofa' and 板凳 'wooden bench', are both existing common words in Chinese. In the context of discussion forums, however, they acquire new meanings in terms of the priority status of one's response to a posting. More specifically, 沙发 and 板凳 represent the first and the second responses respectively to a new posting. Both are significant places as people normally do not scroll too far down the rows of responses after reading the message itself.

Moving on to the second half of the Group 2 items, 灌水 is an existing word, originally meaning 'to pour water into a container (to cause flooding)'. In the context of message posting, this word acquires the new meaning of 'inputting plenty of (meaningless) postings' to state one's opinions or simply to help increase the visibility of a supported posting. 潜水, on the other hand, means 'reading without making any response', just like someone diving underneath the surface of the water without being noticed.

The next few terms in Group 2 are words often used to fill in the content of a posting on a message board. This happens when a person finishes reading a message and does not feel like making any serious response. A comment of some sort is required, however, due to the system's regulations, the demand from the owner of the posting or for the commentator's own good. In such cases, the social networker often simply inputs, in a perfunctory fashion, 路过 'passing by', 飘过 'drifting by', 无言 or 无语 (both meaning 'no comment'). These are not generally regarded as respectful postings in online communities.

The last item in Group 2, 枪文, refers to an article posted to the social network written by someone else rather than the self-proclaimed author. The term is probably derived from an existing word, 枪手 'gun-hand' which means 'ghost writer', often used to refer to an author who writes for others or an impersonator taking an exam for someone else.

Group 3
(Politics related)

美狗 *mei3gou3* 'American-dog'
五毛 *wu3mao2* 'five-cents'
天朝 *tian1chao2* 'imperial kingdom'
和谐 *he2xie2* 'harmonious'
河蟹 *he2xie4* 'river-crab'
扩散 *kuo4san4* 'disseminate'
求扩散 *qiu2kuo4san4* 'beg-dissemination'

An issue which many people are interested in discussing on social networks is politics, treacherous as the topic may be in China. Due to the large population and the incompatibility and clashes between different political thoughts, the positions people take are often extreme. The extreme nature of these is reflected in the political jargon created for use on the web. The Group 4 new words (or words with new senses) in the social networking category all have to do with political identities, political censorship and petitions.

The first item in this group, 美狗, refers derogatively to pro-America and pro-democracy netizens. Conversely, those who speak for the communist government are labeled 五毛, which derives its meaning from the alleged fifty-cent reward from the government for every pro-government posting made. Two sentences extracted from Weibo below illustrate how the two terms are used to label people who take up radically different political positions, the pro-American as 'American dog' in Example 2a and the CCP followers as 'fifty cents' in Example 2b respectively.

Example 2

a 右派、   汉奸、   脑残   **美狗**   等   是
   you4pai4 han4jian1 nao3can2   mei3gou3 deng3 shi4
   'right wing' 'Han-traitor' 'brain-disable' 'USA-dog' 'etc.' 'be'
   'The right wing, Chinese traitors, brain-damaged American dogs are

   美帝   资本   圈养   的。
   mei3di4   zi1ben3 quan1yang3 de5
   'USA-emperor' 'capital' 'feed'   ED
   fed by American capitalism.'

b 只有   你   这个   **五毛**   傻逼   才   去
   zhi3you3 ni3 zhe4ge5 wu3mao2 sha3bi1   cai2 qu4
   'only'   'you' 'this'   'fifty-cent' 'foolish-cunt' 'just' 'go'
   'Only a fifty-cent fool like you would

   宣扬   共产主义。
   xuan1yang2 gong4chan3zhu3yi4
   'promote'   'communism'
   go about advocating communism.'

The next word in the politics group, 天朝, is an older word acquiring a new meaning. The item used to refer to the imperial court that historically governed the whole of China. Nowadays it is used to refer to the central government of China formed solely and controlled fully by the Chinese Communist Party (CCP). The following three sentences from Weibo postings illustrate its usage.

Example 3

a 在   **天朝，**   党   领导   一切，
   zai4 tian1chao2   dang3 ling3dao3 yi2qie4
   'at' 'heaven-dynasty' 'party' 'lead'   'everything'
   'At the imperial kingdom, the Party is in charge of everything,

   包括   宪法。
   bao1kuo4 xian4fa3
   'include' 'constitution'
   including the constitution.'

b 揭穿   **天朝**   谎言   背后   的
   jie1chuan1 tian1chao2   huang3yan2 bei4hou4 de5
   'unveil' 'heaven-dynasty' 'lie'   'behind' AD

   事实   真相。
   shi4shi2 zhen1xiang4
   'fact'   'truth'

   'Exposing the factual truth behind the lies of the imperial court'

c 还有   9   天   Justin 就   要   来   大
   hai2you3 jiu3 tian1 Justin jiu4 yao4 lai2 da4
   'still-have' 'nine' 'day' 'Justin' 'just' 'want' 'come' 'big'

   天朝   了！
   tian1chao2   le5
   'heaven-dynasty' SFP

   'Justin Bieber is coming to the great imperial kingdom in nine days.'

Example 3a shows 天朝 to be used in a relatively calm statement, showing a netizen's understanding of how the 'imperial nation' is run. 3b, on the other hand, shows the word 天朝 to be at the beginning of a bitter criticism. The same word used in 3c, however, is free from political implications. The user in this case, like many other examples seen on Weibo, has accepted the term as equal to the word 中国 'China', much as they have accepted the CCP as the supreme (and for some, acclaimed) governing body of the nation.

The next two terms, 和谐 'harmonious' and 河蟹 'river-crab' are near homophones and recently-made synonyms, the latter being developed to replace the former to avoid its political connotations. Both words refer to the censoring actions taken or directed by the government to remove postings with 'dispreferred' contents; i.e. anything that involves the questioning the authority of the CCP or the running of the central government, certain government policies and their execution, radical advocacy of democracy, or any proposal or report on large scale mass protests, government failures, local riots, and social injustice (see the relevant discussions in Kuhn 2010, Miao 2011 and Wright 2011). The extended usage of this term also includes the justified removal by site moderators of inappropriate materials such as nude pictures, obscene language and so on. Some example usages of the words extracted from Weibo are shown in Example 4.

Example 4

a 早上　　　　的　QQ　新闻　　　报道　　　了！
zao3shang4 de5 q-q xin1wen2 bao4dao3 le5
'morning' AD 'QQ' 'news' 'report' AM
'It was reported on QQ news this morning

几　　　分钟　　　　后　　立马　　被　和谐　　　了。
ji3 fen1zhong1 hou4 li4ma3 bei4 he2xie2 le5
'several' 'minute' 'after' 'soon' PB 'harmony' AM
but was removed swiftly after a few minutes.'

b 这　位　妹纸　　露　　的　刚刚　　　好~
zhe4 wei4 mei4zhi3 lou4 de5 gang1gang1 hao3
'this' Cla 'sister' 'expose' Com 'just' 'right'
'This young girl is exposed to exactly the right extent,

所以　　不　会　被　和谐　　掉。
suo3yi3 bu2 hui4 bei4 he2xie2 diao4
'so' 'not' 'will' PB 'harmony' Com
so (the picture) will not be censored.'

c 真心　　　期待　　google　不　要　再
zhen1xin1 qi2dai4 google bu2 yao4 zai4
'real-heart' 'expect' 'Google' 'not' 'want' 'again'
'I honestly hope Google will not

被　河蟹　　　出　香港　　　了，
bei4 he2xie4 chu1 xiang1gang3 le5
PB 'river-crab' 'exit' 'Hong Kong' AM
be expelled from Hong Kong.

这样　　　天朝　　　　真的
zhe4yang4 tian1chao2 zhen1de5
'such' 'heaven-dynasty' 'really'
If it is, then China is really

就　离　朝鲜　　　不　远　了
jiu4 li2 chao2xian3 bu4 yuan3 le5
'just' 'leave' 'North Korea' 'not' 'far' SFP
not very different from North Korea.'

Example 4a reports a typical result of Chinese censorship where a piece of information survives only a few minutes on a medium (e.g. on TV or the web) before being removed for good − especially posts on social media that involves 'collective action potential' (King *et al.* 2013). The word 和谐 is used as a verb and is preceded by the passive marker 被, meaning 'having been harmonized' (as a euphemism) or 'being removed' in essence. The word is used in the same way in Example 4b except that it refers to the censoring act of the site moderator rather than the government. The word 河蟹 is used as a near homophone of 和谐 in Example 4c, referring to the possible removal of Google from Hong Kong in future.

When removed by Weibo censorship, the original posting is replaced by an official text shown in Example 5, according to the practice at the time of writing.

Example 5

抱歉，　　　　此　　微博　　　不　　适宜　　　对　　　　外　　　　公开。
bao4qian4 ci3　　wei2bo2 bu2　shi4yi2　dui4　　wai4　　　gong1kai1
'sorry'　　'this'　'weibo'　'not'　'suitable'　'toward'　'external'　'open'
'Sorry, this weibo item is not suitable for public viewing.

如　需　　帮助，　　　　请　　　联系　　　客服。
ru2 xu1　bang1zhu4　qing3　lian2xi4　ke4fu2
'if'　'need'　'help'　　　'please'　'contact'　'guest-serve'
If you need help, please contact customer service.'

The last two terms are based on the word, 扩散, which is also an old word acquiring a new meaning on social networks. The original meaning of 'expand and spread' is now concentrated on the spread of an appeal for help or for participation in the work of a charity. Two example usages are shown below:

Example 6

a　刚才　　　东西　　　掉　　了，麻烦　　转　　　一下，
　　gang1cai2 dong1xi1 diao4 le5　ma2fan2 zhuan3 yi2xia4
　　'just now' 'thing'　　'drop' AM　'trouble' 'rotate' 'once'
　　'I just lost something. Can people pass this on please?

　　扩散　　下　　消息。
　　kuo4san4 xia4　xiao1xi2
　　'spread'　'down' 'message'
　　Help spread the message.'

b　女　　　肇事　　　　一家　　　　耍　　无赖　　　呢，**求　扩散**！
　　nv3　zhao4shi4　yi4jia1　　shua3 wu2lai4　ne5 qiu2 kuo4san4
　　'female' 'cause trouble' 'one-family' 'play' 'scoundrel' SFP 'beg' 'expand'
　　'The perpetrator and her family are uncooperative. Please help disseminate!'

Both message senders in Example 6 are pleading for readers to help spread the message. In 6a, the poster asks the readers to help find their lost belongings. In 6b, the message sender asks the readers to support the victims in a hit-and-run accident.

6.2.2 Person naming

This category of words concerns newly conceived terms for people of different social classes, identifiers, traits and functions. All of these terms are used in large quantities on Weibo. Some of them are also active in daily spoken Chinese.

Group 1
(Social class)

高富帅 *gao1fu4shuai4* 'tall-rich-handsome'
白富美 *bai2fu4mei3* 'white-rich-beautiful'
穷矮搓 *qiong2ai3cuo1* 'poor-short-ugly'
土肥圆 *tu3fei2yuan2* 'crude-fat-round'
土豪 tu3hao2 'local tycoon'
屌丝 *diao3si1* 'dick-fans'
女神 *nv3shen2* 'goddess'
剩女 *sheng4nv3* 'remnant-woman'

The first two terms in Group 1, 高富帅 and 白富美, refer to promising young men and women of the highest possible social order – men who are tall, rich and handsome, women who are fair-skinned, rich and beautiful. The next two terms, 穷矮搓 and 土肥圆, refer to men and women at exactly the opposite social stratum, who are either poor, short and ugly or vulgar, fat and round. The word 土豪 'local tycoon' is not new, but has gained new popularity with the recent economic boom of China and the rise of ultra-wealthy individuals. An opposite term is 屌丝, which is created from blending a taboo word with the word 'fans' and refers to young men who come from underprivileged family backgrounds and generally look unimpressive. The word is used either in a derogatory sense or in a self-effacing way.

Example 7

a **高富帅**　　　　　坐　　拥　　几　　　房　　姨太，
  gao1fu4shuai4　　zuo4　yong3　ji3　　fang2　yi2tai4
  'tall-rich-handsome' 'sit'　'own'　'several'　'room'　'concubine'
  'The tall-rich-handsome class sit and own several concubines.

  屌丝　　　却　　　连　　媳妇　的　影子　　也　　找　　不　着。
  diao3si1　que4　lian2　xi2fu4 de5 ying3zi5　ye3　zhao3 bu4 zhao2
  'cock-fans' 'conversely' 'even' 'wife' PD 'shadow' 'also' 'find' 'not' Com
  In contrast, the underclass people cannot even find a wife.'

b 富二代　　　　　　　和　　**白富美**　　　　曾是
  fu4er4dai4　　　　he2　bai2fu4mei3　　　ceng2shi4
  'rich-two-generation' 'and' 'white-rich-pretty' 'was'
  'The second generation rich and the white-rich-beauty used to be

  最　　令　　人　　羨慕　　的　结合
  zui4　ling4　ren2　xian4mu4　de5　jie2he2
  'most' 'order' 'person' 'admire'　AD 'match'
  the most envied matched couple.'

c **屌丝**　　也　　要　　好好　　学　　会　　理财，
  diao3si1　ye3　yao4　hao3hao3　xue2　hui4　li3cai2
  'cock-fans' 'also' 'want' 'well'　'learn' Com 'manage-finance'
  'The underclass person should also learn to manage their own finances;

  否则　　　你　　一辈子　　甚至　　连　　**土肥圆**
  fou3ze2　　ni3　yi2bei4zi5　shen4zhi4 lian2 tu3fei2yuan2
  'otherwise' 'you' 'one-life'　'even'　'link' 'earth-fat-round'

  都　　找　　不　　到
  dou1　zhao3　bu2　dao4
  'all'　'find'　'not' Com

  otherwise they will not find even a vulgar-fat-round (partner) in their
  whole life.'

Example 7a contrasts the fortune of the tall-rich-handsome class with the misfortune of the miserable underclass of 屌丝. 7b contains another social elite term, 富二代, which means young people with very rich parents. A male 富二代 is well placed to marry a 白富美 because of the match in social status. In Example 7c, a 屌丝 is advised to acquire some skills in managing their meager income; otherwise, they cannot even find a woman to marry from the same social class.

The penultimate term in this group, 女神, literally means 'goddess'. As can be imagined, it is normally used to refer to a charming and beautiful woman, especially a celebrity. The final word, 剩女, on the other hand, refers to women over or around 30 years old who are still single. Its use is somewhat derogatory. Example usages of these two words are shown below:

Example 8

a 现场　　　　很多　　粉丝　　拿到　　了　**女神**　　的
　 xian4chang3 hen3duo1 fen3si1 na2dao4 le5 nv3shen2 de5
　 'site'　　　　'many'　 'fans'　 'obtain'　AM 'goddess'　PD

　 亲笔　　　　　签名
　 qin1bi3　　　 qian1ming2
　 'personal-pen' 'signature'

　 'Many fans on the site obtained autographs from the female idol.'

b 白富美　　　　　　为什么　　　　成　　　了　**剩女**?
　 bai2fu4mei3　　　 wei4shen2mo5 cheng2　le5　sheng4nv3
　 'white-rich-pretty' 'why'　　　 'become' AM 'remnant-woman'
　 'Why has a white-rich-pretty become a spinster?'

The sentence in Example 8a is extracted from a Weibo posting (which is itself copied from another media source) in which the 女神 refers to Nicole Kidman who attended the ground-breaking ceremony for the Oriental Movie Metropolis in Qingdao, China on September 22, 2013. Example 8b offers a contrast between two opposite social strata – one symbolizes the most desirable women in the world and the other those left on the shelf.

Group 2
(Personal identity)

御姐 *yu4jie2* 'imperial – older sister'
小罗莉 *xiao3luo2li4* 'little Lolita'
正太 *zheng4tai4* 'lovely young boy'
伪娘 *wei4niang2* 'false-woman'
基友 *ji1you3* (基佬 *ji1lao3*) 'gay man'
腐女 *fu3nv3* 'woman who likes gay men'
小三 *xiao3san1* 'little-three'

This group of new words is more related to a person's identity rather than to a social class. The first term in the group, 御姐, means a young woman with a dominant character. It is exactly the opposite of 小罗莉, which refers to a lovely young girl aged 8–14 or thereabouts. The next term, 正太, is the male counterpart of 小罗莉, meaning a lovely young lad. A man with a feminine appearance or female dispositions is called a 伪娘, a gay man is called a 基友 and a woman who is attracted to gay men is referred to as a 腐女 (literally 'rotten woman').

Example 9

a 　**御姐**　　　　的　外表　　　　下　　有　　颗　**小罗莉**　　　　的　心~
　　yu4jie3　　　de5　wai4biao3　xia4　you3　ke1　xiao3luo2li4　de5　xin1
　　'stern sister' PD　'appearance'　'down'　'have'　Cla　'small-Lolita'　PD　'heart'
　　'Underneath her stern appearance she has the heart of a lovely little girl.'

b 　时而　　　　伪　　成熟　　　　时而　　　　装　　　　**正太**
　　shi2er2　　wei4　cheng2shou2　shi2er2　　zhuang1　zheng4tai4
　　'sometimes'　'fake'　'mature'　　'sometimes'　'pretend'　'lovely boy'
　　'(He) sometimes fakes maturity and sometimes pretends to be a lovely innocent boy.'

c 　看　背影，　　　　我　也　　是　妹子　　好　　么！
　　kan4　bei4ying3　　wo3　ye3　shi4　mei4zi5　hao3　mo5
　　'look'　'back-shadow'　'I'　'also'　'be'　'girl'　　'good'　QM
　　'Looked at from the back, I am also a girl, alright?

　　谁　再　　叫　我　**伪娘**　　　　试试看！
　　shei2　zai4　jiao4　wo3　wei4niang2　　shi4shi4kan4
　　'who'　'again'　'call'　'me'　'fake-woman'　'try-try-see'
　　Whoever wants to call me a fake woman again, dare you try!'

d 　身边　　　　无　　男友，　**基友**　　　一　大　帮
　　shen1bian1　wu2　nan2you3　ji1you3　　yi2　da4　bang1
　　'body-side'　'none'　'boyfriend'　'gay-friend'　'one'　'big'　'gang'
　　'I do not have a boyfriend by my side, but I have a bunch of gay friends.'

e 　我们　　　法语　视听　　　老师　　绝对　　　是　个　**腐女**！
　　wo3men5　fa3yu3　shi4ting1　lao3shi1　jue2dui4　　shi4　ge5　fu3nv3
　　'we'　　　'French'　'see-listen'　'teacher'　'absolutely'　'be'　Cla　'decay-woman'
　　'Our French audiovisual teacher is definitely a gay-loving woman.

　　居然　　　　说　一　　部　基片　　　是　罗曼史！
　　ju1ran2　　shuo1　yi2　bu4　ji1pian4　shi4　ruo2man4shi3
　　'unexpectedly'　'say'　'one'　Cla　'gay-movie'　'be'　'romance'
　　She went so far as to say a gay movie is a love romance!'

Example 9a contrasts the two terms 御姐 and 小罗莉 with 'appearance' and 'inside', which are antonyms of each other. 9b also contrasts the term 正太 with the word 'mature'. Example 9c demonstrates how the word 伪娘 is thought of; that is, a real girl does not want to be called a 'fake woman'. 9d is obviously posted by a woman, who claims to have no boyfriend but is surrounded by gay men friends. Finally, Example 9e demonstrates how the word 腐女 is used. According to the message poster, since the French teacher sympathizes with a gay movie, she must be a lover of gay men as well.

小三 is a relatively recent term in comparison with 二奶 'second wife; mistress', both referring to the woman a married man has a sexual relationship with outside the marriage. Both terms are normally used in a derogatory sense.

Example 10

妻子	撞见	丈夫	幽会	小三
qi1zi5	zhuang4jian4	zhang4fu1	you1hui4	xiao3san1
'wife'	'bump-see'	'husband'	'secret-meet'	'mistress'

'A wife accidentally saw her husband secretly dating his mistress.

拉	其	车门	不	放	被	拖行	致死
la1	qi2	che1men2	bu2	fang4	bei4	tuo1xing2	zhi4 si3
'pull'	'its'	'car-door'	'not'	'release'	PB	'drag-go'	'incur-death'

(She) clung to the car door and was dragged along until she died.'

Example 10 shows the extreme measures taken by both wife and husband in dealing with an incident involving the husband's extramarital affair, costing the wife her life and the husband imprisonment (not shown in the example).

Group 3
(Personal trait)

呆逼 *dai1bi1* 'dumb cunt'
傻逼 *sha3bi1* 'foolish cunt'
苦逼 *ku3bi1* 'bitter cunt'
牛逼 *niu2bi1* 'formidable cunt'
牛人 *niu2ren2* 'formidable person'
二货 *er4huo4* 'a fool'
吃货 *chi1huo4* 'eat-stuff'
怂货 *song3huo4* 'coward'

There are three subgroups of new words in Group 3, divided by the ending morphemes. The words in the first subgroup all end with the morpheme 逼 *bi1* 'compel' which is a euphemistic homophone of 屄 *bi1* 'cunt'. The first two terms, 呆逼 and 傻逼, are similar in meaning; both are nouns referring to persons lacking in intelligence or common sense. 苦逼 is primarily used as an adjective or adverb, but also sometimes used as a noun. Its meaning is no different from the monosyllabic item 苦 which means 'bitter' and normally implies a lot of suffering. The only positive term in this subgroup is 牛逼, which is also used as an adjective meaning 'extremely impressive'. The second subgroup in Group 3 has 人 as the ending morpheme. 牛人 is the only noun example in this subgroup, and it refers to someone who is very extraordinary or outstanding. Some examples illustrating the usages of these terms follow.

Example 11

a 有   个   **呆逼**   买   了   相机   各种   哭。
   you3 ge5 dai1bi1   mai3 le5 xiang4ji1 ge4zhong3   ku1
   'have' Cla 'dumb-cunt' 'buy' AM 'camera' 'various-kinds' 'cry'
   'A fool bought a camera and cried out loud.'

b 什么   共产主义，   有   钱   都
   shen2mo5 gong4chan3zhu3yi4 you3 qian2   dou1
   'what'   'communism'   'have' 'money' 'all'
   'What communism!? (Officials) only

   知道   往   家里   划拉，
   zhi1dao4 wang3 jia1li3   hua2la1
   'know'   'toward' 'home-inside' 'paddle-pull'
   know about sweeping home whatever money they can find,

   拿   人民   当   **傻逼**   了！
   na2 ren2min2   dang1 sha3bi1   le5
   'take' 'the people' 'as'   'fool-cunt' SFP
   treating the people like fools!'

c 创业   很   **苦逼，**   也   很   幸福。
   chuang4ye4   hen3 ku3bi1   ye3 hen3 xing4fu2
   'create-enterprise' 'very' 'bitter-cunt' 'also' 'very' 'happy'
   'Although it is very hard work to start an enterprise, it is also a happy experience.'

d 有钱   真的   可以   很   **牛逼**！
   you3qian2   zhen1de5   ke3yi3 hen3 niu2bi1
   'have-money' 'really'   'can' 'very' 'cow-cunt'
   'Rich (people) can really do impressive things!'

e 真是   **牛人**！   看   完   后   好   励志   啊！
   zhen1shi4 niu2ren2   kan4 wan2 hou4 hao3 li4zhi4   a5
   'real''be' 'cow-person' 'see' Com 'after' 'very' 'encourage-aspiration' SFP
   '(She is) really a formidable person. Reading the posting inspires one's ambition!'

Example 11a is the beginning of a story about a person's hilarious experience of taking photos without removing the lens cover, thereby complaining about the new camera. 各种 in this sentence is an old term acquiring a new function of being an intensifier. 11b illustrates how 傻逼 is used, which is a synonym of 呆逼. Both these terms are used in a derogatory sense. The 苦逼 shown in Example 11c is used as an adjective, describing the hard conditions people endure. The word 牛逼 in Example 11d, on the other hand, is equal to 'awesome' in English, describing impressive persons or experiences. A related term is 牛人 in 11e, which in this instance refers to an extremely high achiever in her academic career (detail not shown in example).

The third subgroup of words in Group 3 all share the ending morpheme 货, whose original meaning is 'commodity' or 'cargo'. The terms in the group are used to refer to persons. 二货 means someone who is a bit foolish. The morpheme 二 itself can be used as an adjective. For example, 很二 describes a person as simple-minded and clumsy. While 二货 is normally used in a derogatory sense, the term 吃货, sometimes used to refer to oneself, simply means 'one who likes to eat'. The last item in Group 3, 怂货, refers to a cowardly person.

Example 12

a

遭遇	超级	大	塞车	外加	**二货**	路盲	司机
zao1yu4	chao1ji2	da4	sai1che1	wai4jia1	er4huo4	lu4mang2	si1ji1
'encounter'	'super'	'big'	'jam-car'	'external-plus'	'two-stuff'	'road-blind'	'driver'

'On top of a super big traffic jam, there is also this stupid driver not knowing which way to go.'

b

二货，	你	真的	忘记	吃药	了。
er4huo4	ni3	zhen1de5	wang4ji4	chi1yao4	le5
'two-stuff'	'you'	'really'	'forget'	'eat-medicine'	AM

'Hey, half-wit! I think you forgot to take your medicine.'

c

许多	想	尝鲜	的	**吃货**	们	已经	等不及	啦
xu3duo1	xiang3	chang2xian1	de5	chi1huo4	men5	yi3jing1	deng3bu4ji2	la5
'many'	'think'	'taste-fresh'	AD	'eat-stuff'	PM	'already'	'cannot wait'	SFP

'Many gluttons who would like to eat fresh food already cannot wait.'

d

怂货，	连	@	他	的	勇气	都	没有
song3huo4	lian2	at	ta1	de5	yong3qi4	dou1	mei2you3
'coward'	'even'	'at'	'him'	AD	'courage'	'all'	'none'

'You coward, you do not even have the courage to give him the message.'

Examples 12a and 12b illustrate the usage of 二货, referring to someone whom the speaker is not satisfied with, hence they are being called 'stupid'. The verb 吃药 in 12b is often used today to imply that someone is 'abnormal' in some way (e.g. being crazy, stupid or forgetful) and requires medical attention. The word 吃货 in Example 12c refers to a person who enjoys eating so much they will jump at any opportunity of a good meal. Example 12d illustrates the use of the word 怂货, which refers to a girl who does not have the courage to approach a boy. Interestingly, the @ sign in Example 12d is used as a verb, synonymous to 艾特 from Example 1a.

Group 4
(Social function)

砖家 zhuan1jia1 'so-called expert'
毒舌 du2she2 'poisonous-tongue'
美眉 mei3mei2 'pretty-eyebrow'
闺蜜 gui1mi4 'boudoir-friend'
童鞋 tong2xie2 'classmate'
平头百姓 ping2tou2bai3xing4 'common people'

The fourth and final group of new words in the person naming category have to do with the roles and functions people take up in society. The first term in the group, 砖家, is a popular orthographic variant of 专家 'expert' on Weibo. Experts are people to be ridiculed and jeered at on the web, especially on China's social networks. One reason may be that so-called 'experts' in China often appear on official media to defend government policies rather than giving unbiased, professional opinions or delivering criticisms. The morpheme 砖 'brick' which replaces the original 专 'specialized' probably comes from another new word 板砖 'concrete brick'. 板砖 has become a fashionable term on social networks which acquires the abstract meaning equivalent to a message posted on the web, especially a punchy message used to attack people or simply to impress others. The evolution of 专家 into 砖家, then, is a derogatory process, probably taking the meaning from 砖 to imply that the so-called 'experts' are only good at making a lot of ungrounded claims. The opinions of 砖家 are just as cheap as the millions of messages netizens throw around on the web every day. Two examples follow to illustrate the usage of 砖家 on Weibo. In Example 13a, the 'experts' are regarded as less useful than pigs. In Example 13b, experts are thought to be as simple-minded as local tycoons.

Example 13

a 要　　致富，　少　　养　　**砖家**　　多　　养　　猪
yao4　zhi4fu4　shao3　yang3　zhuan1jia1　duo1　yang3　zhu1
'want' 'get-rich' 'less' 'raise' 'expert'　　'more' 'raise' 'pig'
'If we want to get rich, we should raise more pigs rather than keep more experts.'

b 现在　　　很多　　**砖家**　　　的　逻辑　思维
xian4zai4　hen3duo1　zhuan1jia1　de5　luo2ji2　si1wei2
'now'　　'many'　　'expert'　　PD 'logic' 'thinking'
'Nowadays many experts' logical thinking patterns are

真　　跟　　个　土豪　　　　似的
zhen1　gen1　ge5　tu3hao2　　si4de5
'really' 'with' Cla 'local tycoon' 'similar to'
surely like those of a local tycoon.'

The word 毒舌 refers to someone who likes to pick on the faults of others and damage other people's confidence. Two example sentences are shown below:

Example 14

a 要　　**毒舌**　　　　请　　嘴　　下　　留　　情
yao4　du2she2　　　qing3　zui3　xia4　liu2　qing2
'want' 'poison-tongue' 'please' 'mouth' 'down' 'reserve' 'sentiment'
'If you want to verbally attack me please have some mercy.'

b 可惜　我　是　**毒舌,**　　　从不　　赞美　　别人。
ke3xi2　wo3　shi4　du2she2　　cong2bu4　zan4mei3　bie2ren2
'pity' 'I' 'be' 'poison-tongue' 'never'　'praise'　'others'
'It is a pity that I have a poisonous tongue and I never praise other people.'

Example 14a shows 毒舌 being used as a verb which means 'to verbally abuse'. The same word in 14b, on the other hand, is used as a noun, referring to someone in the habit of making scathing criticisms.

美眉, literally 'beautiful eyebrow', is a near homophone of 妹妹 which means 'younger sister'. 美眉 keeps the core meaning of 妹妹 – a young girl, but adds the extra implication that a girl qualified for this term should be reasonably good-looking. The word 闺蜜 refers to a girl's best friends with whom she can talk. Example usages of these two words follow:

Example 15

a 爱美　　　　的　**美眉**　　千万　　　不　要　　错过
ai4mei3　　de5 mei3mei2 qian1wan4 bu2 yao4　cuo4guo4
'love-beauty' AD 'pretty girl' 'make sure' 'not' 'want' 'miss'
'Girls who want to stay beautiful, make sure you do not miss this (product).'

b 快　　和　　你的　**闺蜜**　　　　分享　　这　份　喜悦　　吧~
kuai4 he2　ni3de5 gui1mi4　　 fen1xiang3 zhe4 fen4 xi3yue4 ba5
'quick' 'with' 'your' 'room-honey' 'share'　　'this' Cla 'delight' SFP
'Hurry and share this joy with your best girlfriend(s)!'

The word 童鞋 *tong2xie2* 'child-shoes' (also originating from Taiwan) is often used nowadays to replace its near homophone 同学 *tong2xue2* 'classmate' in informal writing. Interestingly, although the original term 同学 can only be used in educational settings, the reference group of 童鞋 is now expanded to cover people from any walk of life, so long as they have something in common. Examples are shown below to illustrate this point:

Example 16

a **童鞋**　　　们，　你　过劳肥　　　　了　吗？
tong2xie2　men5 ni3 guo4lao2 fei2 le5　ma5
'child-shoe' PM　'you' 'over-work-fat' SFP QM
'Hey mates, have you overworked and become too fat?'

b 有　　胃病　　　　　的　**童鞋**　　注意　　　了，
you3 wei4bing4　　de5 tong2xie2 zhu4yi4　le5
'have' 'stomach-sick' AD 'child-shoe' 'attention' SFP
'Those of you who suffer from stomach ache, attention!

8　　个　伤　胃　　坏　习惯
ba1　ge5 shang1 wei4　huai4 xi2guan4
'eight' Cla 'hurt'　'stomach' 'bad'　'habit'
Eight bad habits that hurt your stomach.'

c 很　　不错　　　的　围脖，
hen3 bu2cuo4　　de5 wei2bo2
'very' 'not-wrong' AD 'weibo'
'A very nice Weibo article.

正在　　　减肥　　的　**童鞋**　　快　看看！
zheng4zai4 jian3fei2　de5 tong2xie2 kuai4 kan4kan4
'currently'　'reduce-fat' AD 'child-shoe' 'quick' 'see-see'
Those who are currently losing weight come and have a look!'

Example 16 shows how the title 童鞋 is used to address different groups of people who share something in common. For example, in 16a, 童鞋 addresses the professionals rather than the students as the term 过劳肥 'being fat due to overwork' is normally associated with professional jobs rather than schoolwork. In Example 16b, the title is used to address whoever suffers from stomach ache, not necessarily students. The same is true for 16c, where everybody who is currently trying to lose weight is the potential addressee. Thus, the term 童鞋 'mate' keeps some of the implications of the original word 同学; for example, the social network can now be viewed as a large classroom where some conditions or rules of the school apply. At the same time, the addressed groups of 童鞋 become diversified and dramatically expanded.

The item 平头百姓 is normally used in a contrastive sense, to focus on the disadvantages of being a civilian in comparison to the more powerful government officials and the elite groups. The item is normally used by the underprivileged class rather than by the political elite. Two examples illustrating its usage follow:

Example 17

a　平头百姓　　　　　无　法　　　跟　权贵　　斗　啊
　　ping2tou2bai3xing4 wu2 fa3　　gen1 quan2gui4 dou4 a5
　　'flat-head-civilian' 'no' 'method' 'with' 'bigwig'　'fight' SFP
　　'There is no way for the civilians to contend with the rich and the powerful.'

b　一　个　平头百姓　　　图　的　就　是
　　yi2 ge5 ping2tou2bai3xing4　tu2　de5 jiu4 shi4
　　'one' Cla 'flat-head-civilian'　'strive' AD 'just' 'be'
　　'The only thing that a civilian strives for is

　　安稳　　　过　日子
　　an1wen3　guo4 ri4zi5
　　'safe-steady' 'pass' 'days'
　　to live a safe and uneventful life.'

Example 17 shows the predicaments common people may be facing in China. In Example 17a, the fact that civilians are being bullied by those in power (who are therefore rich) is implied. Example 17b, on the other hand, implies that the minimum goal of a civilian of living a safe and uneventful life is unattainable.

6.2.3 Concepts and terms

Nominal words that represent newly evolved (or popularized) concepts involving government, society, individuals and family are discussed in this section.

Group 1
(Government)

正腐 *zheng4fu3* 'is rotting'
城管 *cheng2guan3* 'city-manage'
房叔 *fang2shu2* 'house-uncle'
表叔 *biao3shu2* 'watch-uncle'

The new word 正腐 has been used by netizens as a substitute for its homophone 政府 *zheng4fu3* 'government' in a derogatory sense. The word itself consists of two morphemes of which 正 is a present continuous aspect marker and 腐 means 'rotten' or 'to rot'. Together 正腐 means 'currently in the process of rotting'. Replacing 政府 with 正腐 gives obvious implications. As this word is on the 'blacklist' of Weibo search, examples cannot easily be found there. The following examples are derived from Google.

Example 18

a 这   个   **正腐**   还有   希望   吗？
   zhe4 ge5 zheng4fu3 hai2you3   xi1wang4 ma5
   'this' Cla 'is rotting' 'still-have' 'hope'   QM
   'Does this government still have hope?'

b 有   好处   的 地方
   you3   hao3chu4 de5 di4fang1
   'have' 'benefits' AD 'place'
   'Wherever there are advantages,

   就   有   **正腐**   人员   的 身影！。
   jiu4   you3 zheng4fu3 ren2yuan2   de5 shen1ying3
   'then' 'have' 'is rotting' 'staff member' PD 'body-shadow'
   there are government employees.'

Example 18a is a general criticism of the 'government' (as being hopeless). 18b, on the other hand, shows why the government is thought to be bad – that is, government officials allegedly flock around the place where there is money to be collected.

The word 城管 'urban law enforcer' can refer to the City Urban Administrative and Law Enforcement Bureau or officers employed by the bureau to carry out the mission of maintaining the order and the outward appearance of the streets. In practice, the word is more often associated with employees of the bureau patrolling the city. Since their job is to crack down on any unauthorized civilian setups or activities which affect the orderliness of the city, they often clash with street vendors, vagabonds and so on and are noted for their use of brutal force. Two examples below illustrate the usage of the word;

Example 19

a 刺死   **城管**   的   小贩   夏俊峰   被   执行   死刑。
ci4si3   cheng2guan3   de5   xiao3fan4   xia4jun4feng1   bei4   zhi2xing2   si3xing2
'stab-dead'   'city-govern'   AD   'vendor'   'Xia Junfeng'   PB   'execute'   'death penalty'

'The vendor Xia Junfeng, who stabbed (a couple of) chengguans to death, was executed.'

b 请问   中国   哪里   没有   **城管，**
qing3wen4   zhong1guo2   na3li3   mei2you3   cheng2guan3
'please-ask'   'China'   'where'   'none'   'city-govern'

'Can I ask: Is there any place in China where there are no chengguan?

还是   移民   到   没   **城管**   的 地方   去
hai2shi4   yi2min2   dao4   mei2   cheng2guan3   de5 di4fang1   qu4
'still'   'immigrate'   'reach'   'none'   'city-govern'   AD   'place'   'go'

It is better to immigrate to a place where there is no chengguan.'

Example 19a involves an incident where a street vendor was arrested by a couple of law enforcers. The vendor later claimed that he was attacked by the two officers back in the bureau and accidentally killed both of them out of self-defense. He was sentenced to death and was executed a few years later. The incident provoked a lot of discussions on social networks and called into question the rightful existence of 城管. The user in Example 19b, for example, expresses their wish to live in a city in China without 'chengguan', although this is impossible.

The next two words, 房叔 and 表叔, were coined as new names for two real people who were government officials. 房叔, 'Uncle House', on one hand, was exposed by netizens to own more than 20 properties under his and his family's names. 表叔, 'Uncle Watch', on the other hand, was spotted wearing many expensive watches in his various official appearances, including one where he smiled happily while being interviewed as a government representative at the scene of a traffic accident. Both 房叔 and 表叔 were later suspended as a result of investigations. The two terms live on after the incidents and may be used to refer to someone else with the same traits.

Group 2
(Society)

潜规则 *qian2gui1ze2* 'hidden rules'
中国梦 *zhong1guo2meng4* 'China-dream'
淘宝体 *tao1bao3ti3* 'scoop-treasure style'
元芳体 *yuan2fang1ti3* 'Yuanfang style'
甄环体 *zhen1huan2ti3* 'Zhenhuan style'
思密达 *si1mi4da2* 'Korean (honorific)'

潜规则 'hidden-rule' refers to the implicit rules players adhere to once they are committed to joining or remaining in the game – which could mean a job with the government or a private corporation, an academic or professional program, an examination or inspection, and so on. The most well-known example is probably where TV or movie actresses have to sleep with directors and producers in order to act in their films. Similar situations might have occurred in government and educational institutions. The term is originally a nominal unit made of a verb/adjective (潜) and a noun (规则), although it is also used as a verb later on. Two examples of its usage follow:

Example 20

a

当	教授	可以	**潜规则**	女	学生，
dang1	jiao4shou4	ke3yi3	qian2gui1ze2	nv3	xue2sheng1
'when'	'professor'	'can'	'hidden-rule'	'female'	'student'

教育	就是	笑话
jiao4yu4	jiu4shi4	xiao4hua4
'education'	'just-is'	'joke'

'When professors can apply hidden rules to female students, education is a joke.'

b

奶粉	企业	贿赂	医生	护士	早
nai3fen3	qi4ye4	hui4luo4	yi1sheng1	hu4shi4	zao3
'milk-powder'	'enterprise'	'bribe'	'doctor'	'nurse'	'early'

已	成为	**潜规则**
yi3	cheng2wei2	qian2gui1ze2
'already'	'become'	'hidden-rule'

'It is already an established practice for formula milk corporations to bribe doctors and nurses.'

The two sentences in Example 20 see the word 'hidden rules' apply to the educational setting (i.e. male professors making females students sleep with them) and the business of marketing (i.e. formula milk sellers bribing the nurses so new-born babies become dependent on a certain brand of dried milk). The word 潜规则 is used as a verb in Example 20a and as a noun in 20b.

中国梦 'China dream' is a term proposed by the leader of the CCP in 2013 as a national goal for the next few decades. The term spawned a lot of bureaucratic toadying, online discussions and a relatively small number of sarcastic comments on Weibo. As the term is very generic, poetic and idealistic, it seems to help hide the weaknesses of authoritarianism and creates a 'mesmerizing effect' for the general public. It is, so to speak, less prone to verbal attack due to its linguistic incompatibility with 'harsh words'. Some examples of socio-political criticisms making use of this term can still be found on Weibo at the time of writing, as shown in Example 21 below:

Example 21

a **中国梦**   就是   老   了   能   捡   垃圾，
zhong1guo2meng4 jiu4shi4 lao3 le5 neng2 jian3 la1ji1
'China-dream'   'just-is' 'old' AM 'can' 'pick' 'garbage'
'China Dream means collecting garbage when one gets old,

有   垃圾   可   捡！
you3 la1ji1 ke3 jian3
'have' 'garbage' 'can' 'pick'
and there is garbage to collect.'

b 天朝   老师   怎么   如此 变态？
tian1chao2   lao3shi1 zen3mo5 ru2ci3 bian4tai4
'heaven-court' 'teacher' 'how'   'such' 'pervert'
'How can the teachers of the Tian Dynasty be so perverted?

中国梦   做   多   了   吗？
zhong1guo2meng4 zuo4 duo1 le5 ma5
'China-dream'   'make' 'many' SFP QM
Have they had too many China dreams?'

c 登基   后， 仅有   的 一点儿
deng1ji1   hou4 jin3you3   de5 yi4dian3er5
'coronation' 'after' 'only-have' AD 'a little'
'After (his) enthronement, the only

言论   思想   自由   也   在   被   压榨！
yan2lun4 si1xiang3 zi4you2 ye3 zai4 bei4 ya1zha4
'speech' 'thought' 'freedom' 'also' AM PB 'squeeze'
freedom of speech and thinking is also being squeezed.

中国梦，   大家   都   懂得，   在 做梦……
zhong1guo2meng4 da4jia1 dou1 dong3de5 zai4 zuo4meng4
'China-dream'   'everybody' 'all' 'understand' AM 'dream'
The so-called China Dream, everybody knows, is indeed
a daydream.'

Example 21a interprets 'China Dream' in an intentionally narrow way to reflect a social issue the speaker is obviously keenly aware of. Note that collecting recyclable materials from the garbage and reselling them for money is a way of earning money for many underprivileged people (especially older people) in Chinese societies. 21b is extracted from a message condemning a child-molesting kindergarten teacher in China. 'Too many China Dreams' is suspected, and therefore degraded, by the author to be the reason for such perverted behavior.

Example 21c accuses the CCP leader of further undermining freedom of speech since he 'ascended the throne' (rightfully reflecting the nature of the communist sovereignty). Thus, according to the author, everybody knows what China Dream means – that you are indeed 'dreaming' about obtaining reasonable freedom of speech and independent thinking under the current political regime.

The three terms, 淘宝体 'Taobao style', 元芳体 'Yuanfang style', 甄环体 'Zhenhuan style', each refer to a special way of writing or speaking using particular linguistic features or key phrases. The first term, 淘宝体, originated from the Taobao Marketplace, the largest online shopping platform in China. Taobao style refers to the online sellers' intimate way of communicating with their customers, which involves the oral address 亲 'darling' and generous use of sentence-final particles. Both 元芳体 and 甄环体 originated from TV dramas. The 元芳体 mainly involves the use of a question 元芳, (此事)你怎么看? 'Yuanfang, how do you look at (the matter)?' often asked by the protagonist detective of his sidekick in the drama. The 甄环体, on the other hand, involves the use of many archaic forms of speech such as 本宫, 臣妾, 哀家 (forms women used to address themselves in the imperial court) and so on.

Example 22

a
这	是	南京	理	工	大学	给	被	录取	考生
zhe4	shi4	nan2jing1	li3	gong1	da4xue2	gei3	bei4	lu4qu3	kao3sheng1
'this'	'be'	'Nanjing'	'logic'	'work'	'university'	'give'	PB	'admit'	'exam-student'

'This is sent from Nanjing University of Science and Technology to admitted students,

发	的	短信	通知,	使用	**淘宝体,**	很	潮!
fa1	de5	duan3xin4	tong1zhi1	shi3yong4	tao1bao3ti3	hen3	chao2
'send'	AD	'short-letter'	'notice'	'use'	'Taobao-style'	'very'	'tide'

a short message notification, written in Taobao style, very fashionable!'

b
众多	网友	大呼,	内幕,	黑暗。
zhong4duo1	wang3you3	da4hu1	nei4mu4	hei1an4
'many'	'net-friend'	'big-call'	'inside-act'	'dark'

'Many netizens shout out loud: foul play! Black-box operation!

元芳,	你	怎么	看?
yuan2fang1	ni3	zen3mo5	kan4
'Yuanfang'	'you'	'how'	'look'

Yuanfang, what do you think?

c
看完	甄环,	文字	用	的	都	是	**甄环体......**
kan4wan2	zhen1huan2	wen2zi4	yong4	de5	dou1	shi4	zhen1huan2ti3
'view-finish'	'Zhen Huan'	'words'	'use'	AD	'all'	'be'	'Zhenhuan-style'

'After seeing the Zhen Huan (TV drama), all the words used are Zhenhuan style.'

Example 22a offers a brief comment (i.e. 'very fashionable') on the admissions letter issued by a university written in Taobao style. The actual notice (followed by my translation) is as follows:

> "亲，祝贺你哦！你被我们学校录取了哦！亲，9月2号报到哦！录取通知书明天'发货'哦！亲，全5分 哦！给好评哦！"
>
> "Dear, congratulations! You are admitted by our university, d'y' know? Darling, be sure to report on September 2! Offer letter will be 'shipped' tomorrow, ok? Darling, the full score is five! Give a good feedback, will you?"

The author of Example 22b summarizes the comments of netizens about the result of a particular episode of the TV singing contest 'The Voice of China', exploring the possibility of an under-the-table arrangement for a weaker contestant to win. The summary is followed by a question written in 元芳体, 'How do you look at it, Yuanfang?' As the assistant Yuanfang always answers 'I think it is suspicious' in the original detective story, the use of 元芳体 implies there is something underhand in the event under discussion. Example 22c shows how popular TV dramas can influence people in their styles of speaking and writing nowadays.

思密达 is the transliteration of a Korean honorific ending which has no content meaning. Chinese language speakers find this interesting and sometimes add it to the end of a sentence just for fun or for imitating the Korean way of speaking. The word is also used to refer to Korea or Korean people.

Example 23

a
韩国	金	老师	的	造型	团队	确实	给力	**思密达**。
han2guo2	jin1	lao3shi1	de5	zao4xing2	tuan2dui4	que4shi2	gei3li4	si1mi4da2
'Korea'	'Jin'	'teacher'	PD	'model'	'team'	'indeed'	'give-power'	SFP

'The team of Korean teacher Jin is really inspiring, I say.'

b
一	入座，	对面	的	大叔	就	和	我	搭讪	聊天，
yi2	ru4zuo4	dui4mian4	de5	da4shu2	jiu4	he2	wo3	da1shan4	liao2tian1
'one'	'enter-seat'	'opposite'	AD	'big-uncle'	'just'	'with'	'me'	'approach'	'chat'

'As soon as I was seated, the mature man opposite me approached me and chatted away.

还是	用	很	蹩脚	的	国语。	原来	他	是	**思密达**
hai2shi4	yong4	hen3	bie1jiao3	de5	guo2yu3	yuan2lai2	ta1	shi4	si1mi4da2
'moreover'	'use'	'very'	'poor'	AD	'Mandarin'	'actually'	'he'	'be'	'Korean'

He spoke very poor Mandarin. He turned out to be a Korean.'

Example 23a is self-completing without the sentence-final element 思密达. The term used in this way does not seem to add any pragmatic implication except perhaps to signal an association with, or awareness of, the Korean element. The 思密达 used in Example 23b though, is different. It clearly replaces the canonical 韩国人 'Korean' as a more contemporary, casual, and possibly amusing, variant.

Group 3
(Person and family)

果照 *guo3zhao4* 'naked photo'
鸭梨 *ya1li2* 'pressure'
回头率 *hui2tou2lv4* 'head turning rate'
小确幸 *xiao3que4xing4* 'small and assured fortune'
失独家庭 *shi1du2jia1ting2* 'lose – only child – family'

The first term in this group, 果照, is created from the existing word 裸照 'naked-photo'. Readers will notice that the character 果 'fruit' is the character 裸 'bare' minus a radical 衤 (the 145th radical of the 214 listed in Paton 2008) which means 'clothes'. Therefore the morpheme 果 is reinterpreted as 裸 without clothes, which means 'naked'. This gives the netizens a fun way of referring to an interesting concept on social networks.

The word 鸭梨, literally 'duck pear', originally meant a kind of pear. As it is a near homophone of 压力 *ya1li4* 'pressure', at some point Chinese netizens began to substitute 鸭梨 for 压力 and the term has caught on since then. A related term is 鸭梨山大 (itself a near homophone of the standard Chinese translation for the English name Alexander, or 亚历山大) which means the pressure is 'as big as a mountain'.

The new term 回头率 refers to the likelihood of people turning around to look at you while walking past you. The term reflects people's concerns about their appearance nowadays, especially the younger generation who are now able to afford fashionable clothes and accessories.

Example 24

a 等   我   到   了   250   粉   我   就   发   **果照**。
   deng3 wo3   dao4   le5   er4bai3wu3shi2 fen3 wo3   jiu4   fa1   guo3zhao4
   'wait' 'I'   'reach' AM   '250'   'fans' 'I'   'then' 'issue' 'naked photo'
   'I will post my naked photo when the number of my fans reaches 250.'

b 就   要   高考   了   **鸭梨**   很   大   吧？
   jiu4   yao4   gao1kao3   le5   ya1li2   hen3   da4   ba5
   'just' 'want' 'high-exam'   SFP   'pressure' 'very' 'big' SFP
   'The college entrance exam will soon be held. The pressure is mounting, right?'

c 让   你   立刻   从   人群   中   脱颖而出，
   rang4 ni3   li4ke4   cong2 ren2qun2 zhong1 tuo1ying3er2chu1
   'let'   'you' 'at once' 'from' 'crowd'   'middle' 'stand out'
   'Lets you immediately stand out from the crowd.

   回头率   超   高。
   hui2tou2lv4   chao1 gao1
   'return-head-rate' 'super' 'high'
   Head-turning rate super high.'

Example 24a is a netizen's typical promise to do something dramatic (in this case, upload their naked photos) once their number of fans passes a threshold. 24b demonstrates how the new word 鸭梨 is used where conventionally 压力 is expected. Example 24c is extracted from an advertisement for iPhone 5S cases posted on Weibo.

The word 小确幸 is a combination of three morphemes, each representing a distinct concept. 小 means 'small', 确 is a short form for 确定 'definite' and 幸 is the short form of 幸福 'happiness and well-being'. Together the term means 'small but definite happiness'.

The term 失独家庭 means a family which has lost its only child, normally referring to older parents who have lost their grownup son or daughter and have no more progeny to depend on. The possibility of this happening is greater in China than in other countries of the world because China is still largely maintaining its one-child policy begun in the 1970s.

Example 25

a   一边   作饭   一边   听   自己 喜欢   的   音乐，
    yi4bian1 zuo4fan4 yi4bian1 ting1 zi4ji3 xi3huan1 de5 yin1yue4
    'one-side' 'make-rice' 'one-side' 'listen' 'self' 'like'   AD 'music'
    'While making a meal, (I) listen to my favorite music

    体会   生活   中   的   **小确幸**。
    ti3hui4   sheng1huo2 zhong1 de5 xiao3que4xing4
    'appreciate' 'living'   'middle' AD 'little-confirmed-happiness'
    appreciating a little assured happiness in life.'

b   中国   **失独家庭**   至少   有   100万   个。
    zhong1guo2 shi1du2jia1ting2 zhi4shao3 you3 yi4bai3wan4 ge5
    'China'   'lose-only-family' 'at least'   'have' 'one million' Cla
    'There are at least a million families who have lost their only child
    in China.'

Example 25a shows how the term 小确幸 is used to represent every little happiness achievable in daily life. 25b is an informal statistic of the number of families which have lost their only child up to the year 2012.

6.2.4 Descriptions

In this section we discuss new words which are mainly used as adjectives. The words are grouped into three subcategories depending on whether they normally imply a positive evaluation, a negative evaluation or no such evaluation (i.e. neutral).

Group 1
(Positive description)

牛 *niu2* 'awesome'
萌 *meng2* 'cute'
给力 *gei3li4* 'inspiring'
有才 *you3cai2* 'talented'
有范 *you3fan4* 'gracious'
碉堡 *diao1bao3* 'blockhouse; awesome'

The morpheme 牛, originally meaning 'cow' as a noun, has now become a popular adjective capitalizing on the distinct traits of the animal: sturdy, persevering and sometimes awe-inspiring. The morpheme 牛 is now used to describe someone or something as particularly awesome and highly impressive. In actual usage it normally couples with an adverbial element such as 很 'very', 太 'excessively', 特 'especially' and 超 'super'.

Example 26

a 一辈子　　　　做好　　　一　件　事　　就
   yi2bei4zi5　　　zuo4 hao3 yi2　jian4 shi4　jiu4
   'one life time'　'do-good'　'one' Cla　'matter' 'then'

很　牛　　　　了
hen3 niu2　　　le5
'very' 'remarkable' SFP

'It is quite remarkable if you can accomplish one thing satisfactorily in a lifetime.'

b 司机　师傅　**太　牛**　　　了，
   si1ji1　shi1fu4 tai4 niu2　　　le5
   'driver' 'master' 'too' 'formidable' SFP
   'The taxi driver is extraordinary.

三　　部　手机　　　同时　　　开　着　约车。
san1　bu4　shou3ji1　　tong2shi2　kai1　zhe5　yue1che1
'three' Cla 'cell phone' 'same-time' 'open' AM 'date-car'
He takes car reservations on three cell phones at the same time.'

c 实拍：　　　**超　牛**　　女童　趴　　　车　下
   shi2pai1　　　chao1 niu2　nv3tong2 pa1　　che1 xia4
   'actual footage' 'super' 'amazing' 'girl'　'lie prone' 'car' 'down'

奇迹　　躲避　　车祸
qi2ji1　duo3bi4 che1huo4
'miracle' 'dodge' 'car accident'

'Real footage: A super fantastic girl lies beneath the car to avoid an accident.'

The adjective morpheme 牛 appears with various adverbial elements in Example 26. It is translated into different English words to reflect the influence of context on its relatively flexible meaning. In 26a 很牛 is used in a predominantly positive sense, and is thus translated appropriately into 'very remarkable'. In 26b, the term 太牛 is not necessarily a compliment; it only describes something as unusual, hence the translation of 'extraordinary'. The term 超牛 used in 26d describes an extraordinary event at the highest possible level (here referring to a girl ducking under a car to avoid being hit). Again, the term is used to express amazement and no appraisal is obviously involved.

The morpheme 牛 can sometimes be used in a negative sense, implying that someone or something is being extraordinary in a bad way. For example, Example 27a refers to the rather inconsiderate behavior of a bus company (i.e.

the unpredictable change of bus routes) in an unpleasant way. Example 27b, on the other hand, applies the term to a student who was insolent enough to ask the invigilator of an exam how to answer a question.

Example 27

a 邯郸 　　公交 　　**很牛，**
　han2dan1 gong1jiao1 hen3niu2
　'Handan' 'bus' 　　'very-wilful'
　'Handan bus is incredible.

　可以 　不 　预告 　　不 　公布 　　就 　随意 　改线。
　ke3yi3 bu2 yu4gao4 　bu4 gong1bu4 jiu4 sui2yi4 gai3xian4
　'can' 'not' 'announce' 'not' 'post' 　'just' 'at will' 'change-route'
　They can change routes at will without notice or announcement.'

b 有 　个 　哥们 　　**特 　牛，**
　you3 ge5 ge1men5 te4 　niu2
　'have' Cla 'man' 　'really' 'great'
　'There is an unbelievable guy

　他 考试 　不 　会 　就 　直接 　问 　监考 　　　老师
　ta1 kao3shi4 bu2 hui4 iu4 zhi2jie1 wen4 jian1kao3 　　lao3shi1
　'he' 'exam' 　'not' 'able' 'just' 'direct' 'ask' 'monitor-exam' 'teacher'
　who directly asks the invigilator about questions he cannot answer.'

The item 萌 'lovely' is another single-morpheme adjective which has recently become popular. It is primarily used to describe younger people, especially girls who appear to be cute and innocent. However, the item is also increasingly being used to describe animals, objects and situations, moving from objective observation to subjective feelings.

Example 28

a 你 　太 　粘人， 　　太 　爱 　卖**萌，** 　　太 　会 　撒娇 　了。
　ni3 tai4 nian2ren2 　tai4 ai4 mai4meng2 tai4 hui4 sa3jiao1 le5
　'you' 'too' 'stick-person' 'too' 'love' 'sell-cute' 　'too' 'able' 'flirty' 　SFP
　'You are too clingy, try too hard to be cute and play the woman too much.'

b 孩子 们 　都 　唱 　的 　好 　可爱，完全 　　**萌 　爆 　　　了！**
　hai2zi5 men5 dou1 chang4 de5 hao3 ke3ai4 wan2quan2 meng2 bao4 　le5
　'child' PM 　'all' 'sing' Com 'very' 'lovely' 'complete' 'cute' 'explode' SFP
　'The kids all sang so lovely. They are totally and explosively cute!'

Example 28 shows the morpheme 萌 incorporated into two frequently used expressions: 卖萌 'play the cute' and 萌爆 'incredibly cute'. The morpheme can also come after standard adverbs to form descriptive units like 太萌 'excessively cute', 超萌 'super lovely' and so on.

给力, literally 'give power' means 'refreshing', 'stimulating', 'energizing', 'inspiring' and so on. Its primary usage is serving as an adjective but it is also used as a verb. The negative form, 不给力, meaning 'unimpressive' or 'not as expected', is said to have come into fashion first and seems to have distinctive meaning and usage.

Example 29

a 这个　　比　　　中　　　彩票　　　**给力**　　　多　　　了
　zhe4ge5 bi3　　zhong4 cai3piao4 gei3li4　　duo1　le5
　'this'　　'compare' 'obtain' 'lottery'　'give-power' 'much' SFP
　'This (program) is much more useful than winning the lottery,

有木有！
you3mu4you3
'yes or no?'
right?'

b 网速　　　　着实　　　**不　给力**　　　啊…
　wang3su4　zhuo2shi2　bu4　gei3li4　　a5
　'web-speed' 'indeed'　'not' 'give-power' SFP
　'Internet speed is really disappointing . . .'

The author of Example 29a is referring to the USA Green Card Lottery Program, recommending his fellow netizens should make an application as obtaining a Green Card in this way is much better than winning a lottery. The author of 29b, on the other hand, is complaining about the speed of the Internet. It can be seen that although 给力 is a very positive adjective (used to describe something better than winning the lottery), its antonym, 不给力, is only moderately negative.

Both 有才 'gifted' and 有范 'graceful' are positive terms describing a person's talents and charismatic appearance respectively. As Example 30a shows, 有才 is often used to describe someone behind an impressive piece of work, such as a video, a joke, a song, an article and so on. 有范, on the other hand, praises someone for their outward appearance or performance. The term is often used in clothing or accessories advertisements, as exemplified by Example 30b.

Example 30

a 这　份　招聘　　谁　写　的?　太　　　有才　了!
zhe4 fen4 zhao1pin4 shei2 xie3　de5　tai4　　　you3cai2 le5
'this' Cla 'recruit' 'who' 'write' ED 'excessively' 'talented' SFP
'Who wrote this vacancy advertisement? So extraordinarily talented!'

b 小小　　　的　饰物,
xiao3xiao3 de5 shi4wu4
'small'　　AD 'ornament-object'
'A small accessory

让　　我们　　　更　　　有范。
rang4 wo3men5 geng4　　you3fan4
'let'　'us'　　'even more' 'graceful'
can make us even more gracious-looking.'

碉堡 'fort' is a near homophone of 屌爆 'cock-burst (amazingly great)'. Because 屌爆 involves a taboo word, its orthographical substitute 碉堡 was picked up by social networkers at some point and it caught on. Both forms are interchangeably used on the web today, their meanings and functions remaining largely the same.

Example 31

a 变　　　鸽子　还有　　这么　多　　玩法,
bian4　　ge1zi5 hai2you3 zhe4mo5 duo1 wan2fa3
'transform' 'pigeon' 'still-have' 'such'　'many' 'play-method'
'There are so many magic tricks involving pigeons,

好　　碉堡~~
hao3 diao1bao3
'very' 'incredible'
how extraordinary . . . '

b 师傅　手艺　真　碉堡　　了
shi1fu4 shou3yi4 zhen1 diao3bao4 le5
'master' 'craft'　'really' 'amazing' SFP
'The master's craft is really incredible.'

The author of Example 31a uses the adjective 碉堡 to express wonder at the magician's skills in manipulating the pigeons. The author of 31b, on the other hand, uses 屌爆 to praise a chocolate maker's handcraft. Both terms are essentially interchangeable.

Group 2
(Negative description)

悲催 *bei1cui1* 'tragic'
蛋疼 *dan4teng2* 'egg-sore'
黑心 *hei1xin1* 'black-heart'
重口味 *zhong4kou3wei4* 'heavy taste'

The word 悲催 is normally used to describe a tragic happening, often one experienced personally by the author, and provides a comic touch like so many social networking new terms do. The first morpheme of 蛋疼 (literally 'egg-ache') refers to the male private parts. The word is therefore mostly used by male authors, although female speakers are using this term increasingly. The word initially means 'being bored' but as it becomes more widely used, it also takes on other meanings like 'not knowing what to do' or 'having a headache'.

Example 32

a　**悲催**　　的　事情　　　发生　　　了，
　　bei1cui1　de5　shi4qing2　fasheng1　le5
　　'sad'　　AD　'matter'　　'occur'　　AM
　　'A tragic thing happened.

　　凌晨　　　4点　　　多　　起床　　　拉肚子　　　了。
　　ling2chen2　si4dian3　duo1　qi3chuang2　la1du4zi5　le5
　　'daybreak'　'4 o'clock'　'more'　'rise-bed'　'pull-tummy'　AM
　　I got out of bed at 4 with diarrhea.'

b　真　　烦人！　　　　一　　放假　　　　就　　闲　　的　　**蛋疼**。
　　zhen1　fan2ren2　　yi2　fang4jia4　jiu4　xian2　de5　dan4teng2
　　'real'　'bother-person'　'one'　'on holiday'　'then'　'idle'　Com　'egg-sore'
　　'It is so annoying! As soon as (I am) on holiday I feel so bored having nothing to do.'

c　个子　　不够　　　　身材　　　也　　不行　　　真是　　　**蛋疼**。
　　ge4zi5　bu2gou4　　shen1cai2　ye3　bu4xing2　zhen1shi4　dan4teng2
　　'build'　'inadequate'　'figure'　　'also'　'not-ok'　'really'　'egg-sore'
　　'I am short, with a poor figure. How annoying!'

Although the author of Example 32a reports the incident of diarrhea as a 'tragic happening' using the word 悲催, this kind of posting is often intended to achieve a self-teasing and comic effect rather than share a truly saddening experience. Example 32b shows the word 蛋疼 used in the sense of 'being bored'; while the same word in 32c most likely means 'being annoyed'. The author of sentence 32c happens to be a female Weibo user complaining about her own appearance.

The term 黑心, literally 'black-hearted', is a long-standing word, originally referring to a person who is 'lacking a conscience', 'heartless', 'merciless' and so on. The term has recently acquired an extended meaning due to a series of industrial scandals in both China and Taiwan where food products and articles for daily use were found to contain a variety of health-damaging materials. The word 黑心 became used extensively for, and understood to mean, commodities or services sold by unethical manufacturers or rogue traders.

The recently popularized term 重口味 also develops new meanings from an original meaning centering on food. The term used to refer to very spicy or salty food or taste. While keeping the original usage, it is now also used in other settings, referring to a person's relatively unusual inclinations and preferences in other aspects of life.

Example 33

a 这　　旅馆　　的　被子　睡　　得　　我　全身　　　　　过敏！
zhe4　lv3guan3　de5　bei4zi5　shui4　de5　wo3　quan2shen1　guo4min3
'this' 'hotel'　PD 'quilt' 'sleep' Com 'I' 'whole-body' 'allergic'
'The quilt in this hotel made me allergic all over after sleeping under it.

是　有　　多　　黑心！
shi4　you3　duo1　hei1xin1
'be' 'have' 'much' 'black-hearted'
How obnoxious they are!'

b 他　这次　　　的　表演　　全裸　　　　出镜，
ta1　zhe4ci4　de5　biao3yan3　quan2luo3　chu1jing4
'he' 'this time' AD 'perform' 'whole-naked' 'exit-lens'
'His current performance involves full nudity in front of the camera,

以　　重口味　　　　的　行为　　揭露　　现实　　的
yi3　zhong4kou3wei4　de5　xing2wei2　jie1lu4　xian4shi2　de5
'with' 'heavy-taste'　AD 'behavior' 'expose' 'reality'　PD

残酷　　与　无奈！
can2ku4　yu3　wu2nai4
'cruelty' 'and' 'no-endure'

revealing the cruelty and helplessness of the reality with somber behavior.'

The author of Example 33a complains about a bad hotel stay experience, where the problematic quilt caused allergic reactions. The word 黑心 in this instance is generally understood to mean the questionable filling of the quilt (黑心棉被 'black-hearted quilt' was widely reported in China to contain industrial and medical wastes and other waste materials inside the well-presented cover and sold as new). Example 33b illustrates the usage of 重口味, referring to an artistic performance involving complete nudity. Although the context of Example 33b does not generate a negative interpretation overall, the term 重口味 itself does normally imply something unusual, such as the nude performance in this example.

Group 3
(Neutral description)

囧 *jiong3* 'embarrassing'
口年 *kou3nian2* 'pitiful'
雷人 *lei2ren2* 'stunning'
羞射 *xiu1she4* 'shy'
劲爆 *jin4bao4* 'astounding'

The character 囧 has only acquired lexical status in recent years. Previously it was an ancient character very rarely used if ever. Nowadays it has become a popular symbol in the media and social networks due to its distinct shape (like a perplexed human face). Its meaning is roughly the same as another character with the same pronunciation: 窘 'embarrassing or being embarrassed'. The morpheme can be used alone or it can form a disyllabic unit with a preceding adverb like 很囧 'very embarrassed' or a following noun like 囧事 'embarrassing thing' in Example 34a.

The item 口年, on the other hand, is a nonsensical combination of 口 'mouth' and 年 'year' used to substitute its near homophone 可怜 *ke3lian2* 'pitiful'. An example usage of this item is shown in Example 34b.

Example 34

a 说   一   件   你   关于   运动   的   囧   事。
  shuo1 yi2 jian4 ni3 guan1yu2 yun4dong4 de5 jiong3   shi4
  'say' 'one' Cla 'you' 'concerning' 'sports' AD 'embarrassing' 'matter'
  'Name one thing in the sports area which embarrassed you.'

b 口年   的   螃蟹   挣扎   的   腿   都   掉   了。
  kou3nian2 de5 pang2xie4 zheng1zha2 de5 tui3 dou1 diao4 le5
  'pitiful' AD 'crab'   'struggle' Com 'leg' 'all' 'drop' AM
  'Poor crab, its legs are detached due to its struggling.'

The new term, 雷人 literally 'thunder-person', refers to something stunning and causing speechlessness. 羞射 *xiu1she4*, another netizen's play of similar sounding characters, replaces its near homophone 羞涩 *xiu1se4*. Both mean 'shy' but the new item has sexual connotations due to the association of 射 'shoot' with the concept of 'ejaculation'. 羞射 thus implies a flirtatious nature underneath the shy appearance. The newly popularized adjective, 劲爆 meaning 'powerfully explosive' can often be found in news, sports or entertainment contexts to emphasize a certain event, person, or object. The word is also used in commercial advertisements to attract potential buyers' attention.

Example 35

a 雷人!　　　　女子　　边　　骑　　电动车
　lei2ren2　　　　nv3zi3　bian1　qi2　dian4dong4che1
　'thunder-person' 'woman' 'edge' 'ride' 'electric-car'

　边　　给　　孩子　　喂奶。
　bian1　gei3　hai2zi5　wei4nai3
　'edge' 'give' 'child' 'feed-milk'

　'Stunning! A woman feeds her child milk while riding an electric bike.'

b 然后　　　伦家　　很　　羞射　　　　的　　跟　　你
　ran2hou4 lun2jia1 hen3 xiu1she4　de5　gen1　ni3
　'then'　　'I'　　　'very' 'shy-shoot' Com 'with' 'you'

　对视　　　　了　几　　秒。
　dui4shi4　　le5　ji3　miao3
　'mutually stare' AM 'several' 'second'

　'And then I shyly stared at you, with you staring back for a few seconds.'

c 超　　劲爆!　　　　胆　小　　慎　　入!
　chao1　jin4bao4　　dan3　xiao3　shen4　ru4
　'super' 'power-explode' 'gut' 'small' 'careful' 'enter'
　'Super explosive! Not suitable for the faint-hearted!'

Example 35a shows the adjective 雷人 'stunning' independently used to describe the ensuing event: a lady breastfeeding a child while riding an electric bike. The author of 35b, on the other hand, shares her feeling of shyness on seeing a handsome young man. The new term 羞射 more competently expresses her underlying flirtatiousness than the canonical word 羞涩. Note that the item 伦家 is a 'spoof' version of 人家 (a supposedly cute, feminine way of referring to oneself), assimilated into mainstream Chinese via a Taiwanese accent. Example 35c is a warning for readers to beware of the video enclosed within the Weibo post which contains violent dog fighting scenes.

6.2.5 Action and interaction

This section deals with new words that are primarily used as verbs (though like other Chinese verbs, many of them can also be used as nouns). For easy presentation, the words are divided into five groups based on the functional domain of their meanings.

Group 1
(Love and marriage)

裸婚 *luo3hun1* 'naked-wed'
闪婚 *shan3hun1* 'quick-wed'
闪离 *shan3li2* 'quick divorce'
稀饭 *si1fan4* 'rice porridge; like'
开房 *kai1fang2* 'check into a hotel room'
人流 *ren2liu2* 'have an abortion'

The first three terms in Group 1 have to do with marriage. 裸婚 'naked wedding' means a marriage without any materialistic conditions being required by the bride's parents of their future son-in-law, such as a property, a car or a sum of money. A 'naked wedding' can even do away with a wedding ring and keeps only the marriage certificate. 闪婚 'lightning marriage' means to get married soon after a couple's first meeting (from one day to three months, for example). 闪离 'lightning divorce' is the opposite of 闪婚, meaning an agreed divorce soon after the marriage (e.g. from one month to a year). Some example usages of these terms are shown below:

Example 36

a 想   **裸婚,**   丈母娘   不   同意。
   xiang3 luo3hun1   zhang4mu3niang2   bu4   tong2yi4
   'think' 'naked-wed' 'mother-in-law'   'not-' 'agree'
   'I would like to have a naked wedding but my mother-in-law does not agree.'

b 一般   情变   不久   的   女星   很   容易   就   **闪婚!**
   yi4ban1 qing2bian4   bu4jiu3   de5 nv3xing1   hen3 rong2yi4 jiu4 shan3hun1
   'usually' 'love-change' 'not-long' AD 'female-star' 'very' 'easy'   'just' 'flash-wed'
   'Generally, when a female star breaks up (with her ex) she is likely to get married quickly!'

c 结婚   两   月   就   **闪离。**
   jie2hun1 liang3 yue4   jiu4 shan3li2
   'marry' 'two' 'month' 'just' 'flash-part'
   '(They) were married for two months and then quickly divorced.'

Example 36a illustrates the situation where a man would like to have a 'bare wedding' but the prospective mother-in-law would not agree. That is, she expects something from the future son-in-law as a guarantee for her daughter's happiness or as a reward for her raising the child. The author of 36b expresses their opinion about female celebrities' romance patterns, specifically, their inclination to get married quickly after breaking up with their ex-boyfriend. The subjectless sentence in Example 36c is part of a story where a couple divorced each other after being married for two months.

The next item 稀饭 *xi1fan4* 'rice gruel' is a fairly 'distant' near homophone of 喜欢 *xi3huan1* 'like' and is a fashionable replacement for the latter on social networks like Weibo. The phrase 开房 is not a new combination but, like many other new terms, has acquired new meanings in contemporary Chinese society. In most cases, 开房 means a couple (generally single or not spouse to each other if married) checking into a hotel room and having sexual intercourse. The term 人流 is a short form for 人工流产 'artificial abortion' and has become much more frequently used than the full form. 人流 can also sometimes be used to mean 'human flow' or large crowds of people.

Example 37

a 嘴巴　甜　　的　小孩子　　　就　是　惹　　　人　　稀饭。
　zui3ba1 tian2　de5 xiao3hai2zi5 jiu4 shi4 re3　　ren2　xi1fan4
　'mouth' 'sweet' AD 'kid'　　　'just' 'be' 'provoke' 'person' 'like'
　'A child with a sweet mouth is just so likable.'

b 女子　　与　　网友　　开房　　　后　遭　　　勒索。
　nv3zi3　yu3　wang3you3　kai1fang2　hou4 zao1　　le4suo3
　'woman' 'with' 'net-friend' 'open-room' 'after' 'encounter' 'blackmail'
　'A woman was blackmailed after being in a hotel room with a friend she met on the net.'

c 少女　　人流　　　前　　晒图
　shao4nv3　ren2liu2　qian2 shai4tu2
　'young girl' 'abortion' 'prior' 'show-picture'

　称　　　舍不得　　　　双胞胎。
　cheng1　she3bu4de2　　shuang1bao1tai1
　'claim' 'abandon-not-get' 'twin'

　'A young girl shows a picture of twin babies before undergoing abortion, claiming reluctance.'

Example 37a shows 稀饭 being used as a verb, replacing the canonical word 喜欢 'like'. The 开房 used in 37b clearly demonstrates the implications normally associated with the word. That is, the reason for the woman to be blackmailed must have something to do with the earlier event of 开房, which is understood to involve sex and sometimes (secret) photographing or videotaping of nudity. In Example 37c a 19-year-old unmarried girl was reported to have posted on the web the ultrasonic pictures of her unborn twin babies. The reported abortion was later verified by the hospital upon the enquiry of a journalist.

Group 2
(Life and society)

北漂 *bei3piao1* 'Beijing-drift'
上访 *shang4fang3* 'up-visit'
强拆 *qiang2chai1* 'forcefully take apart'
维权 *wei2quan2* 'maintain-right'
维稳 *wei2wen3* 'maintain-stable'
双规 *shuang1gui1* 'double-regulating'

The term 北漂, literally 'north-drift', refers to the migration of people from all over China to Beijing to work, study or do something else. 上访 means to bypass the local jurisdiction and directly appeal to the central government in the hope of achieving justice. Some examples are supplied below:

Example 38

a 大学　　毕业　　的　他　决心　　　与　　她　北漂。
　　da4xue2　bi4ye4　de5 ta1　jue2xin1　yu3　ta1　bei3piao1
　　'university' 'graduate' AD 'he' 'determine' 'with' 'her' 'north-drift'
　　'Having graduated from university, he decided to go to Beijing with her.'

b 地方　　官员　　　没　人　　信任，
　　di4fang1 guan1yuan2 mei2 ren2　xin4ren4
　　'local'　'official'　'no'　'person' 'trust'
　　'The local officials are not trusted by anyone.'

　　常规　　　方法　　无法　　　申冤，　　只有　　上访。
　　chang2gui1 fang1fa3 wu2fa3　shen1yuan1 zhi3you3　shang4fang3
　　'regular'　'method' 'no-method' 'right-wrong' 'only-have' 'up-visit'
　　Conventional methods cannot help redress the injustice, so (people) can
　　only go to the top.'

c 祖国　　　　60　　周　　国庆　　　　期间
　　zu3guo2　　liu4shi2 zhou1 guo2qing4　　qi2jian1
　　'grand-nation' '60'　'cycle' 'nation-celebrate' 'period'
　　'In the period of the sixtieth National Day celebration,

　　妈妈　　因　　上访　　　被　打死。
　　ma1ma5 yin1　shang4fang3 bei4 da3si3
　　'mother' 'because' 'up-visit'　PB　'hit-die'
　　a mother was beaten to death for up-visiting.'

Example 38a illustrates some aspects of the concept 北漂 'drifting to Beijing'; that is, it might occur at a turning point of one's life, such as upon graduation from university. Also, it takes determination to do so, implying it is likely to be a tough process. The author of Example 38a is most likely a young man with a long-term girlfriend whom he intends to bring along to Beijing, probably to set up a career together and ultimately a family. Example 38b shows a different kind of trip to Beijing with a completely different purpose. Here 上访 means for civilians to communicate with higher authorities (the highest being the power center in Beijing) than the local government about an injustice they might have suffered which is impossible to correct under the current jurisdiction. 上访 is rarely effective. In fact, it could be fatal, as Example 38c shows, where a civilian was illegally jailed by the local jurisdiction and beaten to death after many failed attempts to 'up-visit', hoping for intervention from higher authorities which never arrived. The term 祖国, literally 'grandparent's country' or 'motherland', is a clever adoption by the communist party to imprint patriotism and inspire loyalty from Chinese people who are unable to separate their love for the homeland from the authoritarian government running it.

The term 强拆 'forcefully demolish' is very poignant indeed for the people involved in this process, which refers to the forceful action taken by property developers to demolish old buildings with the approval of the government, usually with disproportionally meager compensation for, and despite protests from, existing residents. 维权 'defend rights', is another newly evolved term in the twenty-first century due to the partial opening of the socio-political environment of China. It refers to the actions taken by civilians to defend their homes, properties, and other basic human rights. At the other end, 维稳 'maintain stability' is the primary method adopted by the CCP government to tackle the new domestic issues which have arisen due to improved communication and people's awakening. Essentially, this means the elimination of mass protest activities of all kinds to strengthen the control of the government and 'maintain the stability of society'. The word 双规 'double regulating' is an administrative procedure imposed on members of the CCP who may be involved in government corruption or other unlawful activities. The 双规 process is a kind of 'house arrest' which effectively keeps the suspect in custody for an indefinite period of time (perhaps until they break and confess). 'Double' refers to the designated place and time in which to confine the subject and 'get the truth'.

Example 39

a 俩　老人　　　为　阻止　政府　　　**强拆**　　　自焚，
  lia3 lao3ren2　wei4 zu3zhi3 zheng4fu3　qiang2chai1　zi4fen2
  'two' 'old-person' 'for' 'deter'　'government' 'forceful-tear' 'self-burn'
  'Two older people self-immolated to stop the government's demolition act;

  一　死　一　伤。
  yi4　si3　yi4　shang1
  'one' 'die' 'one' 'hurt'
  one dead, one injured.'

b 村民　　　**维权**　　　　遭到　　暴力　　清场！
  cun1min2　wei2quan2　zao1dao4 bao4li4　qing1chang3
  'village-people' 'maintain-rights' 'receive' 'violence' 'clean-venue'
  'Village people protesting were subject to violent site clearance measures.'

c 党　政府　　　对　外　颁布　　　中国　　　人权　　　法。
  dang3 zheng4fu3　dui4 wai4 ban1bu4　zhong1guo2 ren2quan2　fa3
  'party' 'government' 'to' 'external' 'promulgate' 'China'　'human-right' 'law'
  'The party government announced the Human Rights Action Plan of China to the
  outside world.

  实际　　　上　是　用　高压
  shi2ji4　shang4 shi4 yong4 gao1ya1
  'true-edge' 'up' 'be' 'use' 'high-pressure'
  In truth, it uses political oppression to keep

  维稳　　　国内　　　百姓。
  wei2wen3　guo2nei4　bai3xing4
  'maintain-stable' 'nation-internal' 'hundred-surname'
  the civilians at bay at home.'

d 随着　　　民众　　　人权　　　法治　　意识　　增强，
  sui2zhe5　min2zhong4 ren2quan2　fa3zhi4　yi4shi4　zeng1qiang2
  'follow' AM 'civilians'　'human-right' 'law-rule' 'awareness' 'increase'
  'Following the increased awareness of the general public about human rights
  and lawful government

  对　　**"双规"**　　　的　质疑　声音　　逐渐　　多　起来
  dui4　shuang1gui1　de5 zhi2yi2　sheng1yin1 zhu2jian4 duo1 qi3lai2
  'toward' 'double-regulate' AD 'question' 'voice'　'gradually' 'many' 'rise-up'
  the questioning voices about "double regulation" have become louder.'

Example 39a describes a tragic scene of self-immolation in protest against enforced demolition. Other widely publicized incidents involving 强拆 include civilians being run over and 'flattened' by bulldozers while protesting the demolition. Example 39b reports a similar incident where villagers trying to defend their rights were brutally expelled from the scene. Example 39c is a Weibo netizen's posting, apparently as a result of their long-term observation and retrospection. The word 维稳 'maintain stability' collocates with 高压 'high suppression' in Example 39c, implying known oppressive measures such as suppression of dissent and surveillance of potential activists with possible illegal arrest, imprisonment and torture. Example 39d is another Weibo user's observation regarding people's raised suspicions about 双规 due to increased awareness about human rights and the country's need for independent legal systems.

Group 3
(Vulgar)

爆菊 *bao4ju2* 'explode-anus'
装逼 *zhuang1bi1* 'pretend-cunt'
撸管 *lu1guan3* 'rub-tube'
打飞机 *da3fei1ji1* 'strike-airplane'

The term 爆菊 is derived from 菊花 *ju2hua1* (chrysanthemum), which is a synonym for 'anus' due to their similarity in shape (NB this is a vulgar usage, as are the other terms in this group). 爆菊 means the anus 'explodes' as a result of forceful penetration. 装逼 is also written as 装 B (the same is true with 牛逼 → 牛 B) and is used to refer to a person who is disgustingly pretentious, for example pretending to be knowledgeable, innocent and so on. Both 撸管 and 打飞机 mean (male) 'masturbation'.

Example 40

a 今天　　体检　　　被　爆菊。
  jin1tian1　ti3jian3　　bei4　bao4ju2
  'today'　'body-test'　PB　'explode-chrysanthemum'
  'At my health examination today (my) anus was penetrated.'

b 职务　　越高　　越谦虚，　　职务　　越低　　越装逼。
  zhi2wu4　yue4 gao1　yue4 qian1xu1　zhi2wu4　yue4 di1　yue4 zhuang1bi1
  'position'　'higher'　'humbler'　　'position'　'lower'　'more pretentious'
  'The higher the position, the humbler (the person); the lower the position, the more pretentious.'

c 我　劝　　你　莫　撸管　　吧。撸　多　　伤　　视力。
  wo3　quan4　ni3　mo4　lu1guan3　ba5　lu1　duo1　shang1　shi4li4
  'I'　'advise'　'you'　'not'　'rub-tube'　SFP　'rub'　'much'　'hurt'　'eye sight'
  'I advise you not to masturbate. It hurts your eyesight if you overdo it.'

d 不如　　　宅　　　在　家里，　　看看　　片子，　打打飞机，　多好。
  bu4ru2　　zhai2　　zai4　jia1 li3　kan4kan4　pian4zi5　da3da3fei1ji1　duo1hao3
  'had rather'　'stay indoor'　'at'　'home-inside'　'see'　'video'　'hit-airplane'　'much-good'
  'Might as well stay at home, check out the videos and masturbate. It's great.'

Example 40a refers to a procedure in a health examination where the doctor probes into the rectum with a finger to see if there are piles. 爆菊 is a fun way of referring to this process. The term is also used in sexual settings and for cursing others (by wishing their anus to be 'broken' somehow). Example 40b shows how the word 装逼 is seen as an undesirable behavior associated with the lower classes. It generally refers to people of lower status trying to look more important, rich, pretty or innocent than they really are. Example 40c is a joke that connects masturbation to porn viewing. Example 40d, on the other hand, compares masturbation with another activity (i.e. hanging out) and finds it a better option. There are many other terms which mean the same thing, but currently 撸管 and 打飞机 are in fashion.

Group 4
(Casualty)

爆头 *bao4tou2* 'explode-head'
坑爹 *keng1die1* 'entrap-father'
打枪 *da3qiang1* 'hit-gun'
中枪 *zhong4qiang1* 'sustain-gun'
躺枪 *tang3qiang1* 'lie-gun'

The word 爆头 'headshot', like many other new terms, is believed to originate from game playing contexts (e.g. a zombie receiving a gunshot in the head, which explodes). It is now widely used to refer to homicide scenes, such as in Example 41a, or traffic accidents involving serious injuries to the head. 坑爹 means something like 'I have been cheated' and is used to denounce a person, product or experience. Example 41b is a complaint against a commercial product 'milk partner' advertised in China, accusing it of being more damaging than useful.

Example 41

a 女   护士   婚   后   3   天   遭
   nv3   hu4shi4 hun1   hou4 san1 tian1 zao1
   'woman' 'nurse' 'marriage' 'after' '3' 'day' 'encounter'

钢管   **爆头**。
gang1guan3 bao4tou2
'steel pipe' 'explode-head'

'A nurse was fatally injured in the head by a steel pipe three days after her marriage.'

b 奶伴侣   有   害   无   益,   **坑爹**   的 产品!
   nai3ban4lv3 you3 hai4 wu2 yi4   keng1die1   de5 chan3pin3
   'milk company' 'have' 'harm' 'no' 'benefit' 'cheat-dad' AD 'product'
   'The so-called milk partner does more damage than good. It's a fraudulent product!'

The word 打枪, literally 'strike the gun' or to fire a gun, means to reject, defeat or slander someone. It often means to reject approaches from a person of the opposite sex. Example 42a, for example, is said by someone mocking their friend for being turned down by a girl while trying to get a date. Note that the verb morpheme 闲 'unoccupied' in this example is possibly an 'intentional mistake' of 嫌 'pick fault', which is a homophone and the correct verb in this context. Using intentional mistypes and playing on homophones for fun is a common behavior on Chinese social networks today.

Example 42

a　妹妹　　　　　闲　你　老　啦，被　**打枪**　　了　吧
　　mei4mei5　xian2　ni3　lao3　la5　bei4　da3qiang1　le5　ba5
　　'younger-sister' 'detest' 'you' 'old' SFP　PB　'hit-gun'　AM　SFP
　　'The girl finds you too old, man. You are turned down, aren't you?'

b　全球　　　　20　大　水患　　　　城　　中国
　　quan2qiu2　er4shi2　da4　shui3huan4　cheng2　zhong1guo2
　　'whole-ball' '20'　'big' 'water-trouble' 'city'　'China'
　　'Among the 20 cities in the world suffering the most from floods,

　　5　市　　"**中枪**"
　　wu3　shi4　zhong4qiang1
　　'5'　'city'　'sustain-hit'
　　5 cities in China get hit.'

c　他　死　了　五　年
　　ta1　si3　le5　wu3　nian2
　　'he' 'die' AM '5'　'year'
　　'Even though he has been dead for years,

　　还是　　被　人　　拉　　出来　　**躺枪**　　　了　呀
　　hai2shi4　bei4　ren2　la1　chu1lai2　tang3qiang1　le5　ya5
　　'still'　PB　'person' 'drag' 'out'　'lie-gun'　AM　SFP
　　he still cannot escape being implicated.'

d　人行道　　　上　　被　撞，
　　ren2xing2dao4　shang4　bei4　zhuang4
　　'sidewalk'　　'up'　PB　'hit'
　　'Hit (by a vehicle) on a sidewalk,

　　学生　　　　**躺着也中枪**
　　xue2sheng1　tang3　zhe5　ye3　zhong4qiang1
　　'student'　'lie-AM-also-sustain-gun'
　　unlucky student got involved.'

The word 中枪 means something like 'to be hit by a stray bullet'; that is, one probably has not done anything wrong but sustains damage anyway. It is used predominantly in a non-physical sense, referring to a verbal attack rather than a bodily injury. Example 42b illustrates a usage of 中枪, where five of the cities in China are said to be on the list of the 20 most flooded cities in the world. The gun metaphor helps generate an image of five cities (along with China) being hit by bullets, sustaining injury.

躺枪 'receiving a gunshot while lying down' means essentially the same as 中枪 'receiving a gunshot'. A person who is said to 躺枪, though, is even more unlucky and undeserving. Example 42c, for example, shows the victim of the act being already dead. However, he is still dragged out from his grave and verbally attacked. A longer version of 躺枪 is 躺着也中枪 'getting shot while lying down', Example 42d, shows how this phrase is used to describe the bad luck of a student – getting hit by a car on the sidewalk.

Group 5
(Action and reaction)

喷 *pen1* 'spurt'
添乱 *tian1luan4* 'add-confusion'
石化 *shi2hua4* 'petrifaction'
毁三观 *hui3san1guan1* 'destroy-three-view'
hold 不住 *hold bu2zhu4* 'cannot hold'

The monosyllabic verb 喷 originally meant to 'spit' or 'spurt'. In the social network context, it has come to mean 'verbally abuse'. Example 43a is a 'disclaimer' which rules out the possibility that the article in question represents a serious opinion. Therefore, the author should not be subject to any verbal attacks. The verb 添乱 means to 'add more trouble on top of existing confusion'. An example usage is shown in Example 43b.

Example 43

a 娱乐　　　　　之　作···　不　喜　勿　　喷···
   yu2le4　　　　zhi1　zuo4　bu4　xi3　wu4　　pen1
   'entertainment'　AD　'work'　'not'　'like'　'do not'　'attack'
   'This article is only for entertainment. Do not attack it even if you don't like it.'

b 路上　　　　早已　　　人满为患，
   lu4shang4　zao3yi3　ren2man3wei2huan4
   'road-up'　'already'　'people-full-as-worry'
   'There are already lots of people jammed on the road.

   你　　就　　别　　　再　　去　　添乱　　　　了。
   ni3　jiu4　bie2　zai4　qu4　tian1luan4　le5
   'you'　'just'　'do not'　'again'　'go'　'add trouble'　SFP
   No need for you to add to the numbers.'

The word 石化 literally 'turn into stone', describes a person's reaction to something extraordinary. That is, the person is shocked and rendered immobile and speechless. The term 毁三观 'destroy three views' describes something very extreme, very extraordinary and totally incomprehensible. The three views are generally thought to mean a person's views about life, the world and values. The term *hold* 不住 means to 'lose control' of oneself or the situation at hand. The opposite term is *hold* 住 or *hold* 得住, which means to 'keep oneself or things under control'.

Example 44

a　没　　看　　过　　这么　　大片　　向日葵　　的　我
　mei2 kan4 guo4 zhe4mo5 da4pian4 xiang4ri4kui2 de5 wo3
　'not' 'see' AM 'such' 'big' Cla 'sunflower' AD 'I'

　瞬间　　　　石化　　　　了。
　shun4jian1 shi2hua4 le5
　'instantly' 'stone turn' SFP

　'I who have never seen such a large field of sunflowers am instantly petrified.'

b　真是　　　毁三观，　　这么　　多　　人
　zhen1shi4 hui3san1guan1 zhe4mo5 duo1 ren2
　'really-is' 'detroy-3-view' 'such' 'many' 'person'

　维护　　　一个　　杀人犯。
　wei2hu4 yi2ge5 sha1ren2fan4
　'defend' 'one' Cla 'kill-person-offender'

　'All our views on life, the world and values are overturned. So many people defend a murderer.'

c　**hold**不住　　了，太　　　萌　　了！
　hold bu2zhu4 le5 tai4 meng2 le5
　'hold-not-stay' SFP 'excessively' 'cute' SFP
　'I can no longer compose myself. So lovely!'

In Example 44a, the word 石化 describes the reaction of the author at the sight of a magnificent sunflower field. The author of 44b feels amazed at the unusual phenomenon of many people defending a homicide perpetrator. Example 44c shows the author being unable to control their emotion (of admiration) when seeing a lovely child or small animal.

Group 5
(Media exposure)

吐槽 *tu4cao2* 'vomit-trough'
爆料 *bao4liao4* 'expose-material'
自曝 *zi4pu4* 'self-expose'
赚眼球 *zhuan4yan3qiu2* 'earn-eyeball'

The term 吐槽, literally 'vomit into the trough', means to openly reveal someone's weaknesses with no regard for their feelings. 爆料, 'offering explosive materials', means to expose something irregular, unlawful or things like celebrity gossip to the general public. 自曝 'self-expose' means to reveal one's own secret(s) to the public. The term 赚眼球 'earn the eyeball' means to catch the public's attention through media exposure.

Example 45

a 许多　　　新生　　　　　"狂　　吐槽",
　 xu3duo1　xin1sheng1　　kuang2　tu4cao2
　 'many'　'new-student'　'madly'　'speak-ill'
　 'Many freshmen openly spoke ill of their schools,

　 抱怨　　　　校规　　　　　　　太严。
　 bao4yuan4　xiao4gui1　　　　　　tai4yan2
　 'complain'　'school-regulation'　'too-stern'
　 complaining about the stern regulations.'

b 日本　　　女星　　　　爆料
　 ri4ben3　nv3xing1　　bao4liao4
　 'Japan'　'female-star'　'expose-material'
　 'A Japanese female star reveals

　 韩国　　　　男　　偶像　　　　床技　　　　差。
　 han2guo2　nan2　ou3xiang4　　chuang4ji4　cha1
　 'Korea'　'male-idol'　　'bed-skill'　'inferior'
　 the poor love making skills of a male Korean celebrity idol.'

c 地铁　　　乞讨者　　　自曝：
　 di4tie3　qi3tao3 zhe3　zi4pu4
　 'subway'　'beg-person'　'self-expose'
　 'A subway beggar self-reveals that

　 一　　月　　　能　　赚　　　万　　　　　元。
　 yi2　yue4　　neng2　zhuan4　wan4　　　　yuan2
　 'one'　'month'　'can'　'earn'　'10 thousand'　'dollar'
　 they can earn ten thousand dollars a month.'

d 车模　　　争艳　　　　　搔首弄姿　　　　　　　　赚眼球。
　 che1mo2　zheng1yan4　　sao1shou3nong4zi1　　　　zhuan4yan3qiu2
　 'car-model'　'compete-colorful'　'scratch-head-adjust-pose'　'earn-eyeball'
　 'Models at car shows compete with each other, doing their best to get people's attention.'

Example 45a shows how the word 吐槽 is used to describe a group of students' unrestrained criticisms of their new·school. Example 45b may be the title of a piece of gossip news, where 爆料 refers to the revelation of an alleged weakness of a celebrated idol. Example 45c illustrates how the word 自曝 is used in context where someone willingly or involuntarily reveals a secret about themself which is otherwise unlikely to be found out. Example 45d demonstrates a situation where the term 赚眼球 is often used; that is, staging some kind of lively performance or visually appealing scene to catch people's attention.

6.2.6 Colloquial expressions

This category of new words involves colloquial expressions and newly assembled phrases to express novel concepts, complicated ideas, or taboo items on the web. Four groups of new terms are distinguished in this section to facilitate discussion.

Group 1
(Swear words)

尼玛 *ni2ma3* 'you-mother'
TMD (*ta1ma1de5*) 'his-mother's'
卧槽 *wo4cao2* 'oh-fuck'
次奥 *ci4ao4* 'fuck'

The words in Group 1 are new combinations used by netizens to denote taboo meanings. 尼玛 replaces 你妈 which is a short form for 操你妈 *cao1ni3ma1* 'fuck-you(r)-mum'. TMD has come to stand for *ta1ma1de5* or 他妈的 literally 'his mother's' used for light swearing. 卧槽 is a euphemistic replacement for 我操 *wo3cao1* 'I-fuck'. 卧槽 and 尼玛 can sometimes be seen together as 卧槽尼玛 (or 卧槽泥马) on the web, which would be the strongest swearing form in this strand. 次奥 is synonymous with 操 which probably came about through a 'reverse sandhi' process (that is, the original sound *cao* was split into two sounds *ci* and *ao*).

Example 46

a 尼玛，　　　　你的　　脚　　踩　　　住　我的　　脚　　了。
　　ni2ma3　　　　ni3de5　jiao3　cai3　　　zhu4　wo3de5　jiao3　le5
　　'you-mother'　'your'　'foot'　'step on'　Com　'my'　　'foot'　AM
　　'Damn! Your foot is on my foot.'

b **TMD**　　　　是不是　　　心　被　狗　吃　了?
　　t-m-d　　　　　shi4bu2shi4　xin1　bei4　gou3　chi1　le5
　　'he-mother-AD'　'be-not-be'　'heart'　PB　'dog'　'eat'　AM
　　'Asshole, is (his) heart eaten by the dog?'

c **卧槽**　　　　好　美　啊　神　一样　　的　摄影　　　　师。
　　wo4cao2　　　　hao3　mei3　a5　shen2　yi2yang4　de5　she4ying3　　shi1
　　'prone-trough'　'so'　'pretty'　SFP　'god'　'same'　　AD　'photography'　'master'
　　'Fuck me! So beautiful! The photographer is like a god.'

d **次奥**　差点　　给　我　吓　　尿　了。
　　ci4ao4　cha4dian3　gei3　wo3　xia4　　niao4　le5
　　'fuck'　'almost'　　'give'　'me'　'frighten'　'urine'　SFP
　　'Fuck! I was so scared I almost peed my pants.'

The various sentences in Example 46 show the swear words being predominantly used as an independent element at the beginning of a sentence and they do not participate in the syntactic formation of the ensuing sentences. Since they are euphemized forms, they also seem less offensive than the original forms.

Group 2
(Dialect)

神马 *shen2ma3* 'what'
酱紫 *jiang4zi3* 'like that'
肿么样 *zhong3mo5yang4* 'how about'
有木有 *you3mu4you3* 'yes or no'

This group of words is mostly nonsensical combinations which, on the surface, do not offer good semantic interpretations. This is because they originate from non-standard Chinese dialect pronunciations transcribed in similar-sounding Chinese characters. The characters are meant to represent original accents, which nevertheless express meanings different to those normally represented by the orthography. For example, 神马, literally 'god-horse' is a phonetic assimilation of 甚么 *shen2mo5* 'what' pronounced this way in a certain dialect. 酱紫 'sauce-purple' means 'like so', a phonetic assimilation of 这样子 *zhe4yang4zi5* (spoken quickly and with a Taiwanese accent). Likewise, 肿么样 (nonsensical) is an assimilation of 怎么样 'how about?'; 有木有 'have-wood-have', that of 有没有 'have-not-have?'. Example usages of these items are shown in Example 47.

Example 47

a 外界　　　的　**神马**　　都　是　浮云
  wai4jie4 de5 shen2ma3 dou1 shi4 fu2yun2
  'outside' AD 'what'　　'all' 'be' 'float-cloud'
  'Everything in the external world is floating cloud.'

b 8　年　　来　都　**酱紫**,　以后　　也　不会　变。
  ba1 nian2 lai2　dou1 jiang4zi3 yi3hou4　ye3 bu2hui4 bian4
  '8' 'year' 'since' 'all' 'like this' 'afterward' 'also' 'not-will' 'change'
  'It has been like this for eight years, and it will not change in the future.'

c 上班　　　　第一　天　的　你　感觉　**肿么样**?
  shang4ban1 di4yi1 tian1 de5 ni3　gan3jue2 zhong3mo5yang4
  'on duty'　'first' 'day' AD 'you' 'feel'　'how about'
  'How do you feel about being on duty the first day?'

d 好　想　　去　旅游　的　童鞋　　**有木有**?
  hao3 xiang3 qu4 lv3you2 de5 tong2xie2　you3mu4you3
  'very' 'think' 'go' 'travel'　AD 'child-shoe' 'have-not-have'
  'Are there any people out there who would like to go travelling?'

Example 47a shows 神马 appearing in an idiomatic structure 神马都是浮云 (originally 甚么都是浮云) meaning 'everything is transient and temporary'. The nonsensical character combination, 酱紫, a 'spoof' version of 这样子, means 'like this' in 47b. The term 肿么样 (怎么样) 'how about', Example 47c, is used to form a question. The A-not-A structure in 47d, a dialect version of 有没有, also makes the sentence into a question.

Group 3
(Fixed expression)

你懂的 *ni3dong3de5* 'you understand'
伤不起 *shang1bu4qi3* 'cannot afford to be hurt'
给跪了 *gei3gui4le5* 'kneel before you'
长见识了 *zhang3jian4shi4le5* 'knowledge increased'
弱弱的问一句 *ruo4ruo4de5wen4yi2ju4* 'timidly ask a question'

Items in Group 3 are mostly short sentences or phrases that can be used independently. 你懂的 is a short sentence which assumes mutual understanding between the author and the reader(s). When this item is used, it usually implies a lot is left unsaid, which the readers should automatically understand. 伤不起

describes a person or persons as fragile, who 'cannot afford to be hurt'. 给跪了 is a short form for 我给你跪下了 'I hereby kneel down before you' and is used when one feels awestruck and speechless. 长见识了 '(my) knowledge is increased', usually co-occurs with a sentence incorporating a new discovery the author has just made. 弱弱的问一句 'feebly asking a question' expresses a self-effacing attitude accompanying what seems a very stupid question.

Example 48

a
生日	快乐	啦	N年	兄弟	不	多	说	**你懂的**
sheng1ri4	kuai4le4	la5	n nian2	xiong1di4	bu4	duo1	shuo1	ni3dong3de5
'birthday'	'happy'	SFP	'n-years'	'brothers'	'not'	'much'	'speak'	'you-understand-ED'

'Happy birthday! We have been brothers for numerous years. No need to say more. You know what I mean.'

b
10月	份	了	还有	台风	**伤不起**	啊！
shi2yue4	fen4	le5	hai2you3	tai2feng1	shang1bu4qi3	a5
'October'	'portion'	SFP	'still''have'	'typhoon'	'cannot afford to be hurt'	SFP

'It's October and we still have typhoons. Please don't hurt us. We are fragile.'

c
6	格	漫画，	斑马	的	故事。	看	完	我	**给跪了…**
liu4	ge2	man4hua4	ban1ma3	de5	gu4shi5	kan4	wan2	wo3	gei3gui4le5
'six'	'square'	'comic'	'zebra'	PD	'story'	'read'	Com	'I'	'give-kneel' SFP

'Six-panel comic, a zebra's story. I totally gave up after reading it . . .'

d
长见识了，	原来	外国	也	有	小	摊贩	啊！
zhang3jian4shi4 le5	yuan2lai2	wai4guo2	ye3	you3	xiao3	tan1fan4	a5
'grow-knowledge-AM'	'turn out'	'foreign nation'	'also'	'have'	'small'	'vendor'	SFP

'My knowledge has just grown. I did not know there were street vendors in foreign countries.'

e
弱弱的问一句，	碰到	暖气	片	会	被	烫伤	么？
ruo4ruo4de5wen4yi2ju4	peng4dao4	nuan3qi4	pian4	hui4	bei4	tang4shang1	mo5
'weakly ask a question'	'touch' Com	'heater'	'slice'	'will'	PB	'burn-hurt'	QM

'Can I ask a stupid question: will I get hurt if I touch the radiator panel?'

The author of Example 48a, by using 你懂的, implies that his long-term friend knows what he wants to say. The 伤不起 in 48b reveals the fragile nature of humans in the face of a natural disaster. Example 48c refers to a 6-panel comic where a panda transfers some of its blackness to a white horse, turning it into a zebra. 给跪了 shows the author's feeling of awe after viewing the comic – utter admiration and some dumbfoundedness. The author of 48d, on the other hand, obviously thought street vendors only existed in China. After discovering they also live in foreign countries, the author uses the term 长见识了 to show the increase in their knowledge and the impact of this process on their mind. Finally, the author in 48e asks a seemingly unimportant and stupid question. Note that when using 弱弱的问一句, the author is normally asking a genuine question whose answer they are eager to know. They use the expression because they think the answer must be obvious to everyone else.

Group 4
(Abbreviation)

何弃疗 *he2qi4liao2* 'why giving up treatment?'
十动然拒 *shi2dong4ran2ju4* 'very touched then reject'
男默女泪 *nan2mo4nv3lei4* 'man silent woman cry'
人艰不拆 *ren2jian1bu4chai1* 'life is hard: be considerate'
不明觉厉 *bu4ming2jue2li4* 'not understanding but find formidable'
累觉不爱 *lei4jue2bu2ai4* 'feel tired and can longer like'

The new terms in Group 4 are each an 'abbreviation' of a longer phrase, much like English abbreviations. This is a striking new development in the Chinese language as a result of web-based written communication. 何弃疗, for example, is an abbreviated form of **何必放弃治疗** 'why give up treatment?' 十动然拒 stands for **十**分感**动然**后**拒**绝 'Although extremely moved, still declining (the offer)' and is primarily used for a woman to turn down the advances of a man despite his touching courting behavior. 男默女泪 means **男**的沉**默，女**的流**泪** 'Men fall silent; women weep' after reading a story. 人艰不拆 is more difficult to interpret. The phrase originated from the lyric of a pop song **人**生已如此 的**艰**难，有些事情就**不**要**拆**穿 'Life is hard enough; try not to expose certain things (i.e. at least to maintain some dignity)'. 不明觉厉 introduces an interesting concept 虽然**不明**白，但是感**觉**很**厉**害 'Although the message is not understandable, it seems powerful and profound'. 累觉不爱 is the short form for 很**累**，感**觉**自己**不**会再**爱**了 'I am so tired I feel I can no longer fall in love again'. Example 49 shows how these extraordinary new terms are skillfully used in real-life settings by a new generation of Chinese speakers.

Example 49

a 大晚上　　　　　整个　　　寝室　　　　　　打电话
da4wan3shang4　zheng3ge5　qin3shi4　　　da3dian4hua4
'big-night'　　　　'entire'　　'sleep-chamber' 'make phone call'
'On such an evening (she) made phone calls all over the dormitory

让　　别人　　　收　　　快递　　　　　**何弃疗**。
rang4　bie2ren2　shou1　kuai4di4　　　he2qi4liao2
'let'　'others'　'receive' 'special delivery' 'why-abandon-treatment'
asking people to take a special delivery. Why did she give up psychotherapy anyway?'

b 男生　　　　堆　　1314　　　　　　　　　个　　雪人　　　表白
nan2sheng1　dui1　yi4qian1san1bai3yi1shi2si4　ge5　xue3ren2　biao3bai2
'boy'　　　　'pile'　'1314'　　　　　　　　　Cla　'snowman'　'confess'
'A man made 1314 snowmen to bare his heart to the girl,

女孩　　　"十动然拒"。
nv3hai2　shi2dong4ran2ju4
'girl'　　　'very touched but refuse'
who was very touched but declined.'

c 原来　　　　你的　　名字　　　背后　　　藏　　着　　如此　　**男默女泪**　　　的　　故事。
yuan2lai2　ni3de5　ming2zi4　bei4hou4　cang2　zhe5　ru2ci3　nan2mo4nv3lei4　de5　gu4shi5
'turn out'　'your'　'name'　　'behind'　'hide'　AM　'such'　'man silent　　　AD　'story'
　　　　　　　　　　　　　　　　　　　　　　　　　　women cry'
'Never realized a story which makes men silent and women cry is hidden behind
your name.'

d **人艰不拆**　　　　　　宝马　　　停车　　　数　　　小时
ren2jian1bu4chai1　　bao3ma3　ting2che1　shu4　xiao3shi2
'life-hard-not-reveal' 'BMW'　'park-car'　'several'　'hour'
'Life is too hard to bear – A BMW was parked for a few hours and

四　车轮　　　不翼而飞。
si4　che1lun2　bu2yi4er2fei1
'4'　'car-wheel'　'no-wing-but-fly'
all four wheels disappeared.'

e 国宝　　　　　　在　　美国　　　遭遇　　　**不明觉厉**　　　的　　老外　　　围观。
guo2bao3　　　zai4　mei3guo2　zao1yu4　bu4ming2jue2li4　de5　lao3wai4　wei2guan1
'nation-treasure' 'at'　'USA'　　'encounter'　'not-know-　　AD　'foreigner' 'surround-
　　　　　　　　　　　　　　　　　　　　　feel-strong'　　　　　　　　　　view'
'Our national treasure is viewed by crowds in the USA who do not understand but
feel great.'

f 对　　　巴黎　　逐渐　　　**累觉不爱**……
dui4　　ba1li2　zhu2jian4　lei4jue2bu2ai4
'toward' 'Paris' 'gradually' 'tired-feel-no-love'
'(I) gradually feel tired (of my ordeals) and find (I can) no longer love Paris.'

The author in Example 49a uses 何弃疗 to imply that the girl who made indiscreet phone calls all over the dormitory in the night was a psycho and should really resume her treatment (in a mental hospital). 十动然拒 in 49b is used to describe the unhappy ending of a courtship, where the procedure was touching but the result was disappointing. Example 49c refers to the sad story behind a name (a man naming his daughter after his previous girlfriend whom he deeply loved but could not marry). The phrase 男默女泪 refers either to a sad story like this or to any story that contains a negative element which the author feels unable to do anything about. The 人艰不拆 in 49d is mainly used to lament a sad situation and perhaps to call for some sympathy. 不明觉厉, originally used to refer to a post on the web which looks abstruse but seems profound, is applied to people admiring an intriguing foreign object in 49e. Finally, the author of the weibo (as an item of posting on Weibo is called) from which Example 49f is extracted, first complains about several unpleasant incidents she encountered in Paris (passport and money getting stolen, being unjustly fined in the underground, undelivered bank cards, weird landlord...) and then concludes with the remark that she can no longer fall in love with Paris, using the phrase 累觉不爱 to express the frustration.

6.3 METHODS FOR CREATING NEW WORDS

There are several routes from which the new words and phrases discussed in 6.2 are created. Most of the word-formation methods discussed here are only made possible through the web – it is a written language based platform and large quantities of information spread quickly.

6.3.1 Homophones and near homophones

As there are fewer than 2,000 usable syllable-tone combinations in Chinese, many slots in the syllable-tone matrix are incredibly crowded with homophones representing different meanings. For example, the syllable *sha1* (first tone alone) has 30 homophones, some frequently used ones being 杀 'kill', 沙 'sand', 鲨 'shark' and so on, all spoken in the same way. Also, as most of the Chinese input methods are sound-based (using Pinyin), it is easy to pick up homophones instead of the intended characters when typing into the computer. As a result, intentional or unintentional creations of new words appear on the web every day, some of which catch on and become established alternatives to existing words.

A notable example is 杯具 *bei1ju4* 'cup-utensil' originally meaning 'glasses' but now widely used in place of 悲剧 *bei1ju4* 'tragedy' in informal, mostly web-based settings. Sometimes only one character is replaced, such as the nonsensical new combination of 民煮 *min2zhu3* 'people-cook' in place of the canonical 民主 *min2zhu3* 'democracy' in some web postings.

Still more difficult to interpret are the near homophones which do not sound exactly the same as the intended units; for example, 盆友 *pen2you3* 'pot-friend' has become a fashionable replacement for 朋友 peng2you3 'friend' on social networks. 涨姿势 zhang3zi1shi4 'swell-posture' is also a new invention, used by some netizens to replace 长知识 zhang3zhi1shi4 'grow knowledge' which is itself a new term.

In some cases, the new terms differ from the old ones only in tones; for example, 油菜花 you2cai4hua1 'canola flower' is used as a replacement for 有才华 you3cai2hua2 'have talents' by some netizens. A similar case is 草泥马 cao3ni2ma3 'grass-mud-horse' which is used to replace the swear word 操你妈 cao1ni3ma1 'fuck-you(r)-mum'.

Through using homophones the writer allows the reader to access the exact or similar sounds of the intended lexical unit, but the reader fails to retrieve the correct entry immediately due to a mismatch between the meaning represented by the orthography and the meaning dictated by the context. The reader is forced to reprocess the sentence through a direct interaction between phonology (i.e. reconsidering the sounds of the incompatible unit) and the result of sentence processing (i.e. a semantic-pragmatic representation of the rest of the sentence) in order to retrieve the correct item (i.e. the intended lexical unit) from the mental lexicon. By this time the intended effect will have been achieved (i.e. for fun, to baffle the reader, to show one's wit and so on).

By using homophones, the authors also seem to distance themselves from the emotional or attitudinal involvement embedded in the original words. In some cases, using homophones also helps the authors avoid political implications, or bypass the Weibo keyword-based censorship (so the message is not filtered out because it contains politically sensitive words, such as 正腐 'is rotting', 六四 'June 4' and so on, before posting, and can be retrieved after posting by the general public via the Weibo search function as it is not on the blacklist).

Another way of forming new words is to create new meanings for old words or phrases. In other words, an original orthographic representation acquires a new meaning on top of existing meanings. For example, 马甲 'horse-armor (vest)' acquires the new meaning of 'socket puppet account', referring to the extra IDs a person registers on a forum or social network to support the original account or for other purposes. The phrase 不约而同 'coincide with each other by accident' acquires the new meaning of 'unable to get a date so become homosexual'.

6.3.2 Derivational process

New words are also created from derivational processes, as Figure 6.1 shows, where a morpheme in a lexical unit is used to create related words centering around the core concept represented by the original word. When a new word is created, especially when it represents a new concept, more new words will be spawned based on that word and the concept it represents. Again, the example of 粉丝 'fans' illustrated in Figure 6.1 is relevant.

The easiest way to create new terms is perhaps to take the initial portion (e.g. the first morpheme) of a word and add a second part to create a fresh combination. For example, when 腐女 literally 'rotten woman', meaning 'women who fancy boy-boy love', establishes itself as a new term, new words like 腐书 'rotten-book (gay book)', 腐文化 'rotten-culture (gay culture)', 腐国 'rotten-country (referring to the UK due to its gay culture fancied by the Chinese netizens)' follow.

Using the last element of a new term to generate a battery of similar words is also a common process. For example, 淘宝体 is one of the first new terms to be adopted in the 'stylistics' strand of neologisms, all of which contain a suffix-like morpheme 体 'style'. Other new words include 甄环体, 元芳体 – see Example 22, 咆哮体 'shouting style – a style of writing which uses a lot of exclamation marks!!!', *TVB* 体 'a talking style imitating characters in popular dramas broadcast by Television Broadcasts Limited Hong Kong' and so on.

A term quickly coming into fashion, 绿茶婊 'green-tea-prostitute', was coined after the Hainan Sanya Rendezvous sex party scandal disseminated on Weibo in April 2013. The term refers to the many fashionably dressed young lovely girls (looking like pure green tea) appearing on the photos of the suspected sex party allegedly waiting to be picked up by rich 富二代 and male celebrities. Since then a number of similar terms have appeared using the same 婊 ending, such as 星巴克婊 'Starbucks whore', 汉子婊 'man whore', 草莓婊 'strawberry whore' and so on.

6.3.3 Local accents Romanized

Some new terms are Romanized items from regional dialects which share the same meaning with their counterparts in Mandarin but have somewhat different pronunciations. The most popular term may be 有木有, seen in Examples 29a and 47d, which is equivalent to the Mandarin version 有没有 'have or not have'.

Some of the dialect-based new words are easily recognizable if the regional accents for these terms are reasonably close to Mandarin pronunciation, such as the 有木有 above. Others will not be so easily recognizable and will have to be learned; for example, 偶 *ou3* is 我 *wo3* 'I' pronounced with a Taiwanese accent.

The most difficult new terms based on dialects are words and phrases that exist only in that dialect. These have to be learned the hard way, even by native Chinese speakers. The sentence in Example 50, for example, contains a non-standard lexical unit which most Chinese native speakers will not know the first time they see it.

> *Example 50*
>
> 这些　　千奇百怪　　　　的　"世界第一"　的
> zhe4xie1 qian1qi2bai3guai4 de5 shi4jie4 di4yi1 de5
> 'these' 'totally strange' AD 'world' 'first' AD
> 'All these various kinds of world number one,
>
> "面子　　工程"　　　　背后，　究竟　　有　　多少　　　猫腻？
> mian4zi5 gong1cheng2 bei4hou4 jiu4jing4 you3 duo1shao3 mao1ni4
> 'face' 'engineering' 'behind' 'exactly' 'have' 'how much' 'cat-urine'
> pompous-looking constructions, exactly how many dodgy dealings are
> behind them?'

The term 猫腻 'cat-bored', a (popular) typo of 猫溺 'cat-urine', is said to originate from the Beijing indigenous dialect, meaning something hidden, dodgy and suspicious. In Example 50, the author speculates about the underlying reasons for some recently planned 'world No. 1' constructions in China, using the word 猫腻 to imply possible foul deeds.

Another interesting process of forming new words, similar to dialect Romanization, is through the direct transliteration of English expressions. For example, 闹太套 *nao4tai4tao4* stands for 'Not at all', a term coined by netizens to ridicule a Chinese singer's English pronunciation in his song. 爱老虎油 *ai4lao3hu3you2* 'love-tiger-oil' stands for 'I love you'.

6.3.4 Media catchphrases

A lot of new terms and expressions are extracted from TV dramas or certain widely disseminated postings on the web. Often the initial phase of creation involves the direct transportation of the phrase from the media to a post, such as 元芳，此事你怎么看? 'Yuanfang, how do you look at this matter?' taken from 神探狄仁杰 'Detective Di Renjie'. The second phase then sees the original form being modified, usually into a more compact form; for example, 此事 is removed from the original script and the shorter form 元芳，你怎么看? becomes the more popular version. In the third phase, a keyword from the new expression may be further extracted to stand alone and represent the essence of the initial concept or to combine with other elements to form new expressions. For example, in 元芳，那院长，会做何种判断? 'Yuanfang, how will the dean make his judgment?' where only the keyword 元芳 is kept. This process is graphically illustrated in Figure 6.2.

Weibo is itself a giant machine for creating neologisms. A famous sentence, 我和我的小伙伴们都惊呆了 'I and my little companions are all terribly shocked', appears in a weibo in 2011, originally posted as part of the handwritten and photographed text composed by a primary school student. While the original

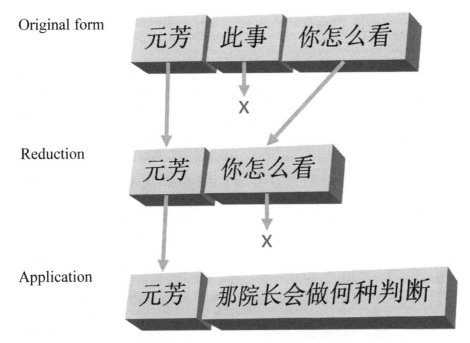

Figure 6.2 The three phases of media catchphrase adaptation

form is still widely used for its idiomatic essence and comic value, netizens quickly developed a compact form 我伙呆 'I-companion-dumb', which is an abbreviated version of the original expression. At the application stage, related expressions using the core elements appear, each with some additional elements nonexistent in the original construction, for example, 我伙已呆, 我伙彻底呆了 and so on.

6.3.5 Abbreviations

Abbreviation as a method for creating new terms has become fashionable recently. The prototypical process is to collect a group of 3–4 words or phrases, and take one character from each word or phrase to form an acronym. For example, the new term 喜大普奔 'happy, big, general, run' is extracted from the set {喜闻乐见、大快人心、普天同庆、奔走相告} taking the first character from each quadrisyllabic unit. Sometimes the process is reversed, and an existing term is given a new interpretation. For example, 蛋白质 'egg-white-material (protein)' has been reinterpreted by some netizens as an acronym extracted from the set of three words {笨蛋、白痴、神经质} 'stupid-*egg* (fool), white-*mad* (idiot), nerve-*material* (apprehensive)'.

Another method in this strand is to take a longer phrase or sentence and select a subset of characters from it to represent the phrase or sentence. 我伙呆 mentioned in 6.3.4 is an example. Other examples include 人干事

'human-do-matter' abbreviated from 这是人干的事吗？ 'Is this something a person is capable of doing?' and 细思恐极 'detailed-think-horrible-extreme' for 仔细想想，觉得恐怖至极 'If you think about it carefully, you will feel extremely terrified'. For these new terms, it is almost impossible for the novice reader to derive their meanings independently without referring to the original expression.

Some new phrases can be expanded into full sentences, such as 火钳刘明, or more accurately 火前留名 'fire-prior-leave-name', being interpreted as 在帖子变火前留下姓名 'leave my name (in the comment region of a promising post) before it gains widespread popularity (so my name will be noticed too)'. However, unlike 人干事 or 细思恐极, the term itself can be understood without referring to the fuller expressions, therefore it is an original term rather than an abbreviation.

6.3.6 Orthographical play

Many Chinese characters are put together by radicals and other basic characters. For example, 明 'bright' is composed of 日 'sun' and 月 'moon'. 李 'plum' comprises a 木 'wood' character on top of 子 'son'. This aspect of Chinese writing is taken advantage of by the netizens to create novel orthographical representations in a fun way. For example, 强 'strong' can be rewritten as 弓虽 and 神 'god' as 礻申. The new dual-character representation takes double space and confounds the reader not used to reading this layout, achieving the desired effect. This is also said to be a deliberate tactic to defeat the Weibo censorship when certain keywords become politically sensitive and are included in the black list.

6.4 CONCLUSION

We have examined around 150 new words and expressions in this chapter, with an extensive range of real examples selected from Weibo to illustrate how the new terms are used in context. New words are being invented and disseminated every day, and new ways of creating new words and expressions discovered every now and then. By familiarizing ourselves with the current neologisms and the different machineries for creating them, we are one step closer to the future Chinese language which may look even more different from traditional Chinese in 100 years' time.

As the main source of new words discussed in this chapter (i.e. the Sina Weibo social networking website) only came into existence in 2009, the work presented here is of a highly pioneering nature. Therefore, the classification method is tentative and the inclusion of new words is by no means exhaustive. In 10, or even as short as five years' time, some of the new words and expressions discussed here will have gone out of fashion. Some will stand the test of time, while still more neologisms will be invented. The Chinese language is evolving at an accelerated speed with the help of the internet.

The Chinese virtual community is a formidable powerhouse, pushing for change in both language and ways of life. This chapter only touches upon vocabulary in a superficial fashion. More subtle and long-lasting changes in syntax and morphology may also be happening which are worthy of further investigation. Obviously, the changes brought about by online social networks are not limited to language. With more and more Chinese people looking for truth, fairness and sustainability in society, cultural and political changes are not only possible but inevitable. Language on the web, while constantly transforming itself, is helping to change everything involving the use of language – which means all human activities in society.

Bibliography

Bai, J. (2009). *Chinese Grammar Made Easy: A Practical and Effective Guide for Teachers.* New Haven and London: Yale University Press.

Baker, M. (1992). *In Other Words.* London: Routledge.

Chao, Y. R. (1968). *A Grammar of Spoken Chinese.* Berkeley and Los Angeles: University of California Press.

Dr. eye dictionary. Available online at www.dreye.com/en/

Duanmu, S. (2007). *The Phonology of Standard Chinese.* 2nd edn. Oxford/New York: Oxford University Press.

Flynn, D. (2010). *Learning Chinese: Pinyin or Zhuyin? Chinese Hacks.* 19th June, 2010. Available online at http://chinesehacks.com/blog/study/learning-chinese-pinyin-or-zhuyin

Fromkin, V. and Bernstein-Ratner, N. (1998). 'Speech Production'. In Gleason, J. and Bernstein-Ratner, N. (eds). *Psycholinguistics.* 2nd edn. New York: Harcourt Brace. pp. 309–346.

Fung, L. and Carter, R. (2007). 'Discourse Markers and Spoken English: Native and Learner Use in Pedagogic Settings'. *Applied Linguistics.* 28(3): 410–439.

Halliday, M. A. K. and Hasan, R. (1976). *Cohesion in English.* London: Longman.

He, P. (2004). *Hanyu Chengyu Cidian.* Chengdu: University of Electronic Science and Technology of China Press.

Heselwood, B. (2013). *Phonetic Transcription in Theory and Practice.* Edinburgh: Edinburgh University Press.

King, G., Pan, J. and Roberts, M. E. (2013). 'How Censorship in China Allows Government Criticism but Silences Collective Expression'. *American Political Science Review.* 107(2): 1–18.

Kuhn, R. L. (2010). *How China's Leaders Think: The Inside Story of China's Reform and What This Means for the Future.* Singapore: John Wiley & Sons (Asia) Pte Ltd.

Li, C. N. and Thompson, S. A. (1981). *Mandarin Chinese: A Functional Reference Grammar.* Berkeley: University of California Press.

Li, D. and Cheng, M. (2008). *A Practical Chinese Grammar for Foreigners.* Beijing: Beijing Language and Culture University Press.

Lin, H. (2001). *A Grammar of Mandarin Chinese.* Munich: Lincom Europa.

Loar, J. K. (2011). *Chinese Syntactic Grammar: Functional and Conceptual Principles.* New York: Peter Lang.

Miao, D. (2011). 'Between Propaganda and Commercials: Chinese Television Today'. In Shirk, S. (ed.). *Changing Media, Changing China.* Oxford: Oxford University Press. pp. 91–114.

Norman, J. (1988). *Chinese*. Cambridge: Cambridge University Press.

Packard, J. L. (2004). *The Morphology of Chinese*. Cambridge: Cambridge University Press.

Paton, S. (2008). *A Dictionary of Chinese Characters: Accessed by Phonetics*. Abingdon, Oxfordshire: Routledge.

Reiss, K. (1981). 'Type, Kind and Individuality of Text: Decision Making in Translation'. *Poetics Today*. 2(4): 121–131.

Schiffrin, D. (1987). *Discourse Markers*. Cambridge: Cambridge University Press.

Searle, J. (1969). *Speech Acts: An Essay in the Philosophy of Language*. Cambridge: Cambridge University Press.

Shei, C. (2005). 'Fixedness in Genre-Specific Language and Intercultural Differences: Comparing English and Chinese Fire News Corpora'. *International Journal of Corpus Linguistics*. 10(2): 199–225.

Shei, C. (2008). 'Discovering the Hidden Treasure on the Internet: Using Google to Uncover the Veil of Phraseology'. *Computer Assisted Language Learning*. 21(1): 67–85.

Shei, C. (2010). *Translation and the Web: Theory, Practice, and Norm*. Taipei: Winjoing Publisher Co. Ltd. (in Chinese)

Shei, C. and Pain, H. (2000). 'An ESL Writer's Collocational Aid'. *Computer Assisted Language Learning*. 13(2): 167–182.

Shi, Z. and Chen, Q. (2011). *China's Culture*. Singapore: Cengage Learning Asia Pte Ltd.

Sun, C. (2006). *Chinese: A Linguistic Introduction*. Cambridge: Cambridge University Press.

The International Phonetic Association. (1999). *Handbook of The International Phonetic Association*. New York: Cambridge University Press.

Wright, D. C. (2011). *The History of China*. Santa Barbara, CA: Greenwood.

Wu, R-J. R. (2004). *Stance in Talk: A Conversation Analysis of Mandarin Final Particles*. Amsterdam/Philadelphia: John Benjamins Publishing Company.

Xiao, R., Rayson, P. and McEnery, T. (2009). *A Frequency Dictionary of Mandarin Chinese: Core vocabulary for learners*. Routledge: London.

Xiao, Z. and McEnery, A. (2004). *Aspect in Mandarin Chinese: A corpus-based study*. Amsterdam: John Benjamins Publishing Company.

Yip, P-C. (2000). *The Chinese Lexicon*. London: Routledge.

Yip, P-C. and Rimmington, D. (2004). *Chinese: A Comprehensive Grammar*. London: Routledge.

Zhao, X-R. (2001). *Dictionary of Chinese idioms*. Taipei: Liu Tong Cultural Enterprise Co. Ltd. (in Chinese)

Index